SAGE was founded in 1965 by Sara Miller McCune to support the dissemination of usable knowledge by publishing innovative and high-quality research and teaching content. Today, we publish over 900 journals, including those of more than 400 learned societies, more than 800 new books per year, and a growing range of library products including archives, data, case studies, reports, and video. SAGE remains majority-owned by our founder, and after Sara's lifetime will become owned by a charitable trust that secures our continued independence.

Los Angeles | London | New Delhi | Singapore | Washington DC | Melbourne

CHILD LABOUR

CHILD LABOUR

GLOBAL CHALLENGES, ISSUES AND POLICY

**ANIL BHUIMALI
PARTHA CHATTERJEE**

Los Angeles | London | New Delhi
Singapore | Washington DC | Melbourne

Copyright © Anil Bhuimali and Partha Chatterjee, 2022

All rights reserved. No part of this book may be reproduced or utilised in any form or by any means, electronic or mechanical, including photocopying, recording, or by any information storage or retrieval system, without permission in writing from the publisher.

First published in 2022 by

SAGE Publications India Pvt Ltd
B1/I-1 Mohan Cooperative Industrial Area
Mathura Road, New Delhi 110 044, India
www.sagepub.in

SAGE Publications Inc
2455 Teller Road
Thousand Oaks, California 91320, USA

SAGE Publications Ltd
1 Oliver's Yard, 55 City Road
London EC1Y 1SP, United Kingdom

SAGE Publications Asia-Pacific Pte Ltd
18 Cross Street #10-10/11/12
China Square Central
Singapore 048423

Published by Vivek Mehra for SAGE Publications India Pvt Ltd and typeset in 10.5/13 pt Bembo by AG Infographics, Delhi.

Library of Congress Cataloging-in-Publication Data

Names: Bhuimali, Anil, author. | Chatterjee, Partha, author.
Title: Child labour : global challenges, issues and policy / Anil Bhuimali, Partha Chatterjee.
Other titles: Child labor
Description: First Edition. | Thousand Oaks, California : SAGE Publishing, 2022. | Includes bibliographical references and index.
Identifiers: LCCN 2022011060 | ISBN 9789354794315 (hardback) | ISBN 9789354794322 (epub) | ISBN 9789354794339 (ebook)
Subjects: LCSH: Child labor–Case studies. | Children–Social conditions–Case studies. | COVID-19 Pandemic, 2020—Influence–Case studies.
Classification: LCC HD6231.B48 2022 | DDC 331.3/1–dc23/eng/20220401
LC record available at https://lccn.loc.gov/2022011060

ISBN: 978-93-5479-431-5 (HB)

SAGE Team: Rajesh Dey, Shipra Pant and Rajinder Kaur

*To those millions of children who dream
for a better tomorrow*

Thank you for choosing a SAGE product!
If you have any comment, observation or feedback,
I would like to personally hear from you.

Please write to me at **contactceo@sagepub.in**

Vivek Mehra, Managing Director and CEO, SAGE India.

Bulk Sales

SAGE India offers special discounts
for purchase of books in bulk.
We also make available special imprints
and excerpts from our books on demand.

For orders and enquiries, write to us at

Marketing Department
SAGE Publications India Pvt Ltd
B1/I-1, Mohan Cooperative Industrial Area
Mathura Road, Post Bag 7
New Delhi 110044, India

E-mail us at **marketing@sagepub.in**

Subscribe to our mailing list
Write to **marketing@sagepub.in**

This book is also available as an e-book.

Contents

List of Tables	ix
List of Abbreviations	xv
Foreword by Sibabrata Das	xvii
Preface	xxi
Acknowledgements	xxv

Chapter 1	Introduction	1
Chapter 2	Child Labour in Scholarly Writings	14
Chapter 3	Post-Industrial Revolution Concern: A Developed Country Context	61
Chapter 4	Child Labour in Sub-Saharan Africa	160
Chapter 5	Child Labour in Asia	203
Chapter 6	The Global Scenario	289
Chapter 7	Grassroots Experience from Rural India	300
Chapter 8	Impact of COVID-19 Pandemic	326
Chapter 9	Conclusion and Policy Recommendations	349

Bibliography	357
About the Authors	359
Index	360

List of Tables

3.1	Child Employment, 1851–1881	73
3.2	Working Children in England and Wales	74
3.3	Most Frequently Recorded First Jobs and Top 20 Jobs for the 10–14-year-old Males in England and Wales (Excluding London), as per the 1851 Census	77
3.4	Percentage of Children Recorded as Working, by Age Range, in England and Wales, 1851–1911	79
3.5	Occupation Status of Children Aged 5–14 in England and Wales as a Percentage in the Total Age Range	80
3.6	Child Labour in Some Ghent Factories	83
3.7	Child Labour in Factories in Various Belgium Provinces, by Age and Gender, 1843	85
3.8	Child Labour in Some Important Belgian Crafts and Industries, by Age and Gender, 1846	86
3.9	Textile Workers in the Voortman Cotton Mill in Ghent, Percentage by Age and Gender, 1842–1902	88
3.10	Statistics of Children According to Age and Sex	90
3.11	Working Hours in Ghent Industries during 1840–1914	93
3.12	Height and Weight of Children Working in the Ghent Cotton Industry, by Age and Gender and Compared with Normal Values, 1843	94
3.13	Wages (Average) Paid to Belgian Children under 16 Years of Age, 1846 and 1880	95
3.14	Daily Wages of Ghent Children under 16 Years of Age, in Cotton, Flax and Steel Industries, before 1896	96
3.15	Literacy in Belgium, by Gender, 1866–1910	97
3.16	Participation Rates of Youth in Selected Communes, 1851	106
3.17	Age-wise Composition of Males and Females in Mills, 1822	107

3.18	Composition of the Industrial Labour Force, after the 1839–1845 Enquiry	109
3.19	Gainful Workers, Aged 10–14, in the United States of America: 1870–1930 (in Thousands)	119
3.20	Distribution of Child Labourers in the Age Group of 10–15 Years in 1900	120
3.21	Occupation of Children 10–15 Years of Age, Inclusive by Age	121
3.22	Selected Non-agricultural Occupations of Children 10–15 Years of Age, Inclusive	122
3.23	Proportion of Children among all Workers in Manufacturing and Mechanical Industries	123
3.24	Passage of Anti-child-labour Laws in Different States of America	125
3.25	Children in Industrial Employment, by Age and Gender, 1899, 1909 and 1914	135
3.26	Child Labour by Factory Size and Gender, 1899, 1909 and 1914	135
3.27	Child Labourers in Select Japanese Industries by Gender, 1900	136
3.28	Characteristics of the Workforce in Selected Industries, 1900	137
3.29	Working Conditions of Japanese Child Workers in Select Industries, 1900	138
3.30	Employment Structure of the Larger Mines in the Chikuho Coal Field between 1906 and 1930	140
3.31	School Attendance: Children in Four Mines in Chikuho in 1905	141
3.32	Reasons for Non-attendance at School among Working Children in Four Mines in Chikuho in 1905	141
3.33	Age Structure of the Deceased in the Ōto Mine Disaster, 1903	142
3.34	Age of Entry of Interviewed Women Who Joined Work at Mines, 1907–1933	143
3.35	Queensland Population and Workforce Participation Rates (Those Aged 19 Years and Under), 1891, 1901	149
3.36	Child Adolescent Participation in Key Economic Sectors: Queensland 1891, 1901	150

3.37	Occupation Characterized by Significant Child Employment: Queensland Censuses 1891, 1901	151
3.38	Percentage of Child Labour: Overall and by Individual and Household Characteristics	157
4.1	HIV/AIDS Prevalence and Children Orphaned by HIV/AIDS	165
4.2	Educational Status of Select African Countries' Children in Rapid Assessments	167
4.3	Effect of Orphanhood on School Attendance, Zambia	168
4.4	Children Aged 5–14, by Sex, Type of Activity and Residence	170
4.5	Percentage of Children Involved in Household Chores, by Age and Sex	171
4.6	Distribution of Working Children Aged 5–14 by Industry and Age Group	171
4.7	Distribution of Working Children Aged 5–14 Years by Industry and Sex	172
4.8	Child Labour and Children's Education	172
4.9	Percentage of Children Aged 5–14, by the Capita Income Quintiles, Sex and Type of Activities	173
4.10	Statistics on Children's Work and Education	174
4.11	Overview of Children's Work by Sector and Activity	175
4.12	Ratification of International Conventions on Child Labour	176
4.13	Zimbabwean Laws and Regulations on Child Labour	177
4.14	Child Labour Estimates Based on National Legislation	182
4.15	Children Aged 14–17 Years in Child Labour	183
4.16	Activity Status of Children Aged 5–13 Years by Sex and Residence	185
4.17	Activity Status of Adolescent Aged 14–17 Years by Sex and Residence	186
4.18	Statistics on Children's Work and Education	188
4.19	Working Children by Sector, Aged 5–14 Years	188
4.20	Child Labour Estimates Based on National Legislation and Global Measurement Standard	189
4.21	Involvement in Child Labour, Age Group of 5–13 Years, by Age, Sex and Residence	190

4.22	Children in Child Labour, Age Group of 14–17 Years	191
4.23	Children's Activity Status, 5–13 Years Range, by Sex and Residence	193
4.24	Adolescents' Activity Status, 14 Years, by Sex and Residence	194
4.25	Out-of-School Children Aged 10–17 Years with Less Than 2 and 4 Years of Education	195
4.26	Statistics on Children's Work and Education	197
4.27	Ivory Coast Children's Work by Sector and Activity	198
4.28	Children's Work and Education in Ghana	202
4.29	Children's Work (Sector-wise)	202
5.1	Child Population and Labour Force Participation Aged 5–14 Years by Sex	208
5.2	Child-labour Participation (10–14 Years) in Agriculture and Non-agriculture Sectors by Gender	210
5.3	Children Aged 5–14, by Sex, Type of Activity and Residence	211
5.4	Children's Activity Status and Household Income Level	213
5.5	Distribution of Child Labour by Industry and Age Group	215
5.6	Distribution of Children in Hazardous Works by Industry and Age Group	217
5.7	Statistics on Children's Work and Education	220
5.8	Working Children Aged 5–11 Years (in Nepal) by Background Characteristics (%)	228
5.9	Distribution of Working Children, by Major Occupational Group, Sex, Sector, Region and Age Group	229
5.10	Distribution of Working Children, Child Labour and Children Engaged in Hazardous Work, by Ethnic Group and Locality	232
5.11	Child Labour and Children Engaged in Hazardous Work, by Ethnic Group	236
5.12	Distribution of Average (Median) Monthly Income and Weekly Working Hours of Working Children, Child Labour and Children Engaged in Hazardous Child Labour, by Sex, Age Group and Urban/Rural Classification	239

5.13	School Attendance of Child Workers, by Age Group, Sex, Locality and Region	240
5.14	School Attendance of Children Engaged in Hazardous Child Labour, by Age Group, Sex, Locality and Region	242
5.15	Distribution of Child Labour, by Major Occupation (in Thousands)	244
5.16	Distribution of Child Workers Engaged in Hazardous Works, by Major Occupation (in Thousands)	245
5.17	Statistics on Children's Work and Education	246
5.18	Child Labourers in Pakistan, 1996	251
5.19	Child Labour Force Participation Rates in Pakistan by Provinces, Age, Sex and Area	252
5.20	Statistics on Children's Work and Education	254
5.21	Overview of Children's Work by Sector and Activity	255
5.22	Statistics on Children's Work and Education	259
5.23	Children's Work by Sector and Activity	259
5.24	Daily Wages of Brick Makers (Child and Adult)	262
5.25	Breakdown of Average Household Debt	263
5.26	Health and Development Risks of Brickmaking	264
5.27	Concentration of Child Labour	273
5.28	Total Children and Their Number in Percentage Terms, 5–14 Years	273
5.29	Distribution of Working Children by Type of Work, 2011	274
5.30	State-wise Distribution of Working Children According to 1971, 1981, 1991, 2001 and 2011 Censuses in the Age Group of 5–14 Years	275
5.31	Expansion of NCLPs	280
5.32	Enrolment: All India—Age Group: 6–14 Years	285
5.33	ASER: Children Enrolled in Different Types of Schools, 2018 and 2020 (Age Group 6–14 years)	286
5.34	Benefits the Vulnerable Children Received	288
6.1	Global Estimate of Child Labour, 2017	291
6.2	Children's Involvement in Child Labour and Hazardous Work 2000–2016	293
6.3	Changes in Rates of Progress against Child Labour since 2000	294

6.4	Regional Profile of Child Labour and Hazardous Work	294
6.5	Child Labour and Hazardous Work by National Income	295
6.6	Child Labour by Sector	296
6.7	Gender Profile of Child Labourers, and Child Labourers in Hazardous Work, 2016	297
7.1	Schools under the NCLP in the Districts of West Bengal, 2007–2008	303
7.2	Child Labour and NCLP Schools in West Bengal	306
7.3	Schools reph the Number of Students (Gender-wise and Caste-wise) in the Northern West Bengal District of Cooch Behar	308
7.4	Income-wise and Caste-wise Surveys of Households	312
7.5	Literacy and Children Size (Caste-wise) in the Household Survey	313
7.6	Educational Status of Parents	314
7.7	Agricultural Survey: Survey with 200 Farm Families	316
7.8	Agricultural Working Children in Activities: Attending Special School, Out of School and Joining High School	316
7.9	Tobacco-growing Village—Tikavita(V-1)	318
7.10	Tobacco-growing Village—Niztaraf (V-2)	319
7.11	Child Labourers Identified at Tea Stalls, Hotels, Restaurants in Cooch Behar Town, 2013	320
7.12	Beedi Rolling in the District of Cooch Behar	321
8.1	Child Labour and Hazardous Work: Trends	330
8.2	Children Aged 5–17 Years in Employment	334
8.3	Experience of Online Study among Online Children	341
8.4	Children's Attendance in Urban and Rural Areas	341
8.5	Students Locked (Community-wise)	342
8.6	Total Number of Child Labour in India under CLPRA during 2014–2016	346
8.7	Budget Allocation under NCLP During 2016–2019	347
9.1	Ten Worst Performing Countries, 2019	354

List of Abbreviations

AFL	American Federation of Labor
AIDS	Acquired immunodeficiency syndrome
ANADER	National Agency for Support to Rural Development
ASER	Annual Status of Education Report
ATIMC	Anti-Trafficking Inter-Ministerial Committee
BBA	Bachpan Bachao Andolan
BBS	Bangladesh Bureau of Statistics
BGMEA	Bangladesh Garment Manufacturers and Exporters Association
BPL	Below Poverty Line
CBS	Community Board schooling
CHNS	China Health and Nutrition Survey
CLAPRA	Child Labour (Prohibition and Regulation) Act, 1986
COCOBOD	Ghana Cocoa Board
CPC	Child Protection Committee
CRIG	Cocoa Research Institute of Ghana
CRPL	Child Rights Protection Law
CRY	Child Rights and You
DEP	Daughters Education Programme
DFID	Department for International Development
FAO	Food and Agriculture Organization
FLSA	Fair Labor Standards Act
GNP	Gross national product
HIV	Human immunodeficiency virus
HSCT	Harmonized Social Cash Transfer
IDSK	Institute of Development Studies Kolkata
ILO	International Labour Organization
IMF	International Monetary Fund
INEI	Instituto Nacional de Estadística e Informática
IPEC	International Programme on the Elimination of Child Labour

LEAP	Livelihood Empowerment Against Poverty
MGNREGA	Mahatma Gandhi National Rural Empowerment Guarantee Act
MNCLS	Malawi National Child Labour Survey
MOLSAMD	Minority of Labour, Social Affairs, Martyrs and Disabled
MPSLSW	Ministry of Public Service, Labour & Social Welfare
MSMEs	Micro, small and medium enterprises
NAPLAC	National Plan of Action
NCLC	National Child Labour Committee
NCLP	National Child Labour Project
NCLS	National Child Labour Survey
NGO	Non-governmental organization
NSSO	National Sample Survey Organization
NTFSC	National Task Force on Street Children
OBCs	Other Backward Classes
OECD	Organisation for Economic Co-operation and Development
PHCs	Public Health Centres
RA	Rapid assessment
RC	Rights of the Child
SDGs	Sustainable Development Goals
SSA	Sub-Saharan Africa
UCW	Understanding Children's Work
UK	United Kingdom
UN	United Nations
UNESCO	United Nations Educational, Scientific and Cultural Organization
UNICEF	United Nations International Children's Emergency Fund
USA	United States of America
VDC	Village Development Committee
WACAP	World Association for Children and Parents
WTO	World Trade Organization
ZRP	Zimbabwe Republic Police
ZUNDAF	Zimbabwe and UN Development Assistance Framework

Foreword*

Two recent reports on child labour give us wake-up calls.
First report on child labour[1]—released ahead of World Day Against Child Labour on 12 June 2021—shows that the declining trend of child labour has stalled, and COVID-19 crisis might have contributed to reversal of years of progress in the fight against child labour during 2000–2016.

The second report from the World Bank[2] shows that more than 40 per cent of children, about 350 million, don't have access to any healthcare, and investments in childcare would increase women's employment and productivity, create new jobs, improve child outcomes and drive economic growth.

Although in numbers child labour fell from 246 million in 2000 to 152 million in 2016, the progress is uneven across Africa, Asia and Pacific, Middle East, Europe and Western Hemisphere. Almost 50 per cent or more of these children work in areas which are hazardous for their health and lives.

Historically, it's a global problem. One can hardly forget how the American, English, French and German litterateurs and social reformers in the 18th and 19th centuries were plaintively calling out for governmental—and even international—interventions to uplift the living conditions of child labourers. The tear-soaked lines of Charles

---

*The views expressed are fully personal and do not necessarily represent the views of the IMF, Board or management.

[1] International Labour Office and United Nations Children's Fund, 'Child Labour: Global Estimates 2020, Trends and the Road Forward', 2021, https://data.unicef.org/resources/child-labour-2020-global-estimates-trends-and-the-road-forward/#:~:text=63%20million%20girls%20and%2097,10%20of%20all%20children%20worldwide.&text=The%20report%20warns%20that%20globally,a%20result%20of%20the%20pandemic.

[2] A. Devercelli and F. Beaton-Day, *Better Jobs and Brighter Futures: Investing in Childcare to Build Human Capital* (Washington, DC: World Bank, 2020).

Lamb and Charles Dickens, condemning child labour, are unforgettable! Globally, the declining trend till 2016 was partly due to various coordinated efforts over the years reflected in Minimum Age Convention (1973, ratified by 172 countries); UN Convention on the Rights of the Child to guarantee the protection of children's rights to grow and thrive (1989); International Program on the Elimination of Child Labour (IPEC; 1992) and Worst Forms of Child Labour Convention (1999, ratified by 186 countries) towards ending practices such as slavery, child trafficking, debt bondage, forced labour and other illicit activities.[3]

The year 2021 has been declared by the UN General Assembly as the Year for the Elimination of Child Labour. Also, the UN Sustainable Development Goals (SDGs—target 8.7) asks 'member states to take immediate and effective measures to eradicate forced labour, end modern slavery and human trafficking, and secure the prohibition and elimination of the worst forms of child labour, including the recruitment and use of child soldiers, and by 2025 to end child labour in all its forms.'[4] With this target ahead of us, the International Labour Organization (ILO) Director-General Guy Ryder aptly mentions: 'The new estimates are a wake-up call. We cannot stand by while a new generation of children is put at risk.'[5]

Needless to say, during this period of alarming increase in the number of child labourers in the post-COVID-19 world, *Child Labour: Global Challenges, Issues and Policy* would highlight some of the major questions, issues and suggestive solutions, which academicians, socio-economic policymakers, government officials and NGOs working in this area would find very helpful.

Dr Anil Bhuimali, whom I had the privilege and honour to know personally from my college days, is a reputed and well-accomplished academician and currently Vice-Chancellor of Raiganj University in West Bengal, India.

Dr Partha Chatterjee, the Hon'ble Minister, Government of West Bengal, having a very wide and first-hand experience in the applied

---

[3] Kathryn Reid, World Vision, 2021, https://www.worldvision.org/author/katreidworldvision-org

[4] International Labour Office and United Nations Children's Fund. 'Child Labour'.

[5] UNICEF, Press Releases, 2021, https://www.unicefusa.org/press/releases/child-labor-rises-160-million-%E2%80%93-first-increase-two-decades/38686

and policy fields of education, industry, trade and commerce, is very knowledgeable about the issues related to legislative and practical actions needed to eradicate child labour.

Hence, like many students, research scholars and public policymakers, we have high hope that this research-based publication, *Child Labour: Global Challenges, Issues and Policy*, would convincingly highlight the measures which are necessary to achieve one of the major targets of the UN SDGs, target 8.7, where the goal is to end child labour in all its forms by 2025.[6]

In this book, Dr Bhuimali and Dr Chatterjee, reflecting on the history of the growth of child labouring practices, have analysed the present condition of the child labourers, in selected countries of Europe, North America, Africa and Asia. The book refers to several published works of eminent scholars in this area. The researchers in this field would find this an important and valuable addition for their own literature review. Analysing the problems being faced by the child labourers worldwide, the authors present statistics related to child labour arising out of micro-studies of different areas of West Bengal—the state of domicile for both the writers. Highlighting the challenges and additional poverty due to COVID-19 pandemic, the authors propose their suggestions and policy prescription in the concluding chapter.

We hope that authors' notable analytical and policy research in *Child Labour: Global Challenges, Issues and Policy* would become an important and valuable publication for academicians, policymakers and all of us who share and echo the same feelings: 'Child labour perpetuates poverty, unemployment, illiteracy, population growth, and other social problems,'[7] and hence, 'There is no place for child labour in society much depends on how we respond. This is a time for renewed commitment and energy, to turn the corner and break the cycle of poverty and child labour.'[8]

We hope that this book will convincingly act as a reminder of the task ahead of us, as we were told by Nelson Mandela: 'Safety and

---

[6] International Labour Office and United Nations Children's Fund, 'Child Labour.'

[7] Kailash Satyarthi, Work, https://www.kailashsatyarthi.net/work

[8] https://violenceagainstchildren.un.org/news/day-african-child-protecting-all-childrens-rights-and-investing- children-paramount-africa

security don't just happen, they are the result of collective consensus and public investment. We owe our children, the most vulnerable citizens in our society, a life free of violence and fear.'[9]

Sibabrata Das
Strategy, Policy, and Review Department
International Monetary Fund
Washington, DC

---

[9] https://violenceagainstchildren.un.org/news/day-african-child-protecting-all-childrens-rights-and-investing- children-paramount-africa

Preface

Of the different socio-economic–cultural 'menaces' threatening the all-around development of the postmodern, 21st-century world, that of warring and sectarianism come first. The second, undoubtedly, is that of child labour. When the little hands—which should have turned the pages of books and scribbled away with pencils—roughen themselves up by picking stones in quarries or shovelling away through hard rocky soil, one could easily understand that not only is the childhood threatened in such a case but also that the country, which 'permits' this to happen, is surely heading to a (socio-economic) disaster. The practice of employing child labourers is obscene, a practice which, in the long run, threatens the economy because an 'underdeveloped' and 'less-educated' individual who matures out of a child labourer is not a boon but a bane for the population resource. 'Child labour' is a menace which needs to be uprooted fully; even if there is a single child who is out of school and working at a building under construction, the society in which they live cannot progress in the true sense of the term.

We are amazed at the way different nations conceal the prevalence of child labourers among their population. No country of the world is free from this social ill. In some countries—for example, those in South Asia, the Middle East and Northern and Central Africa—child labourers are easily identifiable. They work as domestic help and servants, on agricultural lands, as transporter of goods, in brick-laying factories, at automobile-repairing garages, at building sites under construction, at garment-making factories or other industrial workhouses, or as waiters at restaurants and the roadside shanties. They seem to be omnipresent. The condition of the female children working as child labourers is worsened by the fact that they are sometimes obliged to satisfy the sexual lust of their employers or senior acquaintances, and they often end up working in their mature life as prostitutes. And yet the governments of such countries are in a denial mode. Officially, in most of the countries' records, child labourers do not exist! Or they are 'negligible' in number. As we browse through data provided officially by UNICEF on its website, we find that there are, presently, 160 million child labourers working all over the world. Between 2016 and 2020, 8.4 million more children were sucked into the quagmire of underpaid or free labour! And for the first time in recent memories, as the UNICEF exasperatedly notes, the global initiatives to 'end' child labour 'have been stalled' for several reasons—difficulties arising out of the COVID-19-related global lockdown, undoubtedly, being among them. The cursed COVID-19 pandemic, by severely disrupting the global economy, has also led to a marked increase in the number of child labourers. Ironically, even as the ILO decides to observe 'AD 2021' as the 'International Year for the Elimination of Child Labour', we stand at a juncture of time when my own country of origin—that is, India—has been desperately trying to grapple with the problem of resettling more than 10 million child labourers. In fact, in India, financial difficulties arising out of the COVID-19 pandemic have led to the closure of at least 1.5 million schools by June 2021, directly affecting the educational prospects of approximately 247 million children. Who knows how many of these education-deprived children would end up as child labourers at other people's factories and flats?

No country can boast that it does not have any child labourer working in its factories and houses. The only difference—it must be mentioned—is in the degree of obviousness or in the degree of obtrusivity. In India and Pakistan, for example, a child labourer would be pathetically emaciated and pitifully underdressed, with soot covering their innocent face and tender skin. In the West—so 'famously developed'—they would be 'assisting' in the factories, 'serving at restaurants to make money for education' or 'working in free time to make money to realize their dreams'. But the story afflicting the bodies clad in torn pyjamas and 'sleek' jeans is the same: They are 'child labourers' whose work engagements are gradually denying them their childhood and, with every passing day, making them unfit to stand tall in the big, bad world in future. Like the so-called 'impoverished' nations of the East, the West was—and still is—never free from the menace of child labouring. The conditions of child labourers in African countries are perhaps the worst! We could only give our own efforts to solve the problem of child labour in our own ways—we could send a couple of child labourers to school, take up some financial liabilities and, of course, nudge the governments to take relevant steps to curb the problem of employment of child labour.

This is perhaps the most proper time for the publication of *Child Labour: Global Challenges, Issues and Policy*—we would say, rather: 'Desperate times needs desperate measures.' In the background of bludgeoning increase in the number of child labourers in the post-COVID-19 world, *Child Labour: Global Challenges, Issues and Policy* could become the outlet for the hitherto-unheard voices of those pathetic millions who are silently toiling away the prime time of their life at factories and quarries. This book would be successful in motivating further governmental actions and efforts and individual undertakings. Finally, we would like to add that *Child Labour: Global Challenges, Issues and Policy* has exceptionalized itself—even before its publication—through its widespread circulation. It is not a localized take on the problem of child labour. We have carefully sorted out different countries of Europe, North America, Africa and Asia for analysing not only the present condition of the child labourers in these nations but also reflecting on the history of the growth of child-labouring practices in these select countries. There are nine chapters in the book, and each chapter—beginning with a lengthy historical analysis of the beginning of child labour—is in itself a revelation. We have so far tried to substantiate our take on different factors related to the existence of child labour by referring to several works which have earned permanent places on the list of highly respected socio-economic publications. The book has been divided into nine chapters. The introductory chapter gives a historical review of the development of the system of child labour, and how the system was followed in different countries. The second chapter collates different critical and socio-economic approaches on child labour. Taking an exhaustive view of the development of child labour, the third chapter reviews the changes in the system of child labour after post-Industrial Revolution. The fourth chapter takes an all-inclusive view of the umpteen numbers of mysteries of the child labourers in the countries collectively known as 'Sub-Saharan Africa.' The fifth chapter, reviewing the situation in different Asian countries, deals with identifying and exemplifying the worst forms of child labour. The sixth chapter focuses on the problems being faced by the child labourers worldwide, while the seventh brings together statistics related to child labour arising out of micro-studies of different areas of West Bengal—the state of domicile for both the writers. While the eighth chapter paints a grim picture for child labourers in a world ravaged by the COVID-19 pandemic (2020–2021), the concluding chapter, throws away the stupor and reflects on our suggestions regarding how the problem of child labour could still be addressed in the best, sensitive and most sensible way. *Child Labour: Global Challenges, Issues and Policy*, for its exceptional collation of data and statistics, is bound to become a so-called 'unputdownable' publication for those who are really concerned about ending the problem of child labouring.

As artists and sociologists say, a little amount of 'care' usually solves numerous problems. We could hope that the readers of this publication will also be convinced enough to add to their own 'care' for the distressed souls toiling away as 'child labourers'!

Acknowledgements

We are thankful to Shri Rajesh Dey and Shri Biplab Biswas of SAGE. Professor Pinaki Roy, Department of English, Raiganj University, has thoroughly checked the manuscript. We are indeed grateful to him. Shri Soumendu Kumar Dutta of the Office of the Vice-Chancellor, Raiganj University, took all the pains in typing the manuscript in spite of performing his normal duty as Secretary to the Vice-Chancellor. We are indeed thankful to him. Shri Ajoy Mishra, Deputy Librarian, Raiganj University, supplied materials for preparing the book. We are indebted to those who have shown their encouragement to us. We also pay our love and affection to each and every of our family members.

Chapter 1

Introduction

1.1. CHILDREN UNDER STRESS

A (prepubescent) boy or girl under fifteen years of age (seventeen years, as per the law in some countries), who has been forced to engage herself/himself in work at the cost of education, schooling and self-entertainment is usually identified as a 'child labourer'. Underage young people—if they work at all—do not usually toil in adverse environments; there are several economic and social factors involved in a condition where such children are forced to fend for themselves through labour. Internationally reputed scientists, physicians and psychologists have unanimously agreed upon the hypothesis that hard labour before attaining maturity is outrightly detrimental to the physical and mental growth of those who have been assigned or forced to do such work. As per the latest United Nations Educational, Scientific and Cultural Organization (UNESCO) reports, approximately 264 million children worldwide are presently being denied the privilege of going to school.[1] Not only do these hapless children not go to school, but they also do not have any time left to play or enjoy themselves. Instead, they are unceremoniously forced to join the ever-increasing number of international labourers. If, according to the estimates of the

---

[1] Deutsche Welle, 'UNESCO: 264 Million Children Do Not Go to School,' 2017, https://www.dw.com/en/unesco-264-million-children-dont-go-to-school/a-41084932#:~:text=UNESCO%3A%20264%20million%20children%20don%27t%20go%20to%20school,that%20countries%20must%20invest%20a%20lot%20more%20money

World Bank, there are 3.492 billion labourers worldwide in 2020,[2] 152 million are working as child labourers.[3] Most of these children live in underdeveloped, developing or semi-developed countries (sub-Saharan Africa [SSA], Latin America, India, Pakistan, Sri Lanka, Bangladesh, etc.). They work and live in/under hazardous conditions and are not—usually—in the best of their health because of lack of proper nutrition and care. Traditionally speaking, child labour is more prevalent in families living in abject poverty than anywhere else. These families have very limited access to land, credit, food, nutrition and other resources necessary for living well, securing education and enjoying good health. The result is the existence of malnourished and neglected child labourers in large numbers.

The employment of child labour to perform menial errands is not at all a 'new concept'. This has been practised throughout human history and could be traced to earlier ages in primitive agricultural societies. Select passages in the Vedas, Upanishads and Jatakas (particularly in the Vidura-pandita Jataka) reveal the existence of child labourers—especially in the form of the children of slaves (who were born in the houses of the slave owners). As L. B. Punecha writes, during the reign of the Mauryans (321 BC–185 BC), the child-labouring system was practised until the Mauryans abolished it.[4] In *The Arthashastra* (published in the 3rd century BC), Kautilya/Chanakya (375 BC–283 BC) clearly mentions that child labour, slavery and the practices of meting out humiliating treatment to labourers have existed since ancient times. The Punjab-born economist and statesman, L. B. Punecha, severely criticized the purchase and sale of children below the age of eight years and later systematized rules for the abolition of child labour. The intensity and severity of child slavery started declining

---

[2] The World Bank, 'The Labour Force—Total—in 2020,' 21 June 2020, https://data.worldbank.org/indicator/SL.TLF.TOTL.IN

[3] *The Times of India*, 'World Day against Child Labour 2020: Some Facts about Child-labour That Will Leave You Shocked,' 12 June 2020, https://timesofindia.indiatimes.com/life-style/parenting/moments/world-day-against-child-labour-2020-some-facts-about-child-labour-that-will-leave-you-shocked/articleshow/76334853.cms

[4] L. B. Punecha, *Child-labour: A Social Evil* (New Delhi: Alfa Publications, 2006), 1–4.

during the post-Mauryan period.⁵ This trend was noticeable, especially in the societies predominated by the Hindus.

In the epics of the Ramayana (c. 7th century BC) and the Mahabharata (c. 4th century BC), one could find innumerable illustrations of children's engagement in different affairs of the family and their movements away from the families in search of education and monetarily beneficial engagements. Even Lord Rama and his brothers—in the Ramayana—were sent to a hermitage (or 'ashram') at a tender age for their education and training. During their sojourn in the hermitage, they had to perform different menial tasks such as cultivation and domestic chores and so on. In the Mahabharata too, Lord Krishna was sent to a harbourage for his safety and training. It was imperative in ancient India (and many years later) that students residing in hermitage during their educational training should perform free labour and participate in daily chores. However, under the aegis of these ancient Indian systems of education and employment, students did not have to pay for their educational expenses; they earned their living expenses through simple labouring.

Also, during ancient times—especially in South Asia—children helped their family members in various agricultural and familial activities such as protecting the crops and caring for the younger siblings. Most of the artisans and craftsmen would train their children so that they could help their parents augment the family income. Early rural artisans and agriculturists considered all the family members (including the children) as a unit, and they all worked together to augment the family income. Importantly, while doing such work, the concerned children never felt that they were being physically abused and mentally harassed. But this was not applicable to the children of slaves and of bonded labourers. Slaves of tender age (less than eight years of age) were purchased in open markets to work as child labourers; they and the children of bonded labourers (males and females) were used to do low, uncomfortable and/or hazardous work. The sadistic masters and owners of these underage slaves and child labourers treated them as chattels and cattle. These tender-age labourers were born as slaves, lived as slaves and also died as slaves.

---

⁵ Stanley Engerman and Seymour Drescher, *A Historical Guide to World Slavery* (Oxford: Oxford University Press, 1998), 78.

But scarcely any other intellectual of the ancient South Asian region (including India)—with the bright exception of Kautilya—had ever condemned these practices or written against them. As already mentioned, the children of slaves were considered as 'commodities', and were purchased and sold as goods. However, other than the children of slaves and the *mlechchhas* (or the non-conforming foreign settlers), no child could be marketed and mortgaged. However, underneath the daily flow of the society in ancient India, there existed different unobtrusive but humanist approaches to children. Kautilya, for example, mentioned that the purchase and sale of children were unlawful and necessitated the direct intervention of the elderly for the unhindered growth and welfare of children. The joint family system was understood to be the best way to protect the children. But even in such seemingly welfare state systems in ancient India, slave children were the principal source of labour and income.

1.2. THE PROLOGUE TO DISTRESS: CHILD LABOUR IN THE INDIAN PERSPECTIVE

The Aryans—between 900 BC and 600 BC—introduced the *varna* system in India.[6] This system ranked the Shudras at the lowest strata in the Indian Hindu social hierarchy. Men, women and children of Shudras had to serve their masters, who would usually belong to the so-called 'upper class', frankly exploitative in nature and attitude. The parents of the Shudras were ill-treated by the masters who would make it a point that the so-called 'lower-class' people always remained in the muck and mire, with a daily dose of humiliation. The wages sanctioned for/to the Shudras were low—that of their working children's even lower—and they were expected to engage in hours and hours of unrewarded labour. In fact, there was no wage rule for the underage workers who were slave children. The wages would be given in menial cash or damaged kind, or both. These weak and hapless people were routinely and mercilessly exploited. They were principally employed in agricultural and allied activities. Their children were also assigned to perform domestic work.

---

[6] Anjana M. Chandra, *India Condensed: Five Thousand Years of History and Culture*. (Singapore: Marshall Cavendish Editions, 2008), 24.

The concept of 'bonded labour' in India became widespread during the mediaeval period. Bonded labourers had to perform hard work for the houses of large landowners who were prototype feudal lords. The children of the bonded labour were also routinely engaged to boost up the economic activities of the labourers. Besides, these children would also help their families with their traditional craftmaking and family-based activities. During the 5th–15th centuries AD (the European Middle Ages), both the Hindus and the Muslims in India flaunted their affluence by engaging children as servants and slaves to serve their personal errands.[7]

In the Indian agricultural farms too, the children were employed in large numbers because of the gradual shifting of adults to alternative occupations in search of better living. In the mediaeval period, there existed a huge number of landless Indian agricultural labourers, many of whom were 'bonded labourers'. The sons of the bonded labourers were also used as child labourers in agriculture and, later, in industries. Rural indebtedness has been traditionally held responsible for one of the chief causes of the existence of bonded child labour in the Indian subcontinent. Children would be pledged against loans by the children's fathers to prospective loan givers. In the 17th-century Bengal, different Dutch silk factories were known to use about 700–800 weavers, most of whom were bonded child labourers. However, while the parents of these children were given the bulk of the principal weaving works, the child labourers were assigned light tasks. There had been a huge demand for child workers in India over the ages because they were cheap and readily available, ate less, protested even less and worked as a unit under factory systems. As a result of the availability of cheap labour sources, there was a considerable expansion of the European industries in India during 1860–1870, especially in the sectors of tea, coffee and indigo plantations and jute industries, which usually involved child labour.

During the medieval period in India, land possessions became fragmented, and landlessness, consequently, increased. The families of small landholders had to look for alternative occupations beyond their own cultivation. They had to join and work on the estates of large

---

[7] Refer to *The New Encyclopaedia Britannica*, Vol. 7–8 (Chicago: Encyclopaedia Britannica, Inc., 1998), 180.

landholders as bonded labourers. As mentioned earlier, their children, back at home, had to help their family members who engaged in the family-based traditional crafts making and the domestic chores.

Internationally reviewed, the intensity of usage of child labour in Europe seems to have increased considerably during the Industrial Revolution of the 18th century. Simultaneously, different movements to regulate child labour were initiated, particularly in England, at the close of the 18th century. The European manufacturing sector both used and exploited child labourers considerably, and to combat this situation, the first law against child labour was enacted in Great Britain in 1802—specifically directed towards controlling the apprenticeship of pauper children. But due to the lack of enforcement, the law could not be implemented effectively.

Going back to the history of child labour in India, under the Mughal regime (16th–19th century AD), children of commoners had no freedom of their own, and they had to depend on the wishes of their parents. In fact, their familial position was no better than that of a young slave. These children were sold without warning or mortgaged. Thereafter, they were mercilessly exploited and forced to do any work that the owners needed them to do. In short, children were used like movable properties in the interest of their families. The destitute families were forced to sell or mortgage their children in order to redress hunger and extreme misery in the families.

During the time of the English imperial rule in India, one could have easily noticed the tremendous expansion of the European industries—especially during the period of 1860–1970. Children from impoverished Indian families were used in tea, coffee and indigo plantations and jute industries—apart from other European industries.

In the course of time, the handicraft industry, which largely employed child labourers, was replaced by the factory system of production. During this period, the usage of cheap child labour was widely prevalent—principally due to weak governmental regulations on child labour.

Sociologists, economists and political scientists have given many reasons behind the growth of child labour in India over the ages. Some of the prime reasons are given in the following text.

First of all, the breakdown of the family-based handicraft-manufacturing system intensified the demand for child labour. Second, the expansion of European industry in India and internationally necessitated the employment of low-cost child labourers. Third, the increase of population called for the expansion of child labour in India. Fourth, the recurrence of droughts and famines gave rise to what is called 'exploitative child labour practice'. Fifth, due to an increase in landlessness among numerous families, the employment of child labourers increased. Sixth, children were cheap, readily available and easy to handle. Seventh, though the protective legislation for child labour was enforced in India in 1881, it was applicable only to those children who were under seven years of age and was binding for only those workhouses and factories which employed 100 or more employees. Eighth, the agriculture sector and the unorganized sectors were exempted from the enforcement of this law, and this ensured continuation of child labour in these sectors. Finally, in pre-Independence India, child slavery was encouraged by the English monarch themselves! This was because of the fact that slave children were always in high demand internationally, and the English imperialists could monopolize child slavery. Naturally, the British administration in India had no intention to stop or reduce child slavery or child labour.

In fact, in India, child labour—from time immemorial—has been a problem principally associated with the social system. It was perpetuated in early India along with other evil practises such as early child marriage, widow burning and maintenance of caste system. The intensity and severity of the system of child labour are—presently—escalating, especially due to the expansion of agriculture and industrialization. Agriculture is a common sector where children used to, and still work, numerously along with their parents. As mentioned earlier, during the British Raj (1708–1947), there was a huge expansion of industrial organizations—principally due to the Industrial Revolution. Even in the pre-capitalist Indian society, children were employed in traditional guilds and trade occupations. A large number of working parents involved their children with those activities, but their usage was largely informal in nature. They were given easy tasks and no hazardous work was offered. This, rather, was like training and was a part of their socialization.

However, these situations and conditions underwent significant changes with the advent of capitalism and industrialization. Before this, child labour was never a social threat; but during the 18th and 19th centuries, and beyond, child labour emerged as a major social problem. The family-based economy (of traditional agriculture and home-based handicrafts) had been changed, and in its place, people witnessed rapid mechanization in agriculture and industry. Consequently, the owners of the home-based industry were converted into wage-earning workers—both in the agriculture sector and the modern factory system of industrial production.

The new system of industrial production opened the scope for waged employment, and labour unions and labour markets were created as a result. The frequent advent of famines, scarcity of food, extreme poverty, lack of education for children and huge unemployment among the adults shoved children towards the labour market. There was no legislation for child labour. There was no minimum wage and working hours for children. Due to this, there was always a huge engagement of children in agriculture and modern industries. They were limitlessly abused and exploited by their employers.

Importantly, because of uneven industrialization, there had been a change in the socio-economic order, and this was one of the reasons for the destruction of the family-based economy. This also gave rise to extreme poverty, forcing children into the labour market: as mentioned before. In this way, child labour became a significant part of the economy, society and polity of the developing world.

This system continues even today—internationally—in one form or another, even after the enacting of legislation against child labour in/by almost all the countries of the world. During the British rule in India, the uncertainty among the children at work loomed large, especially because they emerged from the so-called 'lower strata' of the society: there was no security for them. To reiterate, these children would not face any mentionable problem while working with their family members and parents, but things became extremely exploitative and abusive when they worked under the factory system. The factory system—as already mentioned—separated children from their families. They were thus exposed to an unhealthy environment. Children were faced with longer hours of work with minimal wages. Naturally, they were not able to develop their mental and physical ability. They were not provided with sufficient food and nutrition. This could not ensure a good health standard of the working children. Not only this, these working children—as already mentioned at the beginning of this chapter—could not get education and time to play.

Large-scale mechanized industries were in existence internationally since the mid-19th century. During this period, there was no labour legislation, and, as already mentioned, the employers enjoyed unlimited bargaining power over the conditions of the workers. Both the adult workers and the children working in industries were mercilessly exploited. They did not have any bargaining power, and thus, the wages, working hours and other conditions were settled on the whims of employers. The children were used in jute mills, coal mines and cotton textiles in plenty. They were even engaged in underground works in mines, which were unhygienic and hazardous in nature. There—consequently—began to crop up the hue and cry in the public domain against the exploitation of child labourers by the employers. In the course of time, widespread public attention was drawn towards the evils of working children in mechanized industries and factories. The bamboozled employers tried to restrict it but failed.

To recapitulate, the first labour legislation was enacted in India in 1881 in the name of the Indian Factories Act, 1881, which, among others, gave some protection to the children (under the age of seven years) working in factories.[8]

Under this Act, some remarkable steps were proposed and included for the benefit of child labourers. In the first place, no children, under the age of seven years, could be employed in any factory system. Second, children could not be employed in two different industries on the same day. Third, the maximum working period of a working child was limited to nine hours a day. Fourth, four holidays were provided to the child labourers in a month. Fifth, a resting time on every working day was specified for every child worker. Finally, factories employing 100 or more workers were forced to have safety measures, such as fencing of dangerous machines. However, the legislation was weak in terms of its enforcement machinery. This was not implementable to agriculture and unorganized sectors. Naturally, child labour was randomly absorbed—as mentioned earlier—in these two sectors because such labour was cheaply available.

The Government of India, in pre-Independence India, appointed a committee known as the Mulock Commission (in 1884) in order to examine the workings and implementations of the Factories Act, 1881. Also, in the same year, another committee, the Bombay Factory

---

[8] S.D. Punekar and R. Varickayil, eds., *Labour Movement in India—Documents: 1891–1917*, Vol. II (Mumbai: Popular Prakashan, 1990), 268–269.

Commission, 1884, was appointed to look into the then status of the factory workers. On the basis of recommendations of this commission as well as the recommendations of the Factory Labour Commission, 1890, the Factories (Amendment) Act, 1891, was enacted. This Act was applicable to factories having 50 or more labourers.[9] Under this Act, the duration of work of a child labourer was further reduced to a total of seven hours a day. It was also mentioned that children would be engaged in factories during the day time and evening time only—between 6.00 AM and 7.00 PM—and they were not allowed to work in night shifts. Under this Act, some provisions directed specifically towards children and women were included. But later on, it was noticed that the provisions for women and children working in industries were inadequate.

The salient features of the 1891 Act were as follows. First of all, the Act was applicable to factories employing 50 or more employees a day. Second, the working hours for children workers were fixed at seven hours. Third, children would be engaged to work between 6.00 AM and 7.00 PM, and no children would be allowed to work in nightshifts. Fourth, the engagement of women in the night shift (i.e., the working hours between 7.00 PM of the previous day and 5.00 AM of the following day) was prohibited. Fifth, the hours of work in factories for women was fixed at 11 hours a day. Sixth, provisions were made for the maintenance of proper space, cleanliness and ventilation in the factories. Seventh, the lower age of children (employable as labourers) was increased from seven years to nine years. Finally, a weekly holiday for workers, including children and women, was introduced. However, due to the inadequate enforcing machinery of the Act of 1891, the working children in factories remained unprotected and, as a result, atrocities against child labourers increased. Also, due to the deficient provisions of the Act of 1891, the exploitation of children and women increased enormously.

1.3. METHODOLOGICAL FRAMEWORK AND ORGANIZATION OF THE BOOK

Before proceeding with the next chapter, it would be pertinent if the methodological framework and organization of this book are discussed briefly.

---

[9] Balwant Singh, *Labour Policy and Administration* (New Delhi: M.D. Publications, 1996), 16.

1.3.1. Methodology

The present study covers a wide spectrum of child labour issues spreading across the globe. It begins with a historical review of child labour from ancient time to the 21st century. The materials used here for study, research and inferences are broad contributions made by scholars, policymakers, civil society organizations, and governmental and international organizations such as the International Labour Organization (ILO), the UNESCO, the World Bank and the International Monetary Fund (IMF), in forms of books, reports, documents and published policy papers. To have a wider and deeper understanding of the problem and origin of child labour, the writers have covered several Western and Eastern countries such as England, Belgium, France, the United States of America, Japan, Australia and China, which have been separately taken up for further analysis. International research has revealed that SSA represents the highest concentration of child labour in terms of percentage. Therefore, the two writers of the present book have selected sub-Saharan countries such as Zimbabwe, Zambia, Tanzania, Malawi, Ivory Coast and Ghana to understand the severity and intensity of child labour under the volatile, impoverished and critical socio-economic, political and cultural conditions of Africa. In the context of Asia, the writers have chosen Bangladesh, Nepal, Pakistan, Afghanistan and India because these are the countries with a high concentration of child labourers. Elaborate discussions have been added with huge data collected from different secondary sources. In a nutshell, the global dimension of working children, with special references to their plight and miseries, has been accommodated in the book to grasp the situation.

1.3.2. Organization

Child Labour: Global Challenges, Issues and Policy begins with finding the existence of child labour in primitive agricultural societies and ancient Indian societies, especially during the reign of the Mauryas (as described in Kautilya's *Arthashastra*). Going back to the two major Indian great epics—the Ramayana and the Mahabharata—children could be found involved in the so-called 'home affairs', which we refer to in post-modern terminology as 'child labour'. Children, in ancient times, helped their parents in various ways—principally to enhance the income of the family. In the course of time, the concept of 'bonded labour' became a common term—especially during the medieval period. Not only the bonded labourers but also their children were forced to manufacture home-based crafts and participate in completing domestic chores. Much later, the Government of India—during the British Raj—enacted several legislations to eradicate child labour from the Indian subcontinent. These issues have been discussed in the introductory Chapter 1.

The usage of children in home activities or as participants in the home-based tiny enterprises, and in factories, mines, agriculture and allied works, and in crime syndicates have been repeatedly focused on by numerous social scientists, activists, policymakers and also through the publication of reports by the world organizations such as the ILO, the UNESCO, the IMF, the World Bank and the governmental organizations of various countries. Chapter 2 is the result of the two authors' thorough study of select contributions made by some internationally renowned scholars in the field of child labour development and the related socio-economic, political and cultural issues.

Chapter 3 discusses, with relevant details, the problem of child labour in the post-Industrial Revolution era. The problem of child labour became acute during the Industrial Revolution. Keeping the rapid industrialization of Europe in the background, the authors seek to highlight here the issue of child labour in the so-called 'developed countries' such as the United Kingdom, Belgium, France, the United States of America, Japan, Australia and China.

The highest percentage of child labour is usually found in the SSA continent. Child labourers in Africa are found in large numbers in the agriculture and domestic sectors. Besides, numerous children have had been sold into slavery, and many more are/were engaged as servants in order to recover their parents' debts. The worst forms of child labour have been practised in SSA, especially in Zimbabwe, Malawi, Tanzania and Ghana. Chapter 4 discusses and extensively reviews these issues and problems.

Chapter 5 analyses the worst forms of child labour in Asia. In this chapter, the authors discuss different aspects of child labour in countries such as Bangladesh, Cambodia, Indonesia, the Maldives, Nepal, Pakistan, Sri Lanka, Thailand and India, invoking relevant details.

The authors are poised to discuss the present scenario of child labour in an international/global context in Chapter 6.

A grassroots experience of child labour has been reviewed in Chapter 7. Chapters 7 and 8—respectively titled 'Grassroots Experience from Rural India' and 'Impact of COVID-19 Pandemic'—are important vis-à-vis the present pandemic situation. The COVID-19 situation has only increased the miseries of the child labourers if that is possible, and Chapter 8 surveys these miseries on an international level. Chapter 9, in conclusion, precisely suggests the measures to be taken immediately and in the long run if the menace of child labour is to be tackled successfully.

Chapter 2

Child Labour in Scholarly Writings

2.1. INTRODUCTION

In this chapter, we have presented an overall idea of what we have gathered from child labour-related studies by some outstanding scholars such as Honeyman, Colin, Vorst, Basu, Lieten, Sally, Matsuoka and Satyarthi. We have also intensively studied an ILO publication titled *Child Labour: A Textbook for University Students*,[1] which lucidly explains different aspects of child labour and other relevant issues.

2.2. KATRINA HONEYMAN

Katrina Honeyman, in her book,[2] depicts the conditions of working children in England during the years of 1780–1820. She writes that before the latter half of the 18th century, English children were used especially in the sector of domestic production activities. All the demands of woollens, worsteds, linens, fustians and cotton, the author pointed out, for domestic as well as trading purposes were produced by the families in their houses or the communal workshops. In course of time, the form of centralized factory production replaced the domestic

---

[1] International Labour Organization, *Child Labour: A Textbook for University Students* (Geneva: ILO, 2004).

[2] Katrina Honeyman, *Child Workers in England, 1780–1820: Parish Apprentices and the Making of the Early Industrial Labour Force* (Farnham: Ashgate Publishing, 1988).

and communal workshop systems of production, and the subsequent participation of textile traders in higher numbers helped the expansion of textile manufacturing.

The early English textile mills usually preferred engaging women and children. For demographic reasons, there was a high dependency ratio during the second half of the 18th century, which accounted for 20 per cent of the children aged —five–fourteen years. Children were employed en masse in factories. It was thought that children should begin working at an early age to acquire knowledge, support their own expenses and also help their families. The high dependency ratio increased poverty, and the poor laws encouraged poor children to join parish apprenticeships and, through this, they ultimately joined the factories.

Honeyman's 1988 study focuses on the contribution of parish apprentices as a special type of working children. During the late 18th century and afterwards, the English parish apprentices were engaged in urban factories. Parishes maintained records of apprentices. During 1780–1820, there was a huge transformation of textile manufacturing capabilities in terms of technological upgradation and centralization of production. Honeyman's study surveys data collected from 164 parishes, which were located in Yorkshire, Lancashire, Derbyshire, Nottinghamshire, Warwickshire and Staffordshire, and in counties like Herefordshire, Worcestershire, Essex, Kent, Lincolnshire and Suffolk.

Honeyman has thoroughly explained the establishment of a parish apprenticeship system. The first step under this system was to identify the available number of poor children and the demand for their labour, and accordingly, the parish factory apprenticeship system was strengthened. Initially, the parishes had to take a major responsibility in advertising for the pauper children. The factory owners had nothing to do with them in the beginning. Data on parish apprentices were available from parish records. The data available were: (a) registration of apprentices in the parish with their full introduction, (b) apprenticeship indentures and (c) minutes of meetings of churchwardens and overseers.

The author has also discussed the patterns of apprenticeship in her study. It has been hinted that the distribution of factory apprenticeship was complex. Placements of apprentices were common within the locality. Not only had the cotton mills but the general textile mills also used parish apprentices in large numbers. The transfer of parish children during the early period of industrialization was not confined only to factory employment. Parish apprentice children were essential also for working at textile factories and other trades for industrial expansion.

Honeyman notes with concern that many London parishes were engaged in the transfer of children to the early factories. Groups of children were sent during pick times—more than 90 per cent of their bindings—to new textile factories. Honeyman studied parish records of Witney, Oxfordshire from 1780 to 1812 and found that a number of apprenticed boys transferred to other trades but the majority of indentures were with local blanket weavers. The St Clement parish apprenticeship records mentioned that the majority of poor children were trained within the parish.

The author notes that parishes of eastern England especially took part in the parish factory apprenticeship system. Poor children in the parishes of the region around Hull were trained for local trades and the boys of Sculwater parish were bound to shipbuilding and associated works and that of girls, though a fewer in number, were mostly to domestic works.

Honeyman has analysed the workings of the textile mills in the south and other parts of England with the help of available data. In these mills, labour was drawn especially from the metropolis. Usually, there would be no movement of children from north to south. It is true—as Honeyman has indicated—those parish children helped in giving quick-start to many enterprises, and without them, the growth of factories would have been delayed. The apprenticeship arrangements continued even after the passing of legislation beyond 1816. After that, the number of registered children in the parishes lessened remarkably. According to recorded data, the parishes of Hull, Edinburg, Liverpool, Leicester and a few in Southwark continued engagement of factory apprenticeship system until the 1820s, and thereafter too. There were some instances of parish apprenticeship practice even during the 1880s and 1890s and this was locally called the 'tragic' tale. The textile firm I and C Calvert in the Calder Valley, for example, brought 100 such children from Liverpool.

During the early years of textile factory production, the apprentice training had not been standardized, and the practice varied between different factories and even within the factory over time. Because of the absence of standard practice, some works required training and some required experience. This was done as per the requirement. According to apprentices' indentures, the children needed to acquire a specific skill. The parishes were interested in the training of children for long-term employment. Since the early period, the parishes had an objective to train children so that they could learn basic literacy skills and facility with general education. Both the parish and the state stressed moral and religious education. However, the working environment of such children was polluted and unpleasant. Children spent long hours—working—in utter discomfiture and frequently suffered from eye injuries due to flying cotton fibres. This also damaged their lungs. Children did scavenging and collected leftover cotton. This involved them moving under machinery and sometimes moving between motive parts. Serious injury could happen for any lapse of concentration. The parish children gained 10- or 12-year experience in factory work. These children, thereafter, were better placed to get factory employment.

There was a gendered division of labour during pre-industrial England. The parish apprenticeship system offered different opportunities to boys and girls. Boys were offered training for skilled work while girls were destined for domestic trades. In this way, gender inequality became prominent in scale and scope. The girls were particularly directed toward domestic activity during the later period of their apprenticeship and in this way, they became competent domestic help.

In her book, Honeyman has also assessed the experience of parish apprentices and other child workers—their working conditions, living condition, corporal punishment they experienced, the sexual abuses they faced, their health conditions and the inadequate diet they were provided. The abused children in fear could not report against the cruel masters to the parish factory victims about torture and exploitation. Children sometimes resisted excessive violence by running away. Many autobiographical accounts provide a description of untold miseries suffered by the working children. The working hours of early parish apprentices were too long—often more than 12 hours. Sometimes they had to do night duty which was unusual for other child workers. The food provided by employers of parish apprentices was different in quality and quantity in different parishes. Parish visitors and children criticized the diets provided in the parishes. The author, in her book, has also had made an assessment of the words/voices of parish apprentices and how these had been interpreted through the parish agencies or institutions.

Honeyman explained that parish children were not independent economically but they were independent as child workers (as referred to by Lumilla Jordanova in the 1989 publication, or by John R. Gillis in his work published in 1974). They were independent workers in the sense that they worked in the factories, not as helpers but they were in sole charge of machines. The author describes how the parish children as apprentices and as workers were sometimes allowed to speak out and their voices were heard. Children of many parishes, including the children of the parish of Chelsea and at Merryweather's Yorkshire factory, complained that very poor quality foods were supplied during dinner time and consequently a large number of working children spent the night without dinner. The issue of working conditions was a more serious issue than food. Children also suffered from homesickness. They were very desirous to see their family, relatives and friends. There was frequent absconding of children. Two issues could be frequently observed. The first issue among these children was a 'deep discontentment with family life', and the second issue was 'yearning to go home', as the author indicated. Children could speak against the ill-treatment they received from the parish and the factories where they worked. They protested in several ways about the level of the chastisement they received. Apart from long working hours, poor food and torture, children were also forced to serve for longer periods as unpaid labour. Initially, the term of apprenticeship was seven years. It extended for 11 or 12 years and this was without any wage. This was another form of exploitation of pauper children by the factories and parishes. The children, in a group, raised their voices and put their complaints, and these were heard through the agency of parish officials. Which complaints would be resolved depended purely on the subject matter. Complaints about insufficient food, for example, were heard and resolved. Complaints even about education were listened to and accordingly acted, but complaints like homesickness were not considered.

The welfare of parish children rested on the officials of the parishes. Minutes of parish meetings, reports of factory visits and business correspondence, etc., showed that the parishes could barely discharge their duty following formal binding. The performance of parishes greatly varied depending upon the care and protection offered to the children. There were some parishes, the parishes of St Mary Newington, for example, who took protective care and expressed concern for the welfare of parish children. There were some parishes, the parish of St Mary Newington, for example, those took protective care and expressed concern for the welfare of Parish Children.

In her work, Honeyman writes that the poor London parishes—that of St George the Martyr, Southwark—optimally utilized the opportunities offered by factory apprenticeship. The majority of children were sent to textile mills in the Midlands and the North for a longer time, and the process continued. The protection of parish children varied and magistrates were active in Poor Law administration. This was responsible for maintaining and checking the children's condition. The 1802 Act empowered justices for inspection of factories using parish children. Both types of parishes—more protective and less protective, and also the most neglectful and least neglectful firms—prevailed. Birmingham and St Merry Newington, for example, chose wisely and were identified as protective firms which were economically successful. Those firms that made provision for their parish children properly succeeded in the longer term, while the other firms did not survive. From Honeyman's study, it is evident that parish apprentices were the part and parcel of the total labour force in England in the 18th and 19th centuries. The pauper children had nothing to do but only to contribute. But in the course of time, the children responded to their unbearable situation in many ways.

2.3. COLIN HEYWOOD

Colin Heywood, in his book,[3] has explained the child labour situation in 19th-century France.

During the 19th century in France, children from agriculture occupations were frequently found on streets, and at workshops and agriculture farms, gossiping with adults. In many factories/workshops, adult workers were assisted by the children (boys and girls). In the rural areas, children were less intellectually developed than those who lived in towns. Many agricultural and allied activities were performed by these children. They were seen working in agricultural operations,

---

[3] Colin Heywood, *Childhood in Nineteenth-century France: Work, Health, and Education among the 'Classes Populaires'* (New York: Cambridge University Press, 1988).

herding animals, collecting dung for manuring the fields, and so on. They also, simultaneously, joined gladly in festive entertainments.

The rampant usage of child labour in French factories during the 19th century came under huge criticism. Schooling for all children, as Heywood has pointed out, was not equally available. For the families of middle and upper classes, it was easier to access educational advantage. The peasant and artisan families barely had those opportunities which were accessed by people of higher echelon. As regards the children in an agricultural setting, their guardians faced the ancient problem of poverty in a rather new form. The author has referred to Olwen Huflon's estimates which showed that in 1787, one-third—or probably half of the French people—lived in poverty. The poorer families living in rural areas had little residential space for their members. Rooms were small with thatched roofs; floors were damp with inadequate heating, lighting and ventilation. There was a perpetual fear of fire hazards. In a nutshell, living conditions were very unhygienic, and due to this, many of them spent winter with coughs and running noses. Poverty-stricken peasant families sent their children to earn money for their living. Children worked as casual workers on local farms or as 'wage labour' for domestic industry including handloom shops.

Weaving was initially a male occupation. It began to include females during the 19th century. Many of children used to leave home at the age of seven or eight years and were engaged as domestic workers, shepherds or drovers with a farmer or as apprentices in domestic industry. When they became adolescents they started working as a farm servant.

There was a provision for elementary education for the children of peasant families. The author has presented data estimated by J. C. Toutain that states that the proportion of school attendance of children aged —five–fourteen years in France was one-fifth in 1815, half in 1850, and in 1881, it was three-fourths. Literacy levels varied between regions, between the sexes and between occupations. Parents had admiration toward school education. Apart from this, they had some elementary instructions for their children. Many of the parents believed in the process of learning by living. In this way, the children acquired skills and knowledge that helped them in everyday living.

The capitalist system of production was widely practised during the Industrial Revolution and afterwards, with free competition in trade and commerce. The condition of employment for children in the manufacturing sector transformed especially during the 18th and

19th centuries. With the advancement in technology, new forms of organization and elaborate commercial networks through the expansion of roads, canals and railways there was a huge expansion of trading within the country and with other countries.

The factory owners had special demand for child labour because (a) children were most suitable for certain jobs due to their physical advantages than the adults, (b) children were cheaply available and (c) they were docile. Also, during the Revolutionary and Napoleonic Wars, mechanized cotton textiles faced a shortage of adult workers. Naturally, the mill owners had to resort to using women and children in the factories. Since the late 19th century, the usage of child labour in factories and mines started declining. The income of working-class people started soaring up and naturally, they thought of securing the future of their children. Children were withdrawn from the labour force and admitted to the school. Naturally, many children of working-class families could experience a new pattern of childhood.

The urban commercial sector provided jobs to children as messengers, delivery boys and street traders. Children deserted by their parents opted for these sorts of jobs as their survival strategy. The author, based on statistical data, indicates that the mortality rate among the working children in the factory located in towns was higher than those working in the countryside. It means that working children in industries were confronted with situations that exerted a destructive influence on their health. Living rooms were dirty and in each house, on average, 30–40 people lived. Conditions of living were thus extremely unhygienic. Children were the main victims, and they suffered from typhoid and diarrhoea. Children and women working in the cotton spinning mills suffered from lungs diseases.

Heywood has referred to the concern of social thinkers about the moral welfare of working-class children in France. Contemporary literature showed that there were many instances of degradation of family life in industrial towns. Most of the investigating authors agreed that domestic virtues associated with peasant farming and handicraft trades were solid if compared with the factory workers in the French cities. It is said that machinery and big capital could bring wealth and civilization to society but could not make the morality of the young working people stronger. They rather became corrupted at their earliest age through the experiences of viciousness, drunkenness and disorder, and ultimately became the head of miserable and demoralized families.

Children working in French factories were exploited in many ways. Wages were low, working hours were longer, living conditions were poor, health facilities were poor and girl children were also sexually abused. During the start of the 19th century, the modern family and schooling for children were restricted to a few numbers of elites. There was slow progress of reforms to help the abandoned children.

The debate regarding the upliftment of children influenced the reformers in the ambit of the publication of Adam Smith's *Wealth of Nations* (1776). Adam Smith and his followers, such as David Ricardo and J. B. Say, expressed their opinion in favour of laissez-faire principle. This created a hostile climate for social legislation. Sismondi, a Swiss-born economist, who was initially the blind supporter of Adam Smith, later on rejected Ricardo and Say's abstract method and asserted that political economy should be a moral science based on experience, history and so much engagement of women and children in factory works. Eugene Buret, in his prize-winning essay 'For the Academy of Moral and Political Science on Poverty of Labouring Classes', asserted that the poor would overcome all the hurdles through their hard labour, not through charity. Like Buret—the author describes—the work of Villeneuve-Bargemont supported Sismondi.

On the issue of child labour, a series of debates were held during the 1820s under the leadership of Bourcart. Louis Vitterme, after his tour of textile manufacturing areas of France during the mid-1830s, announced in 1837 his remarkable conclusions where he stressed the need for enforcing legislation to regulate and improve working conditions for children. Ultimately, the first social legislation in France was enacted in 1841.

The French State also intervened in the lives of children by enacting the Child Labour Law on 19 May 1874. The law mentioned that children and minor girls between sixteen and twenty-one years of age could not be employed in factories and mines. The minimum working age for children was increased from eight to twelve years, and in some specific industries, it was fixed at ten years. Children were allowed to work for six hours a day. Night work was not allowed for children and for girls less than twenty-one years of age.

Heywood mentions that during the inspection of factories, the factory owners tried to hide or evacuate children, and it happened frequently in the smaller workshops. A series of important discussions towards reducing child labour was held during 1874–1892. By the

1870s, few children in France could escape the classroom. Heywood's book mentions that as per the statistics supplied by the Divisional Inspectors, two-thirds of the children aged twelve–fifteen years had the certificate of primary instruction in 1886. However, the worst forms of child labour continued to be found at glassworks and spinning mills where larger numbers of children were employed. The new anti-child labour law of 1892 superseded the law of 1874 which gave formal recognition to changes affecting child workers. Under the law, children could resist to some extent the pressures exerted by the factory owners, school teachers and child labour inspectors. Heywood considers this as an important step towards the emancipation of child labourers.

2.4. BESSIE VAN VORST

The US author and social reformer Bessie Van Vorst (1873–1928) describes, in her book,[4] that in 19th-century America, cotton mills thrived like mushrooms, and in both northern and southern parts of America, millions of children were put to work.

Vorst's *The Cry of the Children* depicts a true picture of the early-20th-century American cotton mills where little children in the age group of seven—fourteen years worked under untold miseries. To conduct her research, Vorst lodged for six weeks at different cotton mill towns of Maine, New Hampshire, Georgia and Alabama. She gathered vivid experiences about the lives, living conditions, working conditions and the tortures little children suffered. All the invaluable accounts that she collected were later presented in her epoch-making book.

In the first part of the book, Vorst presents the account of her visit to the Alabama cotton mills and her interaction with manufacturers and the working children there.

Vorst's first visit began with a quick survey of the cotton mills of the town of Anniston lying among the foothills of the Blue Ridge Mountains. The town is situated half-way between Birmingham and Atlanta. At Anniston, in Alabama, thousands of children worked in the umpteen numbers of cotton mills. The tenements rented by the mills' hands were the property of mills. However, there were several

---

[4] Bessie Van Vorst, *The Cry of the Children: A Study of Child Labour* (New York: Moffat, Yardaw Company, 1908).

schools that were located in the township area, not in the mill areas. The working children, like many other children in the locality, had the choice of going to school. It was optional, and there was no compulsory school law in Alabama State. Education was good in the context of well-to-do families, but it was a problem for poorer households and the mill people.

Vorst writes that most of the Alabama mills were built in 1895 and, in the town she first surveyed, there were 60,000 running spindles where 2,000 'hands' worked. 'Hands', the author explained, 'referred to the little children working in the mills'. The other mills she visited were located at Huntsville near Alabama City. Interviewing the little working children, she became certain that they used two ages while working. In the mills, they hid their actual age. The age was '10' years for a working child in the mill, and whenever the child left the factory premises, s/he 'became' 12-years-old. For these children, the working time was 12–13 hours a day and the wage was very low.

There was little scope for education for the working children, Vorst explains in her study. Their dresses were dirty and teary. In her words, 'Their clothes were flecked with cotton lint, grey and dusky like their ashen faces; they were bowed and drooping with a strange nervous animation that became them as pitifully as friskiness favours an unconscious old age'. The little working child did not have scope for going to school. Vorst's visit to a school at Huntsville mill gave a vivid picture. She saw that in the school's register, there were 600 children; but the total presence that day was 130. When she asked the teacher the reason for so poor an attendance, the lady teacher answered solemnly that the children were working at the mills. This showed that little children were arbitrarily taken out from school and used for work.

Vorst's second visit was to Georgia. In Georgia, she first visited a primary school before her visit to cotton mills. In the register of Georgia school, 250 students had been accommodated. A number of teachers gave a lesson to them and their salary came from the company. During her first visit she found 50 per cent of students in the classrooms. She shared her experience while she was entering the school gate. She saw a boy on the floor near the entrance, who was legless, maimed and twisted. She inferred and ultimately verified that this was due to the company's indifference to human life.

Many of the students were usual absentees because they were performing other tasks at school time. The tasks were different and varied:

Some said that they had to sell newspapers. Some others told that they were sick and some were discontented. They made, the author noted, a pitiful group.

Some children told Vorst that they never thought of joining the school. Her investigation revealed that the mill folks received so low wages that it could not bring the household members out of starvation. The only option left for such children was sending their children to work. During other visits, Vorst found many truants—both boys and girls—not attending schools. Some of them joined mills, and some—especially girls—stayed home to look after the ailing family members. Many of them, during summer, went back to farming. During other seasons they worked in mills. The little children were toiling from early morning to early evening. The author writes that they worked from quarter to six in the morning until quarter past at night, with one half-hour to rest and eat at noon.

During the visit to a factory, Vorst found that over 40 per cent of working children were under the age of 12 years. It was usual, as the author presented, for almost all the southern cotton mills; but an unusual occurrence in the Cartersville factory which had installed new machines. She presents that though there were 100,000 spindles at the Lindale mills, only 1,500 children were employed. At Cartersville, there were 30,000 spindles and 300 children working. Thus, the boys who were essential and indispensable in factory works were fast becoming redundant and were replaced by automation.

Bessie Van Vorst's next visit was to the mills of Griffin—a southern town. The first visit of this tour was to a spinning mill. Entering into the room, she found that there were 20 little children of whom only 2 said that they were over 12. This was one of the spinning mills where she received permission to visit. She also visited a nearby mill without permission, and entering the classroom she found 10 children under the age of twelve years. In other mills, she was not allowed to visit. But she collected information about children from the teachers of the neighbouring schools. She gathered that many little children at the age of eight and nine left school even before completing the first book offered in the school and joined work in the spinning mills. She explains that one day while in the street, she met a 'kind-looking' person, whom she asked the name of the mill superintendent and got the answer. The person, like many staring eyes, said that he worked in the mill for 30 years; but when played out he was played and that was the rule of the game there. As regards wages, he replied that barely little would be left for savings. While being asked about changing his profession, he answered that after joining in the mill and working there for 15 to 20 years they did not dare to quit.

The author also visited two large Columbus factories. Like Southern mills, workers here including the working children were migratory. Thousands of children worked and contributed a lot through which the factory owners earned huge profits. One account divulged by the superintendent of a factory stated that the factory earned a profit of 18 per cent per annum.

Classes for working children were held from 07.30 AM to 10.30 AM and from 01.00 PM to 04.00 PM. During the evening also, classes would be held. In her book, Vorst mentions that in 1901, the Columbus Primary Industrial School—the first Public School in the United States of America—was opened. One hundred and five students got admitted in the school. After the first three months, it was found that not a single student could read a simple English sentence. However, as Vorst presents, things improved remarkably after the Principal of the School, Mr John Sherman, and his wife stayed as 'resident' in the school for five years. During these years, they did many humanitarian works—especially for child labourers—in the South.

Of all the manufacturing establishments in Atlanta, Vorst found that the factories manufacturing cotton cloth were the largest in number. However, in these factories, the rooms built for the workers and their hands in the mill villages were very dirty and dingy. The children at the age of six or seven were sent to mill. When Vorst began asking mothers why the little children were sent to work, one woman answered that it was the only option left to her family to avoid taking to the streets. Such hapless children were sent half-day to school and half-day to Atlanta mills. The wages provided to these children were very low, ranging from $2.50 to $4.50, and this would be against six to seven hours of work. Due to the 'ignorance' and 'dire poverty' of the child workers—the author mentions—the manufacturers fastened the belts of their insatiable greed. In a bag-manufacturing company in Atlanta, the author found that there were around 100 little children out of 160 hands. Most of the workers who did the job of swiping were children of the age of five–nine years. One little child said—the author puts—'I'm five—I'm only he'pin'.

The author also visited Augusta cotton mills—a city country on the central-eastern border of the US state of Georgia. The cotton mills were run by a system of water power canals. The rooms of the mills were dingy and dark and woodwork and stairways were old. Out of 1,400 looms, 400 remained idle. Vorst wanted to visit the mill but was not allowed to interview the little toilers. Asking about the usage of 'coloured people' in the mill, she received answers from the 'guides' that they were used, and were not allowed to mix with the 'white-complexioned children'. The Afro-Americans, 70 in number, became frequent absentees. Most of them remained idle and spent their expenses with the saved money and as and when their money gave out they rejoined the work. The author states that there was no law in Georgia regarding hours of work and the working age. Children suffered due to this and had to face abuse and violence. There was police intervention throughout Georgia and Alabama.

While visiting the North of America especially the mills of Maine, New Hampshire and Massachusetts, Vorst noticed many migratory child workers in the factory. During her Biddeford visit, she found that of the total of 1,600 registered inhabitants, 1,300 were born overseas. The workers could speak different languages, such as French, Italian and Greek, apart from English. It was a common practice to employ children at a very tender age and the working periods, everywhere, were quite long. Vorst decided to interview the mill owners and accordingly visited the mills of Sanford. Like Biddeford, a large number of workers were from other countries at Sanford. One mill owner told that the French-Canadian families helped more than the Americans because the former families had a bigger number of family members than the Americans. She categorically asked the mill owner whether it was profitable to use child labour. His answer was straightforward. He said that the owners could not get on without the usage of children. Children to them were more efficient than the adults. Many children were in work in the mills. The restriction on the use of child labour could be lifted if children were allowed 16 weeks to go to school. But it was not strictly followed. In the mills, more than 50 per cent of inhabitants were French, and only a few Americans were engaged as workers.

Several militant clubwomen of Maine initiated a movement against child labour and forced the amendment of law against child labour, which, ultimately, resulted in the amendment of the law in 1905 and the appointment of inspectors. In practice, however, there was no implementation of the Act. No statistics were officially available on child labour, and in this context, Vorst relied on data supplied by the inspector unofficially. In a Lewiston mill, there were 2,000 hands of which 170 were very little children. She visited a public kindergarten school. The teacher told that there were only two Americans and the rest were Greeks, Jews, Americans, Portuguese, French and Russian.

Vorst next visit was to Dover which consisted of 15,000 population, the majority of whom were foreigners from Europe, America, Portugal, Greece, Poland, Russia, etc. The agent of the mill accompanied the author wherever she visited. While visiting an upper room she found that very little children were working hard to produce extremely fine and perfect thread. It seemed that the little children were very much indispensable in the mill. Interacting with the militant members of the Federation of Women's Club and asking about the conditions of child labour in the New Hampshire mill, the author came to know that many children were working in the mills of Manchester, Nashua and Suncook. The cotton mills at Manchester, New Hampshire, covered 125 acres and 13,704 acres in the world. About 50 per cent of inhabitants living in the Manchester area were foreigners having their large families. Contrarily, the American families wanted two children with a good education. The inhabitants hid their children's age and managed false certificate on age.

During one of her visits, Vorst came across a lady, Landrys by name, who was deserted by her husband. She lived with her four children. She worked in the mill. Her elder daughter left school and stayed home. She did all the domestic work for the family and looked after her two younger brothers and sister. The elder daughter, aged 13, worked in the factory.

Vorst visited mills in Massachusetts and found that the age limit for child labour was ten years and the working time was 10 hours a day. This was as per the 1876 law. The child labour problem in the South was different from that of the North. The South suffered from acute labour shortages especially the shortage of hands. Due to scarcity of workers, not more than three-fourths of the plants could be operated. In the North, what mills required was not the quantity, but the quality of labourers. Since there was an abundant supply of hands, there surfaced urgent implementation of compulsory laws. In this direction, clubwomen played a dominant role and took up the child labour issue.

Britain and other European nations were pioneers in protecting the interests of working-class people including women and children, and later, many states of America took up initiatives to that end through the passing of labour legislations.

2.5. THE ILO

The ILO took a great initiative in publishing *Child Labour: A Textbook for University Students* from Geneva in 2004. The prime objective was to make higher education students understand the concept of child labour and its causes. The major issues highlighted are the family context, poverty and additional factors of the household that allow children to work with the family adults such as working in agriculture or working with family seniors in the home-based cottage workshops. Children are forced to work in many other sectors—manufacturing, fishing, construction, domestic service and the like. Children's involvement is mostly found in the informal sector of the developing countries of the world. Naturally, their work in this informal sector is not formal or official and thus does not have legal implications. There is no job security, wages are low and there is no wage payment if children become ill or are injured at the workplace. All these have been lucidly explained in the book. An informal and formal sector distinction has clearly been made—this says that in the informal sector there is easy entry while formal sector entry in the factory or industry is very restricted due to many legal obligations. A high degree of resourcefulness and family ownership is present in the informal sector, while in the formal sector there is the frequent reliance on external resources and there exists corporate ownership.

Small-scale operation and skills acquired outside the formal school system are absent in the informal sector. The formal sector, on the other hand, is a large-scale operation with skills acquired formally from the school system. In this book, it is discussed in detail, that children globally work more in rural than in urban areas. They are mostly forced to work in agriculture—sometimes in hazardous such as in tobacco production; some are engaged in commercial plantations like fruit production, coffee production, flowers and sugarcane.

All the children working in agriculture are from rural poor families with no scope of education, even the basic education they cannot complete because of poverty or family attitude. Also millions of children in developing countries work in the informal manufacturing sector which is mostly labour intensive. The majority of such undertakings are garments, toys, matches, brassware, soccer balls, etc.

The book mentions that child labour is not a major issue in the developed world today as it was during the 18th, 19th and 20th centuries. Still, there is the existence of child labour, although in lesser measures, in the developed world including the United States of America, Poland, Italy and Portugal. In developed countries, some sorts of work are done by the children illegally which are largely part-time jobs. The children there try to combine work with the school for their survival and for providing partial income to their family.

Children perform two types of worst forms of work, which has been presented in the book—worst form 'by definition' and 'by condition'. Slavery, trafficking, debt bondage, armed conflict, prostitution or pornography, and illicit activities mentioned in Convention Number 182 and in similar other 'Conventions' falls under the first category. In the second category falls works like hazardous manufacturing operations, mining, crushing rocks, deep sea diving, construction, scavenging or rag-picking, carrying heavy loads, etc. A section on commercial sexual exploitation of child labour has also been included; here, it is said that 1.8 million children in the world have been trafficked and sexually exploited.

The second part of the book deals with the causes of child labour, that is, the forces that help to occur the unwanted happening of child labour. In this context, special focus is given on the role of family and economic pressures that lead to child labour. In small farm families, children's help in agricultural operation is very much needed. Even financially sound farmers need their children's help in agriculture. Also, children help their parents in running small shops, and commercial activities or small family-based petty trade and businesses. It is noted that poverty is the cause and a consequence of child labour in a country. Lower-income countries indeed have more representation of child labour.

The households where survival is the main concern—that is, where poverty is extreme and the basic needs of the family are not fulfilled—are forced to devote all their existing resources to production. These households are caught in a survival trap. As the income of the family dwindles, children, in an increased number, are forced to work to earn the familial bread. The internal factors identified for the existence of child labour in poor families are difficult family situations, such as parentless or single parent families, poor family values, low educational levels of parents and low parental skills. External factors found are population suffering from social exclusion, socio-economic dislocation, the effect of human immunodeficiency virus/acquired immunodeficiency syndrome (HIV/AIDS), strong peer groups and external influence, and the special situations of girls.

The book puts much emphasis on education in the context of child labour. It requires time to go to school, and also enough time is needed in the evening for the study purpose. Similarly, enough time is required for working. Both schooling and working cannot be combined. If there is legislation about compulsory basic education, certainly there would be less prevalence of children in the working place. Many experts view that compulsory education, up to a level, can be a necessary condition but not sufficient condition for eliminating child labour. There are certain other issues essentially needed to address the situation. The decision for sending children to school, for example, depends on the household. It depends on the costs and benefits of education. Parents evaluate whether benefits associated with schooling are larger than the costs of education. The returns or benefits to education are a long-term phenomenon and it does not go to parents. It is enjoyed by the children in future. But the costs are being borne by the parents in the short run which completely depends on the affordability of parents. The decision of parents of withdrawing their children from school and sending them for work is compounded by a 'principal–agent' interaction problem related to costs and benefits of education. Here 'principal' is the child and 'agent' is the parent. The child wants his parent to invest in their education, which is expensive for the parent.

As is discussed in the book, the costs which are borne at present by the parent reap the benefits that go to the child in the long run. Naturally, parents do not wish to send the child to school, rather withdraw the child from school and involve him to work. The comparative study of child labour and schooling in Africa shows that one important way to keep children in the educational system is to improve access to credit to the children in education. The family will pay back the money in future.

An important study report by Christopher Heady based in Ghana, 2000, has been presented in the book. This study analyses basically the effects of child labour on learning achievement. It finds that the children's mathematics and writing skills are very low. Those who work in their home do better than those who work outside. The condition of girl students is worse than that of the boys. This is due to the fact that girls work more than boys. It is suggested that education cannot contribute to eliminating child labour unless there is increased access to education, improved quality education, formal and informal education combined with vocational training with basic education.

The book discusses different types of girl child labour as well, which is mainly due to their gender biases. Girls are trafficked for domestic service, armed conflict, sexual services, agriculture and construction. In many countries—it is indicated in the book—girls' education is threatened by the preference of educating sons. It is necessary to make efforts to increase girls' attendance in school. This can help to eliminate child labour.

The third part of the book is about research on child labour. The actions of governments and international organizations on eliminating child labour in an effective manner—have been discussed in this part of the book. It is suggested that the participation of governments and non-governmental organizations is urgently required to present an actual picture of the status and extent of child labour in any country or a specific region of the world. The government's action in this respect in enforcing laws and international standards to protect children from hazardous child labour is very essential. Governments can explore children's needs and accordingly set targets and programmes and arrange funds for achieving those targets.

The book, finally, mentions the role of international organizations' programmes in the elimination of child labour. The organizations, such as the ILO, UNESCO, United Nations International Children's Emergency Fund (UNICEF), the World Bank and the IMF, can play a vital role in eliminating child labour. Actions of employers' organizations, trade unions, non-government organizations (NGOs) and children have also a great role to play in eliminating child labour from the globe. Universities can also influence policymaking through research and publication on child labour. The media —it is said—also can disseminate information on the plight of child labour through newspapers and the Internet, influence public opinion and create awareness about child labour issues. NGOs also have a great role to play in motivating governments to take a decision on working children.

2.6. KAUSHIK BASU

In his essay,[5] Kaushik Basu lucidly distinguishes between 'child' and 'labour', and in defining and distinguishing the terms, he refers to the ILO and Ashagrie. He mentions that child labour is an old problem that persisted in different parts of the world through different stages of history.

Child labour, the author argues, is a part of economic life and child labourers work under hazardous conditions. The use of children in the factories of England and other European nations intensified since the time of the Industrial Revolution and the mid-19th century in America. The author then narrates the world's experience of child labour. He cites the estimate of child labour by Ashagrie in the 1993 publication and shows that there has been a downward trend of child labour between 1980 and 1990 in the world as a whole. Asia—both East Asia and South Asia—has witnessed a decreasing trend of child labour, while an increasing trend was observed in America and Africa during the same period of time. He also cites the works of 1998 publication by Ashagrie, and the 1996 publication by the ILO wherein it was noticed that there was an upward trend of the figures in countries like Ghana, India, Indonesia and Senegal. The ILO estimates mentioned that adding part-time works done by children would make the number of child labour double and that would be 250 million in 1995.

Because of its large population, Asia has always contributed with the largest number of child labour. Basu—keeping this in mind—has surveyed the workforce participation rate of children aged 10–14 years category. Assessing on this basis, it has been found by him that during 1990, the problem of child labour was very serious in Africa representing 27.87 per cent. For Asia, it was 15.19 per cent. He has also analysed the ILO child labour data from 1950 to 1995, along with projections up to 2010. The data has revealed a remarkable decline in the child labour participation rate for countries like China, India and Italy. For many Latin American countries, including Brazil, the trend is declining, but at a lesser rate than expected. The problem, however, remains extremely serious in large parts of SSA. The author mentions

---

[5] Kaushik Basu, 'Child Labour: Causes, Consequences, and Cure, with Remarks on International Labour Standards,' *Journal of Economic Literature* XXXVII (September 1999): 1089–1119.

a contemporary study on child labour conducted by the researchers at Delhi School of Economics and Indian Social Institute, which found that child labour in rural areas was lesser compared to the number of children working in industries. In the rural areas, children can work as well as they can continue their studies because of the light work they perform in the rural sector. In this case, the author has also referred to the 1983 publications—respectively—by Kothari and Kulkarni.

In his essay, Basu asserts that after the enforcement of legislation against child labour and compulsory education for children, there has been a sharp decline in the number of child labourers. Another reason was the increasing prosperity of Europe, America and Japan due to which parents have become determined not to send children to the factory.

The author has referred to Peter Scholliers' study (1995) and stated that there was a reduction in the number of working children during the mid-19th century and it was not due to the enactment of legislation. This happened in Ghent, Belgium. Weiner (1991) has been cited by the author who stated that only banning child labour could do little to solve the problem; rather, compulsory education along with legislative intervention could better handle the problem. In this context, Basu has also referred the 1990, 1996 and 1998 works respectively by the works of Nardinelli, Cunninghum and Viazzo, and Moehling.

Early writers such as Karl Marx, Alfred Marshall and Arthur Pigon—the author mentions—believed in government intervention to curb child labour. Karl Marx opposed the exploitation of child labour but did not believe in a complete ban. John Stuart Mill, Basu points out, opposed the employment of child labour in industrial work. Mill stressed that parents should encourage their children to go to school. He also noted that children should be prevented from overwork and should be restrained from doing work beyond their strength. Mill thus stressed the positive externality of education.

In the context of the battle against child labour, the author discusses three types of interventions and institutions. These are intra-national, supranational and extra-national. Enactment and implementation of laws against child labour come under the ambit of intra-national effort. This is done on the part of the national government's implementation of national boundaries. The enactment of a law prohibiting child labour by the state of Massachusetts in 1837 forced the firms to not employ children below the age of 15 years (who had not attended school at least three months in the previous year). The laws passed by Nepal known as Labour Act of 1992 and The Children's Act of 1992 were such kind of intra-national effort to combat child labour. Basu also cites the act passed by Northern Thailand known as the Daughters Education Programme (DEP). This Act, passed in 1989, prevented young girl children from going into prostitution by providing education. It also required mobilizing local opinion through different ways. The supra-national intervention comes from international organizations such as the ILO, the World Trade Organization (WTO) and UNICEF. These organizations rectify and motivate nations by establishing conventions, the ultimate objective being curbing child labour.

The imposition of the international labour standards, according to Basu, is the most controversial instrument in curbing child labour. Following the imposition of minimum rules and conditions for labour, trade sanctions are imposed on defaulting countries that do not satisfy the minimum standards. The author identifies another type of law that can be imposed by a country on the importation of goods from other countries which used child labour in the production of such goods. He has referred—in this context—to the 'Harkin's Bill', which was much debated in the US Congress. He mentions that such types of interventions might be misused by lobbies and a group of countries representing sectarian interests.

Externality in the context of child labour plays an important part, which had been rightly disused by Grootaert and Kanboor in their 1995 publication, Basu explains. Groetaert and Kanboor state the possibility of externality that the social returns to education might be larger than the private return. In this context, government intervention to direct children away from work and join school might become desirable.

The author has analysed child labour in terms of modelling household behaviour. He has referred in this context to earlier initiatives undertaken, for example, by Mark Rosenzrweing and Robert Evenson (in their 1977 book) and Goldin (in his 1979 publication). They expressed the significance of household decision-making, explaining the decisions of consumption and child labour, and child schooling and fertility. He has also analysed Moehling's Model which considers that each agent in the household is concerned about the consumption of each and every number of the family/household. This has been expressed with the help of the household's utility function which is the weighted average of the utilization of all household members where the weight attached to the parent's utility depends on the incomes earned by the parent and the child. In the household's utility function the weight attached to a person depends upon how much he or she earns. The author, in his collective model, explains the household's decision problem. Basu cites the 'textbook case of selfish individuals', that is, the parent is aimed at his own consumption and so also is the child. It is still the collective model of the household and thus the allocation of resources remains to be Pareto efficient. As he discusses, the child's labour supply depends on adult wage and child wage and wages prevailed in the market. He has also referred to the Gupta Model (1998) to explain extra household bargaining. He cites Gupta's survey on child labour in some West Bengal villages wherein he assumes that parents were uninterested in their children's welfare. Due to the lack of land or cattle, parents could not productively use their child and naturally child is sent to the employer who possessed such resources. In this model, the bargaining between the parent and the employer occurs over the wage to be paid to the child for his /her work and the fraction of income to be paid in the form of food. The author believed that this might be empirically questionable.

The author discusses multiple equilibria and government intervention. He demonstrates the model following what has been delineated in the 1998 work by Basu and Van using two special assumptions. These are luxury axiom and substitution axiom. The luxury axiom states that a household would not send its child out to work if the income of non-child sources is sufficiently high. The substitution axiom states that adult labour is substituted for child labour. Basu elaborates his aims by stating that for every household, there exists a critical wage and the household would send its child out to work if the adult wage prevailing in the market is lower than critical wage and the adult labour and child labour are perfect substitutes, subject to an adult equivalence correction.

Basu has used a competitive model to explain household decisions about child labour. In this model, it was shown in a diagram that if the market wage remains below a critical level, then all the children would be sent to work and if the market wage exceeds that critical level, no child would be sent to work. In the latter case, the total labour supply would go down. As wages increase, households withdraw their children from work and thus the total labour supply is kept decreasing. The author calls such type of supply curve of labour (adult labour + child labour) a 'hybrid supply curve' which is an unusual supply curve, that is, it is not the standard labour supply curve. Here multiple equilibria occur, that is, more than one equilibrium takes place where the wage rate and the labour supply are being determined.

In the discussion, Professor Basu has referred to 'social norm' which was initially analysed by Hirschman in his 1995 work, and also discussed by Partha Dasgupta (1993) and Basu (1998). Sending a child to work—Basu considers—is partly a matter of social norm and it is related to social stigma cost. Sending a child of a household to work is attached to social stigma cost and sending more children represents lower social stigma cost to the household and vice versa.

There is certainly an impact of adult unemployment on child labour and this has greatly been described with the help of a model by Basu. He has presented two questions: Question 1: How many adults will find employment? Question 2: Will children be working, and if so, what will be the incidence of child labour? He answers these two questions together with the help of the model. He explains that wages for child labour are flexible, and that is the reason for which the demand for child labour must be equal to the supply of child labour. If the adult labour market, the author considers, is oligopsonistic in nature, there is every possibility for a declining trend in the number of child labour when there is a rise in the legal minimum wage.

Finally, the author is free to analyse the long-term consequence of child labour, although some economists, Basu mentions, have provided hints for modelling the dynamics of child labour. They were Oded Galor and Joseph Zeira (1993), Abhijit Banerjee and Andrew Newman (1993) and Lars Ljungqvist (1993). The author also develops the idea of 'child labour trap'. To explain this, Basu considers an overlapping generations' model. In this model, each person lives for two periods—the first period as a child and the second period as an adult. In the second period he 'gives birth' to a child. As a person the child has two options—either he can go to work or go to school. In this model, Basu finds three steady-state equilibriums of which two are stable. At a point, it shows a minimum wage for an adult that motivates poor parents to send their child to work the whole day long. Because of the very low income of the household, the parents have to send his child to work for sustenance. This child fails to acquire skills, and when he becomes an adult he makes his child again send to work. He cannot think to send his child to school. The equilibrium that has been enriched is called 'child labour trap'.

There is no scope of avoiding this trap. Here the child labour of today creates another child labour when he becomes an adult and it continues for generations. On the other hand, the other stable equilibrium point—as Basu explains—represents the child going to school, where s/he acquires skills and earns money as an adult. S/he thus can now send her/his child to school. This is called a 'virtuous cycle'. When an economy is caught under 'child labour trap' there is a need for strong government intervention. The children of such households should be provided education with skills so that they become successful in getting employment and earning adequately. It is, therefore, necessary to provide education to children through government intervention. This will educate one generation and this will help the economy rolling towards virtuous equilibrium.

The author, in this context, refers to D. P. Chaudhuri's 1997 discussion on 'virtuous spirals' and through this how child labour gets reduced when a 'tipping point' is attached beyond which a remarkable and often unstoppable effect takes place in the economy. This can only be attained by government intervention. Basu stresses in his study the importance of investment in education. He mentions that the availability of credit on decent terms can save money from the hardships of child labour. He refers to the case of India and cites the frequent dropout of students because of parents losing their job or the death of the breadwinner of the household or for medical ground. In such a helpless situation, the availability of credit at an easier term can best prevent children from joining work as child labour.

Basu discusses the Baland and Robinson model (proposed in their 1998 publication) in relation to the credit question. It is a two-period model of child labour in which there exists inefficiency in spite of parental benevolence. This is due to parents' lack of resources to educate the child. In this case, only one option remains and that is to borrow for a child's education. But this is not usually possible. It requires going beyond providing perfect capital markets. Here comes the enforcement of intergenerational contracts. In such a contract, parents borrow for his/her child's education and the repayment of the loan is made by the child when he/she becomes an adult and earns sufficiently. Basu lightly discussed the issue of fertility decisions. He considers in this study the number of children, as given exogenously. He says that, the number of children a family does have depends on two things—it is partly optimal and it also depends on whether the children can be employed. He has referred to Cain's study of Bangladesh in 1982, which shows that a child's income usually supports the family and by the age of 12 a child becomes a net producer and when he attains the age of 15 years his cumulative contribution exceeds his cumulative consumption.

Basu, in his study, presents a theoretical foundation concerning violence and sexual harassment. He uses the term 'principle of free contract'. He considers that there is no question of a ban on sexual harassment in the workplace if the contract is free. If harassment is allowed then the workers who are averse to harassment will be worse off because the wage they receive will be lower than what it would be if the law does not allow harassment. Here Basu considers a market where there are two types of workers—type-1 workers and type-2 workers. Type-1 workers have a strong aversion to sexual harassment than type-2 workers. He infers, the market wage increases if there is a ban on child labour and if the ban is removed, the wage must fall. It invariably worsens the condition of type-1 households.

Finally, Basu discusses the issue of 'international labour standards' and 'social clause' as a prerequisite for trade. For a long, people have argued the need to enforce some minimum standards of labour such as working conditions, working hours a day, wages etc., for the well-being of workers. International forums, such as the ILO and the WTO, have played a major role in the functioning and improving international standards in developing countries.

Basu seems to be deeply interested in child labour standards, and he refers to the theoretical modelling of child labour standards as discussed in the 1996 publication by Maskus and Holman. He studied the impact of child labour laws on welfare with and without capital mobility. Two alternative situations could be considered here: (a) firms that can freely move from one country to another and (b) firms that are completely country-specific. If a ban on child labour is imposed in one country then large monitoring costs on the ban can be borne by the country. If there is no ban, both the workers and employers will be benefited. The workers are likely to be worse with the ban. Basu considers that if all the nations agree to impose a ban on child labour, there could be no capital flight. The author adds that labour standards may be undesirable for each individual nation but they may be good if the standards are coordinated across a large number of countries. This would certainly help to reduce the volume of child labour globally.

2.7. G. K. LIETEN

In his introductory chapter of the edited book,[6] G. K. Lieten emphasizes that child labour emerged in the late 18th century in Western Europe as a by-product of the Industrial Revolution. In those days, families were forced to be separated from their own means of livelihood such as their plots of own land or their craft and joined to work in the factories with low wages and very long working hours only for their survival. Later on, in the 19th century and afterwards, political and social movements were initiated against child labour in the industrialized nations. Also, different movements against child labour started in the countries which demolished the logic of employing child labour, and ultimately, legislations against child labour were enacted. Lieten mentioned, Myers' four perspectives on child labour wherein Myers rejected child labour, but at the same time appreciated it because of the fact that child labour helped alleviate poverty. Myers rejected child labour for it leads to adult unemployment and lowers wages. Most adverse effect is the intergenerational poverty that has been created by child labour. It is argued that children perform varied activities such as playing, leisure, attending school, doing domestic work and other productive activities.

There is no problem with this. The problem occurs when children are forced to do works which are exploitative and hazardous. Part-time light work is allowed which can be a learning experience. By doing such work, children may acquire skills that will help them in their later life. Also, that would positively help to improve their self-confidence and gain practical knowledge.

Lieten has raised his doubts about the magnitude of child labour. He relies more on the ILO and the World Bank-supplied data on child labour. The data calculation was based on new sampling anthropologies in stand-alone surveys which show more accurate subjects to errors. Based on the ILO data on child labour, 2010, Lieten finds that child labour has started to reduce. But after reviewing the child labour data of Peru, Bolivia and Guatemala, Lieten come to the conclusion that child labour is on the rise. Referring the ILO and Instituto Nacional de Estadística e Informática (INEI) data, Lieten finds that in Peru the incidence of child labour in the age group of 6–11 years has increased

---

[6] G. K. Leiten, ed., 'Introduction: The Worst Forms of Child Labour in Latin America,' In *Hazardous Child Labour in Latin America* (London: Springer, 2011).

from 2.5 per cent to 21.7 per cent between 1993 and 2001 and again, to 32 per cent in 2005. It is observed that the official survey does not cover children involved in informal or illegal labour sectors. He further raised a complicated issue of child employment, as also mentioned by Levison et al., in their 2007 publication. He says that the proportion of children at a particular point of time in a year may be larger than at another point of time within the same year. In this case, the calculation on child work should be multiplied with a factor of 2. It is found that the qualitative data of child labour is poor because the perspectives of working children and their parents are very often excluded.

Lieten presented results of three studies on child labour, that is, (a) Comparative Study on the Worst Forms of Child Labour (2006–2007) in Bolivia, Guatemala and Peru; (b) Worst Forms of Child Labour in Rural Areas of Bolivia and Peru (2008–2009); and (c) a Large-Scale Study on the Phenomenon of Street Children of Lima (2009). The first research objective was to map the working and living conditions of child labour in specific economic sectors and the consequences of this work for their physical and emotional well-being. The second focus was to study the reasons why children work in the worst forms sectors. The third objective was to map the existing policy initiatives and to identify the best practices.

2.8. SALLY ATKINSON-SHEPPARD

In her book,[7] Sally Atkinson-Sheppard presents an intensive investigation on street children's engagement as child labour and in the crime groups of Bangladesh. For this work, the author focuses on the experiences of 22 street children of Dhaka, Bangladesh. This is an interesting study based on participant observation and interviews in the group with the street children who work as child labour and also as weapon carriers, drug sellers and street beggars. They are also hired to commit political violence and conduct contract killings.

In her 2019 work, Atkinson-Sheppard applies the term 'street children' to those young people who have some sort of street connectivity. This means that children have spent some parts of the week on street, and in this sense, they are the 'children of street'. The children with

---

[7] Sally Atkinson, *The Gangs of Bangladesh Mastaans, Street Groups and 'Illicit Child Labourers' in Dhaka* (Basingstoke: Palgrave Macmillan, 2019).

whom interviews were taken all worked on the street before their involvement in the organized crime groups.

Atkinson-Sheppard raises a question: Why children are in the street and what motivates them to involve in such crime? Like many studies, the author finds that it is the poverty and economic circumstances that force them to do so. The core of discussion in the book is the *mastaans* or the mafia groups which operate in a market for crime, violence and social protection. The mafia groups have connivance with the corrupt politicians and the police and they have their involvement in a market for protection. The author investigates that the *mastaan* groups work across Dhaka and the adjacent slums.

The *mastaans* lead organized crime groups and each group consists of many members who are also the *mastaans*. There are, the author says, more than the top 10 *mastaan* bosses operating in Bangladesh. There are various divisions of labour in the *mastaan* groups. Some groups collect extortion money, some conduct killings. They monopolize markets and generate a fund to control areas of Dhaka. Mirpur has been chosen as the case study area. Mirpur is a thickly populated area along with a large slum. There are some mafia groups that operate in Mirpur and its adjacent slums. The area is highly developed in the garment industry and many other businesses are being flourished in Mirpur. Very often crimes take place and there is a notorious mafia gang operating under the control of one Mr Sahadat, a great mafia boss. Mr Sahadat, the author narrates, has been absconding and is now in India. From India, he operates the criminal team in Mirpur. Mr Sahadat's groups control street-based gangs who work for him. The groups, known as 'Mirpur area boys', aged 8–15 years, work on the street and conduct activities such as thefts and extortion. Every mafia group, as told, is looked after by a group leader. In each group, it says, there are five to six members and the group leader is a little bit senior to other members in the group.

Atkinson-Sheppard writes that there is a deep relationship between the *mastaan* bosses and the corrupt politicians. *Mastaans* are used by political leaders for voting purposes. In Mirpur slum areas, the *mastaans*, in collaboration with politicians, control access to gas, electricity, water, hospital appointments and land. They charge inflated prices for access to the facilities. The author collected data from the street children and the feedback received from them reveal that street children consider, the work they perform, is not a crime rather it is the normal work that street children usually do. Also, they consider, they are engaged in business and what they receive from the *mastaan* group is profit from the business. Street children are hired and illicit works such as drug peddling, money extortion and even murders are committed by them. Also, another important criminal work that they perform is land grabbing in the slums. They are used in political violence such as they participate in 'hartals'. The children expressed that they earn more participating in gangs than other jobs they do. The *mastaan* groups also give protection to them.

Mastaans are, in fact, always ready to conduct illegal activities with their gangs in collaboration with dishonest politicians and policemen. Gangs are used to control the areas of the city and the slums. The vulnerable street children work for them at the grassroots level. They form groups in order to face the risk and vulnerability they face. The street children hired and used to commit crimes are exploited. In this system of a market for protection operated by *mastaan*, children are the clients who work for the patrons, the *mastaans*. The street children working for a group are also protected from rival groups. Data collected by the author show that the *mastaans* usually pay an amount of their extortion money to the police. In return, these group members—the street children in the groups—are protected from legal prosecution. In explaining this, the author cited a number of related studies.

The street children involved in the *mastaan* group perform 'illicit work', as the author mentions, similar to that of ILO's definition of worst forms of child labour. ILO's definition refers to children who work under severe and damaging conditions in industries, including trafficking, slavery, armed conflict or using children for illicit activities such as drug selling, fall under 'illicit child labour' category. The author, however, asserts that criminalizing children in Bangladesh has been applied as a last resort. This means that protective measures have been taken to prevent children from involving in criminal activities in any form.

Atkinson-Sheppard repeatedly mentions that the ILO has failed to include children involved in organized crime in the definition of the worst forms of child labour. Also, he finds incompleteness of the legislation on child labour in Bangladesh because there is no particular mention of children involved in organized crime in the legislation. In this context, it requires further research on child labour in this particular aspect and relevant issues.

The crux of the book is found in the last but concluding chapter of the book wherein Atkinson-Sheppard had repeated interviews with Mr Sharif: once a street child and now a benevolent person dedicated his life for the cause of street children. In her final task of the book, Atkinson-Sheppard tries to portray the lives of street children who only think about how to gather food, water, and where to stay and cannot see tomorrow. The author could read the face of Mr Sharif where it was written that the street was his only shelter and joining to *mastaan* group was his last resort. The author managed to sit with him several times and could hear from him how his father was killed in the 1971 Independence War by the Pakistan Military. The whole family, after his father's death, became destitute. His sister was abducted by the Pakistan Military and kept in the Military Camp. She was raped again and again—like the 0.1 million women who were abducted and confined in the military camps in a similar manner. His brother became a drug addict and the whole family was ostracized. Mr Sharif had no option but to fly. He did not know where to go, where to stay and how to live. He left home in 1972 and stayed in the Dhaka railway station with other street children for three-and-a-half years and was involved with them in the crime. He led a miserable life there. Staying in the railway station his only desire was how to leave the street and the illicit work he was committing. A senior Railway Guard once rescued him and took him to his family. He completed his university education and managed a government job. After that, he dedicated his life to the cause of child labour, and particularly the street children. Mr Shariff narrated to Atkinson-Sheppard how street children during the 1970s were ostracized from society and how they faced untold miseries and sufferings in order to just manage the bare minimum necessaries, that is, shelter, water and food.

Mr Shariff used the term 'shelter' to describe the term 'protection'. Criminal groups got protection from very well-to-do and influential persons of the society and in exchange, the groups provided 'criminal muscle' to them. His shifting from the railway station to the house of a railway guard helped him to rebuild his life and as he told Atkinson-Sheppard, he became a completely new man—a person who dedicated the rest of his life to the cause of the poor, downtrodden and the helpless vulnerable street children. The study on street children makes a certain addition to knowledge through the exploitation of a relationship between the vulnerable street children and organized crime in a developing country context.

2.9. ASA MATSUOKA

In *Labour Conditions of Women and Children in Japan*, Asa Matsuoka[8] has presented some valuable accounts of the working conditions that existed among women and children in Japanese textile factories. In addition to this, the international influences in determining the working conditions and in making protective labour legislation had been elaborately discussed.

The author begins the book by analysing the characteristics of Japanese factory conditions. Since the beginning of factory systems, the Japanese government made protective provisions— regulation and legislation on a national scale on the statute books. But these laws covered only the larger factories, not the smaller units.

The Japanese industries used dormitory systems to house the factory workers as living quarters. The living conditions were not hygienic and detrimental to health. The working hours were longer, and food was poor. The textile industries were criticized for their bad recruitment method. Girl children were recruited in exchange for huge wages in advance. They were, however, exploited later in several ways including sexual abuse. The first Factory Act was enacted in 1911; although its implementation was made in 1916. Manufacturing and textile industries were imported and developed in Japan with great care and strong leadership of the government. The night work for women and children was abolished in 1929, but it was not implemented in the unregulated sector.

Remarkable changes took place in Japan in industry and trade and other spheres within a very short period of time just after Meiji Restoration in 1868, replacing feudalism. Before industrialization, Japan was the main producer of rice, and it maintained a self-supporting self-sufficient economic system. Apart from this, tea, liquor, tobacco, soybean sauce, lumber, mats and some building materials were produced. The main export commodities were silk, tea, fish, sea products, copper and cereals. After participating in three wars—The Sino-Japanese War (1894–1895), Russo-Japanese War (1904–1905) and the First World War (1914–1918), Japan experienced a huge industrial expansion. The Factory Act of 1911 was the first legislation that was in force for 30 years.

---

[8] Asa Matsuoka, *Labour Conditions of Women and Children in Japan* (Washington, DC: Government Printing Office, 1931).

The main feature of the Japanese factory labour force, the author indicated, was that 53 per cent of the workers were under the age of 16 years and more than 90 per cent of such workers were girl children. Of the employed girl children, 80 per cent were engaged in the textile industries. Japan's family system and early custom tell that children would inherit their father's occupation. According to this system, a merchant's son became a merchant, and a samurai's son became a samurai. Children, at an early age, were sent into apprenticeship and they remained under training until they became the master workers. With the Meiji restoration, new labour problems relating to wages and working hours arose.

Very low wages were paid to the working children and the factory owners tried to suppress the fact. Longer working hours and night working and child exploitation were common phenomena, as elsewhere, in Japan. According to the study conducted by the Department of Social Education, 1924—as the author discusses—there were 23,000 juvenile workers engaged in Tokyo of which 20 per cent were engaged in the clothing industry, 18 per cent in carpentry and cabinet making, and 11 per cent in metalwork, textile, and food and beverage manufacturing. The excessive exploitation of child labour actually called for the enactment of protective legislation. Matsuoka has analysed Isomura's study (1927) which found that the simple average of the number of working hours was 9 hours and 20 minutes. But actually, they had to offer 11 hours per day. The total number of commercial apprentices was 85,000 in Tokyo. The importance of women workers in regulated factories was vast; because about 48 per cent of total workers were women, but they were also exploited in several ways by the factory owners and senior officials.

The dormitory system was common in Japanese factories, but this system had many shortfalls which had a direct and debilitating influence upon the lives of thousands of young women and boys under the age of 16 years. The author refers to 1928 data regarding the total number of regulated factories, which states that there were 55,041 such factories and they employed 1,869,668 workers. Due to the shortage of dormitories, only 33 per cent of workers could be housed. Over 90 per cent of all workers housed in the dormitories were engaged in textile factories and almost 99 per cent of textile workers were women especially minor young girls. Employers mostly preferred young girls to stay in dormitories. Girls staying outside were more uncertain—they remained absent according to personal convenience. This influenced production activities negatively. Dormitory workers—especially the young girls and minor boys—followed the rules and regulations that prevailed such as meal times, rising and retiring, rest time, recreation time, living quarters, etc. The great advantage in staying at the dormitory was that minor girls and boys could be employed to the maximum legal limit of hours and they could also be used in alternative shifts—day and night. This was absolutely impossible if they stayed outside.

The dormitories—the author has indicated—of modern large-scale industries were good in terms of available living facilities. But, at the old and small-scale factories (of weaving and silk-reeling industries), the inhabitants were faced with enormous problems in terms of sanitation, safety and most importantly, moral conditions.

The facilities available in dormitories largely affected the well-being of younger boys and girls. The living rooms were mostly dark, badly ventilated and overcrowded. There were common bathing facilities for all workers including the dormitory employees. Factories having fewer bathroom facilities provided tickets to the workers to use public bathhouses. Big factories had separate bathrooms for men and women, but smaller factories have common bathrooms. Meals and dining facilities varied. Big factories had well-equipped dining facilities, which was not the case in the smaller factories. In the small factories, dormitories were floored with wood. In some factories, workers were allowed to sit and take food, while in other factories, workers were made to stand and have their meals. The meals served at small factories were very poor and had a direct bearing on the health of workers. Considering the nutritional need of workers, the local authorities had prescribed standard menus which the factories had to follow, and it was prescribed to give 2,000–2,200 calories and 60–70 g of protein per day to the workers.

The author, thereafter, discusses Article 13 of the Factory Act of 1911 regarding the provision of sanitary and moral conditions, injurious to health. This lacked uniform regulations. Considering this, the Department of Agriculture and Commerce drafted orders to regulate factories and submitted them to local authorities and interested parties in the country in 1922. The opinions were not favourable and thus the proposal was dropped. Ultimately, the Bureau of Social Affairs proposed regulations for factory dormitories and it became Ordinance Number 26 of the Department of Home Affairs, Government of Japan in 1927.

The dormitories adjacent to factories were under the control and management of separate factory owners and the employees of the respective factories were accommodated there. There was provision for sanitation and welfare. The following provisions were prescribed: (a) minimum height of ceilings in bedroom, dining room and infirmaries was set as 7 feet; (b) earthen floors of the dining room and kitchen were specified; (c) per person minimum space in the bedroom was specified; (d) restrictions were imposed on the use of one room by workers on relay basis; (e) provisions of cleanliness and clean bedding were understood to be mandatory; (f) consumption of food while standing was prohibited; and (g) health check-up of the workers accommodated at dormitories twice a year.

In the 1931 book, the author discusses the importance of looking after the dormitories in the factories in relation to the moral influence of the dormitory environment. She stresses that matrons looking after the inmates living in the dormitories—especially the minor girls and boys—should be women instead of men.

In the Act of 1927, there was a provision of compulsory physical examinations of every worker. This Act helped to reveal the existence of dangerous and prohibited maladies. The provision was enforced on both the regulated and unregulated factories. The police primarily enforced the regulations, but later on, the task was assigned to the factory inspectors. Many of the working women were young and unmarried, the author discussed. The continuous workload and monotony made them dissatisfied and ultimately had a desire to return home. The employers, on the other hand, wanted to keep them at work in many ways and sometimes some unbecoming situations occurred between the employers and the employees.

In conclusion, the author has stressed further enforcement of regulations regarding issues such as ventilation, sunlight, bathing facilities, food, cleanliness of dining room and sanitation, health facilities, etc. The author gives much importance to the moral influence of the dormitory environment which was not in most cases congenial. The author specifically pleads for the completion of primary education of the younger boys and girls in the textile mills, and in this context, the factories might be obliged to send them to local primary schools and establish more schools for boys and girls nearer to the factory yard.

2.10. KAILASH SATYARTHI

In *Will for Children*,[9] Kailash Satyarthi has presented his lifelong experience on the issues of child labour, child trafficking, sexual exploitation and education.

As the Nobel laureate writes, he began his reformatory journey in the 1980s, taking an active part in solving child-related problems. He became actively involved with the issue of child rights and child labour with the establishment of *Bachpan Bachao Andolan* (the BBA or 'Save the Childhood' Movement) in 1981. Satyarthi and his team of activists started rescuing children from agricultural fields, brick kilns, stone quarries, factories, hotels and restaurants, homes, etc., and since then he began his writing on several aspects of child labour. Many of such articles published in magazines, reports, research journals, have been compiled in the present book. The book has been organized in seven sections—the dream of freedom, childhood freedom, childhood on sale, protecting childhood, the chains of slavery will break, education is the key to freedom and childhood religion.

The beginning of the book is with the painting of the death of a girl child, Gulabo, who worked in brick kilns and had contracted tuberculosis. The brick kiln where she worked along with other 32 children under horrible conditions, was located in Kurukshetra in the Indian state of Haryana.

The author has identified six basic reasons for the existence of child labour. These are—the prevalence of myths to justify child labour, lack of social awareness and sensitization, lack of political will, ineffective legal instruments, ignorance amongst children in servitude and their parents and anti-childhood development policies and programmes. In the first section, issues such as child labour and unemployment, child labour and black money, child labour and poverty, child labour and public health, child labour and population, child labour and illiteracy, lack of political will, hypocrisies under the garb of religion, the blunt state of laws, ignorance of parents, anti-childhood development, struggle against child labour, consumer awareness campaign, mass awareness, and political campaign and religious forum have been discussed. the issue of children and democracy has also been discussed in this section. The author's dream is to spread BBA to hundreds of villages across the country.

---

[9] Kailash Satyarthi, *Will for Children* (New Delhi: Prabhat Prakashan, 2017).

Satyarthi has discussed his experience relating to child labour in the villages of Jaipur district of Rajasthan. He describes a meeting with the villagers where almost all the children, women and men of a village were present. In this village, the Bal Mitra Gram Programme was initiated one year before. In the annual meeting, the local Gram Panchayat and Bal Panchayat were also present. A young girl, Hemlata, was also present in the meeting as a member of the Bal Panchayat.

According to Satyarthi, with the formation of Bal Mitra Gram, a lot of changes took place especially in the minds and attitudes of children, women and men. Hemlata narrated all her problems before the meeting in a very straightforward way. The author thereafter involved many children in the movement who took an active part in setting the children free from child labour and helped in admitting them to schools. He narrated the story of a girl, Santosh, from Jagatpura in Jaipur, who worked as domestic help. Cleaning and mopping was her everyday duty. When the village Jagatpura was converted into a Bal Mitra Gram, not a single girl child was going to school. Santosh was the first girl to raise her voice and tell her parents that she would not go to work. Ultimately, she was successful. After leaving the job, she managed to get admitted to the school. Now Santosh has become a leader who tries to convince children and their parents to leave work and go to the classroom. Within two to three years, Santosh with the help of other activists became successful in liberating 161 child workers, who worked as ragpickers, and got them admitted to the school.

The author thrillingly represents his story of 2010 in the Bal Mahapanchayat meeting. In the meeting, the author mentions, when he asked children to tell their own stories one by one. The whole auditorium became so vibrant with a strange excitement among the children. Almost all the children, 66 in number, present there narrated their stories very excitingly. Those 66 children had pulled 600 other working children out from labour and admitted them in the schools.

The author has had repeatedly thought of creating a labour union in the unorganized sector. He and his team faced a lot of troubles and threats from the factory owners and even faced serious resistance and attacks. In 1982, the first quarry labour union was formed in Faridabad amidst many threats and physical attacks. The union, later on, got a national structure. The author urged the need for a strong judiciary system for the support of helpless child workers.

Satyarthi always wants to generate sensitivity at the highest level to activate the system. He always raises movement against child labour and bonded labour. His organization, he stated, has been committed to organizing movement and has attracted the general public and victims. Many protest movements were organized since 1994 such as marches in 1994 from Palamu in Bihar to Delhi, in 1995 from Kanyakumari to Delhi, and from Kolkata to Kathmandu in 1996. A global march was organized in 1998, and in 2001, a march to campaign for education became very successful. The consumer awareness campaign is another greater initiative against child labour. The consumers—national and international—use items made by children. The examples are firecrackers, carpets, shoes, clothes which are produced by industries employing children—both boys and girls. The industries making such products have a strong relationship with local contractors, brokers, suppliers, companies, agents, foreign importers and sellers.

The BBA, as Satyarthi writes, started a consumer awareness campaign in the 1990s. The movement became highly successful in the carpet manufacturing industry at the international level. At the national level, it was successful in creating awareness in the firecracker industry.

Satyarthi explains in brief about the BBA initiative. The BBA initiative is to eradicate child slavery and child labour. The BBA initiative aims at (a) eradication of child labour, (b) education for all children and (c) abolition of poverty. The vision of the BBA is to make every village a child-friendly village. Such a programme begins with a small unit. Gradually, it can transform the whole society and, ultimately, the whole globe will turn into a child-friendly world.

The author has identified four phases essential for building child-friendly villages:

1. No child should work, and there should not be single child labour.
2. Every child should go to school. Any child-friendly village requires all its children to be enrolled for studies. Access to education, Satyarthi considers, is every child's birth right and it is the duty of the government to provide such right. It is suggested that education should be free up to the age of 18 years, education be made compulsory, all the expenses for uniforms, books, day meals, commuting, etc., be borne by the government. Quality education should be imparted and uniform education should be provided to all sections of children irrespective of their social, economic and cultural status.

3. Child panchayat in every village by the children. Through establishing child panchayat, children should develop collective leadership by working together. Children rescued from factory works fight elections in the child panchayat. They fight for the post of Panchayat President, Panchayat Minister and Panchayat Members. All the children cast votes and elect them. Sometimes it becomes difficult to hold the election. On many occasions, the coalition of guardians, casteism and policies create problems in holding elections.
4. The fourth phase for making child-friendly villages is to establish coordination between local village panchayat and the elected child panchayat. All the four phases just stated can be successful depending on the dynamism of the activists.

The author has also identified the following six basic outcomes that might bring about revolutionary changes in society:

1. Empowerment from top to bottom in the village is the first outcome. In such a move, everyone—teachers, youth, women, children should take part in village affairs. The principal effort would be to make every child aware to work together and in that case, it becomes difficult to engage them in factories by the parents or guardians and the mill owners. Hence, preventing children from going to school will naturally become a difficult task.

    In this context, the author mentions a courageous effort made by the school children of Kukura village in Lakhimpur. In that school, there was a police post. Criminals and unlawful persons were brought there throughout the day and were beaten. The situation adversely affected the school children's mental conditions. They protested against this and went to the Headmaster and then to the police station to remove the police post from the school, but it was in vain. The children did not give up. They ultimately went to the Superintendent of Police and became successful.
2. Sustainable and integrated development is the topmost priority today. This means that any development activity should take care of environmental issues, and development activities should cover all sections of the community. The child leaders of Bal Mitra Gram have been trained in that way and they are equally concerned for environmental conservation, caste-related social problems, gender gap, communalism, etc.

The author has also mentioned in his book the story of a girl child labour, Razia Sultan of Janikhurd village in Meerut district, who earlier worked in a factory of sports items and was sewing the footballs there. She actively participated in the session organized by the National Bal Mahapanchyat. There she learned that school education was free. But a nearby school charged fees from the students. Razia took 10 Bal Sarpanchs (child mayors) and went to the District Magistrate and the District Education Officer of the district and placed deputation. They also informed the incident to the editors of *Dainik Jagran* and *Amar Ujala*. Thereafter, the action was taken with immediate effect.

3. Bal Mitra Gram village can play a vital part, the author mentioned, in forming a true democratic structure. Satyarthi discusses that Indian democracy has been suffering from family syndrome and nepotism at the central and state-level politics. The participation of criminals in politics is also another major problem in our democracy. The members of Bal Mitra Gram villages are well aware of the importance of honesty and integrity and they have the vision to do something new and wonderful for the good of the society together as a team.

4. Child-friendly society demands refinement in the thinking, attitude and mentality of people in the society. The priorities of village panchayats are very often dictated by political consideration. Any development activity that may be either road construction, employment or electrification is done based on caste, vote bank and election. No attention is given to children's priority. Due to the intervention of Bal Panchayat, it becomes hard for the parents to stop their children from going to school. Due to the Bal Panchayat formed in Amarola village of Saharsa district in Bihar, the Bal Mitra Gram Village has been functioning in the proper direction. The Bal Panchayat corresponded with the government officers. The government granted funds for school buildings but there was no land for school buildings. A villager donated the land and the problem was resolved. The Bal Panchayat revolted against the owner of a liquor shop who was involved in criminal activities. This shop not only had an influence upon the children but also had a direct bearing on the family members. The villagers strongly protested against the shop, including the women, and the village pradhan ultimately brought the matter to the notice of higher authorities. Within a short period of time, the shop was closed.

5. Discrimination by one set of people to the other has been prevailing in our society for ages. There exists an inherent desire to prove oneself better than the other, or exploitation of one group of people by another is a common tendency that exists in every society and economy. The author expresses his dissatisfaction with the Indian caste system. He narrated that, even today, the Dalit families are not allowed to draw water from the wells belonging to the Thakurs or the Brahmins. Even today, many villages have been segregated differently for different caste people. Some areas are assigned for the Brahmins, some for the Dalits, some for Muslims and so on. Children are not initially affected by this social division but their minds become contaminated as they grow up and become adults. Children's participation in village affairs, interaction and coordination with each other, freedom of speech; that is, courage to speak up in front of elders, etc., bring about revolutionary changes in society.

The author presents a case study related to Chhitouli village in Alwar district of Rajasthan which was, some years ago, transformed into a 'child-friendly village'. A 12-year-old child, Anand, was made Bal Sarpanch. He noticed a child-marriage incident in the village. The minimum age of marriage is 25 years for boys and 18 years for girls. In this case, both the boy and the girl were minors. He narrated the incident to his Teacher and then went to the house where the marriage was taking place. But they could not convince the family members. Then they went to the Panchayat Chief but they were not able to convince him as well. The children then called up the BBA workers, other children, youth, and a few like-minded people also joined them. They all went to the place of marriage. Finally, the marriage was stopped. Satyarthi also narrated the story of Zenab, a little girl who lives in Chandoura village in Meerut. There was a school in the village up to class VIII but no girl child in the village went to the school. A few girls used to take some education in Madrasas. Zenab was also not allowed to get enrolled in the school. She went against her parents and herself took admission in the junior school. Not only this, she encouraged other girls in the village to go to school. It was not an easy task. The Muslim community does not allow girls to get an education. Zenab and her friends firmly supported her. Finally, the parents and villagers allowed all the boys and the girls to enrol in the school.

6. Child-friendly villages take up the issue of environmental preservation as well. Tree plantation, water maintenance and cleanliness are the most important activities that have been taken up in these villages. Satyarthi states an incident of Wazeernagar village in Khiry district of Uttar Pradesh. The drains in the village remained dirty with contaminated water. The child panchayat raised its voice against the bad drainage system in the village. The village panchayat did not immediately take up the issue. The child panchayat members—Gayatri, Alok, Anuradha and Prempratap—took brooms and went to the panchayat's house and handed them a broom. The panchayat radhan had no option but to accompany the group for cleaning the drains.

The author shares one more experience with the readers. This is an incident of two villages—Narhat and Baranbaans Chougan villages in Alwar district of Rajasthan. The villages share boundaries with a forest. The child panchayats in the villages discussed the issue of deforestation in a joint meeting. They made a plan And the concerned forest officer was informed about it. In the night when a tree-cutting gang entered the forest, the group members, who wore masks, started shouting in animal-like voices. that the woodcutters fled the place out of fear and a few of them were caught by the police. Hence, the tree cutting was stopped.

A major part of the book is about the child labour situations under different production and service sectors in various countries. These are all the experiences he gathered from real-life situations. In this context, he tries to link between child labour and illiteracy, child labour and poverty, child labour and other social parameters. Under no circumstances, the author supports child labour. He says if there is child labour, that is, if poor children contain to work as child labourers, they will remain poor and this will continue generation after generation. They will remain illiterate and will be deprived of all the opportunities for their development. He states that unemployment is linked with child labour. There are 65 million unemployed youths and 60 million child labourers in India; in the world, there are 215 million child labourers and 200 million unemployed adults. He repeatedly stresses that there is no question of employing children in factories and service sectors under the adults. There is a great need for strong social safety net, civil society organizations, religious institutions and corporate sectors to take care of parentless, female-headed and the poorest of the poor family children for their education and well-being.

The author specifically points out that children are more prone to injuries and occupational hazards. Children are badly affected by smoke, dust, chemicals, pesticides and heat, and suffer from incurable diseases. In many cases, children use sharp tools without safety measures and sufficient knowledge. The hours of work per day are more than 12–14 hours. The author and his team have rescued many child labourers. He has apprised that there are many schemes for the rescued child labour and bonded labour run by the Central and State Governments. Also, there are provisions that the parents of such rescued child workers are given the preference for government jobs and welfare housing schemes. Poverty and child labour are directly related to each other and if one exists the other one will invariably exist. Child labour creates a vicious cycle of poverty. Satyarthi stresses that both the issues of poverty and child labour should be equally treated with utmost sincerity. One cannot be eradicated until the other is eliminated.

Satyarthi points out that there remains a very low-level social response towards poor and neglected children and there is a lack of political will also. Adequate funds towards education, health and eradication of child labour have not been allocated by the government. Children are seen working everywhere and even they are seen working on ancestral lands in the villages which they do to support their households. Children are used everywhere because they are cheap and easily available, and are docile. Another important thing, the author mentions here, is that working children cannot form workers' unions. The author says that it is difficult but not impossible to eradicate child labour. He has cited examples of child labour problems in industrially developed countries such as Britain, Norway, Sweden, France, Germany, Japan and the United States of America. But these countries realized the long-term harmful effect of child labour and thus systematically worked on its eradication and ultimately came out successful.

It needs a composite programme, the author stresses, to eradicate child labour as far as the government role is concerned. He has cited the example of the Government of Brazil. Brazil introduced several schemes such as providing school bags, family bags, cash transfers and basic social rights so that poorer families send and keep their children in school. that theThe outcome of government effort was overwhelming and about six million children were withdrawn from work and enrolled in schools. The child labour eradication mission was extremely successful in Mexico, Peru, Tanzania, Sri Lanka, Kenya and Malawi. Mid-day meal scheme in schools has shown a tremendous success in Bangladesh and India. Scholarships and incentives like bicycles, bags, books, pens, shoes, etc., have also worked nicely. Consumer awareness initiatives such as boycotting goods produced by children in developing countries have also played a significant role. The author cited examples of carpet manufacturing factories of Banaras, Bhadoi and Mirzapur in Uttar Pradesh which used children trafficked from Bihar and Nepal and the children worked almost as bonded labourers. The BBA initiated a consumer awareness campaign across the globe. The BBA has invented a social labelling mechanism known as 'Goodweave'. Under this initiative, every rug produced is given a child labour–free label. As a result of such intervention, the number of child labour in the carpet industry sector was reduced by 70 per cent in South Asia. The BBA's initiative also gave wonderful results in the fireworks industry.

The author finds a peculiar relationship between religion and child labour. He says that no religious leaders in the globe did speak about the elimination of child labour. There are more than one billion poverty-stricken children and they work at the cost of their health and education. Thousands of trafficked children end up in the sex trade. Many abducted children's organs are sold in the market. In every religion, children are given high priority in the family and society. In Hinduism, a child is equated with God, and a girl child is worshipped. In Christianity, the child is very dear to the family and in Islam, children are respected in the family and society. The author states that more than 53 per cent of children in India are sexually abused and female foeticide and infanticide are on the rise. Girls are being sold for prostitution. Many girls and boys are recruited by religious institutions and they are trained in such a way that they become terrorists in future. The author narrated the problems and obstacles they faced while rescuing boys and girls trafficked. Yet the religious leaders did not protest a bit.

The author has discussed the issue of domestic child labour and the role of the ILO in protecting their interest. The ILO, in 2012 (Convention Number 189), passed *Decent Work for Domestic Workers*. In the convention, the ILO passed the law to ensure security, rights and to create conditions conducive to dignified work for domestic workers. Domestic labour, the author considers, is a sort of invisible slavery where rich families keep poor girls or women for their own convenience. They do domestic work continuously and very often face abuse and atrocities.

Child labourers are often denied, the author points out, many human rights constitutionally guaranteed by the state. Many children in India, for example, cannot receive compulsory education due to so many obstacles. Human trafficking, forced labour and employment of children in hazardous jobs, all are constitutionally prohibited but all these prevail in most of the developing world. Poverty is the main reason for the continuation of child labour; but at the same time, child labour is the primary cause of poverty which pushes children into the unskilled premature labour force, which, in turn, create a 'child labour trap' leading to poverty and hunger. This situation fails to fulfil the targets of Millennium Development Goals 1 and 2.

Millennium Development Goal 1 states complete eradication of poverty and hunger and Millennium Development Goal 2 calls for achieving universal primary education. The author indicates the lack of data and knowledge on different aspects of child labour. Naturally, it becomes difficult to understand the actual situation of child labour, and based on this inadequate information, decision-making policies cannot be appropriately undertaken by the government organs. The author identifies several gaps such as cultural, financial, political, knowledge, coordination and convergence that hinder the elimination of child labour. There is a belief that employing child labour in households help children earn an additional income to support their families. It needs a complete change in the mindset and attitude of people to come out of such a weird idea. The author believes that the eradication of child labour can be possible through a genuine political will and then public demand and action. International organizations and the government's active participation can help eradicate child labour. The need of the hour, the author asserts, is to create a child-friendly mindset. Citing relevant UNICEF-data Satyarthi writes that about half of India's children below the age of five years are malnourished, about 50,000 disappear without a trace and about 60 million children face hardships as child labourers. Satyarthi notices that children's rights cannot be established with the mere execution of legislation. Our thinking, behaviour and lifestyle need to be reconsidered if we want to end all these. Everybody should learn to respect childhood and children's right. This can be achieved through winning their trust in every sphere—at home, in schools and in the public domain.

The author mentions that the largest number of child trafficking is concentrated in Bihar, and children from Saharsa, Darbhanga, Sitamarhi, Siwan, Madhubani, Madhepura and other places are collected and sent to different industrial locations of India. Thousands of girls from Bihar and Jharkhand are sold as 'child labourers' and 'child prostitutes'. The lack of education and awareness are held responsible for rampant child trafficking in Bihar. With quality education and quality healthcare facilities and through awareness campaigns, the author considers, Bihar can be, with sincere efforts, transformed into a child-friendly state. The author cites some instances of child trafficking. His BBA and associated NGOs organized 'South Asian March Against Child Trafficking' in 2007 in India, Bangladesh and Nepal. This march was about 5,000 km, and thousands of people participated in the march under his leadership. Hundreds of children also took part. The children took part in different programmes and talked to one another. They exchanged their views and shared their tales of misery and pain. Every year, the author mentions, around 700,000–800,000 children, girls and men are traded across countries and innumerable cases of human trafficking take place. In this way, thousands of children, boys and girls, go missing and the majority of such children are from poorer and weaker sections of society. This is happening due to a lack of social awareness, loose administration and improper implementation of the law on human trafficking.

Satyarthi has identified Assam as a very active place of child trafficking, especially girl child trafficking. Assamese girls of poor families are supplied to major metropolitan cities of India and the neighbouring countries. Girls are used as 'domestic help' and some of them are sold into prostitution across the country. Many children from other places are trafficked to Assam. They are used in tea plantations, brick factories and the mining. The BBA and different NGOs together rescued many such children which were employed for domestic works, coal mines and prostitution. The author mentions that due to natural disasters when a huge loss of life and damage of property takes place, thousands of children are affected. They are forced to become child labourers. He cites the Uttarakhand tragedy (2013) and states that the educational infrastructure of 400 villages was completely destroyed due to devastating floods and landslides. Many children were separated from their parents and relatives and went missing. The BBA ran awareness campaigns against child trafficking and organized many relief camps in the villages affected by the flood.

Finally, the author has prescribed stringent laws to protect childhood. Many children face insults, tortures and abuses when they come to their residence from schools, hospitals, playgrounds, temples and departments. Everywhere there is a lack of sensitivity and security of children. The author says it is necessary to create public awareness about the law on child safety and their rights. He laments that millions of children are begging on the streets and living in open railway stations and are being bought and sold like commodities despite being legally entitled to get security and care. They are being deprived of education, play and fun.

Satyarthi, in his book, mentions the love, sensitivity and concern for thousands of child rights of Nelson Mandela. He established—in 1995—the Nelson Mandela Children's Fund to promote democratic values in African children and the youth, eradicate diseases amongst children and ensure a dignified life for the children. Later on, it became a large centre and spread out beyond Africa to America and England. Mandela gave immense support and encouragement towards the movement against child labour. Satyarthi gives high priority towards education and for this, he supports for investment in education. He finds a positive relationship between education and economic growth in the areas of building human capital, enhancing income, increasing productivity and enlarging trade cover. He has narrated about the initiative his BBA and the associated NGOs have taken for making education as a fundamental right. The Shiksha Yatra (Education March) was initiated in 2001. He, finally, recalls an incident. A boy, aged 10–12 years, in a village Pilkhua in Uttar Pradesh came to him and gave him his two days' earnings and said to spend this for liberating a child like him. His aim was to leave work and join the school. The author was quite excited about this incident. He also states details about the Parliamentary Forum on Education which was formed in 1990 and was supported by 166 Parliamentarians of Lower and Upper Houses. This, in fact, strengthened the demand for education for all.

Chapter 3

Post-Industrial Revolution Concern
A Developed Country Context

3.1. INTRODUCTION

Although there are several definitions for 'child labour', that which has been provided by the ILO is usually assumed to be the 'standard' identification. The ILO identifies the economically-active children below the age of fifteen years as 'child labour'.[1] However, if children voluntarily perform some tasks with their parents at their parental residence—especially in the developed countries—this cannot be cited as an instance of 'child labouring'.[2] In 2020, one thinks that it is safe to declare the complete cessation of child labour in the so-called 'developed countries', while many 'developing nations' too seem to have eliminated the menace of child labour.[3] However, long back, when the per-capita income was low in the western world, a considerable number of children were found to be engaged in labour to improve family income. In 1861, for example, about 30 per cent of children in

---

[1] Aleclus, Muriel, Peter Dorman, Janet Hilowitz, Michaelle de Kock, Joost Kooijmans, and Peter Matz, *Child-labour: A Text-book for University Students* (Geneva: ILO Publications, 2004), 16.

[2] Kaushik Basu, *The Intriguing Relation between Adult Minimum Wage and Child-labour* (Washington, DC: World Bank Publishing Division, 1999), 2.

[3] C. K. Shukla and S. Ali, eds., *Child-labour and the Law* (New Delhi: Sarup and Sons, 2006), 233.

England worked for families, with 34 per cent of them being females who, other than working in families, also worked on farms and cultivation grounds.[4]

This chapter proposes to focus on the child labour context in the so-called 'developed countries'. While discussing the aspect, one should give serious consideration to reviewing the role of working children—especially in the Western nations which, usually, are understood to constitute the 'developed world'. Importantly, workers below the age of eighteen years are regularly found to engage in major economic activities in the so-called 'developed countries'. They even work under hazardous conditions. Many of the children of these 'developed countries' are also often involved in prostitution. Precise data on child labour may not be always available—more so, in the case of the 'developed nations'—but children could be found working everywhere: starting from household chores (to go against Basu's definition), restaurants, petty-trade outlets, entertainment sectors and sexual-service providing sectors. It is the general belief that child labour is directly related to poverty and the low-income of the concerned families. But it is also true that in many developed countries of North America, Europe and the Western Pacific, child labouring—in one form or the other—is a serious problem.

3.2. THE CONTEXT

It has already been mentioned that the issue of child labour is not a new problem; it has had existed in its present form or some other garb since the beginning of the agricultural and Industrial Revolutions around the world. However, in the past, dependable data on child labour was barely available, while in the 21st century, a significant portion of such information—though not always incontestable—is readily available to academics and anti-child labour activists. Child labour, it is understood, is a socially undesirable phenomenon, and the chief goal of numerous international organizations is to eliminate it globally. However, what complicates the recognition and rehabilitation of child labourers is that the decision to supply child labour is almost solely taken by the

---

[4] Sally Mitchell, ed., *Victorian Britain: An Encyclopaedia* (New York and London: Routledge, 1988), 866.

parents. The identification and resettlement, therefore, requires their wholesome participation, which, in most cases, is rare. This is chiefly because child labour is directly linked to the income of the household, irrespective of the socio-economic status of the countries to where the child labourers belong.

The *World Report on Child Labour*, released by the ILO in the end of 2015, estimated that there were approximately 168 million children engaged as child labourers worldwide.[5] Counting the number of child labourers properly, one can summarize that in 2020, 152 million children are engaged as child labourers internationally.[6] This is about 7.68 per cent of the total world child population (which, according to Statista, is approximately 1.98 billion in 2020),[7] and it is the SSA region that shows its maximum prevalence.[8] Also, it is traditionally believed that child-labouring incidents are much more numerous in the countries where the general people's standards of living are low and they are more dependent, for earning their livelihood, on agriculture than on any other sector. Numerous global data on child labour, compiled by different reputed statistical organizations in 2020 show that there has been a widespread decline in the trend of employing child labourers over the last few decades. But the percentages of the decline in the numbers of child labourers widely vary according to clusters of nations.

In the late 18th and throughout the 19th century, the engagement of child labour was a usual practice in Europe and North America. But, from the early 20th century onwards, there was a rapidly declining trend of child-labourer engagement in these two continents. Economists and sociologists—especially Pier Paolo Viazzo and Hugh Cunningham in their work[9] have noted that in Europe and North America, the employment of children, during the phase of rapid

---

[5] ILO, *World Report on Child-labour* (Geneva: ILP Press, 2015), xiii.

[6] *The Times of India,* 'World Day against Child Labour 2020.'

[7] Statista, 'Number of Children Aged 0–14 Globally, 1950–2100,' 2022, https://www.statista.com/statistics/678737/total-number-of-children-worldwide/

[8] Peter Hess, *Economic Growth and Sustainable Development,* 2nd ed. (London and New York: Routledge, 2016), 457.

[9] Pier Paolo Viazzo and Hugh Cunningham, *Child-labour in Historical Perspective, 1800–1985: Case-studies from Europe, Japan, and Columbia* (Florence: UNICEF–ICDC Press, 1996).

industrialization, started to increase, and, thereafter, the trend declined, until child labour was almost eliminated.[10]

At the United Nations (UN) Convention on the Rights of the Child, held in November 1989 in New York, the then world leaders made a historic commitment to the children of the world. They promised to protect every child of the world and to fulfil their rights through the adoption and enforcement of an international legal framework which was chalked out during the General Conference of the ILO in June 1973.

The 1989 convention, based (as already mentioned) on the resolutions of the ILO general conference of 1973, outlined that every child has his/her own rights and that childhood, which lasts until the concerned individual reaches 18 years of age, is separate from adulthood. Until s/he attains 18 years of age—which is a special and protection-needing time—every child must be allowed to grow, learn, play, develop and flourish with dignity. This convention was one of the more important historical events (against child-labouring system) to have had taken place internationally. It inspired several governments to change laws and policies, to make investments for the purpose of children's healthcare and nutritional supplies as well as to promulgate legal safeguarding processes to protect children from violence and exploitation.

Although a considerable amount of progress towards safeguarding children from child-labouring practises was made after the convention, all the resolutions were not fully implemented. As a result, millions of children still continue to suffer from the violations of their rights. They are still deprived of healthcare, nutrition supplies, education and protection from violence. Innocent childhoods continue to be cut short when the children are forced to leave school, attend hazardous work, get married, fight in wars, or are locked up in adult prisons.

Due to global changes like the advent of digital technology, environmental changes, prolonged conflicts and mass migration, childhood—in the 21st century—is rapidly undergoing changes. The ILO's most important programme on the elimination of child labour, the International Programme on the Elimination of Child Labour (IPEC), was started in 1992. The sole objective of the programme

---

[10] Quoted in Goete Hansson, *International Labour Standards: A Conference Report* (Stockholm: Almqvist and Wiksell, 2003), 38.

was the progressive elimination of child labour from the entire world through the designing and promulgation of a worldwide movement to combat child labour. Presently, 88 countries of the world have been operating under the IPEC to eliminate child labour.[11] This programme aims at eliminating child labour as a part of ILO's *Decent Work Agenda*. Child labour prevents children from acquiring skills and education, which are essential for building their future. Hence, it could not be a part of 'decent-work'. Apart from this, the practice of employing child labourers perpetuates poverty—generation after generation. Thus, it does not only contribute to bringing personal losses, it also causes harm to the concerned nation in terms of competitiveness, productivity and income. It is believed by experts that withdrawing children from work, admitting them to school, providing training will give them decent standards of living in future.

Since the last half of the 19th century, the so-called 'developed countries' of the world have taken numerous initiatives against child labour. But—as already mentioned—child labour exists in the 'developed nations' even today. In the so-called 'developed world', many children (under the age of eighteen years) from low-income families are compelled to work in order to supplement the family income. In this context, it might be observed that the concerned 'developed nation' has failed to protect those children from physical, mental, social and economic harm. In the ILO Convention Number 182, it has been categorically discussed that the two worst forms of child labour exist everywhere in the world (including the so-called 'developed countries'): hazardous works and prostitution.[12] High-income nations—like the countries of North America, Europe and the Western Pacific—have achieved a high rate of growth on virtually every socio-economic front, but they are still plagued by the menace of child labour. In spite of the introduction of the compulsory school education system by a number of countries, the poison tree of child labour has not been uprooted.

---

[11] Sensagent, 'Child-labour,' n.d , http://dictionary.sensagent.com/child%20labour/en-en/#:~:text=The%20International%20Labour%20Organization%E2%80%99s%20International%20Programme%20on%20the,largest%20program%20of%20its%20kind%20in%20the%20world

[12] ILO, 'Worst Forms of Child Labour Convention, 1999,' n.d., https://www.ilo.org/dyn/normlex/en/f?p=NORMLEXPUB:12100:0::NO::P12100_ILO_CODE:C182

The children, who drop out of schools and work as child labourers, lose time to play and all access to nutrition or care. It has been estimated by international statisticians that over 50 per cent of working children experience the worst forms of child labour like working in hazardous conditions, slavery, forced labour, involvement in illegal activities like drug trafficking and prostitution as well as involvement in armed conflict.[13]

The writers of this book presently propose to discuss the conditions of child labour in Europe and North America, concentrating principally on the United Kingdom, Belgium, France, the United States of America and the countries of the Western Pacific: especially Australia, Japan and China. The discussions would take place one by one, with reference to the incidents during the post-Industrial Revolution era.

As already mentioned, it was thought earlier that child labour is an issue of the past, and presently it is no longer a problem—especially in the case of the so-called 'developed countries'. But there is a strong argument that there are still a large number of child labourers all around the world, and the numbers might as well be increasing with the rise in economic crises and the consequent soaring unemployment in Europe. As a result of recent recessions, many of the European nations have curtailed social aid drastically. This has exerted a deep impact on the socio-economic stability of low-income families. Due to this, the families have been left with no option other than sending their children to work. As per the report of the Council of Europe—Commissioner of Human Rights[14] and according to numerous recently-concluded UN-researches, the child-labour situation in Europe is getting grimmer with each passing day. The researchers unanimously conclude that in the mid-2010s', 29 per cent of children are/were working in Georgia, 19 per cent in Albania, more than one million in the Russian Federation, and 5.2 per cent in Italy. Precise data on child labour in other European countries are not available, as the reports declare. Many of the working children of Europe perform hazardous works. They work in sectors like agriculture, construction, factories, or on the

---

[13] Refer to Regina Don Santos, *Leading Social Entrepreneurs* (Chaguanas: Ashoka, 2003), 171.

[14] Nils Muiznieks, 'Stop Child Labour,' Council of Europe: Commissioner for Human Rights, 20 August 2013, https://www.coe.int/en/web/commissioner/-/child-labour-in-europe-a-persisting-challen-1

streets. Children carry heavy loads (machinery and tools used in agriculture), and are compelled to spread harmful pesticides and insecticides on crops. Child labour is used aplenty in the tobacco industry (e.g., in Bulgaria). An article by Nuno Ferreira—published in *The Conversation* of 4 November 2015—reports that more than 7.5 million children in Europe were working in 2014–2015 for pay, profit and goods for the family.[15] The entire European continent faced a number of unprecedented socio-economic crises in 2008, and since then the problem of child labour has cropped up—aggravated by the continual dropping-out of children from schools. Instead, the school-going children have had started serving as child labours at firms, farms, shops and restaurants. Some of them even joined in prostitution, contacted local mafias and involved themselves with drug trafficking and panhandling.

3.3. CHILD LABOUR IN EUROPEAN NATIONS

3.3.1. The United Kingdom

Child labour was a common feature in the United Kingdom during the Industrial Revolution in the 18th and the early 19th century. During this period, industrial cities and towns expanded rapidly, principally due to the migration of agricultural workers, farmers and their family members who were in search of works at factories and mines for better living conditions and education for their children. However, the living conditions of the factory workers were miserable. Overcrowding, poor sanitation and the lack of daily cleaning and bathing facilities contributed to the onset of pollution and, consequently, bouts of dangerous diseases. The workers were usually offered low wages. The wages were so low that they could not purchase the bare minimum necessities. Under such conditions, these adult workers were forced to engage their children in factories and mines for the survival of the families.

In industrializing Britain, children were employed in industries and mines for several reasons. First, children labourer meant less payment by the employers. These children were paid 10–20 per cent of

---

[15] Nuno Ferreira, 'Child-labour in Europe: A Challenge To Be Tackled, Not To Be Ignored,' The Conversation, 4 November 2015, https://theconversation.com/child-labour-in-europe-a-challenge-to-be-tackled-not-ignored-49992

what adult workers received for the same job. Finding out means to save their capital, British employers engaged an increasing number of child workers. Second, the British child labourers were obedient and could be easily handled and coerced to complete their work. Third, children could easily adjust themselves to the working atmosphere of factories and mines. In the sector of textile manufacturing, for example, children were found to be defter in handling machines than adult workers. Finally, the British working children could be engaged in different works for more hours per day than the adult workers by the sinister factory owners. They usually worked for longer working hours—between 12 and 16 hours—per shift, but were paid a meagre wage, and suffered from abuses at the workplace.

Victorian England was marked by the existence of laissez-faire capitalism. Under this system, the British government had no role to play in the affairs of factories and mines. Naturally, the royal government did not promulgate any legislation to control the atrocities against child labourers. Consequently, the rich British mill owners dictated everything: they decided the wages, working hours and other conditions for working. The workers—adults and children alike—had no bargaining power. Resting houses—where the hapless British child workers lived—and the factories and mines where they worked were really bad in terms of sanitation, cleanliness, etc. There were no rules for the protection of the workers. The British factories and mines were dangerous places with minimum or no safeguarding facilities for labourers. The factory owners could easily exploit the working children or the working adults as there were no rules framed for them to save them from industrial hazards. The spinning mills had open and exposed textile-processing machines, which, when working, posed a great risk and life threat to the children at work. During the English Industrial Revolution in the 18th century, approximately 40–50 per cent of the British child labourers were engaged in mills and mines. They often faced fatal accidents because several powerful machines remained unfenced. The children were forced to work dangerously close to the spinning belts and shafts. Due to their short height, children could not, properly and safely, operate the machines. Protection was routinely denied to them. Due to this, the working children intermittently suffered injuries—sometimes fatal—to their heads and fingers.

Another unhealthy situation that the working children faced in their workplace was the gruelling heat produced by the running machines.

Most of the factories built during the 19th century in Britain were without proper ventilation or windows. This caused intense heat to suffocate workers inside the factories. Due to poor or no ventilation, the temperature inside the machine rooms became unbearable for the minor children working there. It was horrible to work under such asphyxiating conditions. In addition to this, there was no proper compensation for the child workers who would suffer an injury while working in mills and mines.

During the Industrial Revolution in the United Kingdom, children were used in large numbers to work in the coal mines since coal was an essential resource to run the steam engines. In fact, coal was used to power every part of the factories. It was also used to run ships and trains. Several types of works in the coal mines were performed by children, and in doing so, they often suffered hardships because the mine shafts could collapse anytime, and there was suffocating air pollution all around. This led to breathing problems among children, and they suffered silently under such horrible and abusive working conditions.

In course of time, the exasperated Englishmen started protesting against the suffocating and harmful working conditions for the British labourers. They particularly raised a strong voices against the employment of children in factories and mines. Many people—influenced by the idea of utopian socialism coined by Robert Owen—demanded better working conditions, such as the creation of factory stores, limiting of working hours, raising the wages for children and adult workers, providing healthcare facilities and education. These workers were also directly influenced by the economic philosophies of the German thinker, Karl Marx, who was very critical about child labour, and, in his various publications which were immediately translated into English, explained in detail how the child labourers were being exploited by the wealthy British factory owners. As different essays reveal,[16] these protests and debates held in different corners of the English society led to a number of legislations' being enacted during the 1800s.

The first formal labour law in England was passed in 1788: It was called 'the Act of 1788'. The law aimed at improving the working conditions of child labourers, both boys and girls, working at the British factories and mines. This Act was officially known as the Chimney

---

[16] https://www.historychurch.com

Sweepers Act – 1788.[17] It was, in fact, a British Act of Parliament to stop child labour. Prior to the passage of this Act, a large number of boys aged between 4 and 15 years were being used by the mill owners for chimney sweeping. The Act ended these practices.

Thereafter, the Factory Act of 1833 was passed in England to improve the conditions of working children in factories.[18] Its main features are given in the following paragraph.

First, children below the age of nine years were barred from working. Second, the British employers were required to keep the age certificate of the child labourers. Third, the maximum working hours for a working child, aged 9–13 years, was confined to nine hours. Fourth, it was decreed that the children of 13–18 years should not work more than 12 hours a day. Fifth, students were barred from engaging themselves working in night shift. Sixth, four factory inspectors were appointed to enforce the Act. Finally, it was decreed that two hours of schooling should be provided to each child labourer a day.

In the United States of America, the first State Child Labour Law was enacted in 1836 by the State of Massachusetts: it stated that all the American children working in factories are required to attend school for at least three months a year, and each child should work not more than 10 hours a day.[19] The 1876 Labour Movement set the age limit for child workers and suggested a ban on the employment of working children below 14 years. The American Federation of Labour (AFL), founded in December 1886, supported the State Minimum Age Laws and also demanded that the USA-states should ban all children below the age of 14 years from working. The New York Movement 1883, under the leadership of Samuel Gompers, successfully led to the government prohibition of cigar making in tenements where many USA children were secretly forced to work. Subsequently, the Children's Bureau Act of 1912, the Owen Child Labour Act of 1916, and the Walsh-Healey Act, 1936 were passed in the United States of America to protect children working in factories and mines.

In the United Kingdom—to return to the original discussion—after the adoption of the steam engine, the mill owners mostly relied on

---

[17] Benita Cullingford, *British Chimney Sweeps* (Chicago: New Amsterdam Books, 2001), 106–107.

[18] Thoms Tapping, *The Factory Acts* (London: Shaw and Sons, 1855), 9–28.

[19] Eric Arnesen, ed., *Encyclopaedia of U.S. Labour and Working-class History* (New York and London: Routledge, 2007), 946.

cheap sources of labour—the British underage orphans. A huge number of factory-based towns and villages developed in the areas adjacent to Lancashire, and thereafter spread to Manchester, Yorkshire and Cheshire. The cheap labourers—young boys and girls—were hired in large numbers in the mills of these towns. To supplement the dwindling family income, children from the poor working-class were engaged, and they were paid low wages. Toiling on such a meagre wage, these children prepared and weaved cotton, flax, wool and silk at the factories.

In the British textile mills and coal mines, huge numbers of children were employed during the Industrial Revolution. Many historians and economic historians have researched child labour using data from the various British Parliamentary Reports. Based on the data obtained from the *British Parliamentary Report, 1819*, Herman Freuenberger, Frances Mather and Clark Nardinneli, in their article,[20] describe that the British textile mills used 54.5 per cent of child labourers in the age group under 19 years, and only 4.5 per cent under the age of 10 years. Using data from the same source for the situation in 1834, Carolyn Tuttle, in her article 'Child-labour during the British Industrial Revolution',[21] has found that the children under the age of 13 years comprised 10 to 20 per cent of the total workforce, while children from the age group of 13–18 years comprised 23–57 per cent of the workers in mills such as cotton, wool, flax and silk.

The employment of children in the sector of textiles in the United Kingdom was on the rise until the first half of the 19th century. The British Census of 1841 identified boys who were mostly involved in agriculture, domestic chores and cotton manufacturing as child labourers, but this was also true for the girls. Most of the British underage working girls were engaged in domestic chores, and in the cotton manufacturing industry, followed by dress-making. In different coal and metal mines, a large number of children were also engaged. As Joyce Burnette calculates in 'Women Workers in the British Industrial Revolution',[22] their employment ranged from 19 to 40 per cent in 1842 to 30 per cent of the total number of British coal miners in 1851. After

---

[20] Herman Freuenberger, Frances Mather, and Clark Nardinneli, 'A New Look at the Early Factory Labour Force,' *Journal of Economic History* 44, no. 4 (December 1984): 1085–1090.

[21] https://eh.net/encyclopedia/child-labor-during-the-british-industrial-revolution/

[22] Ibid.

the proper execution of the Mining Act of 1842, the employment of British women and girls in mines fell drastically. The Reports (*Sessions: 1847–48 and 1849 Mining Districts I & Sessions 1850 and 1857–58 Mining District II*), referred to by Carolyn Tuttle[23] mention that the children's employment in underground work decreased drastically too.

The writers are presently in a position to explain why child labour was increasing considerably in the mills and mines during the Industrial Revolution in Great Britain, especially during the 18th century and in the first quarter of the 19th century.

It is very difficult to explain the reasons for the quick increase in the number of child labourers until and unless we use the competitive model of the labour market for children. In this context, we require a demand–supply framework (which is used by many sociologists and economists) to properly understand the dynamics of child labour in the United Kingdom.

We are, at first, trying to explain the supply-side condition of child labour. General sense tells that during the period of the Industrial Revolution, there were huge numbers of children who could work at the mills as per the demands. The economic reason that influenced the children to join factories was abject poverty. Due to the lack of money, the impoverished English parents sent their children to mills and mines so that they could become bread earners. It was commonly believed that it was also the duty of the children to contribute financially to their families for better living.

Another reason behind the prevalence of child labour in 19th-century England was that education was not made compulsory for children. The well-to-do families sent their children to quality schools. But there was no mandatory schooling law for children. This, along with poverty, prevented children belonging to low-income families from going to school. In the United Kingdom, compulsory schooling law was enforced in 1876, following which the attitude of families towards employing children at work underwent changes. However, those who were really poor had no option other than to send their children to work. Poverty—to reiterate—was the main hindrance for the poor families to avail quality educational opportunities for their children.

---

[23] Carolyn Tuttle, 'Child Labour during the British Industrial Revolution,' n.d., https://www.bxscience.edu/ourpages/auto/2009/10/19/58704445/child%20labor%20in%20britain%20and%20IR.htm

Another reason for the growth of child labourers in the United Kingdom in the 19th century was due to the rapid and widespread innovations in science, a large number of machines were installed at factories and to work on/with these machines, children were employed cheaply. They were obedient, prompt and fast. Apart from this, there was no clearly defined child labour law initially enforced by the British government. That is the reason why, in spite of laws by the British government for children working at mills, coal and metal mines during the 19th century, a large number of children worked in factories. To understand the situation, one could refer to the following data drawn up by Charles Booth (Table 3.1).

Data presented in Table 3.1 shows a declining trend in the number of child labourers, both boys and girls. Many reasons can be suggested for such a declining trend of child labour in British mining and textiles towards the end of the 19th century.

Table 3.1 Child Employment, 1851–1881

Industry and Age Cohort	Year			
	1851	1861	1871	1881
Mining				
Males under 15	37,300	45,100	43,100	30,400
Females under 15	1,400	500	900	500
Males 15–20	50,100	65,300	74,900	87,300
Females over 15	5,400	4,900	5,300	5,700
Total under 15 as % of workforce	13%	12%	10%	6%
Textiles and dyeing				
Males under 15	93,800	80,700	78,500	58,900
Females under 15	147,700,115	700,119	80,082	600
Males 15–20	92,600	92,600	90,500	93,200
Females over 15	780,900,739	300,729	700,699	900
Total under 15 as % of workforce	15%	19%	14%	11%

Source: Charles Booth, 'Occupations of the People of the United Kingdom, 1801–81,' *Journal of the Statistical Society of London* 49, no. 2 (June 1886): 314–444.

First of all, parents working in industries became interested to send their children to schools and educating them, instead of sending them to work. Second, the then British government enforced the law of compulsory schooling for children. Third, the Industrial Revolution improved the standard of living for British working families. This influenced the parents to keep their children at home, and not permit them to work at factories and started sending their children to school. Fourth, another strong reason was that sophisticated implements and machines were being increasingly used in factories, and these could not be conveniently handled by the children and required strength of adults, especially of males. Finally, the usage of child labourers in industries during the early phase of the Industrial Revolution later led to a hullabaloo among the English intellectuals which, indirectly, led to the decline of child labour in England.

In fact, the Victorian era (1837–1901) in England was infamous for engaging minors en masse in factories and mines. Children, especially the lean and thin boys, were employed as chimney sweepers. During the later years of the Industrial Revolution—in 19th-century England—about one-third of the poor families were either headed by females or were without breadwinners. This exerted tremendous pressure upon the children, both boys and girls, of such families and they had no option but to sell their labour power. Different census data for England and Wales from 1881 to 1911 show the steady prevalence of child labour. Due to death or abandonment, children became orphans and were forced to join work in mills and mines in order to feed the family members and sacrificed their schooling and playtime. Table 3.2 focuses on the number of such child labourers as described.

Table 3.2 *Working Children in England and Wales*

Census Year	Child Labour (%) (Aged 10–12 years)
1881	22.9
1891	26.0
1901	21.9
1911	18.3

Source: Census of England and Wales (London: His Majesty's Stationary Office, 1914), 540.

Due to the Industrial Revolution in England, people migrated en masse quickly to industrial areas. Such large populations were not welcomed by the local populace there, and the newly arrived families were faced with adverse living conditions. Children living with them in the urban/industrial areas encountered deplorable sanitary conditions. Housings built for the workers nearer to the industrial belts in England were badly constructed and suffocating. Two types of children lived there: the parish children and the free workers. The parish children lived in the workhouses or orphanages. Most of them were routinely sent to factories as apprentices. Naturally, they learned a particular form of trade and sometimes became educated. The free children lived with their parents.

However, because the parish children were mostly orphans, errand boys and victims of violent parents, they did not live well in the parishes. They lived under unhealthy conditions, and in many parishes, children were considered as 'commodities', and they were even sold like commodities. Importantly, there existed 'child markets' in different parts of the United Kingdom for buying and selling of parish and free labour children. Parents residing in the workhouses sometimes disagreed with the decision of the parish heads regarding sending the children to factories but they could not strongly oppose it because they were under the control of clergymen. Robert Hessen, in an essay published in 1967, mentioned that the parish apprentice children were sent to virtual slavery by the government bodies.[24] They were sent to apprenticeship for a long period of time for which no payment was made. Only a bare subsistence was provided. The apprenticeship mostly lasted between 8 and 12 years. This was a highly exploitative practice because children's work remained unpaid and only a minimal food and unhealthy shelter were provided. Some of the apprentices were provided basic education through the setting up of some Sunday schools. They had to work for six days a week and for 14–16 hours a day.

In the case of free labour children, it was less easy to educate them wholesomely. They were under the direct supervision of their parents. They were thus less easily disciplined in the factory team. After the

---

[24] Quoted in Routledge, 'Child-labour and the Industrial Revolution,' 2006, http://cw.routledge.com/textbooks/9780415370240/resources/7child.asp

passage of the Health and Morals of the Apprentices Act, 1802,[25] a fine was imposed on the manufacturers (in the United States of America, it amounted to $5 fine per worker) if children were given night shift duties. With the decline of the parish apprenticeship system, the employment of free labour children increased in factories and mines. Children's entry into factory work completely depended on the wishes of parents. If they agreed, minor children could be engaged in factories—and even for doing hazardous works. They could be even involved in night shift duties. After the 1820s, industries could engage children at their own will. Terrible child markets existed as already described, and the parents could take advantage of the system. Families had, in fact, no alternative but to send their children to work. Most of these families were destitute and starving. The only option left to them was to involve women and children to join the factories and mills. The Austrian economist Ludwig von Mises, however, mentioned in a 1949 publication that it was not true that the British factories forced the housewives out from nurseries and kitchens and the children from their play. The reality was that factories helped children and women to work and earn and look after the family members with the wages they earned. In this way, the UK factories saved the destitute families from starvation.[26]

The socio-economist Jane Humphries has extensively worked on child labour in England during the Industrial Revolution. She based her works—the most important of which is *Childhood and Child-labour in the British Industrial Revolution*[27]—on the autobiographies of working men of the 18th and 19th centuries. After several studies, she has concluded that:

1. During the period of industrialization in the United Kingdom (1790–1850), there were increasing numbers of child labourers in factories and mines around England. This observation fully supports earlier works as well as recent studies.

---

[25] Nikki Booth, Clare Robson, and Jacqui Welham, eds., *Tolley's Managing a Diverse Workforce* (London and New York: Routledge, 2004), 49.

[26] Thomas Woods, 'A Myth Shattered: Mises, Hayek, and the Industrial Revolution,' Foundation for Economic Education, 1 November 2001, https://fee.org/articles/a-myth-shattered-mises-hayek-and-the-industrial-revolution/

[27] Jane Humphries, *Childhood and Child-labour in the British Industrial Revolution* (Cambridge: Cambridge University Press, 2010).

2. In the early industrial economy, child labour was endemic. They were entrenched in traditional and modern sectors. They were also geographically widespread (all over the United Kingdom). Referring to data available from the British population census of 1851, Humphries has found out the data related to the most frequently-recorded first jobs and top twenty jobs for males in the United Kingdom during the Industrial Revolution and afterwards, which show the preponderance of child labourers who were of 10–14 years of age.

Humphrey's findings have been summed up in Table 3.3.

Table 3.3 Most Frequently Recorded First Jobs and Top 20 Jobs for the 10–14-year-old Males in England and Wales (Excluding London), as per the 1851 Census

Most Frequently Recorded First Jobs	Top 20 Jobs
1. Agriculture[a]	1. Agricultural labourer (outdoor)
2. Messenger, porter	2. Farmer's, grazier's son, grandson, etc.
3. Cotton manufacture[b]	3. Messenger, porter (not government)
4. coal-miner	4. Farm servant (in-door)
5. Woollen/worsted manufacture[b]	5. Cotton manufacture
6. Shop boy/retail	6. Coal-miner
7. Monitor schoolteacher	7. Labourer (branch undefined)
8. Sailor	8. Woollen cloth manufacture
9. Shoemaker	9. Worsted manufacture
10. Office boy	10. Shoemaker
11. Domestic servant	11. Silk manufacture
12. Hawker/street trader	12. Iron manufacture
13. Printer/compositor	13. Domestic servant (General)
14. Rope/paper manufacture	14. Earthen manufacture
15. Carpenter/joiner	15. Tailor
16. Earthenware manufacture	16. House, stocking, manufacture

(Table 3.3 Continued)

(Table 3.3 Continued)

Most Frequently Recorded First Jobs	Top 20 Jobs
17. Silk manufacture	17. Blacksmith
18. Iron manufacture	18. Carpenter, joiner
19. Blacksmith	19. Mason
20. Tailor	20. Bricklayer

Source: Peter Kirby, *Child-labour in Great Britain, 1750–1870* (Basingstoke: Palgrave Macmillan, 2003), 135.
Notes: a = Every kind of agricultural occupation possible; b = Factory work and domestic manufacturing.

The census data show that child labour was not only prevalent in factories and mines in the 19th-century United Kingdom but it also had its extension to traditional sectors as well, such as those of agriculture, domestic work, street trading, carpentry, tailoring, bricklaying, farm servant, blacksmith, etc. Children were principally engaged in agriculture, small-scale manufacturing, and allied services. Jane Humphries found that though the traditional sectors needed a sizable number of working children, parish children and free-labour children were much more absorbed and engaged by the factories and industries during their early rapid expansions. While analysing the autobiographies, Humphries noticed that child labour was most vital for the English factory jobs where the volume of child labour was approximately twice the size of the adult labour force.

Table 3.4 illustrates the extent of child labour in England and Wales during Industrial Revolution (from 1851 to 1911). The data presented here show the age-wise and gender-wise segregation of classified child labourers.

During the Industrial Revolution, it was thought—as we think today—that the most effective way of ending child labour is by admitting children to school: that is, schooling should be made compulsory. Schooling for all the children was made compulsory in England in 1880, following which there was a gradual decline in child labour. There were some schooling facilities for working children in the United Kingdom even before elementary education had been made compulsory.

Table 3.4 *Percentage of Children Recorded as Working, by Age Range, in England and Wales, 1851–1911*

Boys & Girls \ Year	1851	1861	1871	1881	1891	1901	1911
Boys 5–9	2.0	2.0	0.8	–	–	–	–
Girls 5–9	1.4	1.1	0.7	–	–	–	–
Boys 10–14	36.6	36.9	32.1	22.9	26.0	21.9	18.3
Girls 10–14	19.9	20.2	20.5	15.1	16.3	12.0	10.4

Source: Census of England and Wales, 1851–1911. Refer to Hugh Cunningham and Pier Paolo Viazzo, *Child Labour in the Historical Perspective, 1800–1985: Case Studies from Europe, Japan, and Columbia* (Florence: UNICEF– ICDC Press, 1996), 10.

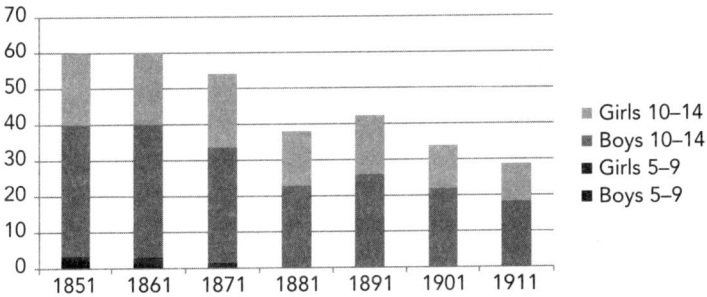

The census data presented in Table 3.5 show the occupational status of children, aged 5–14, in England and Wales during 1851–1871. There are three categories: the general children scholars, those who stayed 'at home', and those who were 'occupied'. Of these, the decline in the number of children staying 'at home' and those in the general 'unemployed' category was faster than the children in the 'occupied' category.

Working people disliked sending their children to government schools even if the educational facilities provided there were free, that is, no fee was charged from the students. Two reasons can be suggested for the working people's reluctance to get their children admitted to government-run schools. First, there was a strict formality to maintain after the students would be admitted. Second, there was a proper and

Table 3.5 Occupation Status of Children Aged 5–14 in England and Wales as a Percentage in the Total Age Range

Category / Year	Boys			Girls		
	1851	1861	1871	1851	1861	1871
Scholars	50.5	57.7	62.2	49.1	58.4	59.7
At home	30.9	23.7	22.1	40.7	31.5	30.3
Occupied	18.6	18.6	15.7	10.2	10.1	10.0

Source: Census of England and Wales, 1851–1871. Refer to K. Schuerer et al., 'Household and Family-structure in England and Wales, 1851–1911: Continuities and Change', Continuity and Change 33, no. 3 (2018): 365–411.

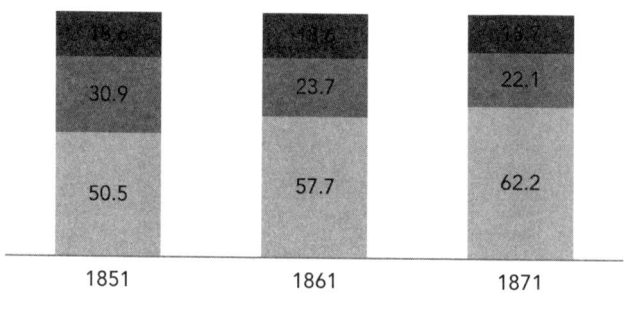

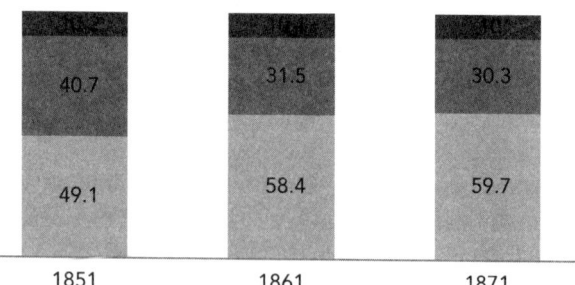

elaborate system for imparting education which dragged on until the examinations commenced. For these two reasons parents preferred private school to government facilities even if the hefty fee was charged. There was no government control over the British private schools, and students could attend school according to their convenience. Referring to the 1979 publication on child labour and schooling in England by the socio-economists Hurt, Cunningham and Viazzo write how the British working-parents thought that schooling would be a place for learning basic skills in reading, writing, arithmetic, sewing and knitting as training for earning a living.[28] Compulsory schooling—as it was thought—was not always good especially for the poor families. It was, in fact, difficult to say that children were better off at school than at work.

Until the 1830s, working children in the United Kingdom were heavily engaged in factories and mines, and the working hours a day lasted between 12 and 19 hours. On one hand, such long working hours increased the productivity of industries. On the other hand, the exhausted child workers faced terrible punishment. Age was another important element in respect to the employment and serviceability of child labourers, as we have already mentioned. The lower the age, the lower was the payment of wage for the concerned child worker. From the beginning of the Industrial Revolution to the end of the 19th century, working children continued to be ill-paid, and their wage was about three times less than an adult earned.

3.3.2. Belgium

The Industrial Revolution began in the United Kingdom, and thereafter spread to the other countries of Europe and North America in the 19th century. The countries which were distinctively influenced and enriched by the Industrial Revolution were Belgium, France, Germany and the United States of America.

Other than the United Kingdom, Belgium was the first country in the European continent that experienced the moulding effects of the Industrial Revolution. This was brought in because of Belgium's rich textile production facilities in the region of Flanders, iron-processing

---

[28] Viazzo and Cunningham, *Child-labour in the Historical Perspective*, 12.

factories in Walloon, and the huge number of coal mines strewn all over the country. The industrious Belgians always maintained close contact with the English, and in 1720 the first steam engine was procured from England and was put into action in Belgium. The increasing number of steam engines led to the rapid growth of coal supplies from different parts of Belgium, and the iron and steel industries multiplied rapidly.

However, the Industrial Revolution and abject poverty in different parts of 19th-century Belgium intensified the problem of child labour until the beginning of the 20th century. Due to the introduction of the steam engine, a considerable number of textile production houses were founded in Verviers and Ghent. These were joined by the steel and mining industries. In 1817, the coke blast furnace was popularized in Belgium by John Cockerill, and the first steamboat was built. As a result, by the mid-19th century, Belgium had become Europe's second richest industrial country. However, the Belgian trade crafts and home industries were under threat due to the modern industrial developments. Home economies were thus in serious trouble, which might have directly influenced—for the worst—the individuals of the families who relied upon the traditional crafts (especially the women and the children). Due to acute poverty, a large number of Belgian children were sent to work at factories rather than to study at schools so that they could contribute to the dwindling family income.

Not only in industries but Belgian children were also engaged in the agriculture sector, especially during the summer months. During summer, there would be a plenitude of cases of school absenteeism. Impoverished Belgian children were used as cattle herders or stable boys and for clearing weeds. Many of the children were also forced to sell milk. Children also were engaged in rural and craft industries. They worked for the whole day in sectors such as rope making, weaving, metal works, basket weaving and leather processing. They also processed straw, made hats and chiselled chairs. But these rural craft industries were severely affected by the rapid Belgian mechanization. In course of time, Belgian women and children were forced to change their traditional occupation and join the mechanized factories and mines as workers. Child labourers in Belgium suffered from the worst working conditions in the coal mines of Wallonia. Children working there were of the age group of 10–12 years. About 10,000 children were forced to work there in spite of low wages and worst working conditions. Only during the Napoleonic regime (1813), children under the age of 10 years were strictly prevented from working in the mines. After 1840, a large number of Belgian children were also used to push to small carts (rectangular-shaped) on iron rails. Children had to work in mines continuously for 36 hours or more without proper rest. Children's earnings were given directly to their parents, and only the supplementary income earned by them was given to them.

In the 19th century, Belgian children also worked in bricklaying industries in a large number. They had to dig up the clay, mix soil with more water, and carry the moulded bricks to the kilns and drying sheds at the brickfields. They had no proper place for sleeping, and they had to sleep in open sheds. Naturally, they could not have the chance to have sound sleep.

Women and children had a maximum contribution to the total workforce in Belgian factories and mining. We hereby present the data of child labour used at the Ghent factories in 1817. The existence of a large number of spinning mills in Ghent in the 19th century gave the sobriquet 'the Manchester of the Continent' to the town. The Ghent factories used about 75 per cent of women and children in mills and mines, and more has been revealed by the following chart.

Table 3.6 shows that on average, 20 per cent of the total workforce at select industries of Ghent came from children below the age of 17 years, and a large number of them (25%) could be found working in spinning mills. But the highest percentage of children (33%) could be found working in tobacco factories, and 26 per cent at paper mills.

Table 3.6 *Child Labour in Some Ghent Factories*

Kind of Factory	Number of Factories	Number of Labourers	Number of Children (Under 17 Years)	Per Cent (%)
Spinning mill	12	1,093	277	25
Weaving mill	5	148	24	16
Textile printing mill	7	360	45	12
Sugar factory	4	71	3	4
Paper mill	3	123	32	26
Tobacco factory	2	18	6	33
Yards	3	131	2	1

(Table 3.6 Continued)

(Table 3.6 Continued)

Kind of Factory	Number of Factories	Number of Labourers	Number of Children (Under 17 Years)	Per Cent (%)
Joineries	2	24	–	–
Hatters	2	25	4	16
Cooperage	1	7	–	–
Roof slating	1	8	1	12
Total	42	2,008	394	20

Source: Stadsarchief Ghent, Reeks K15, 1817. Refer to Cunningham and Viazzo, *Child Labour in the Historical Perspective*, 2.

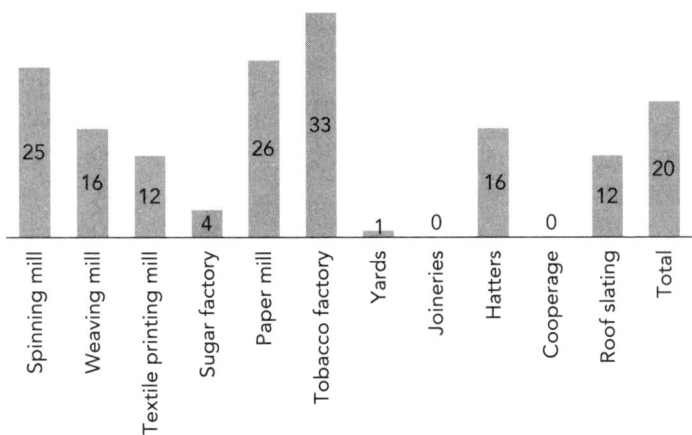

Table 3.7 depicts the number of child labourers at the factories of different Belgium provinces in 1843.

Table 3.7 shows a Belgian government report on the engagement of children at factories located at different places of Ghent. In the table, children in the age group of 9–15 years could be found to constitute 19.5 per cent of the total children's workforce, and the rest is constituted of children/youth of the age group 16–21 years and above.

The first census was carried out in Belgium in 1846 under the leadership of great statistician and astronomer Adolphe Quetelet. The census data presented in Table 3.8 provide detailed information on child labour in the Belgian workforce.

Table 3.7 Child Labour in Factories in Various Belgium Provinces, by Age and Gender, 1843

Age	Male	Percentage of Total Workers	Female	Percentage of Total Workers	Total	%
Under 9 years	532	1	164	0.3	696	1.3
9–11 years	1,615	3	684	1.3	2,299	4.3
12–15 years	5,638	10.4	1,881	3.5	7,519	13.9
16–20 years	5,768	10.6	3,377	6.2	9,145	16.8
21 years over	29,520	54.5	5,002	9.2	34,522	63.7
Total	43,073	79.5	11,108	20.5	54,181	100

Source: Ministère de l'Intérieur, 1848. Refer to Cunningham and Viazzo, Child Labour in the Historical Perspective, 2.

■ Under 9 years ■ 9–11 years ■ 12–15 years ■ 16–20 years ■ 21 years over

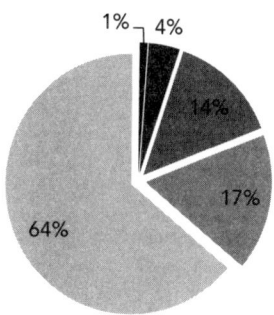

■ Percentage of Total Workers: Male ■ Percentage of Total Workers: Female

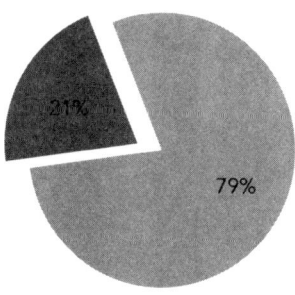

Table 3.8 Child Labour in Some Important Belgian Crafts and Industries, by Age and Gender, 1846

Type of Company	Number of Companies	Number of Labourers by Gender and Age				
		Male	Female	Over 16	Under 16	Total
Coal mines and coal workers	202	39,120	7,066	35,847	10,339	46,186
Craft metal treatment	12,028	15,853	158	13,583	2,428	16,011
Industrial metal treatment	2,419	24,345	1,933	23,674	2,604	26,278
Craft brickyards and potteries	6,786	11,624	165	10,843	946	11,789
Industrial brickyards and potteries	1,613	18,231	1,745	16,367	3,609	19,976
Craft flax and hemp	18,732	13,920	28,874	22,387	20,407	42,794
Industrial flax and hemp	2,401	8,497	8,732	13,591	3,638	17,229
Wool	768	12,210	5,943	14,820	3,333	18,153
Craft cotton processing	43	4	358	101	261	362
Industrial cotton processing	350	10,042	4,276	10,580	3,738	14,318
Silk	27	588	87	438	237	675
Clothing	10,036	7,169	3,888	8,458	2,599	11,057
Craft food processing	7,928	6,979	478	6,725	732	4,457
Craft woodwork	20,636	19,020	215	17,129	2,106	19,235
Industrial woodwork	1,032	1,659	63	1,577	145	1,722
Craft leatherwork	11,841	10,189	270	8,257	2,202	10,459
Industrial leatherwork	968	2,449	243	2,472	220	2,692
Craft paper factories and printing works	611	2,666	39	2,054	651	2,705
Industrial paper factories and printing offices	142	1,582	1,089	2,106	565	2,671

Source: Statistique de la Belgique, Industrie. Recensement général (15 October 1846), Brussels, 1851, x–xi. Cunningham and Viazzo, *Child Labour in the Historical Perspective*, 2.

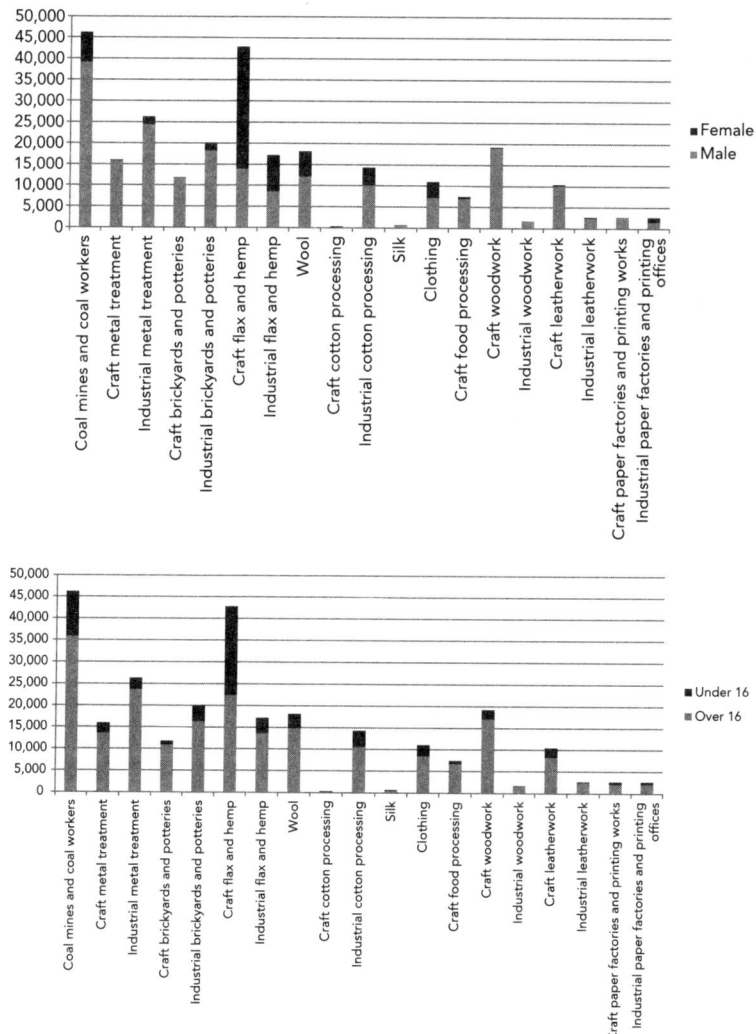

Data presented in Table 3.8 reveal that child labour was widely used in the sectors of textiles, coal mining, brickfields, potteries, food industries, leatherwork, wood and metal works. Working children contributed to 21 per cent of the total workforce. It could be noted that the majority of child labour was found in craft and home-based work and the next was the factories and mines. It is also true that children below 16 years were on the increase in mining, as per the observation of Puissant in his 1976 publication.[29]

A large number of women and children were engaged in the Ghent cotton firm, *Voortman*, as shown in Table 3.9.

Table 3.9 Textile Workers in the Voortman Cotton Mill in Ghent, Percentage by Age and Gender, 1842–1902

Year	1842		1859		1879		1902	
Age	M	F	M	F	M	F	M	F
5–9	0	0.6	0	0	0	0	0	0
10–14	0	3.1	2.6	7.4	1.0	7.0	0	3.8
15–19	4.4	9.5	11.1	9.5	2.0	22.0	6.5	22.7
20–24	7.6	13.3	11.1	13.7	5.0	12.0	7.6	14.6
25–29	3.1	14.5	7.9	5.3	6.0	10.0	4.8	6.5
30–34	8.2	3.8	5.3	3.1	4.0	4.0	3.8	4.3
35–39	5.0	3.1	2.6	0	2.0	3.0	5.4	1.6
40–44	7.6	1.3	5.8	3.1	5.0	3.0	3.8	2.2
45+	9.5	5.0	9.5	1.5	8.0	6.0	10.7	1.5

Source: Scholliers, 1995. Refer to Cunningham and Viazzo, *Child Labour in the Historical Perspective*, 3.

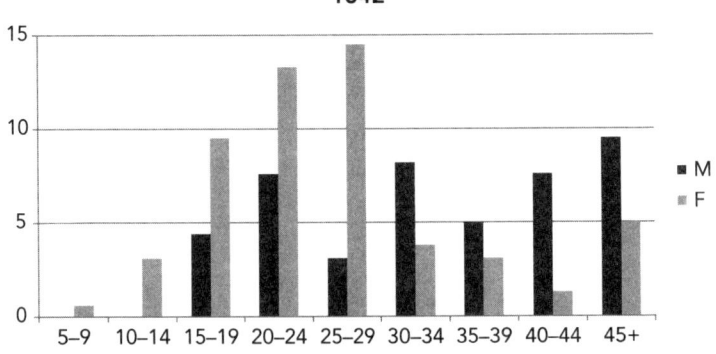

[29] Quoted in Giovanni Vecchi. *Measuring Well-being: A History of Italian Living Standards* (Oxford: Oxford University Press, 2017), 153.

Post-Industrial Revolution Concern | 89

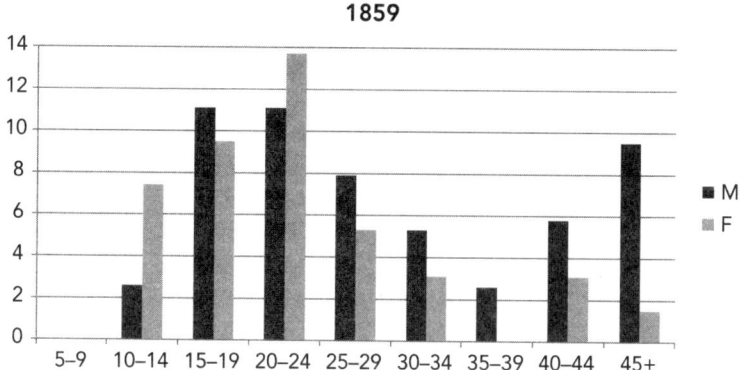

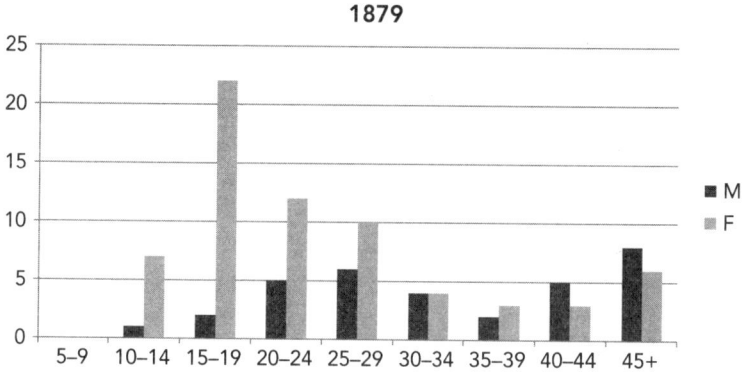

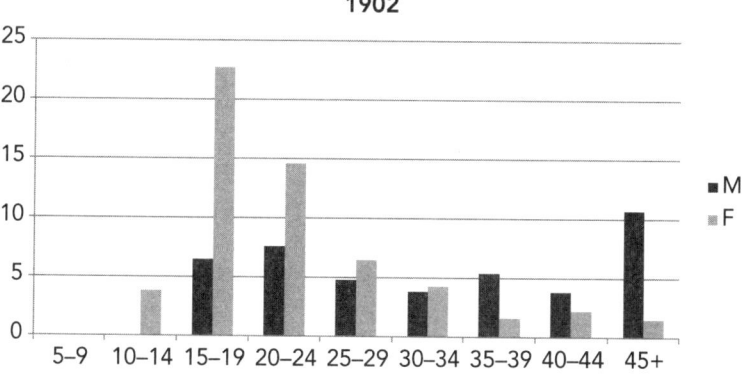

The figures exhibited in table 3.9 and the corresponding chart shows that the women and children were largely employed in order to keep the cost of the production low. Data exhibited in Table 3.9 reflect the constant engagement of child labourers of the age group of 10–16 years. This was particularly noticed during the 1870s, and approximately 20 per cent of total workforce was comprised of child labourers. However, from 1896 onwards, there was a sharp decline in the number of child labourers because of the passing of the Belgian anti-child labour law in 1889, and the improvement in the standard of living in the working families. After the publication of the Belgian industrial census of 1896, the most authentic information of child labourers in Belgium became public. The census data showed that 11 per cent of the total workforce was children aged 16 years. They were principally found working in textiles, mining, clothing and in glass industries. Data show that among 4,681 industrial establishments, 87 establishments employed more child labourers than adults, and these establishments were mainly textile industries, tobacco industries, book manufacturing companies, clothing companies, chocolate manufacturing and wool processing and dress-making mills.

Relevant child labour data from these times (Census of Belgium, 1896) have been represented in Table 3.10.

Data available from Table 3.10 show that 50 per cent of children aged less than 12 years were engaged in the Belgian cloth-making industry. The census carefully determined the actual labour statistics, including the employment of child labour in various Belgian industries. The collected data also show that 61,652 children were employed in industrial establishments. This does not include the number of children

Table 3.10 Statistics of Children According to Age and Sex

| Age Group | No. of Children | | |
(Years)	Boys	Girls	Total
Less than 16	50,493	25,654	76,147
14–16	36,431	18,515	54,946
12–14	13,814	6,948	20,762
Less than 12	248	191	439

Source: Census of Belgium, 1896. Refer to E. Dubois, 'Child labour in Belgium,' *The Annals of the American Academy of Political and Social Science* 20 (July 1902): 203–220.

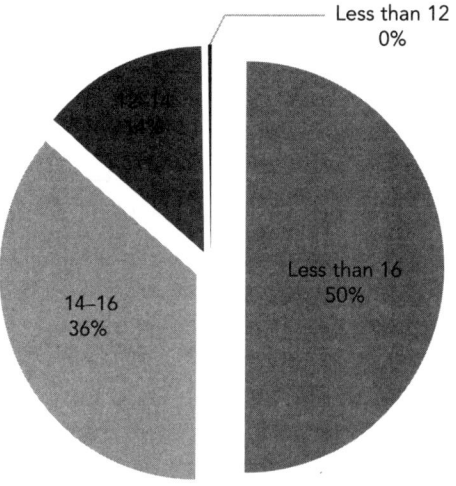

employed in the then coal mines. The working hours ranged between 9 and 12 hours. Both boys and girls had shifting duties of day and night. The coal mines employed 10,167 child workers out of which the duration of labour hours was determined for 9,153 children. Another merit of the Belgian census was that the census was successful in determining the exact wages for both minor and adult workers. The wages of 70,688 children were fixed, and have been shown exactly.

The data also show that about one-fourth of the working children in Belgium earned very little, and their wages were less than 0.50 franc. About half of them earned wages between 0.50 franc and 1.50 franc. Only about one-fifth would earn a little higher than 1.50 franc. The wages received by children and women were far less than what were received by adult males.

Child labour in Belgium faced severe abusive conditions. Efforts were on, especially since 1843, to form statutes for working children. An investigation was made by the Imperial Government of Belgium to assess the extent of unfortunate and abusive working conditions that the children faced while working in mills and mines, but the steps taken by the government did not work and the so-called 'Manchester-ian ideas' prevailed. Despite concerted efforts from enlightened manufacturers, physicians and philanthropists for promulgating legislation against the practice of child labour, it took more than half a century to introduce into the Royal Decree of 1884 regulations related to working in mines and the fixing of the working hours for boys and girls. The decree determined the working age for boys to be less than 12 years, and for girls to be less than 14. Ultimately the Belgium Law against Child-labour of 13 December 1889 was passed for working women, children and adults in industrial establishments. The law was immediately enforced for children working at mines, stone quarries; in workshops, mills and factories; in establishments classified as dangerous, unhealthy or unsuitable; at harbours, terminals and stations; and in the sector of transportation by land or water. The law was enforced for both private and public enterprises.

The law did not, however, affect the family-based enterprises where only the family members were employed under the control of the father, the mother or the guardians. But those family-based undertakings could not be normally classified as being dangerous, unhealthy or unsuitable. The main legal provisions applying to children and youths under the Belgian Law of 1889 were as follows. First, the children's working-age was fixed as 12 years and above. Second, only the Belgian monarch could authorize the employment of children at dangerous or unhealthy enterprises. Third, the working hours of a child per day were fixed at 12. Fourth, children under the age of 16 years were prohibited to work during the night shifts. Fifth, children below the age of 16 years were required to carry a memorandum book which was to be given to them free of cost by their concerned parish—this would contain data regarding their Christian faith, Christian first name and surname, data about the date and place of birth, their residential address, along with the full names of their parents or guardians.

However, one major defect in this legislation was that there was no provision for the education of working children. The Royal Decrees of 19 February 1895, August 1895 and 5 April 1989 further added important legal provisions which were as follows. First, children below the age of 16 years were prohibited to work in industries that manufactured products which could be dangerous for the workers. Second, children were prohibited to work in the *Lucifer*-match factories. Third, children were restricted from working in industries where India rubber was treated with carbon sulphate. Fourth, children under 16 years of age were prohibited to work in factories whose productions and environment were unhygienic. Fifth, children were barred from working at the rag shops. Finally, children were prohibited to work in the places where the hare- and rabbit-skins were processed before being chemically treated, and in all the processes in which the skins underwent after treatment—like carrying, brushing and cutting.

Although different working hours for children prevailed in the Belgian industries, it was more or less the same across factories. The timing was roughly 10–16 hours a day for adult workers. Understandably, it was longer during summer and shorter during winter. The duration of working hours for working children was gradually reducing over the period. Data presented in Table 3.11 focus on the declining working hours for children in Ghent industries during 1840–1914.

Long working hours for children, particularly at night, directly affected their health. Monotonous and repetitive works also affected their health and mental conditions. Working conditions in some of the industries like cotton and flax mills, matchstick factories, tobacco workshops, coal mining, were very deplorable and hazardous and that affected the lungs of the working children.

Historians used height and weight data to measure the well-being of children and the general population in the past. In order to measure the standard of living of working children engaged in the Ghent cotton industry, data regarding their height and weight were collected and analysed. The concerned data have been presented in Table 3.12.

Table 3.11 *Working Hours in Ghent Industries during 1840–1914*

Year	Hours/Day	Hours/Week
1840	13	78
1847	13	78
1859	12	72
1869	12	72
1871	12	72
1892	12	72
1897	11	69
1900	11	69
1904	11	69
1914	11	69

Source: De Neve, 1992, 17. Refer to Cunningham and Viazzo, *Child Labour in the Historical Perspective*, 3.

Table 3.12 Height and Weight of Children Working in the Ghent Cotton Industry, by Age and Gender and Compared with Normal Values, 1843

Age	Boys				Girls			
	Normal Height (meters)	Height of Working Boys (meters)	Normal Weight (kg)	Weight of Working Boys (kg)	Normal Height (meters)	Height of Working Girls (meters)	Normal Weight (kg)	Wight of Working Girls (kg)
10	1.275	1.210	24.52	23.40	1.248	1.204	23.52	22.96
11	1.330	1.300	27.10	26.62	1.299	1.240	25.65	23.80
12	1.385	1.310	29.82	28.47	1.353	1.339	29.82	27.14
13	1.439	1.368	34.38	29.45	1.403	1.372	32.94	29.57
14	1.493	1.367	38.67	31.69	1.453	1.388	36.70	31.23
15	1.546	1.480	43.62	38.49	1.499	1.415	40.37	34.61

Source: De Neve, 1992. Refer to Cunningham and Viazzo, Child Labour in the Historical Perspective, 3.

Table 3.12 shows that the Belgian working children's (boys and girls) heights and weights were considerably lower than the normal standard. This was probably because of their consumption of a low-calorie diet, lack of leisure and less sleep. As we have mentioned, the wages paid to child labourers were very low, and the average working hours were high.

Table 3.13 shows the average wages paid to working children in the Ghent cotton industry during 1846 and 1880.

Wage data presented in Table 3.13 show that meagre wages were provided to children working at the Belgian factories. Wages offered by six industries, viz, ceramics, mining, glassworks, steel, cotton, and

Table 3.13 Wages (Average) Paid to Belgian Children under 16 Years of Age, 1846 and 1880

Sector	Year & Wage Rate	1846 (Belgian Francs)	1880 (Belgian Francs)
Ceramics industry		1.28	1.64
Mining		0.81	1.69
Glassworks		0.72	1.82
Steel industry		0.48	1.76
Cotton industry		0.47	1.36
Flax and hemp		0.33	1.20

Source: De Weerdt D., 1960. Refer to Cunningham and Viazzo's Child Labour in the Historical Perspective, 5.

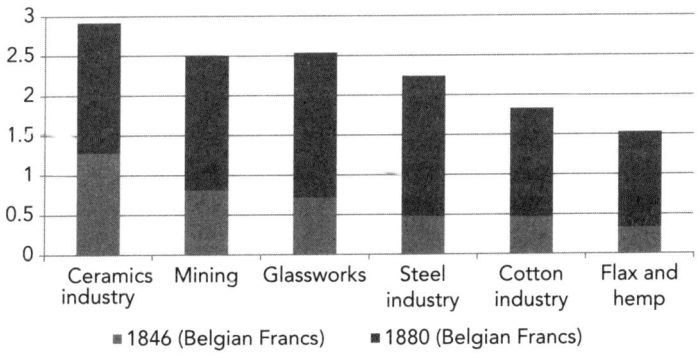

flax and hemp, were very low. It was the lowest—only 0.33 francs—in the flax industry. So was the rate in cotton (0.47 francs) and steel industry (0.48 francs). Comparing the data between 1846 and 1880, one could note a remarkable increase in wage rate in some industries—particularly in the flax and hemp industry, cotton industry, steel industry and glassworks (more than double, three times or more). It was more than double in the mining industry, but there was an almost insignificant improvement in the case of the ceramics industry in 34 years. Low wages existed mainly because of the subcontracting system which prevailed in Belgian industries, especially in the Ghent cotton industry where wages were paid to children not by the factory owners but by the spinners. Also, there was a practice to provide lesser wages to girls compared to that of boys for the same job.

Data exhibited in Table 3.14 echo this.

The Western European kingdom of Belgium was under French, Spanish and Austrian rule for a long time. Different regions of the Belgian province were united by the Treaty of Vienna in 1815 as the 'United Kingdom of Netherlands' at the time of William I, and, eventually, it became an independent kingdom in 1830 under Leopold I.

After the Belgian independence, there was a huge expansion in the sector of school education.[30] This was because of the proliferation of

Table 3.14 Daily Wages of Ghent Children under 16 Years of Age, in Cotton, Flax and Steel Industries, before 1896

Wage Group Belgian Francs	Cotton		Flax		Steel
	% Boys	% Girls	% Boys	% Girls	% Boys
–0.5	3.19	1.51	–	5.42	22.53
0.50–0.99	16.23	38.49	23.07	37.12	45.79
1.0–1.49	54.52	60.00	72.37	57.46	23.76
1.5	26.06	–	4.56	–	7.92
Total	100	100	100	100	100

Source: De Neve, 1992. Refer to Cunningham and Viazzo, *Child Labour in the Historical Perspective*, 3.

---

[30] Refer to Raf Vanderstraeten and Frederik Van der Gucht, 'Geographical Divergences of Educational Credentials in the Modern Nation-state: A Case Study of Belgium, 1961–2011,' in *The State, Schooling, and Identity*, eds. Kari Kantasalmi and Gunilla Holm (Singapore: Palgrave Macmillan, 2017), 61–78.

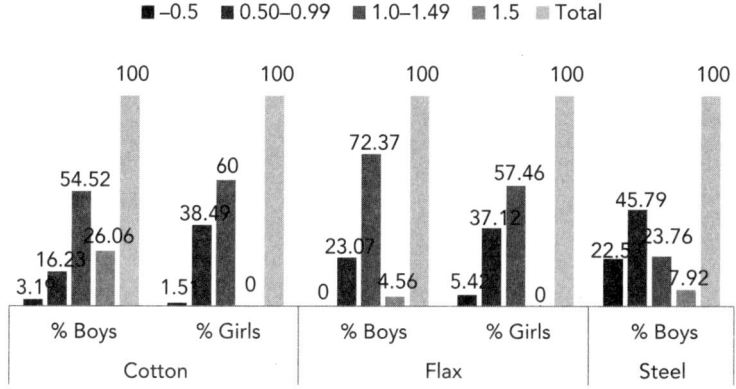

private schools. Earlier (i.e., around 1830), there was one school for every 785 pupils, and after 1840, one school was established for 1,007 people. The first organic law (passed in 1842 with respect to primary education) had the provision of free primary school for poor children. But as already mentioned, parents of working children preferred private schools.

Different types of schools established by the Royal Government of Belgium and private initiatives helped a large number of children receive school education. Thus, the literacy rate was increasing rapidly in independent Belgium. Table 3.15 shows the literacy by gender during 1866–1910.

Table 3.15 Literacy in Belgium, by Gender, 1866–1910

Year	Male Population (000s)	No. of Literates (000s)	% Literate	Female Population (000s)	No. of Literates (000s)	% Literate
1866	2,420	1,209	50	2,408	1,070	44
1880	2,758	1,661	60	2,762	1,527	55
1890	3,027	1,948	64	3,042	1,838	60
1900	3,325	2,309	69	3,369	2,247	67
1910	3,681	2,781	76	3,743	2,765	74

Source: Mitchell, 1981, 29;. Cunningham and Viazzo, *Child Labour in the Historical Perspective*, 6.
Note: All figures rounded.

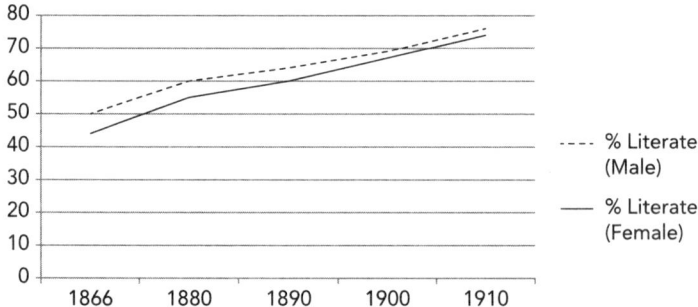

Data for the literacy of both male and female Belgian populations show an increasing growth rate over the years, and no sharp variation in literacy rates between males and females could be noticed. Male literacy, it could be noticed, was 50 per cent in 1866, while it was 44 per cent for females. It rose to 60 per cent for males and 55 per cent for females in 1880. In 1900, the male literacy was 69 per cent and the female literacy rate was 67 per cent, and, in 1910, it was 76 and 74 per cent for males and females, respectively.

In the 19th century, Belgium was one of the more advanced industrialized countries in Europe. But it took a considerable period of time for the Royal Government of Belgium to pass the legislation on child labour although working children were suffering horribly at working places. The government introduced a bill in 1848 that prohibited the employment of children under the age of 10 years from working and restricted the children's (those in the 10–14-year group) working hours to 6.5 hours a day. But the owners of Ghent textile industries remained hostile to the government rules, imposed self-restriction on themselves and engaged children as young as 12 years. With the passage of the Belgian child legislation in 1889—as already mentioned—the employment of (under 12-year-old) children for working at factories became illegal.

3.3.3. France

Like the United Kingdom, France rapidly mechanized her industries in the 19th century, and soon became a great economic power. Impoverished French children and women were employed by the French industrialists in large numbers, and they were pitiably exploited.

In spite of protestations and movements from several corners, it took a long period of time for the French government to promulgate legislation(s) on child labour.

In fact, child labour existed in France even before the onset of the Industrial Revolution in the 19th century—especially in the sectors of agriculture and home-based factories. The French childhood was a brief one, and the children were usually involved in performing domestic tasks and assisted in agricultural and allied activities. Since the Middle Ages, children had been working outside their homes to earn for their impoverished families. As Lee S. Weissbach notes,[31] the French boys usually worked at fields, and the girls performed household works as servants at the houses of the well-to-do families. This situation was not an exception in France—until the 19th century.

For these French working children—until the late 18th century—education was well beyond their reach. Only children from rich and upper-middle-class French families could access quality education. The situation was further aggravated due to the onset of the Industrial Revolution in France. It led to a great demand for labour force including children (both boys and girls). As a result of high demand for labour, there was a large rural exodus—similar to the situation in the United Kingdom—adults (men and women) and children started coming to the industrial areas of France (especially around Paris, Nord, Dunkirk, Lille, Cambrai, Dijon, Marseilles and Lyon) in large numbers, and settled down there. These 'migrants' were massively recruited in mills, mines and construction works. But, as usual, these French workers were provided low wages, and thus they failed to maintain a minimum standard of living. This forced the children to go to the factory with their parents and perform several working assignments, including working under hazardous conditions. Like their English counterparts, the French children engaged in factories and mines were provided with very low wages, and faced long working hours, even 12–14 hours a day with less or no leisure time.

France was known as the 'China of Europe' because it alone comprised 15–16 per cent population of entire Europe. As Peter Mathias and M. M. Postan write, this trend, interestingly, started declining in the mid-19th century: in 1850, France's population was just

---

[31] Lee S. Weissbach, 'Child Labour Legislation in Nineteenth-century France,' *Journal of Economic History* 37, no. 1 (March 1977): 268–271.

35.7 million, and in 1911, the population was further reduced to comprise 9 per cent of the total population of Europe.[32] As an overall assessment, the French population growth accounted for only 14 per cent in 60 years. As against this, it was 78 per cent in England, 64 per cent in the Netherlands, 56 per cent in Belgium and 57 per cent in Germany.[33] Thus, France had to face a long-run decline in the birth rate. Diminishing fecundity was widely identified as the basic reason for a decline in the French birth rate, and the next immediate cause was that of voluntary birth control by the French populace before the onset of the French Revolution of 1789. Political revolution, a part of the French Revolution, was to make way for demographic revolution as well as an enhancement of prosperity of France which was 'sufficiently under-populated'. But, with the rapid decline in population as the French revolution was continuing, an exasperated French (provisional) government vociferously encouraged birth rate, especially by announcing the Pregnancy and Suckling Allowances Policy. In spite of this, there was a sharp decline in the birth rate from 35.9 per cent per thousand in 1791–1795 to 31.6 per cent in 1811–1815.[34] Several historians and social scientists have considered social changes to be more responsible for this declining trend rather than the declared government policies. Many families were broken up by the incidents of divorcing which were fast catching up with the French couples in late 18th-century France. Moreover, social mobility also limited the size of the family. Suppression of customary policies in the rural sites, relaxation of religious customs and increased geographical mobility are also held responsible by post-modern socio-economists for the French 'population-control' during the Industrial Revolution. On the other hand, the French death rate due to epidemics was on the rise, and the larger killers included cholera, diphtheria, small pox and tuberculosis. Moreover, during the Franco–Prussian War (19 July 1870—28 January 1871), 0.138 million French were killed in action,[35] which also took

---

[32] Peter Mathias and M. M. Postan, *The Cambridge Economic History of Europe*, Vol. VII, Part 1 (Cambridge: Cambridge University Press, 1978), 296.

[33] Kevin Kinsella and Cynthia Taeuber, *An Aging World* (Washington, DC: US Government Printing Office, 1993), 21.

[34] Wikipedia, 'Demographics of France,' 24 November 2020, https://en.wikipedia.org/wiki/Demographics_of_France

[35] Frederick Nolte, *Military and Diplomatic Europe in the Nineteenth Century, 1815–84* (Paris: E. Plon, Nourrit et Cie, 1884), 527.

a major toll on the already declining French population—which, in turn, necessitated child labouring at the blooming French industries. Understandably, the declining trend in birth rate also had a major impact on the labour supply in French agriculture and industry. Industrial Revolution in France in the 19th century especially called for the participation of a large number of skilled and unskilled workers and labourers at the French factories and mines. Adults were insufficiently available—many employed militarily or having been conscripted—and this demanded employment of children in industries. French children were recruited en masse in industries. The child labour issue created tremendous problems in France, but little attention was initially paid to this aspect. Consequently, a movement for child labour legislation was initiated at the government level. However, even after the enactment of the legislation, it took a long period of time for the implementation of the anti-child labour law. In the second quarter of the 19th century, a small group of benevolent industrialists of Mulhouse began calling for the legal protection of working children (both boys and girls). The Alsatian entrepreneurs (of Mulhouse) made child labour legislation a crusade, and they were ably joined by the Conservative Catholic writer Alban de Villeneuve-Bargemon (1784–1850), the economist and physician Dr Louis-Rene Villerme (1782–1863) and the Swiss-industrialist (settled in Alsace, France) Daniel Legrand (1783–1859). Ultimately, in 1841, the first legislation on child labour was enacted by the Government of France.[36] The main features of this law were as follows. First, it was applicable to the French shops employing 20 or more workers and those business establishments which relied upon mechanical power or a continuous fire. Second, the working age for a child was fixed at eight years. Third, children below 12 years would be required to work not more than eight hours a day, and for children aged 12–16 years, the working time was 12 hours a day. Fourth, children were not allowed to work at night, on Sundays, and during the notified holidays. Finally, a minimum education was a prerequisite condition for the engagement of factory working children.

By the time the child labour act was passed in France, there remained 12 per cent of underage workers at the French factories. However, the law faced stiff opposition from both the factory owners

---

[36] Hugh Hindman, ed., *The World of Child Labour: A Historical and Regional Survey* (New York and London: Routledge, 2009), 46.

and members of the working-class families. That is why, even after passing the act in 1841, the French government could not enforce the provisions until the 1860s.

Many of the defects of the 1841 law were thoroughly analysed by the concerned officials of the French government and by 1868, the Ministry of Commerce had prepared a new bill related to child labour. But the change of government delayed the adoption of the new anti-child labour law. Ultimately, in 1874, the second child labour law was enacted in France. This law extended the applicability of the regulation to all shops, irrespective of their sizes. Working children's minimum age was determined at 12 (years). A salaried inspectorate was created in 1874. As Weissbach writes in 'Child Labour Legislation in Nineteenth-century France' (268–271), this legislation, once again, could not be implemented in its totality. Many interest groups obstructed the thorough implementation. Only the easier and congenial provisions were obeyed, leaving aside those which would cause greater hardships for the employers.

Before discussing the provisions of the anti-child labour law which was passed in France in 1874, readers need to know the socio-economic status of people living in rural France. In 19th-century France, children from farmers' families and working classes were very often found at the farm, streets and workshop doing nothing and idly socializing with the adults. The majority of agricultural farms had micro-culture, which was not sufficient to support the farm families. To focus on another aspect, the agricultural pattern in the mountain areas was quite different from that of the plains. Naturally, there was a sharp contrast between the societies of mountains and plains. In fact, there was no single model of agriculture in 19th-century France. One thing—related to agriculture—was however common in all the French regions: the slowness of agricultural change. There was no abrupt development in agricultural production and productivity until the 1840s (until the agricultural revolution took place as a result of wider application of improved technology in agriculture and reorganization of land). Spectacular growth in agriculture was particularly concentrated in the northern and eastern parts of France particularly due to those areas' acquaintances with the developments in England and in other coastal regions of north-western Europe, such as Belgium and the Netherlands. Subsequently, widespread growth in agriculture was noticed in the southern and western regions of France. But small-time farmers were barely influenced by the new methods and attitudes. They continued with their traditional polyculture. Under this system, each family tried to support itself by applying its old-age system of production—by producing cereals along with keeping livestock and poultry, maintaining vegetable plots and tending vine. In short, they would maintain a self-sufficient family economy. But this system of production and the irregularly spread economy made rural life very difficult—especially due to spells of illness, unemployment, crop failure and epidemics among livestock. The spread of improved technology in agriculture to all the regions of France was completed only in the late 19th century.

Going back to the history of child labour in 18th-century France, one could find numerous instances of children at the age of seven or eight years leaving 'home to become servants, shepherds, drovers or dindeliers[sic] with farmers or apprentices in a cottage or tiny industry'.[37]

In the then France, children were usually engaged to work for six months, and they stopped working during winter. They were hired by the farmers or artisans from hiring fairs held throughout the year at different places. But, the working children enjoyed a certain level of security, which was not given to the daily-wage workers. The children would typically earn 18 to 20 francs, along with food, clothing and lodging. Most of them had to look after animals, and a few of them were engaged at farmhouses. Their wages would become 20–80 francs per annum after they attained 15–16 years of age.

An interesting system of family economy was noticed at that time. As Olwen Hufton writes,[38] what was problematic in agricultural families in France was that the farmers were unable to support even a family of five people, and, as such, grew indifferent to the family members. Moreover, they always put their own interest before the welfare of their family members. In the agrarian economy of France during the 18th and 19th centuries, the first stage of work of a child would be in the capacity of the role of a shepherd. The French sociologist, Pierre-Guillaume-Frédéric Le Play, in his 1855 study on European Workers, had defined the work of children as 'recreations as much as work'. This has been cited by Gerard Bouchard in his work.[39]

---

[37] Quoted in Heywood, *Childhood in Nineteenth-century France*, 36.

[38] Olwen Hoften, 'Women and the Family Economy in Eighteenth-century France,' *French Historical Studies* 9, no. 1 (Spring 1975): 22.

[39] Gerard Bouchard, *The Immobile Village in the Eighteenth Century* (Paris: Plon, 1972), 321.

If Le Play's point is taken into account, one could say that the French children working as shepherds enjoyed pleasure along with their works. It seems that little efforts were required in looking after the animals which were grazing in the field. In this case, the distinction between labour and leisure could not be established. Sometimes they had to face problems such as attacks by wolves and rampaging by frightened sheep. Moreover, they would have to always ensure that their flock should not damage crops in the field and stay in the meadows. Apart from a couple of emergency situations, the duties of shepherds were more or less relaxed affairs. They had plenty of time for amusement among themselves. When they looked after many flocks together in close proximity, they could easily find time for play or pleasure. Fierce dogs were sent out sometimes to protect cows and sheep. Under such circumstances, shepherds could do alternative work such as wood carving, hunting or even reading books. They could also enjoy the movement of travellers while herding flocks around the river bank. They enjoyed the fresh air and the sun, but at the same time, they had to face cold wind and rain that might sometimes cause health hazards—particularly during winter.

When the French children attained their early teens, they barely did shepherding. Their parents would shift them to farm. Gradually they had to move away from home to work for farming, and at previously-unknown places, they faced different problems of living. Most of them met with inhospitable living conditions. These problems were not encountered by them at where the host family members behaved with the working children as their own family members. The young farm servants had to live in the farmhouses and the child cow-attendees were often unfortunate enough to find sleeping places at the stables and survival provisions as meagre as bread and meat. Very often they had to move from one farm to another and thus had to adjust with the masters and face humiliation from their employers. Rural children who went out on the French towns' streets also faced a hard life. They had to do chimney sweeping which was, in fact, a hazardous job—sometimes ending in disasters. Working children in the agricultural field would sometimes complete vocational training. This was often rewarding for them. This system of informal training helped them to achieve their desire to join the world of established adults. That is how the developments in the industrial sector due to technological innovation in France in the 18th and early 19th centuries led to the mentionable upliftment of women and children.

Due to mechanization and technological innovations, the capitalist system of production emerged in France during the 18th and 19th centuries. This transformed the conditions of work for children working at factories. The working children faced separation from their families while being shifted to the factory system of production in the urban sector. They would be engaged in cotton spinning and cloth printing. Working hours at cotton mills would range between 12 and 15 hours, and in the cloth-printing sector, the range was 8–12 hours as it required natural light. Interestingly, child law could not be implemented in the small and petty shops which employed a larger number of adults. Moreover, these adults were in desperate need of the services of children who would work with them as helpers. Child labour reforms tried to show that children had to face more hazards and hardships under the new factory system than working at family-based industries. In the case of cloth printing, child workers preferred to work with their parents, but the parents usually did not want to work with their children in the same factory. Rather, they were generally happy to work at different workshops. The valid economic reason was that they might face hardship if the factory closed down due to some reason. Children had to perform stressful work and suffered much pain and strain in the process of factory production. Social reformists and political economists believed that working children received attention and love neither from the factory owners nor from their parents. They could only hope that the government would come forward and take some protective measures for their welfare.

As already mentioned, both the French social Catholics and political economists were of the view that the mechanized factory system of production significantly undermined the moral values of workers: both the adults and minors working in the factory. Government intervention was thus very much required to restore their moral values. Gradually, the parents felt that it was necessary to send children to school instead of sending them to factories for work. This would ultimately make a stable working-class family, which, in turn, would bring peaceful industrial order to the French economy and society.

With the wider application of improved technology in the factory system of production, there was a progressive decline in child labour at the turn of the 19th century in France. As per the French Census of 1851, it was found that there was a slight decline in the employment of children. The census data of 1851 presented in Table 3.16 show the declining trend of minor workers in France.

Table 3.16 *Participation Rates of Youth in Selected Communes, 1851*

	Munster (Haut-Rhin)	Sotteville-les-Rouen (Scine Inf.)	Caudebec-les-Elbeuf (Seine-inf.)	Tau Lignan (Drome)	Dieuefit (Drome)	Beccarat Meurthe)	Conton of Lune Ville SE (Meunthe)
Age group 10–14							
Occupation listed	34.69	34.62	50.80	43.48	45.59	44.62	40.96
Living on parents	3.06	2.88	18.25	56.52	54.41	55.38	59.04
No information	62.25	62.50	30.95	–	–	–	–
Total	100.00	100.00	100.00	100.00	100.00	100.00	100.00
Age group 15–19							
Occupation listed	62.34	68.38	89.84	92.21	83.95	96.25	84.49
Living on parents	2.37	3.42	3.13	7.79	16.05	3.75	15.51
No information	35.29	28.20	7.03	–	–	–	–
Total	100	100	100	100	100	100	100

Source: Census Registers for 1851; see, for example, Esteban Ortiz-Ospina and Max Roser, 'Child Labour,' n.d., https://ourworldindata.org/child-labor

Data exhibited in Table 3.16 show that majority of French children aged between 15 and 19 years worked in industries, and also about half or one-third of children aged 10 and 14 years were involved working in factories.

Women were found to be more efficient in some works particularly in tailoring, glove-making and ribbon-weaving in 19th-century France. Data provided by the local governance at Haut Rhin (1822) is reproduced here in Table 3.17 to show female and children workers majority (e.g., about 40% of the total workforce) in mills.

During the first half of the 19th century—in the field of tailoring—big merchant houses started making readymade garments. For this, they began to pressurize the skilled artisans for increasing their workload. By the mid-19th century, nearly 50 per cent of the French looms were active in rural areas. The common practice during this time was that

Table 3.17 Age-wise Composition of Males and Females in Mills, 1822

Age Group (Years)	Males	Females	Total	% to Total
8–11	11	16	27	11
12–15	29	52	81	31
16–25	21	102	123	47
25 and above	25	4	29	11
Total	86	174	260	100

Source: AD Haut-Rhin, 1822; refer to *The Mechanics' Magazine – Gazette* (7 April–29 September 1838), Vol. XXIX, p. 405.

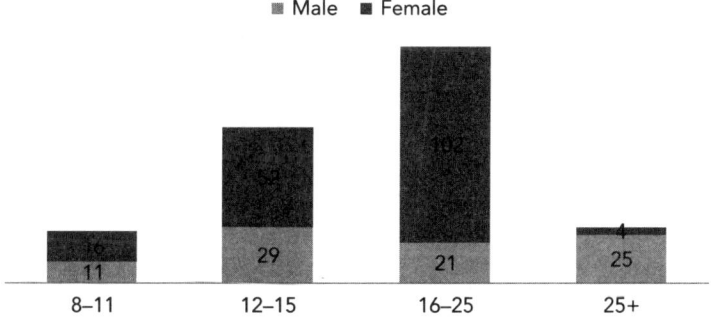

while the parents worked in the agricultural fields, the looms were taken care of by their older children whom the younger brothers and sisters helped. With the advent of the powerloom, the division of labour within the impoverished French families changed completely. The socio-economist, Marie M. Kahan-Rabecq, in her 1839 publication on the economic history of France, explained that during the mid-19th century, the French men outnumbered women in a 3:1 ratio, while at the mechanized sector, women—contrarily—outnumbered men in a 2:1 ratio. In the sector of spinning, it was noticed that three-fourths of the workers in linen-spinning, two-thirds of workers in cotton-spinning, and half of the workers in wood-based industries were women and children.[40] Madelene Guilbert[41] has written extensively on this issue. The writers present the related data in Table 3.18.

Table 3.18 exhibits that cotton, wool, mixed fibres, and linen and hemp were some of the industries where the French women and children were largely concentrated in the workforce participation. Women and children together contributed their highest concentration as workers, that is, 55 per cent for women, and 18 per cent for children. The second sector where women's share as workers was 49.6 per cent and that of children was 18.6 per cent was that of the mixed fibres. The overall contribution of women in all the industries together was 35 per cent of the total workforce, and that of children was 12 per cent.

Women and minor children's engagement in mining, basic metallurgy, machine building, chemicals, glassmaking, printing and grain-milling—as the chart reveals—was nominal. Also, in other industries where the pace of mechanization was slow, women and children's participation was quite limited. In industries, such as quarries, shipyards, tanneries, there was the dominance of adult males. So was the case with the construction industry. Therefore, it could be stated that women and children's engagement was largely concentrated in the localized industries during the 19th century. Women were a big threat to the male skilled workers during the second half of the century, especially in metal works, leather and printing. It may be mentioned here that children's opportunities to work in industries started declining, especially since the 1840s. As per Madelene Guilbert estimation in

---

[40] See, for example, Wikipedia, 'Women in France,' 3 September 2020, https://en.wikipedia.org/wiki/Women_in_France.

[41] Madlene Guilbert, *The Functions of Women in Industry* (Paris: Mouton, 1966).

Table 3.18 Composition of the Industrial Labour Force, after the 1839–1845 Enquiry

Industry	Number of				Percentage of	
	Men	Women	Children	All	Women and Children	Children
1. Textile						
Cotton	109,344	90,647	44,828	244,819	55.3	18.3
Wood	72,678	44,668	26,800	144,146	49.6	18.6
Linen & hemp	33,067	15,868	7,232	56,167	41.1	12.9
Silk	109,662	46,127	9,326	165,115	33.6	5.6
Mixed fibres	47,062	21,471	15,803	84,336	44.2	18.7
2. Mines, quarries	69,243	5,786	6,256	81,285	14.8	7.7
3. Basic metallurgy	63,066	3,287	6,340	72,693	13.2	8.7
4. Metalworking	41,864	4,458	6,315	52,637	20.5	12.0
5. Leather	11,751	9,320	751	21,822	46.2	3.4
6. Wood	5,150	425	262	5,837	11.8	4.5
7. Ceramics	25,187	4,222	4,089	33,498	24.8	12.2
8. Chemicals	7,547	930	606	9,083	16.9	6.7
9. Construction	26,825	2,449	2,930	32,204	16.7	9.1
10. Lighting	1,239	262	71	1,572	21.2	4.5
11. Furnishing	–	–	–	–	–	–
12. Clothing	4,147	1,945	410	6,502	36.2	6.3
13. Food	115,368	14,163	6,889	136,420	15.4	5.0
14. Transport	4,838	13	223	5,074	4.7	4.4
15. Paper, publishing	13,518	8,370	2,841	24,729	45.3	11.5
16. Luxuries	1,199	57	95	1,351	11.3	7.0
17. Miscellaneous	5,153	4,369	1,598	11,120	–	–
18. Total	767,908	278,837	143,665	1,190,410	35.5	12.1

Source: Colin Heywood, 'The Market for Child-labour in Nineteenth-century France,' *History* 66, no. 216 (1981): 34–49.

The Functions of Women in Industry, in the Haut-Rhin region, children's involvement in the total workforce in spinning mills during the 1820s and 1840s was one-third, which fell down to one-fifth by the 1860s. In the final quarter of the 19th century, children's presence in industrial work dwindled rapidly.

Readers could usually notice that there was an overall declining trend in the engagement of child labour in the second half of the 19th century, but in certain industries, it was found that employers had engaged a large number of teens without bothering to adhere to legalities. Some of the reasons which favoured the employers to employ child labour were as follows. Madelene Guilbert writes about these factors in her book *The Functions of Women in Industry.*

First, the French children's physical condition allowed them to perform those works in a factory which could not be done by the adults. In such jobs, adults could not be substituted for children. In spinning mills, for example, there were some works that could only be well performed by younger boys and girls. Children's fingers could be quite helpful in tying threads and handling some parts of machines easily. Children were, therefore, in high demand because of their physical advantages. Second, child labourers were cheaply available compared to women and adult males. Normally, in France, a child earned only one-third of what was earned by an adult male, although there was a significant variation according to industry, location and due to the conditions of business activities. During the mid-19th century, children's wages were ranging between 40 and 75 centimes, while the range was 1.25–1.50 francs for adult males. Children were very ill-paid, and they were recruited to some industries in huge numbers. Third, the 19th-century French factories faced a lack of disciplined factory workers. The factory owners thought that it would be proper if younger workers (minor boys and girls) were employed in factory production in large numbers because of their docile character. This was felt even more necessary because a large number of the French adult males were subsumed into the French military forces during the Revolutionary and Napoleonic Wars. The cotton mills, for example, had to resort to the use of women and children.

As Martine Benoit writes in the 1976 publication on labourers in France, a large number of young girls, particularly from the age of 12 years, were recruited in the silk industry and they worked under the complete supervision of nuns. Young girls and adult females were exclusively recruited around the mountain areas of Bugey, Savoy, the Auvergne and the Bresse because they were more docile, forlorn and had fewer demands compared to ones living in plain areas. According to an estimate by Reybaud, and quoted by Dominique Vanoli in his 1976 publication,[42] 40,000 French girls worked in the south-east in 1860, and by 1900, their numbers had increased to 100,000. Sometimes the youthful stubbornness of children made them hostile, and they would become unruly.

There was a great debate regarding the plight of child workers in 19th-century France with the industrial development. It was a fact that the working conditions of children deteriorated with the progressive growth of industries. Their hours of work were 16–17 hours a day. They had to stay continuously in an enclosed space and had to work without shifting their position. It was indeed torture to work like this. Children of six to eight years of age—especially—had to experience these conditions. They were badly fed, badly clothed and badly paid. As Louis Rene Villerme wrote,[43] excessive working hours formed one of the prime drawbacks in the French factory system, and to reduce its intervention of government was vitally required.

The employers in France used to think that the miserable hardships the proletariats suffered in the towns had been significantly reduced due to the expansion of factories, and this was beneficial to both the employers and the workers (including the children). It was a fact that families which had shifted from rural areas to urban areas had initially suffered from immense poverty. This forced them to employ their children in the industry. Importantly—however—the French industry was less capable of providing jobs than the French sectors of agriculture. The gamins of Paris got jobs as messengers, delivery boys and street traders. They were also used for opening carriage doors, lowering steps or hiring out umbrellas and opera-glass. They were involved in street singing, acrobatics and travelling circuses. Little children from the age of five or six were hired in the textile industries of Mulhouse, Roubaix, Rouen, Cholet, Lyons and Vienne. They were mostly used in the handloom weaving industry to wind bobbins. In the silk

---

[42] Dominique Vanoli, 'The Silky Convents,' *Logical Revolts* 2 (1976): 19–39.

[43] Louis Rene Villerme, *Table of the Physical and Moral Conditions of Workers employed in the Cotton, Wool, and Silk Factories*, Vol. I (London: Forgotten Books, 2017), 91.

industry, they helped the weavers. In most of the factories, the working hours for children were 12–13 hours a day. It was the same hours as the adults performed. The longer hours of work was prevailing in spinning mills, ironworks, paper mills, glassworks and construction works. The engagement of child labourers was on the rise in some industries such as paper mills and textile factories. The factory owners wanted to reduce the high cost of operating machines and thus started a double-shift working systems in their factories. This required a huge number of workers including children. But the French law prohibited nightwork for children. This necessitated working for longer hours during the daytime.

A strong state intervention—hitherto unseen—was observed when the child labour legislation of 1874 was enacted. Debates over the 1847 bill clearly and distinctly called for the replacement of the 1841 law. A detailed scheme for a new child labour law was put forward by the *Counseil General de l'Agriculture, des Manufacture et du Commerce* in 1950. But it was not implemented. Eugene Rouher (1814–1884), the French Minister of Commerce, again placed the issue in 1855, but it again failed to materialize. Therefore, the law's introduction was abandoned in 1862. Again, in 1870, Louvet, a new French Minister of Commerce, presented the bill in the Senate. But the proceedings were hampered due to the outbreak of war and the collapse of the Empire. Again in 1871, government action was taken to reform the child labour law, and finally, in 1874, the law was passed (on 19 May 1874). This law stipulated that children and minor girls should not be employed in manufacturing, plants, factories, mines, etc., except under certain conditions. The minimum working age was fixed at 12, and in some specific cases, it was set at 10 years. They had to work six hours a day instead of eight hours as specified by the 1841 law. Younger children aged 12–16 years would work 12 hours, with gaps for resting times. Child female workers were not allowed to work at night. They would be free during holidays and Sundays. Children aged below 12 years were allowed to attend school for a minimum of two hours a day. The new law created another salaried Inspectorate. Again, there were stiff opposition to this law.

While performing inspection services, the French inspectorate faced two types of problems. First, in the cities of Paris and Lyons, small workshops remained hidden in obscure tenements and backstreets. It was assumed that the total number of working children covered by the law in the capital was a meagre 7,600 from approximately 3,300 firms. This estimation was later proved to be absurdly inaccurate. The then Divisional Inspector, Maurice, in one of his 1875 reports, mentioned that the total number of children was close to 25,000. Second, the Inspectorate faced a particular problem while visiting the so-called 'developing' regions of the south and west. In these regions, firms were thinly dispersed over the large area. It was, therefore, very difficult to implement the new law of 1874 in the yet-to-be-developed industrial belts. As Doll estimates in an 1881 publication, in such thinly-dispersed areas, the Inspector could visit just a few numbers of firms in a day. Naturally, constant contact between inspectors and the industrial population was an impossibility. Inspectors faced ignorance, hostility and indifference from the persons having vested interests, and they urgently felt for a uniform policy to guide them in their everyday activities. The antichild labour inspectors wanted to enforce the law through the persuasive methods. For example, Inspector Mauvice in Paris anticipated a strong opposition from the glass manufacturers, and thus, called a meeting for them in 1875. The response was depressing. The glass manufacturers were about to close down their plants. The Inspector granted six months' grace before implementing the law in totality. The Inspectors had to tolerate many unlawful practices too. Children under 12 or 12–15 years were allowed to work full day under the condition that they would attend school in the evening. Children from poor families were sometimes permitted to perform such work which was against the law. It took a long period of time to enforce the law, and the Inspectors could well understand that the full execution of it would depend on the goodwill of the employers. It was in an experimental stage for long and after the passage of the 1874 legislation, it took quite a few years for its proper implementation. The law had a provision that working children would work six hours a day in a factory system of production, and attend school on a regular basis. Despite this, a few of them joined classes which were quite evident at the end of the 1870s and even by 1884, only 50 per cent of the working children were attending school part time, while the other half could not. Factory schools, instead of obeying the law, slyly avoided the legislation. The French government hesitated to take stronger initiatives in this respect, and the employers had a strong desire to take the working children back from school to the workplace. The parents were readily sacrificing the education of their children in order to survive. Employers and parents were, therefore, hand-in-hand delaying education from spreading among the working children in the French factories and mines.

3.3.4. The United States of America

In the United States of America, rapid industrialization began in 1790 when Samuel Slater (1768–1835) opened the first British-style textile mill in Rhode Island. He borrowed the design from the British model. This was a technology that had been pirated, but it greatly increased the speed with which cotton thread could be spun into yarn. Although in the United States of America, Industrial Revolution reached its zenith during 1820–1870, the Slater Mill is presently considered by the postmodern historians to be the first spark that first set the USA-wheel of industrialization rolling. The spectacular growth of industries on American soil was made possible due to increased productivity, capital investment and re-investment, the rapid expansion of businesses, and the rise of corporation. The American Census of 1790 estimated that more than 90 per cent of the total workforce was engaged in farming and farm-related activities.[44] The agricultural productivity was low, and commensurately, low was the wage rate that was offered to the farmworkers. Wages prevailing in the factory system were far better (by several times) than wages offered in agriculture. Naturally, low-paid and hard-working agricultural labourers happily shifted to relatively high-paying factories located in the urban areas.

Samuel Slater, who is usually referred to as the 'father of American manufacturing', worked as an apprentice at a cotton spinning mill in England. When he migrated to Rhode Island, he did not carry any model or drawing of the machine with him. He built the machinery just applying his memory of the machines which he had operated in Great Britain. Before the 'advent' of Slater's machine, despite huge imports from England, the growth of the American cotton industry was relatively slower. John L. Bishop[45] mentions that there existed

---

[44] *Wikipedia,* 'The History of Agriculture in the United States of America,' 25 November 2020, https://en.wikipedia.org/wiki/History_of_agriculture_in_the_United_States

[45] John L. Bishop, *A History of American Manufactures from 1608 to 1860* (Philadelphia: Edward Young and Company, 1866).

only four cotton mills in America in 1803.[46] After the invention of powerloom in 1804, the first independent cotton processing factory was installed at Waltham, Massachusetts, which was, in fact, a complete factory for the conversion of cotton into cloth. Previously, in 1797, a factory had been established for spinning and weaving flax, hemp and tow. In such an early stage too, children—especially the boys—began to be employed in such factories. After the industries multiplied, iron industries were concentrated in the eastern part of the Allegheny Mountains. Numerous furnaces and rolling and slitting mills were being built in the eastern part of Pennsylvania. After 1800, the iron industries began developing in Western Pennsylvania. The growth of iron industry, nevertheless, was very slow despite the huge import of raw ore from Europe. The tariffs were high, but the importation continued. Moreover, the demand for iron rails for the newly inducted railways increased steadily, and increased mobility through railways helped the iron industries to flourish in America especially after 1840. All these would converge into a mentionable increase in the demand for child labourers in the near future.

Indentured servitude and child slavery were present in America much before the onset of the American part of the Industrial Revolution. Indentured servitude was a common affair in British North America before the late 18th century. In fact, the impoverished Europeans migrated en masse to the different American colonies where they worked as indentured labourers, getting engaged as farm workers, domestic servants and apprentices of craftsmen. They became free after the expiry of their indenture, and thereafter they could work for themselves or could be hired by other employers. A large number of European immigrants—approximately half or two-thirds of the total number of migrants in the 17th–18th century—came to the American colonies between the 1630s and the American Revolution under indentures, but they experienced inhuman sufferings and exploitation. They were found in plenty in the Virginia North and New Jersey regions. Among them, a large numbers were children (boys and girls together) and women. These women were sexually abused by their masters, and so was the condition of the young girls. Tortured and abused women and minor girls had little or no access to the magistrates

---

[46] See *The Pennsylvania Magazine of History and Biography*, Vol. VIII (Philadelphia: The Historical Society of Philadelphia, 1884), 374.

to register their grievances. The American Revolution, however, restricted these immigration to America, but the condition of the children and women did not improve immediately. Later, both the American and British governments passed several laws to reduce and eliminate this bad practice.

Since the Industrial Revolution in America, children used to be regularly employed. They were present on a considerable scale even in the 19th and 20th centuries. They were—chiefly—the daughters and sons of the poor migrants but were not slaves at least.

The trans-Atlantic slave trade was a very common phenomenon in America during the 17th–19th centuries. As Philip Curtin writes, the trans-Atlantic slave trade officially ended in America in 1808, and by this time, about one million slaves were imported, and, after 1807, illegal trading in slaves turned the number of slave importations up to 3,952,760, of which more than 50 per cent were children.[47]

In the American sweating industries, the working conditions for the labourers (including children) were very poor and deplorable. Strictly estimated, there were two types of sweat-works performed in early America: the first type being the small shops managed by contractors/subcontractors in treatment or dwelling houses; and the second type being those found in homes where individuals, with the help of family members, set up 'factories' in the living and sleeping rooms. The first type of sweating was decreased due to the development of factory industries. Some factory products—such as machine-made garments and other allied products—were sent to homes for finishing. This helped the concerned firms to reduce the cost of production which would be necessary for supervision, lighting, heating, paying rentals and purchasing equipment. The second type of sweatshop—as already mentioned—depended on home-finishing and made the clothing industry cheaper because the process would involve—in large numbers—women and children who would be cheaply available.

As F.T. Carlton writes, the second form of the American sweat industry also produced artificial flowers, sewing tapes, kid gloves, millinery work, garters and involved shelling nuts, putting cords in pencils for souvenir cards, stringing beads, sewing men's neckties, finishing corset covers, producing false hair, assembling switches, rolling

---

[47] Philip Curtin, *The Atlantic Slave Trade: A Census* (Madison: The University of Wisconsin Press, 1969), 6–7.

cigarettes, etc.[48] But the most important products of the sweating industry were the finished clothing items.

Wages paid to women and children in the American sweat industries—as usually—were very low, especially in cases where work was done at home. But the hours of work were long, indefinite and irregular. The present writers have traced four features involving the manning and growth of the clothing industry (which also involved child labour) in America.

First, the journeyman was the key person: the skilled mechanic who would look after the entire establishment and often made the entire garment by himself. Second, the division of labour was usually followed in the home shops. Third, the 'task system' was introduced. The Jewish immigrants to New York City originated this system. The given amount of work to be done within a definite period of time was called 'task'. This task could be completed within a day, and the work was so gigantic in terms of volume that its completion took usually 12 to 14 hours of labouring per day. The fourth stage in the manning and growth of the American clothing industry was the factory system. It involved the participation of the 'sweaters'. The 'sweater' was such a man who was familiar with his neighbours, able to speak the language of the immigrant, and motivate them (including women and children) to work with him. The sweaters took advantage of the immigrants' ignorance and helplessness and often exploited them by providing low wages and long hours of work.

Initially—and usually—the American boys and girls—in the age group of 10–16 years—willingly, and with pleasure, made valuable contributions to the garment and other material-making works. But such works quickly became routine works for them, took long hours, and had to be performed under unfavourable conditions so the American children began to find them intimidating, hazardous and humiliating. Such long hours of labouring under stress in factories and sweat-shops deprived the concerned children of education and playtime. These factors ultimately retarded the overall growth process of the country, and caused the labourers (especially the children) to fail to maintain a high standard of living.

---

[48] Frank Tracy Carlton, *The History and Problems of Organised Labour* (Boston: D.C. Heath and Company, 1920), 362.

Before the popularization of the factory system in America, children were engaged in different types of household industries as apprentices. The factory system brought them outside their home, trained them up and shoved them towards working as labourers at various industries. The employers thought that since their wages were low and the contribution made by them was as good as the adults, these factors would contribute mellifluously to the national growth of the country. It was thought that such employments would not only benefit the manufacturers but would also benefit commerce and agriculture as well. Interestingly, the factory owners never thought that the American children would encounter any sort of danger while working under the factory system. The textile industries in America—especially—engaged a large number of women and children. Importantly, with the expansion of the iron and steel industries in the United States of America, the demand for women and children did not increase—rather it was reduced. But the children continued to have high demands in mines, glass factories, textile industries, home works, agriculture, canneries, and were variously and increasingly employed as newspaper delivery boys, messengers, shoe shiners and peddlers. Children of immigrants from Africa and Europe were especially engaged in industries in large numbers. Also, the impoverished Americans living in the rural areas had great attractions towards mines and factories in urban areas. They all began to shift to the American cities in search of a job—especially in factories and mills—and in search of higher standards of living. They created a huge labour force. But after they reached the cities and settled down there, all their hopes and aspirations were being broken into pieces. The jobs and contracts, which were available, required long hours of work and provided lower wages. They had to work 12–14 hours a day, and six days a week. They could barely have any leisure-time while at work. The conditions under which they worked were unhealthy and unsafe. Very often they were grievously injured while handling unsafe machinery. The working children (the sons and daughters of these workers) did not have any playtime or any time to attend school. They remained uneducated. Moreover, due to unhygienic working places, they became infected and thus suffered from serious bouts of illnesses.

Importantly, pre-1870 data regarding child labour in America is not available anywhere. The census of 1870 onwards began to count the approximate numbers of child labourers. One such child labourer–related data (collected for the period of 1870–1930) have been shown in Table 3.19.

The census of 1870 documented that the American children aged 10–14 years who were engaged in the factory system of production

Table 3.19 Gainful Workers, Aged 10–14, in the United States of America: 1870–1930 (in Thousands)

Year	Workers (Age) 10–14	% Non-farm	Population (Age) 10–14	Total Workers	Children as % of Work-force	Activity Rates of Children (%)
1870	765	47.00	4,786	12,925	5.92	15.96
1880	1,118	50.64	5,715	17,392	6.43	19.56
1890	1,504	57.38	7,034	23,318	6.50	21.38
1900	1,750	62.47	8,080	29,073	6.02	21.66
1910	1,822	68.98	9,107	37,371	4.34	17.81
1920	1,417	73.02	10,641	42,434	3.34	13.22
1930	667	78.55	12,005	48,830	1.37	5.56

Source: Historical Statistics of the United States of America, Colonial Times to 1970 (U.S. Census Bureau, 1997), Series A 119–134 and D75–84. See Hugh Hindman' *Child Labour: An American History* (New York and London: Routledge, 2015), https://www.google.co.in/books/edition/Child_Labor/I5cYDQAAQBAJ?hl=en&gbpv=1&dq=Gainful+workers,+aged+10-14,+in+the+United+States:+1870-1930+(in+thousands)&pg=PT39&printsec=frontcover

were 765,000 in number. They were occupied principally by manufacturing establishments (114,628), and they were also engaged in other industries and allied occupations at urban locations. In 1880, the total number of children engaged in different types of occupations was 1,118,000, and their activity rates, in terms of percentage, were 19.56. Children's involvement rose to 1,504,000 in 1890, which, again, was 21.38 per cent in terms of their activity rates. In 1900, the bread-earning children were 1,750,000 in number, and their activity rates were 21.66 per cent. This number rose to 1,822,000 in 1910 but started declining since the census of 1920 (1,417,000), falling to 667,000 in 1930. However, the census figures presented in Table 3.19 are not adequate in revealing the true and overall situation of child labourers. The Maryland Law of 1906 mentioned that every child under 16 years of age needs to obtain work permits before joining a factory.

Child labour data of the age group 10–15 years in 1900 have been presented in Table 3.20.

Data portrayed in Table 3.20 show that more than 50 per cent of children working in the urban sector were in the age group of 14–15 years, and only 17 per cent were in the age group of 14–15 years. Children aged 12 or 13 years constituted 27.9 per cent of the total working force among children.

The present authors are displaying the number and distribution of child workers by industry and occupation, as per the USA Census, 1920 in Tables 3.21–3.23.

Table 3.20 *Distribution of Child Labourers in the Age Group of 10–15 Years in 1900*

Age	Number	Percent	Percent
15	552,854	31.6	54.8
14	406,701	23.2	
13	268,427	15.3	27.9
12	221,313	12.6	
11	158,778	9.1	17.2
10	142,105	8.1	

Source: Carlton, 1920, 456. Refer to George B. Mandold, *Child Problems* (New Delhi: Prabhat Books, reprint, 2016), 177.

Table 3.21 Occupation of Children 10–15 Years of Age, Inclusive by Age

Occupation	Children Number	Children Percent Distribution	Boys Number	Boys Percent Distribution	Girls Number	Girls Percent Distribution
Total	1,060,858	100	714,248	100	346,610	100
Agricultural pursuits, forestry and animal husbandry	647,300	61	459,238	64.3	188,071	54.3
Farm labour (home farm)	569,824	53.7	396,191	55.5	173,633	50.1
Farm labour (away from home)	63,990	6	51,000	7.1	12,990	3.7
Other pursuits	13,495	1.3	12,047	1.7	1,448	0.4
Non-agricultural pursuits	413,549	39	255,010	35.7	158,539	45.7
Manufacturing and mechanical industries	185,337	17.5	104,335	14.6	81,002	23.4
Clerical occupations	80,140	7.6	59,633	8.3	20,507	5.9
Trade	63,368	6	49,234	6.9	14,134	4.1
Domestic and personal service	54,006	5.1	16,082	2.3	37,924	10.9
Transportation	18,912	1.8	15,617	2.2	3,295	1
Extraction of minerals	7,191	0.7	7,045	1	146	(2)
Professional service	3,465	0.3	1,979	0.3	1,486	0.4
Public service (not elsewhere classified)	1,130	0.1	1,085	0.2	45	(2)

Source: Fourteenth Census of the United States, 1920, Vol. IV (Washington, DC: Population Occupations, 1923), 480. Refer to Child Labour Amendment to the [American] Constitution (Washington, DC: United States Congress Senate, 1923), 33.
Note: (2) Less than one-tenth of 1 per cent.

Table 3.22 Selected Non-agricultural Occupations of Children 10–15 Years of Age, Inclusive

Occupation	Children 10 to 15 Years of Age Engaged in Non-agricultural Pursuits	
	Number	% Distribution
All non-agricultural pursuits	413,549	100
Messenger, bundle, and office boys and Girls[a]	48,028	11.6
Servants and waiters	41,586	10.1
Salesman and saleswomen (stores)[b]	30,370	7.3
Clerks (except clerks in stores)	22,521	5.4
Cotton-mill operatives	21,873	5.3
Newsboys	20,706	5
Iron and steel industry operatives	12,904	3.1
Clothing industry operatives	11,757	2.8
Lumber and furniture industry operatives	10,585	2.6
Silk mill operatives	10,023	2.4
Shoe factory operatives	7,545	1.8
Woollen worsted mill operatives	7,077	1.7
Coal mine operatives	5,850	1.4
All other occupations	162,722	39.2

Source: Children in Gainful Occupations at the Fourteenth Census of the United States, 1920 (Washington, DC: The Bureau of the Census, 1924), 30.
Notes: [a] Except telegraph messengers.
[b] Includes clerks in stores.

Marie Van Vorst, in her 1908 survey with women and children in Alabama, penned down the plights and discomforts children and women suffered as a result of leaving their rural homes and finding occupations in urban factories.[49] She, for example, asked a question to a minor girl,

[49] Refer to Christopher Nichols and Nancy Unger, eds., *A Companion to the Gilded Age and Progressive Era* (Hoboken: Wiley Blackwell, 2017), https://www.google.co.in//books/edition/A_Companion_to_the_Gilded_Age_and_Progre/SGHoDQAAQBAJ?hl=en&gbpv=1&dq=Vorst+1908+Alabama&pg=PT590&printsec=frontcover

Table 3.23 Proportion of Children among all Workers in Manufacturing and Mechanical Industries

Persons Engaged in Manufacturing and Mechanical Industries

Industry and Occupation	Total 10 Years of Age and Above	Children 10 to 15 Years of Age, Inclusive			
		Both Sexes		Boys	Girls
		Number	%		
Total	12,818,524	185,337	1.4	104,335	81,002
Labourers and semi-skilled operatives (n.o.s.)	6,576,571	164,064	2.5	86,623	77,441
Building and hand trades	693,725	7,476	1.1	7,009	467
Chemical and allied industries	124,630	2,158	1.7	1,119	1,039
Cigar and tobacco factories	180,379	4,938	2.7	1,269	3,669
Clay, glass and stone industries	209,978	4,968	2.4	3,939	1,029
Clothing industries	422,137	11,757	2.8	2,288	9,469
Electrical supply factories	91,630	1,892	2.1	1,013	879
Food industries	348,430	9,934	2.9	4,633	5,301
Iron and steel industries	1,419,593	12,904	0.9	10,617	2,287
Other metal industries	159,178	3,766	2.4	2,181	1,585
Lumber and furniture industries	489,332	10,585	2.2	9,159	1,426
Paper pulp mills	106,932	1,273	1.2	730	543
Paper box factories	23,836	1,790	7.5	464	1,326
Printing and publishing	91,839	4,023	4.4	2,048	1,975

(Table 3.23 Continued)

(Table 3.23 Continued)

	Persons Engaged in Manufacturing and Mechanical Industries				
	Total 10 Years of Age and Above	Children 10 to 15 Years of Age, Inclusive			
		Both Sexes			
Industry and Occupation		Number	%	Boys	Girls
Rubber factories	137,671	2,106	1.5	1,167	939
Shoe factories	225,435	7,547	3.3	4,374	3,171
Tanneries	59,706	781	1.3	584	197
Textile industries	945,707	54,649	5.8	21,917	32,732
Cotton mills	378,769	21,875	5.8	10,498	11,377
Knitting mills	119,547	7,991	6.7	2,087	5,904
Silk mills	125,801	10,023	8	3,220	6,803
Woollen and worsted mills	148,645	7,077	4.8	3,009	4,068
All other textile mills	172,945	7683 (2)	4.4	3,103	4,580
All other	846,433	21,519	2.5	12,112	9,407
All other occupations	6,241,953	21,273	0.3	17,712	3,561

Source: *Fourteenth Census of the United States, 1920* (Vol. IV: Population Occupation; Washington, DC: Government of the United States of America Press, 1923), 378 and 480.
Note: (2) includes 6,980 apprentices to building and hand trades, 12,343 apprentices to other industries and 1,950 children engaged in other occupations.

'How do you like school?' Her reply was, 'I sure I love school'. Her statement about the mill where she worked was, 'I've worked in the mill, but I don't love it. I'm the only one up home that ain't workin' new. Jeff and Musie and Loona and Dashie is all 't work'. The curious author, thereafter, asked her, 'Does your father work?' She replied, 'He died', and went on saying, 'the week after we come here. He had asthma. His job was awful hard; he worked nights in the dye-room. He used to have to keep the windows open so that he could get air enough'.

The survey depicts that there were five members working in the mill, and the respondent—the minor girl—told the surveyor that it was her evil day when she was forced to move from the school bench into the spinning room. It is heart-rending to learn how an 11-year-old (minor) American girl was expected by the family member to be the bread-earner. A situation soon developed in the United States of America when everybody working at the mills wanted the promulgation of compulsory school laws which would be beneficial for every minor.

The US state of Massachusetts first enacted a child law that regulated the conditions of children engaged in manufacturing industries in 1836. In 1842, the American children's working hours were restricted to 10 hours—for those who were below the age of 12 years. Table 3.24 represents the years of enactment of child labour law in different US states.

The child labour legislation passed by different states of America were not elaborate and were specifically targeted to set the age limit of

Table 3.24 *Passage of Anti-child-labour Laws in Different States of America*

State	Year
Massachusetts	1836
Ohio	1852
Massachusetts	1866
Massachusetts	1867
Illinois	1877
Wisconsin	1877
Michigan	1885

Source: Frank Tracy Carlton, *The History and Problems of Organised Labour* (Boston: D.C. Heath and Company, 1920), 459–460.

children's employment to factories and to prohibit child labour employment in hazardous occupations. The legislation had provisions for penalties for instances of violation. But, to socio-historians like F.T. Carlton, the acts were inadequate in terms of enforcement, and thus were somewhat indefinite. But there were certain 'definite' issues as well. Three months' schooling was made compulsory for all the working children. Children below the age of 15 years could not be engaged in manufacturing establishments. The provisions of inspection and the submission of child employment reports to the governor on a regular basis were made compulsory, and any violation of the act was to be penalized.

The then United States of America gradually promulgated anti-child labour laws for all the states, while adjoining/umbrella nations like Columbia, Alaska, Hawaii and Puerto Rico had their own statute books. The laws, however, were not uniform. In some states, the constitutional statutes were elaborate, while in others, the laws were inadequate. In the US states like Massachusetts, New York and Ohio, the anti-child labour laws were elaborately laid out. But many southern US states had inadequate laws, and those laws were also poorly enforced.

The most important aspects of the laws enforced in all the states were as follows. First, the minimum age for working at the factories was fixed at 14 years. Second, the certificate of completion of a certain amount of school education had to be produced by the prospective worker(s) before joining the mills. Third, the child was required to be in sound health and was to be declared by the physicians to be physically fit to work in a factory. Fourth, school attendance of working children for a minimum period of time was made compulsory. Fifth, the working hours for children were fixed at eight hours per day, and 48 hours per week on a six-days-a-week basis. Sixth, children under 16 years of age were prohibited from doing night duties. Seventh, the US Department of Labour and corps of factory inspectors were given the responsibility of looking after the enforcement of child legislation. Eighth, in the legislation, there was a provision for collecting vital statistics—especially the birth records—over certain periods of time. Finally, there was a provision of scholarships to be granted to children of families in distress.

In his essay,[50] Edwin Markham narrates the instance of an old Native American chief travelling to the New York City, who abundantly

---

[50] Edwin Markham, 'The Child at the Loom,' *The Cosmopolitan* (September 1906): 80–87.

found the 'little children working'. Young children were found by him to be working in street trades, and at the mines, cotton mills, factories, home workshops and farms. The simple-minded chief was both perplexed and flabbergasted.

Actually, the American Industrial Revolution led the children to work for long hours under hazardous conditions and against poor wages. As already mentioned, legislations on protecting the child labourers by different US states were not all-encompassing, and naturally, it was high time to enforce uniform labour legislation for the country. To this end, the National Child Labour Committee (NCLC) was formed by the American government in 1904, and it was incorporated in 1907. The objectives of the NCLC were as follows: (a) investigation and submission of reports concerning child labour; (b) raising of the standards of public opinion and of the responsibility of parents vis-à-vis the employment of children; (c) protection of children by legislation against harmful employment; (d) securing of opportunity for elementary education; and (e) securing physical development which was required for the industrial efficiencies.

In fact, child labour in factories and industries had both good and bad effects. To examine these, different viewpoints were taken.

In 1916 the first federal child labour law was signed by the then US President Woodrow Wilson (1856–1924). However, due to restrictions imposed by the US Supreme Court, it could not be implemented. In 1924, the US Congress approved an amendment to the US constitution and authorized Congress to regulate provisions related to the labour of persons under the age of 18 years. It was submitted to the state legislators for ratification. It took some time, and by 1937, all the US states had given their approval. Next, in 1938, the Fair Labor Standards Act (FLSA) was passed by the US government. After passing the Act, the oppressive employment of child labourers was further prohibited. The law was enforced by the US Labour Department's Wage and Hour Division.

The provisions under the FLSA were as follows.[51] First, the law prohibited or restricted the employment of underage children wholesomely for factory workings. In the second place, the minimum working age for a child to work in factories was fixed at 14 years. But in the case of

---

[51] Refer to *Amending the FLSA of 1938* (Washington, DC: U.S. Government Printing Office, 1999), 2–6.

hazardous works, the age was to be 18 years. Third, there was a provision for minimum wage. Fourth, all states and the federal government required proof of age by the working children before they joined mills or mines. Fifth, a hefty fine of up to $50,000 was to be imposed on the employers violating the FLSA. Sixth, adequate fire-safety measures were required to be provided in factories. Finally, working at sweatshops was completely prohibited for children.

Needless to say, the provisions of the FLSA were highly instrumental in causing the number of child labourers in the United States of America to dwindle.

3.3.5. Japan

The end of the *Shogunate* and that of feudalism in Japan, especially after the Meiji Restoration of 1868, marked the beginning of a modern Japanese state. The Meiji government abolished Japan's domains in 1871 and replaced them with prefectures subordinate to the centre. The Meiji leaders made the government the sole political power in order to secure control over the entire country. The prime task was to give Japan a different status and transform it into a post-modern kingdom. Japan feared that it might be attacked and colonized like the cases of India and Southeast Asia. Accordingly, it started hurriedly to modernize its economy, besides frantically post-modernizing its military power to protect itself from foreign invasions. To attain this avowed objective, the Japanese government sent a high-level team, the famous 'Iwakura Mission' (comprising government officials, students and other dynamic persons) to Europe and America to observe and learn from their wonderful industrial stride. It was a highly successful step that post-modernized Japan.

As Isabella Lucy Bird traces,[52] Japan emphasized constant infrastructural growth, beginning with the expansion of the telegraph line between Tokyo and Yokohama and later on from Nagasaki to Hokkaido. Later, the laying of an undersea line further linked Nagasaki to Shanghai. The sluggish courier service was replaced by the modern postal service in 1871. Japan took a historic decision by joining the Universal Postal Union, and thereafter linking its postal service to the

---

[52] Isabella Lucy Bird, *Unbeaten Tracks in Japan* (London: John Murray, 1880).

world in 1877 by importing telephones. Rail services were duly started with the assistance of England.

For overall growth of industries in Japan, the Royal Government-assisted private company Mitsubishi, and other companies like Mitsui and Ono. The government also set up many factories and establishments like the light industries and those of the agricultural sector to help expand privately owned industries like Shinagawa Glass Factory, Aichi Spinning Mill, Fukagawa Cement Works, Sapporo Brewery and Tomioka Silk Mill. To modernize its industries in line with Europe and America, Japan also invited more than 3,000 foreign specialists and technocrats over several years.

But this rapid modernization came as a great shock to the low-income Japanese, and people became especially dependent on agriculture when the government introduced deflation policies. These policies brought the prices of agricultural commodities tumbling down, which ultimately bankrupted the farmer communities. They had a direct impact on land price—especially the prices of cultivable land. Agricultural land became cheap. Many urban rich people, mostly the city merchants, started buying and selling stocks and setting up companies. The years 1886–1888 were a good period for establishing different Japanese companies. Many light industries such as spinning and silk-making flourished. This led to high demand for labour to work in the industries. Workers working in industries had to work for longer hours than ever, and in return, received a little wage. The children of bankrupt farmer families joined the factories and fell victim to deflation policies.

However, the Industrial Revolution in Japan created ample job opportunities for low-wage workers, including women and children. The Royal Japanese Government banned abortion and infanticide in 1869. This, in turn, led to an increase in population. Labour supplies—naturally—were to increase very soon.

Two major studies were conducted on Japan during the early stages of industrialization. The first one was done by Gennosuke Yokoyama, and it was published in 1899 in the form of a book titled 'Nihon no kasoshakai' (The low classes of Japan). The second study was conducted by the Ministry of Agriculture and Commerce, Royal Government of Japan and the book was published in 1903 under the title of 'Shokkojijo' (i.e., the Factory Workers' Conditions).

Both the books described that children were engaged in large numbers at the matchbox and rug factories, and at the reeling and spinning mills.

The survey conducted by the Ministry of Agriculture and Commerce stated that more than 40 per cent of workers were children working in matchbox factories and 50.7 per cent in rug industries.[53] The factories of this kind were largely located in the slum areas of Kobe and Osaka. These factories enjoyed the cheap labour of children who were paid by the piece. However, this type of job helped the children to join work even after schooling hours. These factories employed female workers comprising women and girls too; but they would be paid a meagre amount of wages. Little children, aged seven or eight years, were involved in the matchbox-making works. Their conditions in the rug and silk-reeling industries too were not mentionably good.

However, a sizeable number of child workers in Japan were very kindly treated, and much attention was devoted to them. There is an old Japanese saying: 'the children are treasures'. Japan—much before the Industrial Revolution—had put emphasis on primary education, and, 4 years of schooling was made compulsory for every Japanese child in 1879. As a result, when Japan passed its first Factory Act, 1911, it was estimated that 98 per cent of children aged between 6–11 years were studying at schools.

During school hours, the Japanese villages remained silent. Isabella L. Bird, in different portions of her *Unbeaten Tracks in Japan*, praises this. She narrates, for example,

> The village is very silent early, while the children are at school; their return enlivens it a little, but they are quiet even at play; at sunset the men return, and things are a little livelier; you hear a good deal of splashing in baths, and after that they carry about and play with their younger children, while the older ones prepare lessons for their following day by reciting them in a high, monotonous twang.[54]

In the family, the Japanese children were petted and much loved—even if they laboured. Bird again observes,

> I never saw people take so much delight in their offspring, carrying them about, or holding their hands in walking, watching and entering into their games, supplying them constantly with new toys, taking

---

[53] Hugh Hindman, *The World of Child-labour* (New York and London: Routledge, 2009), 882.
[54] Bird, *Unbeaten Tracks in Japan*, 139.

them to picnics and festivals, never being content to be without them, and treating other people's children also with a suitable measure of affection and attention. Both fathers and mothers take a pride in their children. It is most amusing about six every morning to see twelve or fourteen when sitting on a low wall, each with a child under two in his arms, fonding and playing with it, and showing off its physique and intelligence. To judge from appearances, the children form the chief topic at this morning gathering.[55]

The children, as Bird observed, were very gentle, docile and obedient. She narrates,

For some reasons they prefer boys, but certainly girls are equally petted and loved. The children, though for our ideas too gentle and formal, are very prepossessing in looks and behaviour. They are so perfectly docile and obedient, so ready to help their parents, so good to the little ones, and, in the many hours which I have spent in watching them at play, I have never heard an angry word, or seen a sour look or act.[56]

The usual social customs of the Japanese family system required that children would mostly inherit their father's occupation, and it was evident prior to the Meiji Restoration. During the feudal system in Japan, merchants' children became merchants, and the children of farmers became farmers. Very often children of low-income families, later, were sent to factories as apprentices. They lived in their masters' houses like family members. They stayed and worked as apprentices until and unless they became mature to work like adults. However, contrarily, there were innumerable instances where children were ill-treated in factories. They were tortured by employers, and they sometimes experienced fatal injuries or fatal diseases. Due to meting out of excessive torture and punishment, minor children, in some circumstances, lost their lives. Their working hours were long, lower wages were provided, and sometimes, they had to work in night shifts. These were the evil effects of the Industrial Revolution as experienced by the working children of different European and North American countries, and, later, Japan. These unhealthy working conditions were

---

[55] Quoted in Gail L. Bernstein, ed., *Recreating Japanese Women, 1600–1945* (Berkeley: University of California Press, 1991), 32.
[56] Bird, *Unbeaten Tracks in Japan*, 75.

experienced by the Japanese children during the transition from home factories and 'native employments' to the factory system of production. These issues were well known to the parents of the children working under the modern factory system. They bowed down to poverty and sent their beloved children for work, depriving them of education, health-facilities and playing opportunities.

The benevolent statesmen of the Meiji era noticed these issues and became very active to stop the evils of the Japanese Industrial Revolution. Child labour was one such form of industrial abuse. They realized this danger, and in the late 1980s of the 20th century, they approached the government to enforce protective measures to stop child labour. The government began to draft child labour legislation, with the help of the British and other western legislations. The legislation thus framed for Japan was based on three important aspects: education, health and the national education policy. The first child labour act, the Factory Act of 1911, came into being in 1916, but its actual implementation could occur only after the establishment of the Bureau of Social Affairs in Tokyo in 1922. The (Japanese) Industrial Employment Act of 1923, which became effective on 1 July 1926, considering aspects such as scope and limits of application, minimum age needs, registration of juvenile workers, legal aspects of inspection of factories, issue of census-register and imposing of penalties.[57] The minimum age of a Japanese child to work in the factory was fixed at 12 years. But in certain cases, children of 10–12 years of age were allowed to work under prior permission from governmental authorities. Children, who could not complete their elementary education, were provided with school facilities in the factories, and if this facility was not available on the factory premises, they were sent to nearby district schools. But this made them unhappy—this was a sort of double-burden to them in the sense that they had to work for long hours, following which they were required to study at the district schools.

Under this revised law, the working hours for the Japanese children below the age of 16 years were restricted to 11 hours a day, and their night duties at factories were completely banned: no such work could be performed by them between 10 PM of the previous night to 5 AM of the next dawn. Also, a provision for two days rest in a month,

---

[57] Refer to Janet Hunter, *Japanese Economic History, 1930–60*, Vol. V (New York and London: Routledge, 2000), 142–143.

and a worktime rest of not less than 30 minutes a day was approved. The Factory Legislation of 1923 provided special protection for the apprentices. The apprentice system was developed in order to provide training and education to working children. However, as Asa Matsuoka writes in *Labour Conditions of Women and Children in Japan*,[58] the factory owners used this system for the purpose of exploitation by paying low wages and engaging little children for longer hours.

Therefore, as per the Factory Legislation of 1923, and through the 4th chapter of the *Japanese Imperial Decree Number 13*, dated 5 June 1926, special protection was provided to apprentices.[59]

The protective measures given to them were as follows. First, the workers, especially the child workers, were to be employed for acquiring knowledge in a trade. Second, training and education were to be provided to the apprentices under special guidance. Third, ethical education was to be compulsorily provided. Fourth, data was to be strictly maintained and periodically handed over to local government representatives with reference to the total number of apprentices, their age(s), the qualifications of the trainers, the subjects and periods of training, the applied methods of training, the time spent each day on such trainings, the extent of holidays and rest periods, the quality of supervision of moral and ethical education, the wage payment method, the provisions of the contract for the apprentices, etc.

A large number of underage children in Japan were also employed in unregulated factories, and at industrial, commercial and different trade occupations. In absence of protective regulations in those industries, conscious violation of the legislation was made. A study undertaken by the Department of Social Education, Imperial Government of Japan, in Tokyo in 1924 was successful in collecting accurate statistics on an apprenticeship in unregulated factories in Tokyo, and the data was horrible. E. Isomura,[60] mentions that in 1922, 23,000 minor workers were employed in Tokyo of whom 20 per cent were working at cloth industries, 18 per cent in carpentry and cabinet making, 11 per cent in

---

[58] Asa Matsuoka, *Labour Conditions of Women and Children in Japan* (Washington: Government Printing Office, 1931), 26–28.

[59] See *Wages and Hours of Labour in the Men's Clothing Industry, 1911–30* (Washington, DC: United States Government Printing Press, 1933), 76.

[60] E. Isomura, 'Juvenile Employment in Japanese Towns,' *Kyocho-Kai Social Reforms* (November 1927): 155; see *Wages and Hours of Labour in the Men's Clothing Industry, 1911–30*, 28.

printing and bookbinding, and the remaining were engaged in textile processing and manufacturing and processing of food and beverages. Juvenile workers had to perform excessive hours of work, and no concession was given to them. In fact, they had to perform works that were fit to be done only by the adults. Their average working hours were 9 hours and 20 minutes, and they were more in the textiles sector than in the sector of machine manufacturing. In the Japanese industries, such oppressive working hours were unjust for the minor workers.

It is generally known that Japan's rapid industrialization was dependent, initially, on Western technology. Soon, parliamentary debates on various aspects of such West-dependent factory systems started. Nevertheless, the introduction of factory legislation took time, and finally, in 1911—three years prior to the beginning of the First World War—the first Japanese Factory Law was enacted.

The writers here are trying to review the statistical data available on child labour in the Japanese industry during the period of 1899–1914. The data sources are the papers released by the Ministry of Agriculture and Commerce, Imperial Government of Japan, in 1914.

Table 3.25 displays data regarding the industrial employment of children—boys and girls—divided into three categories according to their ages: under 12 years of age, under 14 years of age, and under 20 years of age. It could be seen that the employment of boys whose age is less than 20 years is largest among all the three categories during 1899, 1909 and 1914. When one compares boys and girls of all the categories, it becomes evident that the representation of girls less than 20 years of age is the highest in Japanese industries during 1899, 1909 and 1914 (58% in both 1909 and 1914), when compared to the employment of the boys (26% in 1909 and 27% in 1914).

Table 3.26 shows the condition of the Japanese child labour by factory size and gender during 1899, 1909 and 1914. Data presented here show that boys were usually not employed en masse at large factories. But in the case of engagement of female child labourers, the picture is somewhat different. During 1899 and 1909, the cases of employment of females under 14 years of age were quite considerable. The minor girls' engagement in textiles, and, more specifically, at cotton spinning mills (1000+ categories), was larger than their male counterparts. It is thus clarified that Japan's tremendous industrial development was solely responsible for the employment of minor children in large numbers during the Japanese Industrial Revolution.

Table 3.25 Children in Industrial Employment, by Age and Gender, 1899, 1909 and 1914

Year	Proportion (%)			Total Workforce (All Ages)
	Under 12	Under 14	Under 20	
Males				
1899	–	6	–	138,119
1909	0.4	3	26	307,139
1914	0.3	3	27	383,957
Females				
1899	–	13	–	254,790
1909	1	7	58	493,498
1914	0.4	6	58	564,308

Source: Ministry of Agriculture and Commerce (MAC), 32-nen Zenkoku kōjō tokeihyo (1902), Meiji 42-nen kojo tokeihyo (1910), and Taisho 3-nen kojo tokeihyo (1916). Refer to Cunningham and Viazzo, *Child Labour in Historical Perspective*, 14.

Note: The 1899 survey covered factories (kojo) with 10 operatives or more, while the 1909 and 1914 surveys also included those with 5–9.

Table 3.26 Child Labour by Factory Size and Gender, 1899, 1909 and 1914

Factory size (Operatives per establishment)	Proportion under 14 (%)					
	Males			Females		
	1899	1909	1914	1899	1909	1914
5–9	–	4	4	–	6	6
10–29	6	3	3	13	8	8
30–49	7	3	3	12	7	8
50–99	6	3	2	12	7	7
100–499	8	3	2	12	6	5
500–999	4	4	2	14	8	5
1,000+	4	2	1	17	10	5

Source: Ministry of Agriculture and Commerce (MAC), 32-nen Zenkoku kōjō tōkeihyō (1902), Meiji 42-nen kōjō tōkeihyō (1910), and Taisho 3-nen kōjō tōkeihyō (1916). Refer to Cunningham and Viazzo's *Child Labour in Historical Perspective*, 4.

Note: The 1899 survey covered factories (kōjō) with 10 operatives or more, while the 1909 and 1914 surveys also included those with 5–9 operatives.

We can review the condition of this particular issue of Japanese child labour in a more distinct way by considering the numbers of child labourers employed at some of the major industries (70 industrial categories) such as cotton spinning, silk reeling (Group-I), rug weaving, rope braiding, matchmaking (Group-II), glass-making and manufacturing of paper-made products (Group-III). Data supplied by the Ministry of Agriculture and Commerce, Imperial Government of Japan and others (1903) have been presented in Table 3.27, and it shows the proportion of child labourers (boys and girls) in the major seven industries in percentage.

Table 3.27 depicts that the number of child labourers and their percentage of employment as per age, gender and industrial sectors varied widely in the late 19th and early 20th centuries. In the sector of cotton spinning, for example, female engagement was larger than male. In the case of rug weaving, in contrast, boys were largely engaged: their employment was 42 per cent while the girls' involvement in this

Table 3.27 Child Labourers in Select Japanese Industries by Gender, 1900

Industry	Proportion of Workers Under 14 (%)			Total Number of Workers
	Males	Females	Total	
Group-I Cotton spinning	9	12	11	55,511
Silk reeling	4	10	10	124,241
Group-II Rug weaving	42	13	20	1,031
Rope braiding	22	30	28	1,107
Matchmaking	38	35	36	12,804
Group-III Glass-making	26	0	24	2,573
Paper products	15	24	20	1,085

Source: Ministry of Agriculture and Commerce (MAC), Meiji 33-nen Zenkōku kōjō tokeihyō (1903). Also, refer to Carnegie Institution of Washington Publication 85, no. 7 (1902): 151.
Notes: 1. Only factories (kojo) with 10 or more operatives were surveyed.
2. Workers include not only shokko (operatives) but also totii (apprentices).

Table 3.28 *Characteristics of the Workforce in Selected Industries, 1900*

Industry	No. of Workers per Factory	Sex Ratio	Proportion of Apprentices to	
			Total Workers (%)	Workers under 14 (%)
Group-I Cotton spinning	495	0.27	0.05	0.3
Silk reeling	49	0.07	4	18
Group-II Rug weaving	16	0.29	0.04	0
Rope braiding	43	0.33	1	1
Matchmaking	70	0.35	1	1
Group-III Glass-making	50	18.79	25	43
Paper products	32	1.02	7	16

Source: Ministry of Agriculture and Commerce (MAC), Meiji 33-nen Zenkoku kōjō tōkeihyō (1903). Refer to Carl Mosk, 'Japanese Industrialisation and Economic Growth,' https://eh.net/encyclopedia/japanese-industrialization-and-economic-growth/
Note: Sex ratio (M/F) refers to that of the workers, including of apprentices.

industry was only 13 per cent. Again, in the case of silk reeling and rope braiding, the participation of girls was much more than that of boys'.

Table 3.28 demonstrates characteristics of the workforce in select Japanese industries, comparing the total number of workers with child workers under 14 in terms of percentage during 1900. It, again, considers the employment of children in seven categories of Japanese industries during the Industrial Revolution.

Table 3.28 depicts the mass employment of workers under 14 years of age. The number of engaged apprentices was quite large in the sectors of silk reeling and of paper products (18 and 16% respectively), and the largest number of apprentices was found in the glass factories (43%).

Working conditions of boys and girls under the age of 14 years—expressed in terms of the number of hours of work per day and daily wages received in Japanese factories such as cotton spinning, silk reeling, rug weaving, rope braiding, matchmaking, glass making and paper products—have been registered statistically in Table 3.29.

Table 3.29 Working Conditions of Japanese Child Workers in Select Industries, 1900

Industry	Power-driven Establish-ments (%)	Days in Opera-tion (Per Year)	Hours in Opera-tion	Daily Wages for under 14	
				Males (Sex)	Females (Sex)
Group-I Cotton spinning	95	329	12 (21.8)	12.6	10.4
Silk reeling	83	186	10	11.7	9.6
Group-II Rug weaving	0	289	9.5	7.0	6.7
Rope braiding	27	308	11	9.9	9.2
Matchmaking	3	313	10	9.2	7.7
Group-III Glass-making	16	323	9.5	12.7	10.5
Paper products	3	300	10	11.7	9.7

Source: Data available from the Ministry of Agriculture and Commerce (MAC), Meiji 33-nen Zenkoku kojo tōkeihyō (1903).
Note: The figure in parentheses in the column for hours in operation includes the night shift.

Table 3.29 clearly demonstrates that the working hours for both the male and female child workers under 14 years of age were excessive, but the wages received by the girls were far less than their male counterparts.

We have mentioned earlier that Japan has a long tradition of educating its children even before the Meiji Restoration. This had a far-reaching impact on the overall education scenario of Japan. Before the introduction of modern education, there was an old and traditional system of education known as 'terakova', which prevailed in Japan at the primary level. As a result of continuity of education, especially at the primary level under this system, the enrolment rate was quite high since (and during) the Meiji Restoration. As per the education data supplied by the Ministry of Education's *Mombusho nenpo* and Ministry of Wars' *Rikugunsho fokei nenpo*, the enrolment of male children was 51 per cent at the beginning of the reformation, which rose to 64 per cent in 1889. A huge escalation in enrolment occurred in 1895, and the extent of enrolment reached 77 per cent. A higher rate of enrolment was noticed in 1905—1998 per cent—and, subsequently, in 1915 and 1925, it was 99 per cent. In the earlier years, there were huge gaps in the proportion of those who could write and those who completed compulsory schooling (e.g., in 1889 and 1895, the divisions were 77 per cent and 42 per cent, and 89 per cent and 66 per cent, respectively). Gaps crept in since 1905. In 1905 and 1915, the gaps were 10 per cent (98 − 80 = 10%; 99 − 89 = 10%). In 1925, the enrolment gap was just 1 per cent (i.e., 99 − 98=1%). Also, there were all-out efforts from the government and factory owners to provide basic education to the working children, especially after the enforcement of the anti-child labour law in Japan in 1917.

In Japan, as we have seen, child labour was very important in sweatshop and coal mining industries in the late 19th and early 20th centuries. As Sachiko Sone writes,[61] at the Chikuho coalfield, for example, family labour—comprising parents, children and other members—characterized the enterprise. The writers present in Table 3.30, the employment structure in the Chikuho coalfield.

Table 3.30 represents the usage of employment of adults and children in the famous Chikuho coalfield between 1906 and 1930. Later days' data show that the employment of children in the coalfield had decreased. This might perhaps be partially true due to the usage of machines and stringent enforcement of the anti-child labour law. Another reason might be a desire on the part of the record keepers to keep the small army of child labourers unobtrusive in labour records.

In regard to educational arrangements for working children undertaken in Japan, the writers have found that the arrangements were sufficient, and the children could conveniently enroll at the district government schools. In the case of Chikuho coal mines, a survey conducted in 1905 shows that the school-attendance level among the coal miners' children was only 53.4 per cent when compared with the national-level school attendance, which was very high, that is, 95 per cent. Seeing this depressing condition of school attendance among the workers' children, the Furukawa Mining Company provided school fees and other expenses. This had a remarkable impact upon the school attendance, and very quickly it reached 82.7 per cent in May 1905.

---

[61] Sachiko Sone, 'Exploitation or Expectation? Child Labour in Japan's Coalmines before the Second World War,' *Critical Asian Studies* 35, no. 1 (2003): 33–58.

Table 3.30 Employment Structure of the Larger Mines in the Chikuho Coal Field between 1906 and 1930

Year (No. of Mines)	Category	Below Ground				Above Ground	Total Above & Below Ground	Average per Mine	Average Child per Mine
		Hewer/Haulier	Timberer	Misc.	Total				
1906 (25)	a	25,886	2,711	5,652	33,249	9,222	42,471	1,700	0.47
	c	115		3	118	86	204	8	
1913 (40)	a	38,780	4,198	15,191	58,161	17,426	75,407	1,885	0.37
	c	80		14	94	179	273	7	
1917 (42)	a	55,067	6,781	11,312	73,160	20,923	94,083	2,240	0.10
	c	61		7	68	32	100	2.4	
1925 (46)	a	58,629	6,954	16,408	82,002	27,118	109,120	2,372	0.92*
	c	406		127	533	469	1002	22	
1930 (58)	a	25,036	10,187	8,502	43,716	13,713	101,154	1,744	n/a**
	c	n/a	n/a	n/a	n/a	n/a	n/a	n/a	

Source: 1906 figures from Nōsōmu, kōfu Taigū Jinei; 1913, 1917 and 1925 figures from Shōkōmu Shō kōzan k roku (Ministry of Commerce and Industry, Office of the Mines), Hampō Juōyo Kōzan Yōran (Table of large mines in Japan); 1930 figures from Ogino Yoshihiro, Chukuho Tankō Rōshi Kankei Sni, p. 273 (originally cited in Chikeech Sekitun Kogyo Kumari Shozoku Tanko Genkyō Chōsa Hyō, December 1930). Refer to Sachiko Sone, 'Exploitation or Expectation? Child-labour in Japan's Coal-mines before the Second World War,' https://www.tandfonline.com/doi/abs/10.1080/14672710320000061479?journalCode=rcra20

Notes: (Adult = a, Child = c).
*This increase may be explained in part by the definition of an adult being raised from 15 to 16 years of age).
**Women and children were officially banned from the mines beginning in 1928.

Table 3.31 School Attendance: Children in Four Mines in Chikuho in 1905

Number of Children Attending School	Number of Children Not Attending School	Total
March 228 (53.4%)	199 (46.6%)	427
May 412 (82.7%)	86 (17.3%)	498

Source: Chikuho Sekitan Kōgrō Kumiai Geppō 1.13 (1905): 73–77.

Table 3.32 Reasons for Non-attendance at School among Working Children in Four Mines in Chikuho in 1905

Reasons	Number of Children	Specific Details of Individuals
Illness	5	Eye infection (2); cripple (1); of delicate disposition (2), employed (3); nursing own sibling (3)
Poverty	55	
Other	26	
Total	86	

Source: Chikuho Sekitan Kōgrō Kumiai Geppō 1.13 (1905): 73–77.

School attendance at four different mines in Chikuho in 1905 and the reasons for non-attendance have been shown in Tables 3.31 and 3.32, respectively.

Child labour was a common phenomenon in the factory system of Japan during the Industrial Revolution. Working children intermittently met with accidents, especially those working in mines. Sometimes major accidents took place and caused huge casualties. One such accident took place on 5 March 1903 at the Ōto Mine in Tagawa district of Chikuho. In that accident, 123 underage workers narrowly escaped from death, but 65 workers lost their lives—as shown in Table 3.33.

Official statistical data, as Sachiko Sone writes,[62] were not reliable indicators of child labour in the Japanese coal mines. Oral accounts and newspapers supplied plenty of data on child labour working in factories and mines, but all of them could not be relied upon. Data derived from *Tajima Masami, Tankō Bijin* (Beautiful coal mining women) indicates

---
[62] Ibid.

Table 3.33 *Age Structure of the Deceased in the Ōto Mine Disaster, 1903*

Age (Years)	Miners Male	Miners Female	Unknown	Other Trades Male	Total + (%)
Unknown			2	1	3 (4.7)
5	1				1(1.6)
7	1				1(1.6)
9				1	1(1.6)
10	1				1(1.6)
13	1				1(1.6)
14	1				1(1.6)
15–19	5			1	6(9.5)
20–29	12	7		3	22(35)
30–39	19	6		1	16(25)
40–49	7			1	8(13)
50–59	2				2(3.2)
Grand total	38	18	2	7	65(100)

Source: Various reports published in the *Moji Shimpō* (*The Moji Newspaper*), 5, 7 and 8 March 1903.

that even in early 20th-century Japan, there were quite a large number of girls involved in coal mines. This is reproduced in Table 3.34.

While representing data, Sone also indicated that employment of children below the age of 15 years was not legal after 1916 in Japan.

3.3.6. Australia

Australia became a manufacturing giant during 1800 as a result of tremendous advancements in the fields of science, engineering, communications and transportation. Human and animal powers were replaced by wind power in the Australian colony of the English in the early 1800s. John Dickson (1774–1843), a Scottish engineer, brought over, from the United Kingdom, the newly-developed steam engine to Australia in 1813, and by 1815, numerous such engines began operating

Table 3.34 Age of Entry of Interviewed Women Who Joined Work at Mines, 1907–1933

Birth Year	Year of Entry	Age at Entry to Mine	Employment
1898	1907	19	Mining
1903	1915	12	Mining
1903	1916	13	Mining
1903	1916	13	Mining
1903	1916	13/14	Mining, with furniture
1904	1916	12	Mining, with brother
1905	1919	14	Mining
1906	1914	8	Helper, Mining at 13
1907	1919	12	Mining
1907	1922	15	Mining with mother
1907	1922	15	Mining
1908	1923	8	Helping mother, mining at 15
1909	1923	14	Mining
1909	1924	15	Mining
1909	1924	15	Mining
1910	1913	3	With two brothers underground
1910	1922	12	Mining
1913	1927	14	Mining
1916	1921	5	Looking after brother, Mining at 25
1918	1931	13	Mining
1923	1933	10	Mining

Source: Tajima Masami, Tankō Bijin (Beautiful coal-mining women; Tokyo: Tsukiji Shoten, 2000). Refer to Sachiko Sone, 'Exploitation or Expectation?

under his supervision all over Australia. The manufacturing of small steam engines in Australia began in the early 1930s. Australia, for its industrial development, depended heavily on foreign technologies, especially those from England and the United States of America. Some of the technologies imported from abroad were modified according to the local conditions—following trial-and-error methods. Spinning machines, too, were imported and coped with fine Merino wool; but the imported iron and copper furnaces had to be altered to operate with local ore impurities. It was very difficult to adjust imported machines and technologies with the hot Australian climate. Naturally, the Australian scientists, engineers and entrepreneurs had to mould and rectify such technologies to make them suitable for Australian conditions. Successive Australian governments had encouraged the setting up of new printing and locomotive construction enterprises. They also encouraged and supported the local manufacturing agencies to produce or process pig-iron, woollen clothes, paper and glass. Governments in New South Wales, Victoria and South Australia—for the expansion of their individual infrastructural facilities—offered hefty contracts to local manufacturers for building tram cars, hospital beds, railway tracks, portable lockups and many more things. These initiatives by local governments and entrepreneurs required a strong workforce that would sustain the continuous growth of the Australian economy.

Through frantic efforts for post-modernization, the Australian country towns were eventually transformed into self-reliant stations. Local and surrounding areas were well served with products produced at meatworks, boiling-down works, soap and candle factories, iron foundries, engineering works, agricultural implement makers, sawmills, brickworks, flour mills, cordial works, breweries, ice works, etc. Manufacturing output increased manifold, mainly due to mass production and importation of numerous machines. These, in fact, helped to decrease the cost of production, and ultimately the price of goods went down. Most of Australia's production units were located near the capital cities and Newcastle. These were close to shipping and rail hubs. In the course of time, a new group of middle-class mill owners emerged, and these mill owners hollered for the steady supply of industrial workers to operate their machines. Interestingly, the slum areas were developed for the working class so that the members could live well and healthily participate in the production processes. Previously, houses built in city slums (where the factory workers lived) close to factories were unhygienic and dirty. These were frantically rebuilt and cleaned. Thus, the Australian workers were duped into working for long hours and supplying their children to the factory owners to work as child labourers.

Due to the huge expansion of factories and mines in Australia, the demand for labour increased. Women and children formed a major part of the total workforce. Children—girls and boys—worked in factories in spite of the fact that school education was compulsory for every child. These Australian children suffered from injuries, and experienced the worst conditions at the workplace, along with long working hours at a lower wages.

The indigenous Australian child workers (males and females) had 'mellifluously' supplied a huge amount of labouring hours during Australia's colonial past. They were employed as domestic servants (mostly the girls), or laboured in the pastoral industry (mostly boys), and many of them worked in the sea-cucumber industries off the coastal areas of Queensland and Western Australia. They were employed in large numbers in the early 19th century, and by the 1870s, most of the Australian colonies had enforced regulations towards compulsory education for indigenous Australian children up to 14 years of age. Like in other countries, it took a long time to implement the legislation. The minimum age of work for the aboriginal children was firmly set as late as in the early 20th century. In Queensland, for example, it was set in 1919.

Importantly, the Australian female children were largely employed in domestic services, and they were physically, emotionally and sexually abused—quite arbitrarily. Boys were engaged in pastoral industries. Marine pearling and sea-cucumber industries of Queensland and Western Australia engaged many young children. These industries had high casualty rates. The immigrated Europeans were reluctant to perform such works, and a large number of aboriginal children, who performed jobs in maritime industries, suffered casualties. The colonial governments, deplorably, did not maintain records of working children in such industries. Different approximations reveal that about one-third of the total number of Australian workers in the late 19th and early 20th centuries consisted of aboriginal children. As Shurlee Swain writes,[63] the indigenous (or, aboriginal) children were in high demand because they were ready to work anywhere in the country. Morcover, they

---

[63] Shurlee Swain, 'Development of Child Welfare Policy in Australia,' in *The World of Child Labour: A Historical and Regional Survey*, ed. Hugh Hindman (New York: M.E. Sharpe, 2009), 949–952.

were cheap, 'civilized', and were considered 'pliable workers' by the immigrated European capitalists.

However, the indigenous children were denied their basic needs such as education and other requirements for children's development. Benevolent souls from the Australian colonies sought to rectify the wrongs being done to these children. Their first rectifying step was to thoroughly train the poor indigenous children before they joined work in domestic service or in the rural sector. Pauper apprenticeships were given legal authority by the then Governor of New South Wales in 1834. Similarly, South Australia passed an anti-aboriginal-child labour act in 1842, and the Swan River Colony had introduced a like ordinance in 1845. Almost all the colonies—by the 1860s—passed different forms of legislation establishing and administrating industrial schools, especially those for the aboriginal child labourers. Neglected children or children abandoned by their parents could be admitted to such schools initially for a term of seven years, and later, until the age of 18 years, they would continue to attend these schools. But the legislations towards the education of the aboriginal child labourers were not implemented uniformly throughout Australia—especially in the wake of numerous invasions and dispossessions. The indigenous communities were understandably disturbed. While many adults and children were dying of starvation, diseases and violence, the surviving adults and children were absorbed in pastoralism. No wages were provided to these workers, and only food and shelter were given. No inspection was made to assess these indigenous child labourers' conditions. The children would toil while being detached from their parents or their communities.

Child legislations passed between 1890 and 1911 at different Australian colonies gave special attention to the welfare of working children. It was seen that even after the passing of legislation, working children were being engaged increasingly especially in street trades and entertainment industries, where they faced exploitations. To rectify such wrongs, the anti-child labour legislations prohibited the employment of Australian children of school-going age in factories and workshops during school hours. Not only this, the legislations introduced penalties for employers who employed such children into their factories. The legislations also directed that all underage girls be removed from Australian brothels. The legislations thus controlled the employment of juvenile children—especially after introducing compulsory education and stringent anti-child labour laws. However, education and legislation did not, initially, have a remarkable impact upon the children of lower economic strata. Moreover, these legislations allowed the so-called 'protectors' to control the lives of the indigenous people, including their children. Applying their powers, the White 'protectors' separated the indigenous children from their parents and sent them for work in domestic service or at rural sectors. This system, instead of controlling child labour, only helped to increase the number of indigenous working children. Legislation could not save the working children from exploitation in the form of lower wages and increased working hours, and, as a result, all these indigenous people could not—for generations—come out of impoverishment.

With industrialization spreading all around Australia—as also described earlier—there was a greater demand for labourers in factories and mines in industrialized countries such as England, the United States of America, Belgium, France, Japan, China, Australia and Canada. There was a view—for example, of Clark Nardinelli's[64] that the adoption of technology reduced the demand for child labour. But there were also counter-arguments (e.g., of Carolyn Tuttle[65] and of Jane Humphries[66]) which stated that advancing technology created huge job opportunities in industries for children, and for that purpose, the child labour legislation could be implemented properly for the children's betterment and protection.

Technological advancement and the discoveries of gold in Victoria and New South Wales during the mid-19th century in Victoria and New South Wales attracted a large number of immigrants with women and children. As Madeleine Johnston sums up,[67] these were the same problems associated with child labour in Australia as could

---

[64] Clark Nardinelli, 'Child-labour and the Factory Acts,' *Journal of Economic History* (December 1980): 739–753.

[65] Carolyn Tuttle, *Hard at Work in Factories and Mines* (Boulder: Westview Press, 1999).

[66] Jane Humphries, *Childhood and Child-labour in the British Industrial Revolution* (Cambridge: Cambridge University Press, 2010).

[67] Madeleine Johnston, *The Role and Regulation of Child Factory Labour during the Industrial Revolution in Australia, 1873–85* (Cambridge: Cambridge University Press, 2020).

be noticed in the industrialized countries everywhere else. The problems were: low wages, children working at school age, bad working conditions, unstable and unsuitable factory work, etc. The liberal politicians of Australia, since the early 1870s, had been calling for a Royal Commission to inquire into conditions in factories, including the conditions of working children. Accordingly, the Royal Commission was set up in Victoria in 1881. The Commissioners frequently visited the factories and many smaller establishments of food, drink, tobacco, clothing and footwear, household goods, etc. They found underage children working everywhere in the factories and establishments. The Commission members conducted interviews with the factory owners, firemen, workers and underage children, and soon diagnosed a critical child labour problem prevailing in Australia. The problems that the members identified included: (a) lower working age, (b) low attendance in school, (c) long working hours, (d) low wages, (e) children being employed in the lowest skill jobs, (f) boys addicted to smoking and chewing, (g) deplorable plight of factory girls, (h) unhygienic workplace and (i) abject poverty. All these factors contributed to the 'blossoming' of child-labouring systems.

In the late 19th century, like the other colonies of Australia, Queensland was a rapidly developing economy, with a rapid growth of population, which is immediately evident from the *Queensland Census Data* of 1891 and 1901. Although there was a rapid expansion of population and industrialization, the participation of children in the industrial works in this area was quite limited.

Data presented in Table 3.35 shows that Queensland, in the last quarter of the 19th century, was a dynamic and growing society—reflected by a dynamic growth of population from 393,718 in 1891 to 503,266 in 1901. This shows a one-fourth increase in population. This was due to the competitive advantage that other parts of Australia and Queensland enjoyed in the pastoral and mining sector. There was also tremendous growth in the manufacturing sector. Children aged 19 years or less represented higher workforce participation than children aged 14 years or less. It is suspected that children below the age of 14 years were perhaps not recorded while they were working in either rural or non-rural workforce.

Table 3.36 shows children's participation in mining, industries, agricultural and pastoral was meagre. There was a negligible increase

Table 3.35 *Queensland Population and Workforce Participation Rates (Those Aged 19 Years and Under), 1891, 1901*

	1891	1901
Total population	393,718	503,266
Population aged 19 years or under	181,892 (46.2%)	213,944 (42.5%)
Population aged 14 years or under	146,564 (37.2%)	184,469 (36.6%)
Total workforce	56,365	68,323
Total workforce aged 19 years or under	28,408 (17.1%)	38,396 (18.1%)
Total workforce aged 14 years or less	4,804 (2.9%)	6,418 (3%)
Total rural workforce	56,365	68,323
Rural workforce aged 19 years or under	8,569 (15.2%)	11,135 (16.3%)
Rural workforce aged 14 years or less	1,479(2.6%)	2.424 (3.5%)
Total non-rural workforce[a]	110,059	143,671
Non-rural workforce aged 19 years or under	19,839 (18%)	27,261 (19%)
Non-rural workforce aged 14 years or less	3,325 (3%)	3,994 (2.8%)
Workforce participation rate, aged 19 years or less	28,408 (15.6%)	28,369 (18.1%)
Workforce participation rate, aged 14 years or less	4,804 (3.3%)	6,418 (3.5%)

Source: Queensland Census of 1886, 1891, 1901. Consult *Early Australian Census Records*, https://guides.slv.vic.gov.au/earlycensus/qld
Notes: Figures in parenthesis represent percentages of total population or workforce
[a] Includes mining

in the number of child participants aged 14 years or less. Children aged 19 years or less worked less in mining in both 1891 and 1901. In 1891, their involvement was only 4.1 per cent, and in 1901, it slightly improved to 7.5 per cent. But the number of children of 14 years or less, who worked at the mining sector in 1891, was less than 1 per cent (7%), and in 1901 too, their contribution was less

Table 3.36 Child Adolescent Participation in Key Economic Sectors: Queensland 1891, 1901

	1891	1901
Mining—total workforce	11,627	16,375
Mining—aged 15–19 years	474 (4.1%)	1,231 (7.5%)
Mining—aged 14 years or less	71 (0.7%)	113 (0.6%)
Industrial (including building)—total workforce	47,148	51,716
Industrial-aged 15–19 years	6,660 (14.1%)	8,935 (17.3%)
Industrial-aged 14 years or less	1,201 (2.5%)	1,119 (2.2%)
Agricultural and pastoral—total workforce	67,992	68,323
Agricultural and pastoral—aged 15–19 years	7,493 (11%)	8,711 (12.7%)
Agricultural and pastoral—aged 14 years or less	1,550 (2.3%)	2,424 (3.5%)
Commerce and transport—total workforce	20,386	34,694
Commerce and transport—aged 15–19 years	3,777 (18.5%)	5,383 (15.5%)
Commerce and transport—aged 14 years or less	843 (4.1%)	1,169 (3.4%)
Domestic service—total workforce	20,386	25,210
Domestic service—aged 15–19 years	5,633 (27.6%)	7,167 (28.4%)
Domestic service—aged 14 years or less	1,111 (5.4%)	1,419 (5.6%)

Source: Queensland Census of 1886, 1891, 1901. Consult *Early Australian Census Records*, https://guides.slv.vic.gov.au/earlycensus/qld
Note: Figures parentheses represent percentages of the total occupational workforce.

than one per cent (6%). The employment of children aged 19 years or less in the case of industries was slightly higher in 1891 and 1901, which was 14.1 per cent and 17.3 per cent, respectively, and in the case of children of age 14 years or less, it was 2.5 per cent and 2.2 per cent, respectively during 1891 and 1901. Children aged 15–19 years and that of 14 years or less worked in agricultural and pastoral works during 1891 and 1901 at the rate of 11 and 12.7 per cent, and

Table 3.37 Occupation Characterized by Significant Child Employment: Queensland Censuses 1891, 1901

	1891	1901
Boot and shoe manufacture-aged 14 years or less	149 (8.5%)	66 (3%)
Printing-aged 14 years or less	41 (7.9%)	64 (9.6%)
Textile manufacture-aged 14 years or less	425 (5.7%)	325 (3.3%)
Clothing manufacture-aged 14 years or less	237 (4.8%)	224 (3.3%)
Food and drink manufacture-aged 14 years or less	119 (5.2%)	158 (2.8%)
Grocery retail-aged 14 years or less	51 (4.9%)	109 (4.1%)
Diary assistants-aged 14 years or less	62 (12.9%)	114 (21.3%)
Domestic service-aged 14 years or less	1,111 (5.4%)	1,419 (5.6%)

Source: Queensland Censuses of 1891 and 1901. *Early Australian Census Records*, https://guides.slv.vic.gov.au/earlycensus/qld
Note: Figures in parentheses represent percentages of the total occupational workforce.

2.3 and 3.5 per cent, respectively. In the commerce, transport and domestic services, children aged 15–19 years were involved more than the children aged 14 or less years. Children aged 15–19 years represented 18.5 per cent and 15.5 per cent during 1891 and 1901, respectively as the workforce in commerce and transport, while children aged 14 years or less represented 4.1 per cent and 3.4 per cent respectively during the respective census periods. Children aged 15–19 years were represented more (27.6 and 28.4%, respectively) during the same periods, while children aged 14 years or less worked 5.4 and 5.6 per cent, respectively.

The Queensland Censuses of 1891 and 1901 as depicted in Table 3.37 show that children aged 14 years or less represented less than 10 per cent of the workforce during 1891 and 1901, respectively, in industries such as boot and shoe manufacturing, printing, textiles, clothing, food and drink manufacturing, grocery retail, and domestic service. The only exception was the case of the diary works where they represented 12.9 and 21.3 per cent during 1891 and 1901, respectively.

3.3.7. China

Child labour has had existed in China ever since ancient times. In the case of slavery, the slave mothers were the main suppliers of child labour. It was during the Qin Dynasty (221 BC—206 BC) when the captured people—men, women and children alike—were made slaves. In ancient times, these slaves experienced hardship and led a miserable life. They were abused in several ways. Many of the slave children, who worked in the agriculture sector along with the general peasants, did not enjoy equal rights. They had to face the worst of situations when they worked for the emperor, royal families and rich families. On several occasions, they were treated with extreme cruelty. There are many Chinese stories about the cruelty on the slave children by their masters. They were killed when their masters died and were buried with their master. The people of ancient China had a belief that, after death, the slave children would serve the master. During the Han Dynasty rule (206 BC—AD 220), slavery was no longer encouraged and thus did not remain popular. Child labouring was completely banned during the Tang Dynasty rule (AD 618—AD 907). But after the Tang rule, it again got momentum with the support of some rulers. Over the centuries, there was an effort on the part of many Chinese rulers to control child slavery and to abolish the system of slavery.

In China, children traditionally took part in agricultural and household activities, and especially after the Tang dynasty rule ended, they joined as apprenticeships in brickfields and weaving. But child labour got its momentum when China started industrializing. Large numbers of women and children could be found working in packing matchboxes. J. Howard, in a 2009 publication on Chinese child labour, writes about how it intensified after 1895—as a result of the rapid growth of textile mills in China (especially in Shanghai) in collaboration with Britain and Japan.

The practice of Chinese child labouring strengthened and reached its zenith at the end of the 1920s. For this, the Chinese industries were severely criticized and condemned later by the Marxist intellectuals and Christian reformers. Poverty and population pressure aggravated the child-labour problem during China's Republican Era (1911–1949). The Chinese government schools were not sufficiently available for millions of children, and naturally, millions could not avail the opportunity of schooling. Approximately, more than 40 million Chinese children were deprived of schooling during the early 1930s. Poverty and lack of educational opportunity pushed them to the world of child labour.

We can put some of the arguments in black and white to understand the logic of increasing child labour. First, the poverty of people in rural districts forced them to send their children to factories to work as child labourers. Second, low wages earned by the adults in the family forced parents to engage their children in factories for a living. Third, parents thought that the factories were safer places for their children than roaming in the street without doing anything. Fourth, the lack of public schools made millions of Chinese children illiterate and forced them to join work in factories. Fifth, the female-headed families, due to poverty, deprived children from enjoying the opportunity of education, play and fun.

In China, children were amply used in smaller factories, sweetshops, handicraft industries, household factories and street shops. However, actual data on child labour are not available due to the lack of surveys by the government at different small production and service units in China.

The coastal Chinese cities used child labourers in large numbers, and it constituted a normal component of the total labour force. Working children were leased out to modern factories such as textiles and light industries. Drug addiction severely increased in China by the end of 19th century, and it was found that one of the ten adults was drug-addicted. This gave rise to the demand for child labour in the newly established industries in China—especially Shanghai and other treaty ports. The miseries of Chinese child workers seemed to be much more than that of the general working children during early industrialization. Fourteen hours were the working time per day, and on all the seven days they were engaged in industries. Children of minor age (five years or more) worked in industries on a very poor wage. The intensity of child labour was reduced in the Mao Zedong's People's Republic of China. But in many corners, it continued for many decades with excessive inhuman exploitation. Child labour was extremely prevalent in rural areas, special economic zones (SEZs), in the Pearl River Delta, and in the Guangdong Province. In 1988, as G. K. Lieten and Hugh Hindman note,[68] child labourers in China

---

[68] G. K. Lieten and Hugh Hindman, 'Child-labour in China: An Overview', in *The World of Child Labour: A Historical and Regional Survey*, ed. Hugh Hindman (New York: M.E. Sharpe, 2009), 860–866.

amounted to over 10 per cent of the total working force (as per the information from the Ministry of Labour, People's Republic of China, in 1988) in country-township and town enterprises. Their numbers, in some industries, were as high as 20 per cent. The one-child policy and compulsory education for up to nine years remarkably reduced the supply of child workers. The one-child norm was strictly followed in urban areas, and there was a relaxation in the rural areas, especially where the first child was a girl. In that case, the two-child norm was followed particularly in the rural areas.

China, at present, has a population of nearly 1.44 billion,[69] and thus, is very conscious of overpopulation. But, simultaneously, to protect its children from hazardous jobs, sex trafficking and abuse, China has also signed many treaties internationally, and passed its domestic legislations.

In 1991, China passed its remarkable legislation on Child labour: the PRC Law on the Protection of Minors, 1991. The law was again revised in 2006. Also in 1991, Regulations Forbidding Child Labour, 1991, and the Law on Labour, 1994, were passed and enforced. These two acts were, in fact, enacted in order to fix the minimum wage age of a child at 16 years. But these regulations had a problem. It did not cover the informal sector, and there were complexities while enforcing the legislation. But these legislations, coupled with compulsory education up to nine years of schooling, the one-child norm, and the laws against child trafficking and selling of children have drastically reduced the number of working children under the age of 16 years in China.

Under the Chinese child labour legislations, the state organs, social bodies, private enterprises and the non-governmental organizations were/are not allowed to employ children, and in cases of exception, the concerned body would be heftily fined by the labour protection authorities. Not only this, the adults workers are also protected from participating in over-strenuous, harmful or dangerous operations.

Many reasons can be cited for the mass employment of child labourers in the Chinese industries. These are as follows. First, several centuries earlier, the impoverished Chinese children were used by rich families and agrarian societies for performing domestic chores and for participating in the agricultural production purposes. Second, Chinese children themselves felt guilty if they did not assist their family-owned

---

[69] Worldometers, 'Population of China,' n.d., https://www.worldometers.info/world-population/china-population/

business enterprises. Cultural values prevailing in China motivated children of poorer families to support their families through their engagement in family enterprises. Third, the various local governments in China perceived that wholesome enforcement of child labour legislation strictly could have a negative effect on business enterprises. They, in contrast, favoured child labour which they thought could be an effective strategy for spurring economic growth in rural China. Fourth, the Chinese views regarding industrial rights were different from those in the West. Parents in China—especially those living in rural areas—were unaware of the provisions of the children-protection laws. Moreover, they themselves did not know about their own rights. Fifth, in China, like in many other countries of the world, poverty forced children into modern slavery and propelled poor people into bonded labour. These people would easily shove their own children towards hazardous and risky jobs. Sixth, rampant corruption led to forced labour and child labour abuses. The officers responsible for the implementation of child labour laws were, very often, the worst abusers. Businessmen and the factory owners had an unholy alliance with the officials for using child labour in business enterprises and industries. Seventh, there was a widespread lack of public perceptions of children's rights. About one-fourth of parents in China—a recent study reveals—were unaware of the protective powers of the child's /children's legislation. Eighth, there had been huge school dropouts among the rural children because of the deplorable state-run school environment. As a result of economic reforms in China huge investment was made in the education sector, particularly to produce a highly skilled labour force. But, as usual, the rural sector was being deprived. Rural schools received minimum financial support from the government. On the other hand, urban schools received large amounts of financial grants/aid from the central government. Naturally, due to poor economic conditions and lack of governmental support, the rural children had to leave schools and join factories and business enterprises as child workers. Ninth, as Liaol Hong writes in one of the 2010 publications on the Chinese education system and child labour, due to the Chinese parent's poor economic conditions, coupled with their low educational level, they could not understand the long-term benefits of education. Yuanyuan Pan[70] also

---

[70] Yuanyuan Pan, *Education in China: A Snapshot* (Paris: OECD Press, 2016), 8–16.

supports this. Tenth, many rural areas exported children, especially girls, to affluent areas located in southern and eastern coastal provinces of China. Eleventh, (as hinted earlier) as a result of China's transition to a socialist market economy, poor peasants living in rural areas lost their land and became destitute. This forced them to depend on other family members to make a living, and by sending their children to factories.

The root cause of child labour in every country is poverty. It is very difficult to eliminate child labour globally unless children are made free from earning for living. Reducing poverty requires a long term strategy from the concerned governments, along with numerous economic measures.

Child labour data are barely available in China. Whatever data is available is found in the newspapers as reports and case studies. However, macro-data on child labour usage in Chinese factories are available since 1991. We present below child labour data from the China Health and Nutrition Survey (CHNS) of 1991, 1993, 1997, 2000, 2004, 2006, 2009 and 2011.

The data exhibited in Table 3.38 show that for a period of 20 years from 1991 to 2011, 10.6 per cent of Chinese children were engaged as child labourers. The data over the period indicates a declining trend of incidents of child labour for both boys and girls. It is revealed, the engagement of children increases with the increase in their age. Children of the age group 16–17 years have the highest overall engagement in the total workforce. The immediate reason is that after the nine-year compulsory education, children become free and can be engaged in the workforce. By 15, children complete their education and fulfil the minimum age (for working) of 15 years. The data show that children were more used in the rural sector than in the urban sector (12.3% and 5.8%, respectively). The educational status of parents was not good. Their number in percentage was very low at the junior or above level (4.7%)—at the junior level (9.3) and at a primary or lower level it was, on an average, 19.7 per cent during 1991–2011. Parents with poor family income and low education had to send their children to workplaces in order to make a living.

We have seen that the child labour problem was and is widely prevalent in China, like in many countries of the world, and it kept on/keeps on increasing with the growth of industries, technological innovation and trade expansion. We are now trying to discuss the possible solutions to the problem, with reference to the Chinese perspective.

Table 3.38 Percentage of Child Labour: Overall and by Individual and Household Characteristics

	1991	1993	1997	2000	2004	2006	2009	2011	All
All	14.1	12.9	9.3	10.9	10.8	10.9	6.8	6.0	10.6
Gender									
Boys	12.9	12.2	8.6	10.7	11.2	11.1	6.8	7.8	10.4
Girls	15.5	13.7	10.0	11.0	10.4	10.5	6.8	3.9	10.8
Age									
6–12	0.1	0.1	0.4	0.8	0.3	0.9	05	0.7	0.4
13–15	9.3	3.5	6.2	6.9	6.7	7.0	4.5	5.1	6.3
16–17	52.2	61.7	44.4	42.4	33.8	32.1	27.6	22.3	41.2
Location									
Urban	8.5	7.5	5.3	4.8	4.7	5.7	5.3	3.0	5.8
Rural	16.0	14.8	10.9	13.1	12.9	12.6	7.3	6.9	12.3
Parents' Highest Education									
Junior high or above	2.8	3.4	3.4	8.7	5.6	6.8	1.6	20.0	4.7
Junior high	9.6	9.7	7.3	9.3	11.1	11.7	7.9	6.9	9.3
Primary or below	21.8	22.6	19.0	19.4	21.3	16.8	11.3	9.9	19.7
Household Income per Capita, Excluding Own income									
Upper third	9.6	8.3	5.3	6.2	5.6	7.5	5.7	3.8	6.7
Middle third	13.6	14.0	9.8	12.1	13.3	12.0	7.4	6.1	11.4
Lower third	19.2	16.4	12.9	14.5	13.5	13.1	7.6	7.9	13.8
Number of observations	2,549	2,540	2,747	2,591	2,169	1,914	1,587	1,527	17,624

Source: Can Tang, Liqiu Zhao, and Zhong Zhao, Child-labour in China (Bonn: I.Z.A. Papers, 2016).

The usage of minors in hazardous jobs is a crime, and the employers engaging children in such enterprises could be severely punished. It is an obligation for the employers and the state to protect child labourers. Here, we may also highlight some of the possible solutions to the problems of child labour faced by the Chinese economy and society. First, in order to come out of the impasse, the causes of the child labour problem need a proper diagnosis. Literature survey and analyses of child labourers clearly reveal that poverty is the root cause of child labour. It is important, therefore, to find out the causes of poverty, and to find out ways to eradicate poverty. Second, the PRC Law on the Protection of Minors (1991, and revised in 2006) needs to be enforced rigorously and strictly. Third, the PRC Law on Compulsory Education (1986 and amended in 2006) needs to be implemented in all the regions with due importance—especially in the so-called 'developing' parts of western China, including the rural areas. Fourth, there should be more aware of children's rights at every corner of Chinese society. The roles of the voluntary organizations, including women's associations, cannot be denied in this respect. The role of media is also very important. Media is a source that can expose the corrupt productive enterprises exploiting the minors of the labour force. Fifth, China has been experiencing a rapid expansion in trade especially after economic reforms since 1978. China's 'open-door' policy really helped in the rapid expansion of industries and is creating ample employment avenues for cheap and unskilled child labour. Can Tang, Liqiu Zhao and Zhong Zhao, as they write in *Child-labour in China* (2016), have found an inverse relationship between tariff rate and child labour. They, with the help of supportive trade data, show that a 1 per cent decrease in tariff rate accentuates a 1.3 per cent increase in the incidence of child labour in China. The effects, they found, are far greater for girls, older children and rural children. Thus, it has been noticed that the larger the children's participation in industries, the greater was the dropout rate of school-age children. What is needed immediately are stricter legislations and their immediate implementation against child labouring. Sixth, the Chinese government had restricted child labour in factories since 1949. Instead of reducing the intensity of it, the practice appears to be on the rise. This needs to be stopped immediately.

Another difficulty, as already mentioned, in assessing the extent of Chinese child labour is the lack of transparency in statistics. Also, there is a lack of monitoring of enterprises. One reason for this might be that privately owned small enterprises use most of the child labour in their enterprises, and they are not under the purview of child labour legislations due to the negligence of Chinese lawmakers in enforcing child labour legislation. Child labour, therefore, is increasing in the informal sector, and it is the migrant labour force that helps to increase the number of child labourers in this sector. Seventh, only a limited number of empirical studies have—so far—been conducted on Chinese child labour. It is of utmost importance on the part of the government and voluntary organizations to conduct research on the issue of child labour in a more comprehensive way, covering a nationally representative sample and incorporating more variables such as mental health, social support, human capital, education, etc., and comparing them with commensurate issues of those children who are not working as child labour.

Chapter 4

Child Labour in Sub-Saharan Africa

4.1. INTRODUCTION

Excepting eight African countries—Algeria, Egypt, Libya, Morocco, Tunisia, Western Sahara, Sudan and Djibouti—form the 'SSA'. It consists of countries located south of the great Sahara desert. The United Nations excludes Mauritania from being identified as a part of 'SSA'. In contrast, the Library of Congress's *Africana Collections*[1] lists as many as 50 countries within the region of 'SSA'. They are Angola, Benin, Botswana, Burkina Faso, Burundi, Cameroon, Cape Verde, Central African Republic, Chand, Comoros, Congo (Brazzaville), Congo (Democratic Republic), Côted' Ivorie, Djibouti, Equatorial Guiana, Eritrea, Ethiopia, Gabon, the Gambia, Ghana, Guiana, Guinea-Bissau, Kenya, Lesotho, Liberia, Madagascar, Malawi, Mali, Mauritania, Mauritius, Mozambique, Namibia, Niger, Nigeria, Reunion, Rwanda, Sao Tome and Principe, Senegal, Seychelles, Sierra Leone, Somalia, South Africa, Sudan, Swaziland, Tanzania, Togo, Uganda, Western Sahara, Zambia and Zimbabwe. The *Royal Society–DFID Africa Capacity Building Initiative*[2] excludes South Sudan and Western Sahara from the list. The US Census Bureau's *2015-American Community Survey*[3] has formed categories such as 'Western Africa', 'Eastern Africa' and 'Africa' to 'define' the outlines of 'SSA'.

---

[1] https://www.loc.gov/rr/amed/guide/afrillguide.html
[2] https://royalsociety.org/grants-schemes-awards/grants/africa-capacity-building/
[3] https://www.census.gov/acs/www/data/data-tables-and-tools/data-profiles/2015/

4.2. SOME STUDIES

Historically, child labour in Africa was found in the agricultural and domestic sectors. Children were very often sold into slavery, and many of them were engaged as servants in order to recover their parents' debts. They were used as child labourers in agriculture, and would often be engaged in the sector of rural crafts to acquire skills and efficiency. In some of earlier writings regarding child labourers in Africa, it has been categorically and repetitively mentioned that the African economy was self-sufficient (i.e., non-surplus' economy) during the pre-colonial era. But, strictly reviewed, it had had never been so.

The tag of 'self-sufficiency' was attached in the sense that every community in Africa was a surplus economy, having complex patterns of production and trading-relation with the neighbours. As Philip Curtin notes[4] the barter economy was in existence, and there was a steady exchange of animal products for cereals. Cereals were also exchanged for salt, cattle, shea butter, kola nuts or dates coming from long distances as trading goods. These might have, together, earned the 'self-sufficiency' tag.

During the successive colonial rules in Africa, children formed an integral part of the African workforce. Along with the adults, they worked in farming, trading, hunting, mining, manufacturing, domestic chores and even participated in militia organizations. Though most of these children were free, some were bought from the markets or transformed into slaves. The children were in high demand in the pre-colonial period and during the initial periods of the colonial rule. They were trafficked, transported and sold in the cash-crop farm of oil palm, cotton, groundnuts and rubber. Adults and children were also used to carry crops to the coasts and to ferry imported goods such as cloth, sugar, flour and farm implements back to the village market in the remote interior areas. Trafficked girls were in higher demand because they not only worked on land but they were also potential 'wives'. With the growth of commercial agriculture, the pawning system increased. In Ghana and Nigeria, for example, the unmarried younger daughters or nieces were pawned for cash in order to buy land and other property.

---

[4] Philip Curtin, *The Abolition of the Atlantic Slave Trade: Origins and Effects in Europe, Africa, and the Americas* (Madison: University of Wisconsin Press, 1981).

The impoverished African boys worked in the towns, cities and mines. Many of such working boys migrated, with their parents, to towns, while some of them migrated to cities. There were numerous children who were directly born in the town. According to Beverly Grier,[5] a number of boys also migrated to cash-crop farm areas without the permission of their guardians. In towns and cities, boys worked in mining at a large number, and some of them worked for Europeans and rich Africans as domestic servants and shop assistants. A sizeable number of these children found work in the growing African cities as hawkers. They also worked as assistants to traders, craftsmen and other entrepreneurs. A few of them lived on streets, whom we, these days, call 'street children'. These minors lived their lives by any means, that is, through legal and illegal means such as theft, gambling and commercial sex.

In the eastern and southern parts of SSA, where the Europeans settled permanently, child labour was an integral part of the economy. The oldest colony in Africa was founded by the Dutch in 1652 at Cape Town. The slaves were imported there from West Africa, and the children of the slave women were also treated as slaves. They were used as child labourers in agriculture, wine-making, herding, domestic service and factories. They worked here as bonded labourers, and could not move from their workplace at their will. Slavery was abolished in A.D. 1800 when the British captured Cape Colony. The English imperialists, instead, introduced the system of apprenticeship. Under this system, the children of parents who signed contracts for them, or the orphaned or abandoned children were made bonded labourers and made to serve the White farmers until they attained the age of 18–20 years.

The discovery of diamond and gold in the last quarter of the 19th century gave rise to the demand for child labour in the African regions enormously. The quick expansion of the urbanization of South Africa, along with the rapid extension of factories, opened wide scopes for employment for both African adults and children. Growing poverty in the rural areas and increasing landlessness among the peasants due to landlords' malevolent policies on tenancy farms forced many children—boys and girls—to migrate to the African towns. Children were also in demand in other colonies of Eastern and Southern Africa. They

---

[5] Beverly Grier, 'Child-labour and Africanist Scholarship: A Critical Overview,' *African Studies Review* 47, no. 2 (September 2004): 1–25.

were recruited in Zimbabwe and Namibia in large numbers after 1890. Kenya, Zimbabwe and Malawi recruited boys en masse, but they were prohibited from hazardous jobs and night duties. They were allowed to sign labour contracts, and penalties were imposed in the case of violations of the contract. In many colonies, there were provisions of schooling for working children. Governments collaborated with the mission schools to teach the African adolescents different industrial skills free of cost. The boys grew food crops for the school residents, and the surplus crops were forwarded for sale in the towns. Boys also learned carpentry, and girls did needlework. Girls also did cleaning work and cooked for the staff. However, many of the mission schools were more interested in making a profit out of the labour offered by the students rather than educating them. Sometimes students would protest against such attitudes of the school authorities by boycotting classes and refusing to do manual work. Children admitted to the farm schools had to work to attend classes free of cost. However, their labour brought meagre wages for them. During the full agricultural seasons, the schools remained closed and students had to work for the whole day on land.

Beverly Grier writes[6] that child labour during colonial Africa was in high demand; because children possessed some good qualities which the adults did not have. They were cheap and easier to handle. They could also handle certain crops such as tea, tobacco and cotton with their nimble fingers. That is why the colonial government facilitated child labour through tax and through ill-defined labour laws.

Children working in Africa could be categorized into two subdivisions. The first one is of children working in commercial agriculture (constituting about 10% of the total number of working children). They were involved in the cultivation of cocoa, coffee, tea, tobacco, sugar cane, rubber, sisal, vanilla and flowers. The usage of chemicals in plantations regularly caused health hazards. Children living in the plantation areas with their parents frequently fell ill. Schools for working children were also built nearer to the plantations, and they had to work in the plantations before and after school hours. Their usage at the plantations was on the rise because large numbers of adults were being affected by HIV/AIDS. The affected adults would be quickly replaced by these children. We shall discuss this part in detail after some time. The second group was comprised of children working with their families.

---

[6] Grier, 'Child-labour and Africanist Scholarship: A Critical Overview.'

They were very often attacked by poisonous insects, reptiles and wild animals. They had to work on hard soil, use archaic tools and had to travel long distances. Migrated children worked hard at towns, and usually worked as street vendors, shoe-shiners or assisted small trades. Children working in large industries were barely found in Africa. Working children of the urban areas were/are of two types: the child servants and the children in small trades. Children, especially girls working as maids, had to depend on the mercy of their masters. They had little connection with the outside world other than with the family where they worked, and naturally, their plight could not be monitored. The second category, the majority of whom were boys, worked in small trades and offered services principally in mobile businesses. Many children joined apprenticeships in crafts and small business enterprises. Under this system, there were provisions for part-time schooling for children from where they could take basic education. According to M. Bonnet and B. Schlemmer,[7] these educational facilities for the African children acted as stepping stones to jobs, and also helped to act as a process of specialization.

HIV/AIDS has been a severe problem in different African countries since the 1980s, especially in the impoverished Sub-Saharan region. Even in 2020, 35 million Africans are suffering from HIV/AIDS.[8] The deadly AIDS has led to increased African mortality and morbidity, and it has deeply impacted the adults' lives and the economy of SSA. This disease has also influenced child labourers. The death of one or both of the parents makes children orphans, and their normal sociocultural growth is stunted. The opportunities for schooling, nutrition and healthcare facilities all—immediately—go beyond their reach. As Bill Rau writes,[9] instead of receiving the aforesaid benefits, they are forced to join work to feed themselves and their family members. Sometimes the children are sent to extended families for proper care. When that does not happen due to certain causes, the oldest child of the family becomes the principal bread-earner.

---

[7] M. Bonnet and B. Schlemmer, 'Insights on Child-labour,' *Developing Worlds* 37 (2009): 11–25.

[8] Wikipedia, 'H.I.V./A.I.D.S. in Africa,' 19 October 2020, https://en.wikipedia.org/wiki/HIV/AIDS_in_Africa

[9] Bill Rau, *HIV/AIDS and Child-labour in Sub-Saharan Africa: A Synthesis Report* (Abuja: IPESL, 2003).

In SSA, children are usually the worst sufferers in every society due to sociocultural norms, poverty, and the negative impacts of HIV/AIDS and many other diseases. They are found to join work from an early age. Orphanhood due to HIV/AIDS brings social ostracism for these helpless children. They perennially suffer from ill health and malnutrition. They may also face high risks of HIV/AIDS infection and almost regularly lose different opportunities for education.

An ILO/IPEC-commissioned study conducted throughout AD 2002 in four countries in SSA (South Africa, Tanzania, Zambia and Zimbabwe) immediately revealed complex relationships arising from the impact of HIV/AIDS on African child labourers: the impacts include illness, death of bread-earners and the chances of infection. Data related to the HIV/AIDS prevalence and children orphaned by the HIV/AIDS is shown in Table 4.1.

Data represented in Table 4.1 shows that the highest prevalence of HIV/AIDS infection among adults (33.7%) is found in Zimbabwe, and it is the lowest (7.8%) in Tanzania. The projected increase in percentage shows the alarming prevalence of HIV/AIDS in South Africa (106%) and Zimbabwe (45.8%). Zambia was at the second-highest position in terms of prevalence in 2002 (21.5% and the projected percentage was 34.4%), followed by Tanzania (20.1% and the projected percentage was 33.7%).

Table 4.1 HIV/AIDS Prevalence and Children Orphaned by HIV/AIDS

Country	National Adult HIV/AIDS Prevalence, 2002 (%)	Estimated Number of Children Orphaned by HIV/AIDS, 2001	Projected Number of Children Orphaned by HIV/AIDS, 2005	Projected Prevalence Increase, 2001–2005 (%)
South Africa	20.1	662,000	1,328,000	100.6
Tanzania	7.8	815,000	1,090,000	33.7
Zambia	21.5	572,000	769,000	34.4
Zimbabwe	33.7	782,000	114,000	45.8

Source: UNAIDS, Epidemiological fact sheets for individual countries, 2002 (e.g., consult https://data.unaids.org/publications/fact-sheets01/djibouti_en.pdf and https://data.unaids.org/publications/fact-sheets01/dominicanrepublic_en.pdf?preview=true).

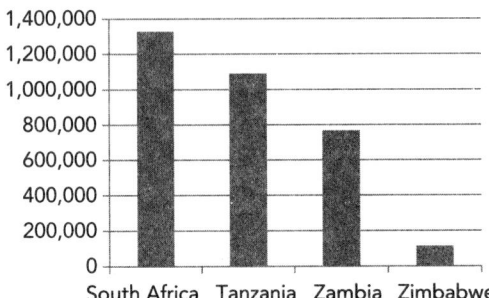

Projected Number of Children Orphaned by HIV/AIDS, 2005

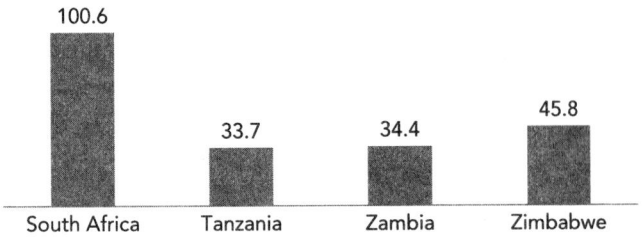

Projected Prevalence Increase, 2001–05 (%)

The HIV/AIDS pandemic in SSA has created socio-economic inequalities and mass poverty. This has directly affected women and children. Children, in particular, have been forced to join in the workforce, sometimes in the worst forms. Most of these children work in the informal sector of the economy, where the wage rate is low and the job is insecure with no other benefits as are usually found in cases of formal sector employment.

The ILO/IPEC conducted qualitative rapid assessments (RAs) and intensively studied the impact of the HIV/AIDS pandemic on working children's education. The concerned officials assessed and examined enrolment, rates of school completion, and other educational data for primary school students for a number of African countries—with reference to the situations in the 1990s. The studies together found an inverse correlation between HIV/AIDS prevalence and school enrolment. The studies together showed that once the admitted students moved upwards from one class to another, they would not, normally, leave the studies. It was also found that among the four African countries—South Africa, Tanzania, Zambia and Zimbabwe—school

Table 4.2 *Educational Status of Select African Countries' Children in Rapid Assessments*

Country	National Net Primary School Enrolment Rates (UNESCO Data)	Children Involved in RAs		
		Currently in School (%)	Once Attended, But No Longer Attended School (%)	Never Attended School (%)
South Africa	88.9	60.0	NA	NA
Tanzania, United Republic of	46.7	37.7	37.7	23.6
Zambia	65.5	25.8	58.2	16.0
Zimbabwe	79.6	72.2	27.8	NA

Source: UNESCO, 2003. Refer to UNESCO-officer, Mr T. R. Pant's *Education for All: 2000–15*, https://www.unesco.org/new/fileadmin/MULTIMEDIA/FIELD/Kathmandu/pdf/GMRLaunch_TRP.pdf

attendance among working children remained relatively high throughout the study period in South Africa and Zimbabwe; two to three times higher than in Tanzania and Zambia. The related data are shown in Table 4.2.

During the stated survey, it was reported that there was a large number of dropouts among the children of families where one or more members were HIV/AIDS-infected than the case in the non-HIV-infected families. The data presented in Table 4.3 shows that there was consistently lower school attendance among the orphaned children in Zambia. There were also evidence for the existence of child-headed households in SSA due to HIV/AIDS deaths, as was revealed by the study of the RA team and this further gave rise to the practice of child labouring.

Children's chance of attending school decreases with the death of parents due to HIV/AIDS or other reasons. Also, the orphans attending schools usually spend lesser time in school than when their parents/parent were/was alive. A child who has become an orphan is less likely to attend school and more likely to become a child labourer. However, a child who has lost either of her/his parents is more likely to attend schools than the complete orphans.

Table 4.3 Effect of Orphanhood on School Attendance, Zambia

Age (Years)	All Children	Orphan Children
Up to 6	19.8	13.1
6–7	37.2	27.3
7–8	58.0	47.0
8–9	72.2	62.1
9–10	76.9	67.2
10–11	79.8	70.5
11–12	81.4	72.4
12–13	77.1	67.3
13–14	70.6	59.8

Source: L. Guarcello and F.C. Rosati, 'Orphans and Child labour,' Presentation at the I.L.O./I.P.E.C.-Workshop on H.I.V. /A.I.D.S. and Child Labour, Lusaka, May 2003. Refer to Brigitte Nshimyimana, 'Perception of Support Provided to Orphan Children in Foster-care-placement in an Urban Setting of Windhoek in Namibia,' Linkoeping, 2008.

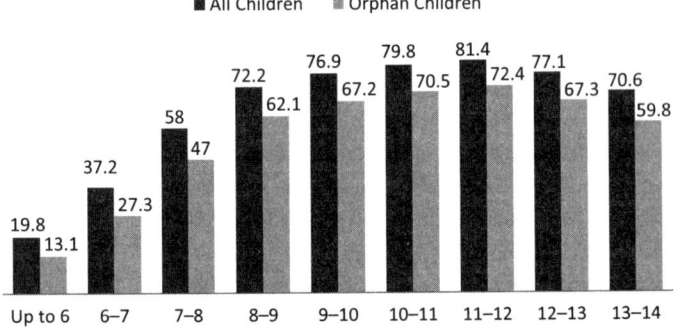

In a 2009 study, the socio-economist Guarello finds that in the Gambia, a complete orphan's school attendance has been reduced by 21 per cent, while in Burundi it is 14 per cent, and it is 10 per cent in Angola, Côte d'Ivoire and Kenya. This study also shows that being a double orphan increases the risk of underage-work involvement in five sub-Saharan countries, while in other five countries the effect is less significant. Another important aspect detailed in the study is that orphanhood makes children inactive: They do not study and do not work. Not only that, they are no longer interested in doing any household work anymore. However, the study reveals the necessity of further research to find the link between African children's orphanhood and their inactivity.

According to an ILO estimation of 1996, one-third of African children in the age group of 10–14 years were part of the then active labour force, and boys were more in number than girls. Another survey—the National Child Labour Survey (NCLS) conducted by the reputed Ghanaian Statistical Service, 2001—indicated that about 10.9 per cent of children in Ghana (0.57 million) aged 5–14 years participated in the labour force and did not attend schools. After segregating the data available for boys and girls, it was found that the non-school-going percentages for boys and girls were 11.2 and 10.5, respectively. These findings are available over the Internet, and in essays digitally archived in the JSTOR.

Table 4.4 presents the children's activity and study sex-wise and area-wise (rural–urban).

Children aged 5–14 years involved in household activities are shown in Table 4.5.

Data presented in Table 4.5 shows that about 88.3 per cent children were involved in household activities, among which the representation of girl children was more than boys (90.9% and 88.9%, respectively).

The characteristics and conditions of child labour in Ghana are exhibited in Tables 4.6 and 4.7.

The data presented in Table 4.6 show that the agriculture sector is the highest service provider to the working children in all the age groups (i.e., 76.3%, 68.6% and 71%, respectively, among the 5–9, 10–14 and 5–14 years age groups), followed by the general service sector (18.3%, 24.6% and 22.6%, respectively) and the least service provider being the industry (5.4%, 6.8% and 6.4%, respectively).

Data showing the sex-wise distribution of working children aged 5–14 years reveal that agriculture is the highest service provider among working children in all categories, that is, 81.5, 59.5 and 71.0 per cent, respectively, followed by the service sector (13.6%, 32.5% and 22.6%). The lowest service provider among the working children was the industry.

Working children's educational status in Ghana (2001) has been presented in Table 4.8.

Data represented in Table 4.8 show that economically active children are less likely to attend school than children who are not economically active. School attendance among non-economically active children is the highest, that is. 91.7 per cent in the age group of 10–14 years, and lowest in the age group of 5–9 years, that is, 82.7 per cent,

Table 4.4 Children Aged 5–14, by Sex, Type of Activity and Residence

Sex	Activity	Urban %	Urban No.	Rural %	Rural No.	Total %	Total No.
Male	Work only a	1.8	16,830	16.0	287,082	11.2	303,912
	Study only b	87.4	811,738	53.2	953,140	64.9	1,764,878
	Work and Study c	6.8	62,912	21.5	384,149	16.4	447,061
	Total work*	8.6	79,742	37.5	671,231	27.6	750,973
	Total study**	94.2	874,650	74.7	1,337,289	81.4	2,211,939
	Neither	4.0	36,850	9.3	166,116	7.5	202,966
Female	Work only a	4.0	38,741	14.6	224,560	10.5	263,301
	Study only b	81.4	782,913	53.9	829,069	64.4	1,611,982
	Work and Study c	9.5	91,811	19.6	302,267	15.8	394,078
	Total work*	13.6	130,552	34.2	526,827	26.03	657,379
	Total study**	90.9	874,724	73.5	1,131,336	80.2	2,006,060
	Neither	5.1	48,888	11.9	183,180	9.3	232,068
Total	Work only a	2.9	55,571	15.4	511,642	10.9	567,213
	Study only b	84.3	1,594,651	53.5	1,782,209	67.7	3,376,860
	Work and Study c	8.2	154,723	20.6	686,416	16.1	841,139
	Total work*	11.1	210,294	36.0	1,198,058	27.0	1,408,352
	Total study**	92.5	1,749,374	74.1	2,468,625	80.8	4,217,999
	Neither	4.5	85,738	10.5	349,296	8.3	435,054

Source: National Child Labour Survey (NCLS), Ghana Statistical Service, 2001, https://www2.statsghana.gov.gh/nada/index.php/catalog/10
Notes: *Total work' refers to children that work only and children that work and study, that is, atc.
**Total study refers to children that study only and children that work and study, that is, btc.

Table 4.5 Percentage of Children Involved in Household Chores, by Age and Sex

Age	Male	Female	Total
5	61.9	69.8	65.6
6	74.9	81.7	78.4
7	80.0	90.4	84.9
8	88.7	90.6	84.9
9	88.9	95.7	92.1
10	90.4	95.9	93.0
11	93.2	95.3	94.2
12	93.8	96.6	95.1
13	93.7	96.4	95.0
14	95.6	96.7	96.2
Total	86.0	90.9	88.3

Source: National Child Labour Survey (NCLS), Ghana Statistical Service, 2001, https://www2.statsghana.gov.gh/nada/index.php/catalog/10
Note: Children performing household chores for at least one hour per day

Table 4.6 Distribution of Working Children Aged 5–14 by Industry and Age Group

Age Group	Industry (% of Working Children)		
	Service	Industry	Agriculture
5–9	18.3	5.4	76.3
10–14	24.6	6.8	68.6
5–14	22.6	6.4	71.0

Source: National Child Labour Survey (NCLS), Ghana Statistical Service, 2001, https://www2.statsghana.gov.gh/nada/index.php/catalog/10

172 | Child Labour: Global Challenges, Issues and Policy

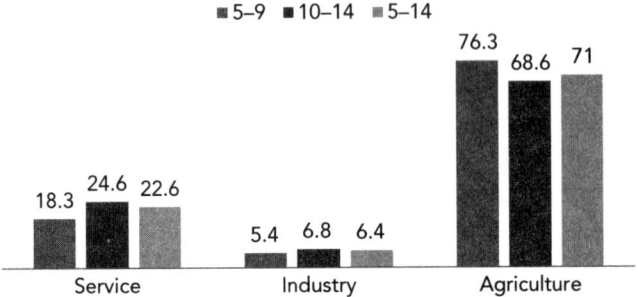

Table 4.7 *Distribution of Working Children Aged 5–14 Years by Industry and Sex*

Industry	Sex		
	Male	Female	Total
Service	13.6	32.5	22.6
Industry	4.9	8.0	6.4
Agriculture	81.5	59.5	71.0

Source: National Child Labour Survey (NCLS), Ghana Statistical Service, 2001, https://www2.statsghana.gov.gh/nada/index.php/catalog/10

Table 4.8 *Child Labour and Children's Education*

Age Group	Economically Active(% of Children Attending School)	Not Economically Active (% of Children AttendingSchool)
5–9	52.7	82.7
10–14	63.2	91.7
5–14	59.7	86.5

Source: National Child Labour Survey (N.C.L.S.), Ghana Statistical Service, 2001, https://www2.statsghana.gov.gh/nada/index.php/catalog/10

Economically active children attending school is the highest, 63.2 per cent, in the age group of 10–14 years.

Children's activity status whether they are working or attending a school is shown in Table 4.9. Children from impoverished families are more likely to be engaged in the working force. Many of them sacrifice schooling and join work for the family—normally not observed among the children of higher-income groups.

Table 4.9 Percentage of Children Aged 5–14, by the Capita Income Quintiles, Sex and Type of Activities

Sex	Type of Activity	Quintile 1	Quintile 2	Quintile 3	Quintile 4	Quintile 5	Total
	Work only	20.3	15.0	9.3	7.9	2.2	11.3
	Study only	55.2	60.6	64.6	68.3	82.1	65.7
Male	Work and Study	17.5	17.1	18.8	17.5	11.8	16.6
	Neither	11.5	7.5	7.6	6.5	3.7	7.6
	Working	17.8	14.1	9.0	8.0	4.3	10.6
	Studying	54.5	59.5	64.2	68.4	77.3	64.9
Female	Work and study	16.5	13.9	18.9	17.1	12.8	15.9
	Neither	14.9	12.5	7.7	6.5	5.5	9.3
	Working	19.2	14.6	9.2	8.0	3.3	11.0
	Studying	54.9	60.1	64.4	68.3	79.7	65.3
Total	Work and Study	17.0	15.6	18.9	17.3	12.3	16.3
	Neither	13.1	9.8	7.6	6.5	4.6	8.4

Source: National Child Labour Survey (NCLS), Ghana Statistical Service, 2001, https://www2.statsghana.gov.gh/nada/index.php/catalog/10

Notes: Totals may not add to 100.0 due to rounding.
The household expenditure is used as a proxy for income.
'Quintile1' represents lowest expenditure category and 'quitile5' the highest.

We shall presently discuss the issue of the existence of a number of child labourers and their plights due to their association with tobacco cultivation and tobacco industries in SSA. Children involved in this sector usually do not want to work in this difficult field. In fact, throughout the tobacco-cultivation world, children are engaged in work. This industry leaves severe and several immediate and long-term impacts upon children and society. Previously, the United States of America took the lead in global tobacco production. This continued up to the 1960s. Presently, the scenario has been changed, and the entire global market is dominated by China, Brazil and India. In 2020, 125 countries around the world produce tobacco, including Argentina, Guatemala, Indonesia, Italy, Kenya, Pakistan, Poland, Thailand, Turkey, Zimbabwe, Malawi, South Africa and Tanzania.

4.3. ZIMBABWE

Zimbabwe has made several efforts to eliminate the worst forms of child labour. Apart from the tobacco industry there are some other sectors where children perform the worst forms of child labour. These sectors include commercial sexual exploitation, mining, harvesting of sugarcane, etc. Table 4.10 shows data on children's work and several indicators of education.

Based on the information available from ILO (Article 3(d) of ILO—C.182 and Article 3(a)-(c) of ILO—C.182) Table 4.11 represents data related to the children's work by sector and activity in Zimbabwe.

Table 4.10 *Statistics on Children's Work and Education*

Education	Age (Range)	Per Cent (%)
Working (%)	5–14	40.4
Attending school (%)	5–14	90.7
Combining work and school (%)	7–14	42.0
Primary competition rate (%)		98.5

Source for primary competition rate: Data from 2013, published by the UNESCO, Institute for Statistics, 2020. Refer to https://data.unicef.org
Source for other data: ILO's Analysis of Statistics from the UNICEF, *Multiple Indicator Cluster Survey* 6 (M.I.C.S. 6), 2018. Refer to https://data.unicef.org

Certain factors such as deteriorating economic conditions, cholera outbreaks, drought and food shortages make children more vulnerable to child labour. Children living in the border areas are forcibly trafficked to South Africa, Mozambique and Zambia, and they become

Table 4.11 Overview of Children's Work by Sector and Activity

Sector/ Industry	Activity
Agriculture	Farming, including the production of tea, cotton, tobacco, corn and sugarcane
	Fishing, including casting nets, hauling fish loads and sorting fish
	Work in forestry, such as dragging logs from felling sites and loading logs for transport
	Cattle herding
Industry	Mining and panning of gold and chrome, using dangerous chemicals such as cyanide and mercury, and extracting material from underground passages and quarries[a]
Services	Street work, including vending, begging
	Domestic work
Categorical worst forms of labour[b]	Use in illicit activities, including selling drugs
	Commercial sexual exploitation, sometimes as a result of human trafficking
	Forced labour in agriculture, and mining for the production of gold and chrome and domestic work, each sometimes as a result of human trafficking

Source: For details, one could download from JSTOR archives or refer to ILO's data given on https://www.ilo.org/ipec/Regionsandcountries/Africa/WCMS_618949/lang--en/index.htm; 'Cigarette-Consumption and the Leading Tobacco-producing Countries,' *Countries Today*, 16 December 2018, https://www.countriestoday.com/leading-tobacco-producing-countries/#:~:text=%20Cigarette%20Consumption%20and%20Leading%20Tobacco%20Producing%20Countries,tobacco%20produced%20in%20the%20country%20is...%20More%20

Notes: [a] Determined by national law or regulation as hazardous and, as such, relevant Article 3(d) of ILO—C.182.
[b] Child labour understood as the worst forms of child labour per se under Article 3(a)-(c) of ILO—C.182.

victims of commercial sexual exploitation and other work assignments—especially forced work in domestic chores. Sometimes orphans are sent to large African cities with hopes that they would be given education or would be adopted. But, there too, they are often forced to work in domestic chores, while some of the boys are sent to work in the sectors of mining or drug smuggling. The girls are forced to act as commercial sex workers.

Zimbabwe has been trying hard to reduce all forms of child labour and, for this purpose, has ratified almost all the key international conventions on child labour. This is shown in Table 4.12.

The Zimbabwean government has passed several laws and regulations with utmost sincerity related to child labour. In spite of this, there remain several gaps in legal framework for protecting the interest of working children. It desperately needs to protect the working children from worst forms of work and to shift them to free public school for education.

Laws and regulations established in Zimbabwe towards these protective activities have been presented in Table 4.13.

The Zimbabwean government has, with great efforts, established mechanisms to enforce child labour laws, and as said, there exist several gaps within the enforcing authority which regularly hinder the enforcement of these laws. The Ministry of Public Service, Labour, and Social Welfare (MPSLSW), Government of Zimbabwe, tries to enforce labour and anti-human trafficking laws and investigates labour-related complaints, including complaints involving child labour. The Zimbabwe

Table 4.12 *Ratification of International Conventions on Child Labour*

Convention	Ratification
ILO C.138, Minimum age	√
ILO C.182, Worst forms of child labour	√
UN CRC	√
UN CRC Optional protocol on armed conflict	√
UN CRC Optional protocol on the sale of children, child prostitution and child pornography	√
Palermo protocol on trafficking in person	√

Source: Data available from the online-uploaded-proceedings of different ILO conventions.

Table 4.13 *Zimbabwean Laws and Regulations on Child Labour*

Standard	Meets in International Standard	Age	Legislation
Minimum age for work	Yes	16	Section 9 of the Labour Relations Amendment Act; Section 10A(1) of the Children's Act (39, 40, 41)
Minimum age for hazardous work	Yes	18	Section 9 of the Labour Relations Amendment and 10A(4) the Children's Act (39, 41)
Identification of hazardous occupations or activities prohibited for children	Yes		Section 3(1) of Labour Relations (Employment of Children and Young Persons) Regulations and Sections 2 and 10A(4) of the Children's Act (41, 42)
Prohibition of forced labour	Yes		Section 54–55 of the constitutions; Section 6 of the Labour Relations Amendment Act (39, 43)
Prohibition of child trafficking	Yes		Section 3 of the Trafficking in Persons Act (44)
Prohibition of commercial sexual exploitation of children	No		Sections 61, 83, 86, and 87 of the Criminal Law Act; Section 8(2)a of the children's act; Section 3 of the Trafficking in Persons Act (41, 44, 45)
Prohibition of using children in illicit activities	Yes		Section 156 of the Criminal Law Act; Section 10 of the Children's Act (41, 45)
Minimum age for voluntary state military recruitment	Yes	16	Sections 5, 9, and 10 of the National Service Act (46)
Provision of compulsory recruitment of children by (State) military	Yes		Section 9 of the National Service Act (46)

(Table 4.13 Continued)

(Table 4.13 Continued)

Standard	Meets in International Standard	Age	Legislation
Prohibition of military recruitment by non-state armed groups	No		
Compulsory education age	No	12[a]	Section 5 of the Education Act (47)
Free public education	No		

Source: U.S. Department of Labour, Bureau of Industrial Labour Affairs; Child Labour and Forced Labour Reports, Zimbabwe. Please refer to 'International Child-labour and Forced-labour Reports,' https://www.dol.gov/agencies/ilab/resources/reports/child-labor
Note: [a] = Age calculated is based on available information (48).

Republic Police (ZRP) is responsible for enforcing laws relating to the worst forms of child labour with the help of MPSLWS and the Ministry of Justice, Legal and Parliamentary Affairs. The Ministry of Justice, Legal and Parliamentary Affairs supervises all court activities and addresses the cases of human trafficking and child victimization through victim-friendly courts.

The Government of Zimbabwe has sorted out mechanisms to coordinate its efforts to address child labour issues. To this end, the National Steering Committee has undertaken to address the worst forms of child labour and provide education (primary and secondary levels) to working children. Ministry-level committees, such as the Child Protection Committees (CPCs), operate at the village-, ward-, district-, provincial- and national-levels to discuss issues affecting working children. The Zimbabwean Anti-Trafficking Inter-Ministerial Committee (ATIMC) takes actions to combat women and children trafficking. The National Task Force on Street Children (NTFSC) adopts strategies to feed street children at drop-in centres, reunite them with their families, and arrange counselling sessions for them. The Zimbabwean CPCs, comprising ministers, civil society, local volunteers and teachers, seriously review and discuss issues affecting children including child labour. The key policies which have had been lately adopted by the Government of Zimbabwe are National Action Plan to Combat Child Labour, Trafficking in Persons, National Plan of Action (NAPLAC, 2009–2011) and the Zimbabwean and UN Development Assistance Framework (ZUNDAF, 2016–2020). The Zimbabwean government has adopted various social programmes such as the Harmonized Social Cash Transfer (HSCT, 2012–2019), the Basic Education Assistance Module, the Mobile Birth Registration Programme, the National Action Plan for Orphans and Vulnerable Children (2016–2020) and the Donor-Funded Programmes such as projects funded by the DREAMS, the PEPFAR, the US-AID and the Department for International Development (DFID) to address child labour issues.

4.4. MALAWI

Malawi is another important tobacco-growing economy of SSA, which primarily depends on agriculture. It has some of the most fertile areas of the southern part of Africa. Agriculture contributes about 40 per cent of the gross national product (GNP), of which 10 per cent comes from tobacco (as per the data available from the Malawian Centre for Tobacco Control Research and Education in 2006). Tobacco cultivation largely depends on efforts by the Malawian child labourers. A study conducted in three tobacco-growing districts of Malawi in 2011 (available in the ECLT Baseline Study Report, 2011) reports that children's contribution in the total labour force in tobacco production accounted for 55 per cent in 2011. Also, the UNICEF's population statistics, 2009–2010, reveals that 53 per cent of Malawi's children were below the age of 18 years, among whom 13 per cent were orphans who worked in agriculture and the allied sector.

Malawian children working in tobacco farms are always highly prized and are usually engaged by people who are not their relatives. They are forced to work for their survival and are mercilessly exploited by the farm owners who give them meagre wages. They experience the worst forms of child labour. Some children, however, willingly join work in the tobacco farms in order to support their families. Another form of child labour found in tobacco farms in Malawi involves the children in the small-scale tobacco-growing families voluntarily helping their parents because their parents cannot bear the cost of hired labour.

Even in 2020, Malawi is one of the poorest countries in the world in terms of human development indicators and average incomes.[10] Infant mortality rate is very high and the literacy rate is very low. As per a report,[11] when one compares the Gini coefficients of Malawi to other neighbouring countries, one could observe that there exists a wide gap between the rich and poor in Malawi but the tobacco farms and tobacco contribute the Malawian economy in various ways. Tobacco companies are determined to address the child labour and tobacco growers' issues by improving the working conditions of children and contracted tobacco farms; providing training and acting as guarantors for loans from banks for farmers; supporting the communities to improve their living conditions; raising awareness among children on sociocultural aspects; and creating a regulatory environment.

Malawi is famous for tobacco production, and it has its own long and relevant history. In ancient times, an elite group of farmers, owned and leased large parts of lands, controlled the early markets of tobacco and sold the products directly to the industrial buyers through an official auction. The small growers, on the other hand, had to face restrictions while selling tobacco in the open market. The only option before them was to sell tobacco to government agencies. Small-time landholders having farm sizes of 0.4–2 hectares were primarily family labours themselves, along with their women and children, and employed hired labourers, if finances permitted. In course of time, the successful small cultivators purchased land and improved their status to that of estate-owners. But, while doing so they were subjected to further regulations. Till now, the tenancy system exists in the Malawian tobacco production; but there exists no standard agreement between the local authorities, the farm-owners and the workers, and in most cases the agreements are oral.

---

[10] Refer to data available on https://www.atlasandboots.com/poorest-countries-in-the-world-ranked/#:~:text=Poorest%20countries%20in%20the%20world%20%20%20,%20%201%2C604%20%2099%20more%20rows%20#:~:text=Poorest%20countries%20in%20the%20world%20%20%20,%20%201%2C604%20%2099%20more%20rows%20

[11] L. Eldring, S. Nakanyane, and M. Tshoaedi, *IUF/ITGA/BAT Conference on the Elimination of Child-labour at Nairobi on 8–9 October 2000*, 2000, https://www.fafo.no/index.php/en/publications/fafo-notes/item/child-labour-in-the-tobacco-growing-sector-in-africa

The Malawian small-time tobacco-growers produce tobacco under a certain quota system, usually up to 10,000 kilograms per season. They can form cooperatives and for this, a levy could be paid. As S. Jaffe estimates, at the beginning of the 21st century, about 315,000 to 330,000 small-growers produced and sold tobacco through some 23,000 cooperatives.[12] Malawian tobacco farming is both profitable and highly remunerative, but poverty in this sector is widespread—especially among women and children who are the vulnerable labour force. Children are found working with their parents at various tobacco estates. Tenant farmers play a dominant role in the production of tobacco. Tenant farmers are recruited from the villages with their wives and children to the tobacco growing areas, and they are leased with plots of land, usually of two-acre sizes, to cultivate tobacco. Sufficient food, plants, fertilizers and other inputs are given to them, and payment is made at the end of the season when harvested tobacco is sold back to the estate owners. However, many of the Malawian tobacco estate-owners charge excessive input prices from the tenant farmers and fix a very low purchasing price of grown tobacco. Tobacco cultivation, thus, does not remain profitable for the tenant farmers, and they are not able to overcome poverty.

Child labour in the sector of Malawian tobacco farming is usually prohibited. However, due to poverty, tenant farmers use their wives and children for working at the farms. There are usually no formal contracts signed between the tenant farmers and the owners, and due to their ignorance and illiteracy, these tenants are deprived and are burdened with debts, especially after the season's harvest is over. In this way, they forever remain in the poverty trap. However, they do not have alternative livelihood sources, and, consequently, very few workers, including children and women, abandon this sector. Children participate in tobacco production activities with their parents; they spread pesticides and do other hazardous works. A large number of working children cannot go to school. Only impoverished children below five years are usually sent to schools in Malawi. The student enrolment was remarkably low before the introduction of free primary education for children in Malawi in 1994. It was half of the total number of Malawian children. As per a 2006 survey by the ILO which was done at different Malawian tobacco

---

[12] S. Jaffe, *Malawi's Tobacco Sector: Standing on One Strong Leg Is Better than on None* (Washington, DC: World Bank), 2003. http://www.worldbank.org/afr/wps/wp55.pdf

plantations, the school enrolment rate went up high, and the dropout rate lowered in the regions after the introduction of free primary education. Interestingly, gender disparity is never the major source of concern in impoverished Malawi. Boys, nevertheless, are a little bit higher in number than girls in terms of their involvement in work. Table 4.14 depicts child labour estimates made by Malawian National Child Labour Survey, 2015.

Child labour in the age group of 14–17 is very high in Malawi, and their involvement in different types of works including hazardous work is about 30 per cent. Data collected by Malawi National Child Labour Survey (MNCLS) 2015 state that child labour among adolescent

Table 4.14 *Child Labour Estimates Based on National Legislation*

	Children Aged 5–13 Years in Child Labour		Children Aged 14–17 Years in Child Labour		Total Child Labour Children Aged 15–17 years	
	%	Number	%	Number	%	Number
Male	42.1	883,155	30.7	211,575	39.3	1,094,730
Female	40.2	834,139	26.5	189,762	36.7	1,023,900
Urban	33.6	195,600	21.6	47,975	30.3	243,575
Rural	42.4	1,521,693	29.9	353,362	39.3	1,875,055
North	40.1	218,335	15.4	28,979	33.8	247,314
Centre	36.0	638,716	25.8	148,938	33.5	787,654
South	46.5	860,242	35.0	223,420	43.0	1,083,662
Total	41.2	1,717,294	28.6	401,337	38.0	2,118,630

Source: Calculations based on: The *Malawi National Child Labour Survey* (MNCLS), 2015. Refer to *Understanding Child-labour and Youth-employment in Malawi* (New York: UNICEF Publications, 2018), 1–64, https://ucw-project.org/attachment/01102018412Malawi_child_labour_youth_employment.pdf

Notes: Child labour for this age group consists of hazardous work. Working children are considered to be in hazardous work if they are found to be in any one of the following categories: children working in designated hazardous industries (mining, quarrying and construction); children working in designated hazardous occupations (they refer to the list of hazardous work established by the national legislation); children working long hours (40 hours or more per week); children working under other hazardous conditions such as night work, using hazardous tools and being in an unhealthy work environment.

children is also high in hazardous work (about 42%). Children's (aged 14–17 years) involvement in work (sex-wise and residence-wise) has been presented in Table 4.15.

Adolescent children involved in different forms of work mostly experience hazardous working conditions. The Malawian National Child Labour Survey, 2015, shows that over 85 per cent of children work in agriculture in Malawi, and 10 per cent of them are found employed in the domestic services. Many of the working adolescent children are routinely exposed to extreme weather and also to flames or fumes.

According to the MNCLS 2015, most of working children have to sacrifice their schooling. The MNCLS has subdivided the interaction

Table 4.15 *Children Aged 14–17 Years in Child Labour*

	Percentage				
	Sex		Residence		
Age	Male	Female	Urban	Rural	Total
14 years	25.3	27.9	26.9	26.6	26.7
15 years	29.1	25.4	14.8	29.3	27.2
16 years	35.1	25.2	27.4	30.9	30.2
17 years	35.4	28	18.2	34.9	31.7
Total 14–17 years	30.7	26.5	21.6	29.9	28.6

	Number				
	Sex		Residence		
Age	Male	Female	Urban	Rural	Total
14 years	45,363	54,662	13,043	86,981	100,024
15 years	62,828	58,054	9,484	111,398	120,882
16 years	58,374	40,797	16,448	82,723	99,171
17 years	45,010	36,249	9,000	72,259	81,259
Total 14–17 years	211,575	189,762	47,975	353,362	401,337

Source: The *Malawi National Child Labour Survey* (MNCLS), 2015. Refer to *Understanding Child-labour and Youth-employment in Malawi*, 1–64.
Note: Child labour constitutes (a) children working over 40 hours per week, (b) children working during the evening and night and (c) and children exposed hazardous forms of work irrespective of working hours.

between children's employment and schooling into four non-overlapping activity categories, that is, children in the child labour category only, children in school only, children combining school and work, and children in neither.

Data presented in Table 4.16 show that 52 per cent of the children attend schools, 38 per cent combine schooling and work, only 3 per cent are exclusively in child labour, and the remaining 7 per cent are neither in school nor in work. The data also reveal that rural children are more in disadvantageous conditions in terms of attending school or in shouldering the responsibility of the family.

Table 4.17 shows that only 27 per cent of Malawian adolescents in the age group of 14–17 years go to school, 14 per cent work, while the majority of them combine both activities (study + work), and they represent 54 per cent. It is also revealed that 9 per cent of such children do not study, and also do not go to work.

The Government of Malawi has taken a number of legal steps regarding child labour and the schooling of impoverished children. The ILO Convention Number 182 was ratified. This targets the worst form of child labour. Also, the ILO Convention Number 138 relating to minimum age, the provisions of the UN Convention on Rights of the Child, and the international legal standards on child labour were also ratified. The Malawian government banned the involvement of children in armed conflict, sale of children, child prostitution, child pornography, forced labour and trafficking of children. The Constitution of Malawi, in 2002, was amended to protect children from economic exploitation, and from any kind of ill-treatment that might harm their mental and physical health, and social development.

The existing legal framework related to child labour in Malawi can be listed as follows: (a) The Trafficking in Persons Act, 2015, (b) The Employment (Prohibition of Hazardous work for children) Order, 2012, (c) The Amendment to Malawian Penal Code related tom Protection of Children's Rights, 2011, (d) The Child Care, and the Protection of Justice Act, 2010, and (e) Constitution of Malawi, 2002 version.

The Government of Malawi has undertaken various measures, such as providing basic awareness, social mobilization and campaigning, to address the grave issue of child labour. To attain these, the Malawian government, within the framework of the National Education Sector Plan, 2008–2017, and the National Girls' Education Strategy, 2014, has increased the scope of children's education, health and nutrition.

Table 4.16 Activity Status of Children Aged 5–13 Years by Sex and Residence

Characteristics		Percentage						
		Activity						
		Only in Employment (a)	In School Exclusively (b)	In Employment and School (c)	Neither in Employment nor in School (d)	Total in Employment (a) & (c)	Total in School (b) & (c)	Total out of School (a) & (d)
Sex	Male	3.2	50.5	38.9	7.4	42.1	89.4	10.6
	Female	3.1	53.4	37.1	6.4	40.2	90.5	9.5
Residence	Urban	2.2	61.7	31.4	4.7	33.6	93.1	6.9
	Rural	3.4	50.3	39.1	7.2	42.4	89.4	10.6
Total		**3.2**	**51.9**	**38.0**	**6.9**	**41.2**	**89.9**	**10.1**
Sex	Male	67,950	1,008,889	815,204	155,092	883,155	1,874,093	233,043
	Female	65,300	1,106,602	768,839	132,295	834,139	1,875,441	197,595
Residence	Urban	12,793	359,588	182,808	27,387	195,600	542,395	40,180
	Rural	120,457	1,805,903	1,401,236	260,000	1,521,693	3,207,139	380,458
Total		133,250	2,165,490	1,584,044	287,387	1,717,294	3,749,534	420,637

Source: The Malawi National Child Labour Survey (MNCLS), 2015. Refer to Understanding Child-labour and Youth-employment in Malawi, 1–64.

Table 4.17 Activity Status of Adolescent Aged 14–17 Years by Sex and Residence

Characteristics		Percentage						
		Activity						
		Only in Employment (a)	In School Exclusively (b)	In Employment and School (c)	Neither in Employment Nor in School (d)	Total in Employment (a) LC	Total in School (b) KK	Total Out of School
Sex	Male	14.3	24.3	58.0	3.5	72.2	82.3	17.7
	Female	14.3	29.0	50.6	6.2	64.9	79.6	20.4
Residence	Urban	13.3	39.8	37.5	9.5	50.8	77.3	20.7
	Rural	14.4	24.2	57.4	4.0	71.8	81.6	18.4
Total		**14.3**	**26.7**	**54.2**	**4.8**	**68.5**	**80.9**	**19.1**
Sex	Male	98,136	167,450	399,192	23,755	497.328	566,642	121,891
	Female	101,998	207,214	361,959	44,129	463,958	569,173	146,127
Residence	Urban	29,436	88,200	83,188	21,004	112,624	171,389	50,441
	Rural	170,699	286,464	677,963	46,880	848,662	964,427	217,578
Total		**200,135**	**374,664**	**761,152**	**67,884**	**961,286**	**1,135,816**	**268,019**

Source: The Malawi National Child Labour Survey (MNCLS), 2015. Refer to Understanding Child-labour and Youth-employment in Malawi, 1–64.

4.5. TANZANIA

Like Malawi, Tanzania is also among the poor countries in the world, with a sizable number of its population living in abject poverty. Since its independence in 1963, Tanzania has been desperately trying to improve the economic plights of its child labourers through several welfare measures. Numerous opportunities have been created to enhance education, and measures have been adopted to protect the rights of children. The majority of people are Africans, Asians, Europeans and Arab minorities.

About three-fourths of Tanzania's population depends on agriculture, and majority of them are small landholders. Children—both boys and girls—work on their family farmland. The Government of Tanzania ratified the ILO Convention Number 138 concerning the minimum working age, in 1998, and the ILO Convention Number 182, one concerning the worst forms of child labour, in 2001. Tanzanian children, as a result, are strictly prohibited from working in hazardous jobs. Along with these children, the impoverished Tanzanian women are largely engaged in agriculture.

As the anthropologist Karen A. Porter estimates in one of her 2009 studies—in Tanzania, the intensity of child labour is much more in rural areas than in urban areas—one in three in rural areas and one in ten in urban areas work as the child labourer.[13] Apart from traditional agriculture, child labourers en masse are found working in commercial agriculture such as tea, coffee, sisal, sugar, cotton, tobacco and flower plantations. The wage of each child labourer is half of that of an adult. The remaining children in Tanzania routinely engage in domestic work, sex work, trafficking and mining.

The Government of Tanzania, in 2017, published regulations and identified hazardous work in children and prohibited children from doing work in the fishery industry. Children are also engaged in hazardous work of mining, quarrying, domestic work and agriculture. Table 4.18 depicts statistics on children's work and education.

Data exhibited in Table 4.18 show that children's involvement in work is more than 29 per cent and their school attendance is 74 per cent. It is a matter of satisfaction that the primary education completion rate is above 72 per cent.

---

[13] Quoted in Hugh Hindman, *The World of Child-labour: A Historical and Regional Survey* (New York: M.E. Sharpe, 2009), 277.

Table 4.18 Statistics on Children's Work and Education

Children	Age (Years)	%
Working (% and population)	5 to 14	29.3 (3,573, 467)
Attending school (%)	5 to 14	74.3
Combining work and school (%)	7 to 14	24.6
Primary completion rate (%)	7 to 14	72.4

Source for primary completion rate: Data from 2013. Published by the UNESCO Institute for Statistics, 218 (7).
Source for all other data: Tanzania National Child Labour Survey (NCLS), 2014 (5).
Note: Please refer to https://uis.unesco.org/en/country/tz for statistical-details.

Table 4.19 Working Children by Sector, Aged 5–14 Years

Sector	%
Service	4.9
Industry	1.0
Agriculture	94.1
Total	100.0

Source: Tanzania National Child Labour Survey, 2011. Refer to the ILO report regarding the same on https://www.ilo.org/ipec/Informationresources/WCMS_IPEC_PUB_28475/lang--en/index.htm

Sector-wise engagement of working children has been shown in Table 4.19.

An estimate of child labourers in Tanzania by Understanding Children's Work (UCW), UNICEF 2017, gives us a clear understanding of the situation of child labour in post-modern Tanzania. This estimate is based on the data available from the Tanzanian National Legislation and global measurement standards. It gives sex-wise and residence-wise segregation of child labour. The data have been reproduced in Table 4.20.

Data portrayed in Table 4.20 show wide variation of child labour by sex, residence and region. It has been noticed that the difference is very small in the age group of 5–11 years, and the involvement of boys are slightly higher than girls. In the age group of 5–13 years the

Table 4.20 Child Labour Estimates Based on National Legislation and Global Measurement Standard

Categories	Children Aged 5–11 in Child Labour (in Employment)		Children Aged 12–13 in Child Labour (in Employment and Not in Light Work)		Children Aged 5–13 in Child Labour		Children Aged 14–17 in Child Labour		Total Child Labour 5–17 Years	
	%	Number	%	Number	%	Number	%	Number	%	Number
Male	22.6	1,008,074	37.6	458,884	25.8	1,466,958	39.8	745,380	29.3	2,212,338
Female	21.5	922,164	34.1	374,984	24.1	1,297,148	41.6	721,433	28.4	2,018,581
Urban	9.4	250,948	17.7	127,750	11.1	378,698	23.1	294,932	14.4	673,630
Rural	27.7	1,679,290	44.2	706,118	31.1	2,385,408	50.4	1,171,881	35.6	3,557,289
Total	22.1	1,930,238	36.0	833,868	25.0	2,764,106	40.7	1,466,813	28.8	4,230,919

Source: UCW calculations based on Tanzania Integrated Labour & Force Survey (ILFS), 2014, of child labour. Refer to https://ghdx.healthdata.org/record/tanzania-integrated-labour-force-survey-2014

involvement of boys is 3 per cent larger than that of the girls', and in the age group of 14–17 years, girls' involvement is 2 per cent larger than the boys'. Child labour also varies widely across regions.

Child labour data in Tanzania based on the 2000–2001, 2006 and 2014 rounds of the Tanzania Integrated Labour Force Survey show that it increases with age, and it is more in the rural areas than the urban areas. The surveys also show that Tanzania has performed far better in reducing child labour than other SSA countries whose per capita income is higher than Tanzania. In this context, Tanzania is a better performer than countries like Cameroon, Chad, Congo, Côte d' Ivoire and Nigeria vis-à-vis their efforts to reduce child labour. Nevertheless, there are some other countries like the Democratic Republic of Congo, Ethiopia and Rwanda who are also performing well in this field, as the survey says.

The data presented in Table 4.21 show a wide variation of child labour by age and region.

Table 4.21 *Involvement in Child Labour, Age Group of 5–13 Years, by Age, Sex and Residence*

	(a) Percentage				
	Sex		Residence		
Age	Male	Female	Urban	Rural	Total
5–11	22.6	21.5	9.4	27.7	22.1
12–13	37.6	34.1	17.7	44.2	36
Total 5–13	25.8	24.1	11.1	31.1	25
	(b) Number				
	Sex		Residence		
Age	Male	Female	Urban	Rural	Total
5–11	1,008,074	922,164	250,948	1,679,290	1,930,238
12–13	458,884	374,984	127,750	706,118	833,868
Total 5–13	1,466,958	1,297,148	378,698	2,385,408	2,764,106

Source: UCW calculations based on Tanzania Integrated Labour & Force Survey (ILFS), 2014, of child labour. Refer to https://ghdx.healthdata.org/record/tanzania-integrated-labour-force-survey-2014

In Tanzania, adolescents aged 14–17 years regularly get involved in hazardous works, including going to sea, mining, quarrying, transferring heavy loads, working at manufacturing industries, producing chemicals, working in factories, working in hotels, bars, working at night, and doing hard work for long hours. Data presented in Table 4.22 show that the female involvement in such works is two per cent more than that of males', and rural adolescents' involvement in work is more than double that of the urban adolescents' (50% and 23%, respectively). In terms of number, the rural adolescents outnumber the urban working adolescents by 877,000 (1,172,000 to 295,000).

Children's activity status (work and school), expressed sex-wise and residence-wise, shows that 56 per cent of them attend school

Table 4.22 Children in Child Labour, Age Group of 14–17 Years

	(a) Percentage				
	Sex		Residence		
Age	Male	Female	Urban	Rural	Total
14	32.2	35.1	14.8	43.2	33.6
15	37.4	44.1	24.1	51.4	40.6
16	46.6	45.5	28.3	54.5	46.1
17	47.0	44.3	28.5	56.1	45.7
Total: 14–17	39.8	41.6	23.1	50.4	40.7
	(b) Number				
	Sex		Residence		
Age	Male	Female	Urban	Rural	Total
14	191,976	191,958	57,183	326,751	383,934
15	178,234	199,029	88,151	289,113	377,263
16	211,676	200,480	81,082	331,074	412,156
17	163,494	129,966	68,516	224,944	293,460
Total: 14–17	745,380	721,433	294,932	1,171,881	1,466,813

Source: UCW calculations based on Tanzania Integrated Labour & Force Survey (ILFS), 2014, of child labour. Refer to https://ghdx.healthdata.org/record/tanzania-integrated-labour-force-survey-2014
Note: Child labour constitutes (a) children working over 40 hours per week, (b) children working during the evening or night and (c) children exposed to hazardous forms of work irrespective of working hours.

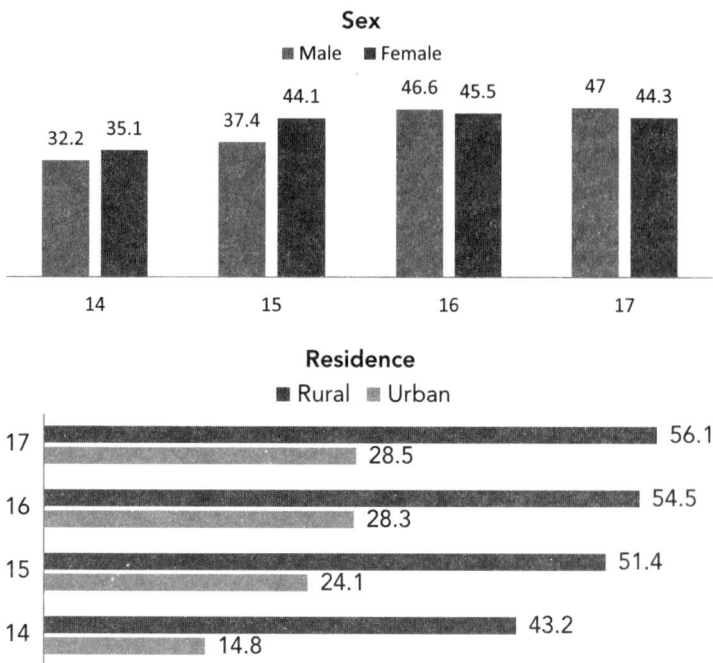

only, 20 per cent combine employment and school, 7 per cent are exclusively in employment, and the remaining 17 per cent are doing nothing. This is described in Table 4.23.

There are differences in two different age groups of children, aged 5–13 years and 14–17 years, in terms of study and work. The younger age group has more involvement in school and less in work, and the reverse is true in case of children aged 14–17 years as shown in Table 4.24.

The UNESCO defines children who have not completed four years of school education as 'children falling in the group of education poverty', and those who have not completed two years of schooling as 'children falling in the group of extreme education poverty'. The Tanzanian ILFS, 2015, as shown in Table 4.25, finds that among the out-of-school children in the age group of 10–17 years, 38 per cent suffer 'education poverty' and 28 per cent suffer from 'extreme education poverty'. This is very alarming, and it has exerted a long-term effect on the Tanzanian economy and society.

Table 4.23 Children's Activity Status, 5–13 Years Range, by Sex and Residence

		Activity (a) Percentage						
Characteristics		Only in Employment (a)	In School Exclusive (b)	In Employment and School (c)	Neither Employment Nor in School (d)	Total in Employment (a) & (c)	Total in School (b) and (c)	Total Out of School (a) & (d)
Sex	Male	7.9	54.8	19.8	17.5	27.6	74.6	25.4
	Female	6.6	56.4	19.7	17.4	26.3	76.1	23.9
Residence	Urban	2.3	80	9.9	7.8	12.2	89.9	10.1
	Rural	9.4	44.8	24.1	21.7	33.5	68.9	31.1
Total		7.2	55.6	19.7	17.4	27.0	75.3	24.7
(b) Number (in thousand)								
Sex	Male	448	3,114	1,122	996	1,570	4,236	1,444
	Female	353	3,033	1,061	934	1,414	4,094	1,287
Residence	Urban	77	2,716	337	266	414	3,053	344
	Rural	723	3,431	1,846	1,663	2,569	5,276	2,387
Total		801	6,147	2,183	1,930	2,984	8,330	2,730

Source: UCW calculations based on Tanzania Integrated Labour & Force Survey (ILFS), 2014, of child labour. Refer to https://ghdx.healthdata.org/record/tanzania-integrated-labour-force-survey-2014

Table 4.24 Adolescents' Activity Status, 14 Years, by Sex and Residence

Characteristics		Only in Employment (a)	In School Exclusively (b)	In Employment and School (c)	Neither in Employment Nor in School (d)	Total in Employment (a) & (c)	Total in School (b) and (c)	Total Out of School (a) & (d)
(a) Percentage								
Sex	Male	39	32.5	19.3	9.3	58.3	51.7	48.3
	Female	34.7	31.4	22.5	11.4	57.2	53.9	46.1
Residence	Urban	21.4	54	11	13.6	32.4	65	35
	Rural	45.5	19.9	26.2	8.4	71.7	46.1	53.9
Total		37	32	20.8	10.3	57.8	52.8	47.2
(b) Number (in thousands)								
Sex	Male	731	608	361	173	1,092	970	905
	Female	602	545	389	197	991	934	798
Residence	Urban	273	690	141	174	414	831	448
	Rural	1,059	463	610	196	1,669	1,072	1,703
Total		1,332	1,153	751	370	2,083	1,903	2,151

Source: UCW calculations based on Tanzania Integrated Labour & Force Survey (ILFS), 2014, of child labour. Refer to https://ghdx.healthdata.org/record/tanzania-integrated-labour-force-survey-2014

Table 4.25 *Out-of-School Children Aged 10–17 Years with Less Than 2 and 4 Years of Education*

Age	Extreme Education Poverty (Out-of-school Children) with Less than 2 Years of Completed Education		Education Poverty (Out-of-school Children with Less than 4 Years of Completed Education		Total Out-of-school Children
	Number	% of Total of Out-of–school Children	Number	% of Total of Out-of–school Children	
10	137,903	72.9	185,593	98.2	189,039
11	111,785	74.8	133,189	89.2	149,360
12	105,157	55.8	134,502	71.4	188,420
13	73,423	33.8	111,371	51.2	217,376
14	86,539	21.6	114,579	28.6	400,308
15	57,523	13.8	97,398	23.3	418,327
16	74,838	15.6	104,494	21.8	479,480
17	39,045	9.7	51,830	12.8	404,544
Total	686,212	28.1	932,954	38.1	2,446,854

Source: UCW calculations based on Tanzania Integrated Labour and Force Survey (ILFS), 2014, of child labour. Refer to https://ghdx.healthdata.org/record/tanzania-integrated-labour-force-survey-2014

Huge numbers of child labourers are found involved in the production of cocoa of which chocolate is a product. This product grows mostly in the tropical climates of SSA (broadly, in the Western African region), Asia and Latin America. Ghana, which we have already assessed, and Ivory Coast supply about two-thirds of the world's total supply of cocoa.

Cocoa is sold to multinational food manufacturing companies such as Hershey, Mars, and Nestle. These industries have links to hazardous works, child trafficking and slavery. As in Ghana and Ivory Coast, several other states of Western Africa produce cocoa with the help of child labour. A September 2017 UNICEF report, titled *Child labour and the Youth: Decent-work deficit in Tanzania* (prepared on behalf of the UCW), states that due to low income, impoverished Tanzanian children are regularly sent to farmers producing cocoa. Many of such children are even sold off to chocolate companies. Child labourers working in the production of cocoa earn less than $2 a day, which, on an international assessment scale, is an income very much below the poverty line. Very often, young children are abducted from the villages of the neighbouring African nations. Most of them are taken away from the two poorest African countries—Burkina Faso and Mali—and are engaged in cocoa cultivation. They are so unfortunate that they cannot meet with their parents and near and dear ones for years. Children begin their work in the cocoa fields early in the morning, and they continue until the evening, doing some 10 hours of work each day.

The usage of knives by the Tanzanian children to cut bean-pods violates international labour laws and the provisions of the *United Nations Convention on Eliminating the Worst-forms of Child-labour*. Eradication of child labour in this part of the world is indeed a very difficult and daunting task because the roots lie in poverty.

4.6. IVORY COAST

Ivory Coast-based cocoa farms are mostly small, having less than 10 acres of land. Different UNESCO studies have focused on the fact that about 60 per cent of the country's rural population have no electricity connection, and the literacy rate is far below 50 per cent. Due to their miserable income, the Ivory Coast parents cannot afford the cost of education for their children and send them to work at farms. Trafficking of children occurs and children with traffickers regularly come to Ivory Coast impersonating cocoa farmworkers. On the other hand, the exploitation of the Ivory Coast child labourers continues unabated. A 15-year-old boy, for example, is paid less than $1 a day.

The eradication of child labour in the cocoa industry would be a long endeavour on part of the international communities and will continue as long as the farmers are paid a fraction of the cost of sustainable production. Even if fair trade is brought in successfully, it cannot provide a permanent solution. A solution towards the end of child labour could be possible only if higher prices for cocoa is charged determinately by the child labourers, and the farmers unitedly and spontaneously come together to form farmer cooperatives. These can help, to some extent, alleviating the root cause of child labouring: the poverty.

The Ivory Coast children of cocoa farmers routinely experience exploitation, violence and lack of legal identity. The Government of Ivory Coast has taken a number of steps to improve children's health and well-being, including raising the minimum age for working from 14 to 16 years, adopting and implementing the 2012–2014 and 2015–2017 National Development Plans to combat the Worst Forms of Child Labour, funding National Child Protection Programmes, enforcing the law regarding compulsory education for children aged 6–16 years, imposing stringent law against the trafficking of children, the promulgation of decrees prohibiting hazardous work for a child under 18 years of age, and so on. These have been mentioned in Jessica Davis Pluess.[14]

Ivory Coast took a stride in eliminating the Worst Forms of Child-labour in 2019 through the initiation of 143 prosecutions. The law-enforcing authorities were instructed to fine, arrest and prosecute the perpetrators of child labour and traffickers. Despite this, children in Ivory Coast have to work under extremely hazardous conditions. Combining work and study, and their numbers were 21.8 per cent according to a survey conducted in 2016. Table 4.26 provides some key indicators on child labour in Ivory Coast.

Table 4.26 *Statistics on Children's Work and Education*

Children	Age Group	%
Working (%)	5–14	25.6
Attending school	5–14	70.1
Combining work and school	5–14	21.8
Primary completion rate		71.6

Source for primary completion rate: Data from 2017, published by UNESCO Institute for Statistics, 2020.
Source for all other data: International Labour Organization's analysis of statistics from Multiple Indicator Cluster Surveys, 2016.
Note: Refer to the statistical data given in 'Child-Labour and Force-Labour Reports of Ivory Coast,' The U.S. Bureau of International Labour Affairs, Washington, DC, https://www.dol.gov/agencies/ilab/resources/reports/child-labor/cote-divoire

---

[14] Jessica Davis Pluess, *Children's Rights in the Cocoa-Growing Communities of Ivory Coast: Synthesis Report* (New York: UNICEF Press, 2018), 1–39, https://www.unicef.org/csr/css/synthesis-report-children-rights-cocoa-communities-en.pdf

Children in Ivory Coast are engaged in varied forms of work including hazardous works. All such works, performed by them, are listed below in Table 4.27 in order to provide readers a chance to assess the situation.

The World Association for Children and Parents (WACAP) programme in Ivory Coast was started with the financial support of the Department of Labour, Government of the United States of America, to contribute to the prevention and elimination of the Worst Forms of Child labour in commercial agriculture in Cameroon, Ivory Coast, Ghana, Guiana and Nigeria. In Ivory Coast, two pilot initiatives—one of which is funded by the US Ministry of Labour and US Bureau of Statistics, along with the WACAP—have been extensively planned to monitor working children in 24 villages. The second one, by the Ivory Coast Prime Minister's Office, along with the WACAP, is using child labour monitoring tools and training manuals. The objective of

Table 4.27 *Ivory Coast Children's Work by Sector and Activity*

Sector	Activity
Agriculture	Mining + including crushing and transporting stones, blasting rocks, digging, working underground, sieving, and extracting gold with mercury or cyanide
	Manufacturing, including repairing automobiles
	Construction + activities unknown
	Domestic work
	Working in transportation and carrying goods
	Street vending and commerce
	Work in restaurants
Industry	Mining + including crushing and transporting stones blasting rocks, digging, working underground, sieving and extracting gold with mercury or cyanide
	Manufacturing, including repairing automobiles
	Construction + activities unknown
Services	Domestic work
	Working in transportation and carrying goods+
	Street vending and commerce
	Work in restaurants

Sector	Activity
Categorical worst forms of child labour + +	Forced labour in mining, carpentry, construction, domestic work, street vending, restaurants and agriculture, including the production of cocoa, coffee, pineapple, cotton and rubber, each sometimes as a result of human trafficking
	Commercial sexual exploitation, sometimes as a result of human trafficking
	Use in illicit activities, including drug trafficking
	Forced begging as talibes by Koranic teachers, sometimes as a result of human trafficking

Source: Refer to the statistical data given in 'Child-Labour and Force-Labour Reports of Ivory Coast,' The U.S. Bureau of International Labour Affairs, Washington, DC, https://www.dol.gov/agencies/ilab/resources/reports/child-labor/cote-divoire

Note: + Determined by a national law or regulation as hazardous and, as such, relevant to Article 3(d) of ILC.182.
+ Child labour is understood as the worst forms of labour.
+ Child labour per se under Article 3(a)-(c) of ILC 182.

such child monitoring is to identify the child labourers involved in hazardous works in cocoa farms/plantations and draw them away to provide educational opportunities. The National Agency for Support to Rural Development (ANADER) was commissioned in order to develop a mechanism for a child labour monitoring system. It noticed that there was little scope for children's education and training. The ANADER initially faced resistance while sensitizing people. It sought/ seeks to involve local people by instigating them to reconsider their own cultural and local traditional habits and end child labour. Training modules have been prepared to guide the trainers involved in the monitoring process. The modules have several steps such as an interview guide, information on how to set up index cards of child labour, documentation of the activities of their employers, and questionnaires adapted in the context of Ivory Coast. Twenty-four monitoring units have already been set up in the central villages. Data collected by the monitors are also used in sensitizing activities and to identify projects for funding. Ivory Coast—village committees headed by chiefs and members from the groups of employers, workers organizations and local governments are responsible for monitoring child labour. The *sous-prefecture*-units coordinate data, compile those collected from the villages and implement training and sensitization programmes at the village level. Different development-level committees supervise training programmes and sensitizing activities and make corrections of data thus collected. The National-level Child Labour Unit formed by the Ministry of Labour and Employment, Government of Ivory Coast, coordinates the overall labour-monitoring process.

4.7. GHANA

Like Ivory Coast's, the economy of Ghana largely depends on cocoa production and trade. Ghana became independent in 1957, and at that time it was rich in mineral resources. There prevailed a well-functioning government and a good educational system. This was possible due to the growth of cocoa production and the development of a prosperous cocoa industry.

Presently, the economy of Ghana is rural and is largely dependent on cocoa, timber and pineapples and all these are export crops. Another important source of foreign-exchange earnings is gold. Cocoa trees were first planted by the Dutch missionaries in the coastal areas of Ghana sometime in 1815, but the overall cultivation expanded after 1879. It was, for many years, Ghana's principal source for foreign exchange. The exports fell sharply, especially since 1970s when the world prices of agricultural crops fell abnormally. This left the Ghanaian farmers to grapple with tremendous hardships and poverty. Moreover, Ghana experienced a severe drought in 1982, and it slowed down the production of cocoa for several years leading to a sharp decline in exports.

Another shock for the Ghanaian farmers came in 1984 when a sudden bushfire destroyed a huge area of cocoa farms. Considering its economic importance, the Ghanaian government took a number of steps to revive the cocoa cultivation. The Ghana Cocoa Board (COCOBOD) was set up to encourage production, internal marketing and export of cocoa along with coffee and peanuts. The buying monopoly exercised by the COCOBOD was, however, lifted in the mid-1990s', but still it determines the producer price of cocoa, along with other fees and rates. The world market price of cocoa always fluctuates, and this depends on demand-and-supply conditions. In order to protect the interest of cocoa-growers (and their underage labourers), the Ghanaian government guarantees a minimum price. The much-reputed Cocoa Research

Institute of Ghana (CRIG) conducts high-level research on pests and diseases, soil fertility and agricultural practices. The Ghanaian government has undertaken myriad measures to increase cocoa production and its marketability, and the 2020 results are quite encouraging.

Child labour has been a major issue of concern to the Ghanaian government for quite some time. To end child labour, the Government has ratified the ILO's Convention Number 182, and passed several laws strengthening the rights of children and protecting them from exploitation. Poverty is the root cause of child labour in Ghana, and one needs to recognize the importance of legislation and access to education in ending child labour in the African nation. Several surveys have identified that child labour contributes to the economic welfare of the Ghanaian household, and hence, has been perpetuated.

Many of the Ghanaian cocoa farmers usually hire specialized workers to apply pesticides. Without skills, the spraying machines cannot be used. Only adult persons with such skills can operate the machines. But, in Ghana, hiring of labour involves very high costs, and the prices often are beyond the reach of the farmers. Due to this, farmers try to limit costs by engaging 'home labourers', especially the women, children, relatives and friends. The concerned Ghanaian children attend school, and they normally work on land after school, and during holidays and on the weekends.

Ghana's fishing industry is very promising and provides huge employment to adults and children. Children trafficking is a common phenomenon and trafficked children are mostly engaged in the fishing industry as bonded labourers. Children working in this industry start working as soon as from the age of four years. Children paddle boats, haul nets, perform domestic works in the hours of fishermen. Their working hours are longer and the wage is meagre. They cannot go to school. They are ill-treated everywhere: malnourished, abused and experience water-borne diseases. The Food and Agriculture Organization (FAO) and the ILO have pointed out that 60 per cent of the world's child workers are involved in agricultural activities, livestock raising, forestry, fishing and allied works. About 10 per cent of children work in agriculture and 2 per cent in fishing and altogether 12 per cent children are being denied education and they cannot stay with their parents at home. The Government of Ghana has announced free and compulsory education. The agricultural families cannot provide school uniforms and books to their children due to very low family income. Many NGOs, as mentioned, have constantly been working to rescue the trafficked and bonded child workers and engage them in school. In this way, thousands of children have been enslaved. Tables 4.28 and 4.29 attest to this condition.

Table 4.28 Children's Work and Education in Ghana

Children	Age	%
Working (% and population)	5–14	13.0 (927,591)
Attending school (%)	5–14	89.9
Combining work & school	7–14	13.2
Primary completion rate (%)	–	93.8

Sources: 1. UNESCO Institute for Statistics, 2020
2. ILO's Living Standard Survey, 2016–2017
Note: Refer to The 2019 Findings on the Worst Forms of Child-labour, https://www.justice.gov/eoir/page/file/1323771/download

Table 4.29 Children's Work (Sector-wise)

Sector	%
Agriculture	79.2
Industry	5.0
Services	15.8

Sources: 1. UNESCO Institute for Statistics, 2020
2. ILO's Living Standard Survey, 2016–2017
Note: Refer to the 2019 Findings on the Worst Forms of Child-labour, https://www.justice.gov/eoir/page/file/1323771/download

Chapter 5

Child Labour in Asia

5.1. INTRODUCTION

Some of the Asian nations employing child workers are Bangladesh, Cambodia, India, Indonesia, the Maldives, Nepal, Pakistan, Sri Lanka and Thailand. All these countries have been trying hard and have already made advancements to eliminate child labour through the enforcement of legislation. Not all countries have progressed equally. Some countries have successfully lowered the level of child labour, but still, many more reforms need to be done to eliminate it. The child labour force participation rate is the highest in Africa and Asia, which, combinedly, becomes more than 60 per cent of the total working children in the world. The nature, magnitude and decline of child labour vary distinctly across different Asian nations. East Asia represents the lowest number of cases of child numbers, while it is very high in South Asia and some parts in Southeast Asia.

Child labourers in the Asian nations are involved in different kinds of work, including hazardous works in factories, agriculture and allied activities. The sectors of employment are factories laying, manufacturing or processing bricks, beedi, footwear, garments, glass, leather, matches, poultry, salt, shrimp, soap, steel furniture, textiles, alcoholic beverages, fish, meat, rubber, sugarcane, timber, tobacco, brassware, carpets, cotton, fireworks, gems, leather goods, locks, silk fabrics, silk thread, soccer balls, garments, rice, stones, gold, oil, tin, glass bangles and surgical instruments. Child labourers also suffer from sex trafficking, acting in pornography, etc. It might be recapitulated that as per the ILO the Worst forms of Child-labour are child prostitution, factory work, bonded labour, children in armed forces, construction, industry, brick kilns, tea plantation and manufacturing industry. All these forms are unscrupulously perpetrated in the case of child labour in Asia.

The ILO, the UNICEF, the World Bank, and many NGOs have initiated different programmes for fighting against child labour in Asia. UCW has been constantly working with utmost sincerity for ending child labour.

According to Bhavin Patel,[1] many reasons can be cited for the prevalence of child labour in Asian countries. First, poverty is one of the prime contributing factors for the perpetuation of child labour. Children join work in order to add up to their family income. This especially happens to families which have an unpredictable income base, that is, an income that does not guarantee an amount necessary for a family for its minimal survival and for supporting minimum requirements such as education and health. Second, the children in the poorer families of Asian nations are vulnerable and passive, which contribute to the existence of child labour in the labour market. Employers prefer child labourers because children can be easily handled, and they do not generally complain while doing demeaning and exploitative work. Children are unaware of the rights and privileges they are entitled to get for the work they do. Moreover, Asian children are more capable of doing certain types of work than adult, and thus they are preferred over adults in some works such as carpet making, textile and gem cutting industries. Third, many of the Asian nations lack adequate schooling facilities for children, which may be another important reason for the problem of child labour. There is a direct relationship between education and child labour. More and more number of children in school consequently lessens the number of children at work. It is education that can restrict the flow of child workers into the workforce. Thus, educational opportunities to the least-privileged, along with provisions for mid-day meals (better meal) can help children to attend school, and this can, to some extent, restrict the involvement of children with work. However, a sizeable number of children are always bound to resort to work than to attend school for earning money to meet their family expenses. Fourth, there is a belief in many Asian nations that it is a virtue to send children to work. Parents believe that children

---

[1] Bavin Patel, 'Effects of Child Labour on the Family in Asian Countries,' *Tulsa Journal of Comparative and International Law* 7, no. 2 (1999): 481–511.

should work with them for the family. This will not only benefit the family economically but it can also provide some skills to the children involved in work. Fifth, in many Asian nations, it is believed that allowing and engaging children to participate in the working force before they attain mature working age could be a virtue because it can work as a socializing device. It helps them to acquire skills, adds income to the family and earns respect from the other family members. The earning children feel they are performing vital work for the family. The income that they earn as 'child labour' can save the family from hunger and poverty, at least temporarily.

As Ranjan Ray writes,[2] when someone minutely examines various data of child labour in Asian countries, there seems to be a wide variation in children's participation in various labour markets, which is contrary to the context in SSA.

In Pakistan, for example, children are involved in making soccer balls and working in the hand-woven carpet industry, and they spend eight to ten hours per day against meagre wages. In many Asian countries, children are engaged to work as bonded workers to repay their parents' incurred loans. In India, children work under stress and strain in brickfields, construction works, tea stalls and restaurants, tobacco production, carpet industry, beedi making, collecting rags and other waste materials from dirty places. In Thailand, children work in the canned food industry under hazardous conditions. In Vietnam, girls are recruited in making Nike tennis shoes. They are ill-paid and are often sexually abused by employers. They work hard in industries that do not have an air-conditioning systems or proper ventilation systems. They also work at the cold storages. All such works are done under asphyxiating conditions.

There are also wide regional variations in terms of children's involvement in hazardous and exploitative works. In this context, one can surely say that rural Asian children face greater challenges than urban children. In Bhutan and Nepal, for example, children aged 7–17 years from the rural areas are found involved in exploitative works, and their number is about double the number of children living in the urban areas. In terms of school attendance, children in rural areas in

---

[2] Ranjan Ray, *Child Labour in Asia: A Survey of the Principal Empirical Evidence in Selected Asian Countries with a focus on Policy* (Australia: School of Economics, University of Tasmania, 2004).

Bangladesh, Nepal, India and Bhutan attend school in a number less than urban children. As per the ILO estimations, in agriculture alone, the highest number of children is engaged in Asian nations.

The writers, underneath, want to discuss the current situation of child labour in some of the prominent Asian nations.

5.2. BANGLADESH

Bangladesh, a fast developing country in Asia, is experiencing the severe problem of child labour, with the underage labourers (5–14 years) numbering approximately 4.7 million. As sources reveal,[3] among these child labourers, 83 per cent are employed in rural and 17 per cent in urban areas. They are largely employed in the fields of agriculture and allied sectors (including poultry breeding and fish processing), followed by employment in the garment-making sector, leather industry and shoe-making factories.

International organizations such as the ILO, UNICEF, IMF and the World Bank have unanimously identified poverty as the main cause for the existence of child labour in Bangladesh. There always exists a negative correlation between the income level and the incidence of child labour: that is, the higher the level of income of a family, the lower is the incidence of child labour and vice versa. Also, child labourers in rural areas in Bangladesh have usually outnumbered those in urban areas, and, again, boys outnumber girls in terms of labour force participation rate. However, in recent years, Bangladesh has made significant improvements in reducing poverty. Bangladesh had 71 per cent of people living below the poverty line in 1973–1974 (HIES, 1973), which was reduced to 24.3 per cent in 2015, and which further dropped to 21.8 per cent in 2018.[4]

A study undertaken by UNESCO in 2012 revealed that working children in Bangladesh in the age group of 5–14 years were thus engaged (by percentage) in different sectors: agriculture: 45.5 per cent;

---

[3] *Baseline Survey for Determining Hazardous Child-labour Sectors in Bangladesh – 2005* (Dhaka: The Press of the Government of Bangladesh, 2006).

[4] Basharat Hossain, 'Poverty-reduction during 1971–2013: Success and its recent trends in Bangladesh,' *JOUR* (June 2019), https://www.researchgate.net/publication/333918204_Poverty_Reduction_during_1971-2013_Periods_Success_and_its_Recent_Trends_in_Bangladesh

service sector: 36.0 per cent; manufacturing: 16.2 per cent; and, in others: 2.3 per cent.[5] As is revealed, the majority of children in Bangladesh are involved in agriculture, and these children perform a variety of tasks, including some risky works such as handling dangerous machinery and implements (threshers, harvesters and power tillers). Children also take part in spraying pesticides and insecticides and bear heavy loads—both of which are hazardous to their health. As Shituma Zaman, Sabrina Matin and Ashiq Mahmud Bin Gholam Kibria write,[6] those who are involved in manufacturing salt, soap, matches, bricks, cigarettes, footwear, steel-furniture, glass, jute, leather and textiles, are required to work with dangerous chemicals and instruments in unhygienic working conditions poor lighting and air for long hours.

The scenario of child labourers (in the age group of 5–14 years) in Bangladesh during the years 1983–2000 in the age group of 5–14 years has been reproduced underneath. The total child population, child labour force, child labour participation rate and child labour as per cent of total labour force have been represented in Table 5.1.

According to the 1983–1984 LFS, the total child labour participation rate was 15.9 per cent in Bangladesh, of which children in the age group 5–9 years represented 4.2 per cent while that of 10–14 years represented 23.9 per cent. There is a huge difference between boys and girls in the workforce participation where boys outnumbered girls. It was 13.3, 4.2 and 23 per cent respectively in the 1984–1985 LFS. It went up to 19.3 and 36.4 per cent respectively in 1989 LFS. In 1990–1991 LFS, the total labour-force participation rate was 19.3 per cent, and for the age group of 10–14 years, it was 42 per cent. In 1995–1996 LFC, it was 18.7 per cent, 4.5 per cent and 33.3 per cent, respectively.

Table 5.2 clearly shows a gender-wise declining trend in children's labour force participation in agriculture, and an increasing trend to participate in a non-agriculture sector with a variation in some years.

---

[5] *UNCTAD-report: The Least-Developed Countries Report*, https://vi.unctad.org/resources-mainmenu-64/digital-library?view=show&doc_name=1033_the_least_de

[6] Shituma Zaman, Sabrina Matin, and Ashiq Mahmud Bin Gholam Kibria, 'A Study on Present Scenario of Child Labour in Bangladesh,' *IOSR Journal of Business and Management* 16, no. 6 (January 2014), https://www.researchgate.net/publication/272984307_A_Study_on_Present_Scenario_of_Child_Labour_in_Bangladesh

Table 5.1 Child Population and Labour Force Participation Aged 5–14 Years by Sex

Source, Period and Age Group	Total Child Population 5–14 Years (000)			Child Labour Force 5–14 Years (000)			Child Labour Participation Rate			Child Labour and % of Total Labour Force
	Both Sex	Male	Female	Both Sex	Male	Female	Both Sex	Male	Female	Both Sex
1983–1984 LFS										
Total	23,812	14,218	13,594	3,782	3,108	674	15.9	21.8	4.9	13.3
05–09	14,563	7,369	7,194	608	468	140	4.2	6.3	1.9	2.1
10–14	13,249	6,849	6,400	3,174	2,640	534	23.9	38.5	8.3	11.1
1984–1985 LFS										
Total	28,316	14,413	13,903	3,774	3,098	676	13.3	21.5	4.7	12.8
05–09	14,594	7,384	7,207	612	452	160	4.2	6.1	2.2	2.1
10–14	13,722	7,026	6,696	3,162	2,646	516	23	37.8	7.7	10.7
1989 LFS										
Total	30,971	16,310	14,661	5,979	3,537	2,442	19.3	21.7	16.6	11.8
05–09	19,301	10,123	9,177	1,734	1,006	728	9	9.9	7.9	3.4
10–14	11,671	6,187	5,484	4,245	2,531	1,714	36.4	40.9	31.3	8.4

1990–1991 LFS										
Total	30,633	16,751	13,882	5,923	3,844	2,079	19.3	22.9	15	11.6
05–09	16,913	8,689	8,224	166	118	48	1	1.4	0.6	0.3
10–14	13,720	8,062	5,658	5,757	3,726	2,031	42	46.2	35.9	11.2
1995–1996 CLS										
Total	34,455	17,862	16,593	6,455	3,856	2,599	18.7	21.6	15.7	11.5
05–09	17,398	8,798	8,600	778	440	338	4.5	5	3.9	1.4
10–14	17,057	9,064	7,993	5,677	3,416	2,261	33.3	37.7	28.3	10.1
1999–2000 LFS										
Total	—	—	—	—	—	—	—	—	—	—
05–09[a]	—	—	—	—	—	—	—	—	—	—
10–14	17,439	9,314	8,125	6,777	4,029	2,748	38.9	43.3	33.8	11.2

Source: Bangladesh Bureau of Statistics (1996: Table 7.8 and Table 7.11) and Bangladesh Bureau of Statistics (2002). Data for 1999–2000 come from Bangladesh Bureau of Statistics (2002); Rasheda Khanam, 'Child-labour in Bangladesh: Trends, Patterns, and Policy Options' (April 2005), https://www.researchgate.net/publication/24115749_Child_Labour_in_Bangladesh_Trends_Patterns_and_Policy_Options

Note: [a] Data for children aged 5–9 years are not available.

Table 5.2 Child-labour Participation (10–14 Years) in Agriculture and Non-agriculture Sectors by Gender

Period and service	Agriculture			Non-agriculture		
	All	Boys	Girls	All	Boys	Girls
1983–1984 LFS	64.1	97.6	2.4	359	58.3	41.7
1983 LFS	74.5	61.2	38.8	25.5	54.3	45.7
1990–1991 LFS	75.1	58.4	38.8	24.9	84.5	15.5
1995–1996 CLS	65.4	61.4	38.6	34.6	57.1	42.9
1999–2000 LFS	64.2	62.2	67.1	35.8	37.8	32.9

Source: Bangladesh Bureau of Statistics (1996: Table 7.14) and Bangladesh Bureau of Statistics (2002). Data for 1999–2000 come from Bangladesh Bureau of Statistics (2002); Rasheda Khanam, 'Child-labour in Bangladesh: Trends, Patterns, and Policy Options' (April 2005), https://www.researchgate.net/publication/24115749_Child_Labour_in_Bangladesh_Trends_Patterns_and_Policy_Options

The children's activity status (aged 5–14 years) derived from NCLS, Bangladesh Bureau of Statistics (BBS), 2002–2003, could be thus displayed in Table 5.3.

Table 5.3 shows that children's workforce participation rate is greater among the boys and girls in rural areas than in urban areas (boys: rural—19.3%, urban—15.5%, girls: rural—3.5%, urban—2.4%). The total workforce participation rate is also higher in the rural areas than the urban areas (rural—13.4%, urban—11.1%).

This is an international phenomenon that children of poor families usually join the child labour force. This is true for Bangladesh too. These children, understandably, sacrifice schooling. The writers present, underneath, child labour data and information regarding their school attendance compiled by the BBS, 2002–2003. This has been shown in Table 5.4.

Table 5.4 shows that families representing Quintile–1 has the highest involvement of boys in the workforce while the highest Quintile–5 shows the lowest involvement. Higher Quintile shows higher involvement in studies, and vice-versa. One can notice a similar trend in the case of girls' involvement in work and studies. The total workforce participation for children is lower in the higher expenditure Quintile, and vice versa. Children's (total) studies are higher in expenditure

Table 5.3 Children Aged 5–14, by Sex, Type of Activity and Residence

Sex	Activity	Urban %	Urban No	Rural %	Rural No	Total %	Total No
Male	Work only (a)	9.4	375,956	9.9	4,409,950	9.8	1,785,906
	Study only (b)	73.9	2,966,904	70.5	10,046,505	71.2	13,013,409
	Work and Study (c)	6.1	244,464	9.4	1,342,305	8.7	1,586,769
	Total work *	15.5	620,420	19.3	2,752,255	18.5	3,372,675
	Total stucy **	80.0	3,211,368	79.9	11,388,810	79.9	14,600,178
	Neither	10.6	426,886	10.2	1,453,145	10.3	1,880,031
Female	Work only (a)	3.9	141,215	4.8	626,735	4.6	767,950
	Study only (b)	83.5	3,028,483	82.0	10,797,935	82.3	13,826,418
	Work and Study (c)	2.4	87,507	3.5	462,920	3.3	550,427
	Total work*	6.3	228,722	8.3	1,089,655	7.8	1,318,377
	Total study **	85.9	3,115,990	85.5	11,260,855	85.6	14,376,845
	Neither	10.2	369,937	9.8	1,286,070	9.9	1,656,007

(Table 5.3 Continued)

(Table 5.3 Continued)

Sex		Activity	Urban		Rural		Total	
			%	No	%	No	%	No
Total		Work only (a)	6.8	517,171	7.4	2,036,685	7.3	2,553,856
		Study only (b)	78.5	5,995,387	76.0	20,844,440	76.5	26,839,827
		Work and Study (c)	4.3	331,971	6.6	1,805,225	6.1	2,137,196
		Total work *	11.1	849,142	14.0	3,841,910	13.4	4,691,052
		Total study **	82.8	6,327,358	82.6	22,649,665	82.6	28,977,023
		Neither	10.4	796,823	10.0	2,739,215	10.1	3,536,038

Source: Bangladesh Bureau of Statistics, 2002–2003; One can compare data available in Wikipedia, 'Child-labour in Bangladesh,' 5 April 2021, https://en.wikipedia.org/wiki/Child_labour_in_Bangladesh

Notes: *'Total work' refers to children that work only and children that work and study, that is, a + c.
** 'Total study' refers to the children that study only and children that work and study, that is, b + c.

Table 5.4 Children's Activity Status and Household Income Level

Sex	Type of Activity	Quintile 1	Quintile 2	Quintile 3	Quintile 4	Quintile 5	Total
Male	Work only	12.3	11.2	11.5	9.6	5.6	10.2
	Study only	67.6	70.0	69.7	73.6	80.3	71.9
	Work and study	7.9	9.1	10.4	10.0	8.7	9.1
	Neither	12.2	9.7	8.3	6.8	5.4	8.8
Female	Work only	6.3	5.2	5.3	3.2	2.4	4.7
	Study only	78	81.4	81.9	86.3	89.7	82.9
	Work and study	3.5	3.5	3.9	3.3	2.7	3.4
	Neither	12.3	9.9	8.9	7.1	5.2	9.1
Total	Work only	9.3	8.3	8.5	6.6	4.1	7.5
	Study only	72.8	75.5	75.6	79.6	84.7	77.2
	Work and study	5.6	6.4	7.3	6.9	5.9	6.3
	Neither	12.2	9.8	8.6	7.0	5.3	8.9

Source: Bangladesh Bureau of Statistics, 2002–2003; BBS–IPEC, *Report on National Child-labour Survey in Bangladesh* (October 2003), https://www.ilo.org/ipecinfo/product/download.do?type=document&id=746.
Notes: (a) The household expenditure is used as a proxy for income. 'Quintile' represents lowest expenditure and quintiles the highest. (b) The total may not add to 100.0 due to rounding.

Quintile (e.g., 84.7% in Quintile-5) and lower in lower expenditure Quintile (e.g., 72.8% in Quintile 1).

Bangladesh's National Child Labour Elimination Policy 2010 identified several reasons for the prevalence of child labour in the country. The major causes identified are economic impoverishment, socio-economic adversity, unemployment, resource scarcity, social insecurity and recurrence of natural calamities. There is a provision in the Constitution of the People's Republic of Bangladesh for ensuring compulsory primary education for children. The Children Act 1974 (Act XXXIX of 1974) of Bangladesh also ensures the protection of children and their rights.

Among other issues, the National Child Labour Elimination Policy 2010 aims at attaining objectives such as withdrawing children from work (especially from hazardous work), involving children's parents in the income-augmenting activities, providing a stipend to working children who attend school, enacting laws and strengthening institutional capacity for their enforcement, sensitizing guardians, people and civil societies about harmful consequences of child labour, and formulating different policies for eliminating different forms of child labour from Bangladesh by 2015.

According to the Bangladesh Child Labour Survey 2013, the largest sector employing child labour in the country is that of mining and quarrying (33.3%), followed by agriculture (29.9%), wholesale and retail trade of vehicles and motorcycles (10.6%), construction (6.9%) and transport and storage (5%).

The sectoral distribution of child labour has been displayed in Table 5.5 demonstrates more detailed segregation.

Data shown in Table 5.5 explains that the manufacturing sector absorbs the highest number of child labour, that is, 33.3 per cent, followed by agriculture and allied sector, that is, 29.9 per cent.

Working children engaged in hazardous works are summarized in Table 5.6.

The UNICEF has identified that there are many forms of child labour in Bangladesh, and many children experience grievous tortures while doing work at the hands of owners of factories, hotels, tea stalls, restaurants, etc. In spite of the fact that legislation for the prohibition of child labour has been strictly enforced, it still exists in different working places such as hotels, motels, launches, buses, brick-kilns, garages,

Table 5.5 *Distribution of Child Labour by Industry and Age Group*

Industry Classification (BSIC Major Group)	Child Age Group				
	5	6–11	12–13	14–17	Total
Agriculture, forestry, fishing	8,106	231,755	3,482	263,834	507,176
	42.0	53.6	90	21.8	29.9
Mining and quarrying	0	0	0	3,309	3,309
	0.0	0.0	0.0	0.3	0.2
Manufacturing	8,812	73,394	29,259	453,612	565,077
	45.6	17.0	755	375	33.3
Electricity, gas, steam & air conditioning supply	0	3502	0	3,949	6,551
	0.0	0.8	0.0	0.3	0.4
Water supply and sewerage	0	0	0	1,640	1,640
	0.0	0.0	0.0	0.1	0.1
Construction	956	5,290	3,950	107,174	117,370
	5.0	1.2	10.2	8.9	6.9
Wholesale and retail	496	42,384	0	136,919	179,798
	2.6	9.8	0.0	11.3	10.6
Transport and storage	0	1,867	0	83,502	85,368
	0.0	0.4	0.0	6.9	5.0
Accommodation food	0	16,751	0	18,746	35,497
	0.0	3.9	0.0	1.6	2.1
Information and communication	0	0	0	1,851	1,851
	0.0	0.0	0.0	0.2	0.1
Financial and insurance	0	0	0	306	306
	0.0	0.0	0.0	0.0	0.0
Real-estate activities	0	0	0	286	286
	0.0	0.0	0.0	0.0	0.0
Administrative and support service activities	0	1,216	0	3,407	4,623
	0.0	0.3	0.0	0.3	0.3
Public administration	0	4,968	0	6,977	11,945
	0.0	1.2	0.0	0.6	0.7

(Table 5.5 Continued)

(Table 5.5 Continued)

Industry Classification (BSIC Major Group)	Child Age Group				
	5	6–11	12–13	14–17	Total
Education	0	0	0	6,514	6,514
	0.0	0.0	0.0	0.5	0.4
Human health and society	0	0	0	2,816	2,816
	0.0	0.0	0.0	0.2	0.2
Other service activity	0	7,393	1,248	35,270	43,911
	0.0	1.7	3.2	2.9	2.6
Activities of households	951	43,669	826	79,410	124,857
	4.9	10.1	2.1	6.6	7.4
Total	19,320	432,188	38,766	1,208,620	1,698,894
	100.0	100.0	100.0	100.0	100.0

Source: Bangladesh National Child Labour Survey, 2013, https://www.ilo.org/ipec/Informationresources/WCMS_IPEC_PUB_28175/lang--en/index.htm

factories, mills, homes, sweet-shops and bakeries, tobacco industry, leather industry and garment industry. Many of these sectors provide very risky occupations for children.

The UNICEF has suggested that the following issues could be resolved to eliminate child labour from Bangladesh. First, impoverishment has been indicated as the prime reason for child labour. It is thus necessary to eliminate poverty completely to stop child labour from the soil. Second, society has a great role to bear to stop child labour. Responsible Bangladeshi citizens are expected to report to local administration and civil society organizations if a child is employed as labour in nearby areas. They should also look at whether proper care is being given to children who are working instead of going to school. Third, child labour prohibiting legislation should be implemented very carefully, and the administration—beginning at the local level and extending up to the district level—should be made aware of the existence of child labour in the locality—at home, in agriculture, or in factories. Fourth, more projects for the rehabilitation of child labour should be undertaken in order to stop child labour. The projects should

Table 5.6 Distribution of Children in Hazardous Works by Industry and Age Group

Industry Classification (BSIC Major Group)	Number				%			
	6–11	12–13	14–17	Total	6–11	12–13	14–17	Total
Agriculture, forestry and fishing	9,511	3,482	263,833	276,827	29.0	9.0	21.8	21.6
Mining and quarrying	0	0	3,309	3,309	0.0	0.0	0.3	0.3
Manufacturing	16,486	29,259	453,612	499,358	50.3	75.5	37.5	39.0
Electricity, gas, steam and air condition			3,049	3,049	00	00	0.3	0.2
Water supply, sewerage and waste management			1,640	1,640	00	00	0.1	0.1
Construction	5,099	3,950	107,174	116,223	15.5	10.2	8.9	9.1
Wholesale and retail trade, repair of motor vehicles and motorcycles	1,713	0	136,919	138,631	5.2	0.0	11.3	10.8
Transportation and storages	0	0	83,502	83,502	0.0	0.0	6.9	6.5
Accommodation and food service activities	0	0	18,746	18,746	0.0	0.0	1.6	1.5
Information and communication	0	0	1,851	1,851	0.0	0.0	0.2	0.1
Financial and insurance activities	0	0	306	306	0.0	0.0	0.0	0.0
Real estate activities	0	0	286	286	0.0	0.0	0.0	0.0

(Table 5.6 Continued)

(Table 5.6 Continued)

Industry Classification (BSIC Major Group)	Number				%			
	6–11	12–13	14–17	Total	6–11	12–13	14–17	Total
Administration and support service activities	0	0	3,407	3,407	0.0	0.0	0.3	0.3
Public and ministration and defence compulsory social activity	0	0	6,977	6,977	0.0	0.0	0.6	0.5
Education	0	0	6,514	6,514	0.0	0.0	0.5	0.5
Human health and social work activities	0	0	2,816	2,816	0.0	0.0	0.2	0.2
Other service activities	0	1,248	35,270	36,518	0.0	3.2	2.9	2.9
Activities of households as employed undifferentiated groups and service producing activities of households for own use	0	826	79,410	80,236	0.0	2.1	6.6	6.3
Total	32,808	38,766	1,208,620	1,280,195	100.0	100.0	100.0	100.0

Source: Bangladesh Child Labour Survey, 2013, https://www.ilo.org/ipec/Informationresources/WCMS_IPEC_PUB_28175/lang--en/index.htm

look at the issues concerning the children's parental socio-economic status, that is, their income, education, social demography, etc., in order to identify the real causes of child labour. Fifth, many short-term and long-term plans should be framed by the government and executed wholeheartedly to ameliorate the condition of the impoverished children engaged in hazardous work in their teenage. Sixth, media has a greater role to play through the publication of reports on child labourer abuses and making people aware of the bad effects of child labour in society and the country as a whole. Seventh, many factory owners, including those of garment industries and other small and medium-sized industries, deprive children of their basic claims by offering lower wages and demanding long hours of work per day. This should be completely banned by enforcing the existing regulations on child labour. If the employers are found guilty of employing child labourers, they need to be punished. Eighth, education should be made compulsory for every child. The Government of Bangladesh has made legislation for the enrolment of every child in primary education. Even then numerous children are engaged in household and hazardous works. The UNICEF, the ILO and the UNESCO are of the opinion that students fit to be enrolled in Grade-I have the highest dropout rate in Bangladesh, and, understandably, they become potential candidates for the labour market. In light of this, the ILO adopted the policy for eliminating child labour in Bangladesh by placing as many working children in schools as is possible. Finally, many children in Bangladesh have missed out on their right to education. This is primarily due to poverty and hunger. They themselves withdraw from schools and join work. Data collected by the UNICEF and the ILO show that the children's working hours are negatively correlated with school attendance and this intensifies poverty.[7]

Table 5.7 represents the statistics on children's work and education in Bangladesh during 2011–2019.

Data depicted in Table 5.7 show that the proportion of children in the age group of 5–14 years engaged in various works remained constant at 10.1 per cent from 2011 to 2014, and it went down to 4.3 per cent and again remained constant at that point from 2015 to 2019.

---

[7] See *A Matter of Magnitude: UNICEF's Report on the Impact of the Economic Crisis on Women and Children in South Asia*, 2009, https://www.childimpact.unicef-irc.org/documents/view/id/58/lang/en

Table 5.7 Statistics on Children's Work and Education

Year	Working (%) (5–14 Yrs.)	Attending School (%) (5–14 Yrs.)	Combining Work and School (%) (7–14 Yrs.)	Primary Completion Rate (%)
2011	10.1	81.2	6.8	NA
2012	10.1	81.2	6.8	NA
2013	10.1	81.2	6.8	74.6
2014	10.1	81.2	6.8	74.6
2015	4.3	81.2	6.8	73.5
2016	4.3	89.4	1.9	98.5
2017	4.3	89.4	1.9	98.1
2018	4.3	89.4	1.9	118.6
2019	4.3	89.4	1.9	67.8

Source: Bureau of Industrial Labour Affairs, U.S. Department of Labour; also see 'List of Good Produced by Child-labour or Forced-labour,' https://www.dol.gov/agencies/ilab/reports/child-labor/list-of-goods

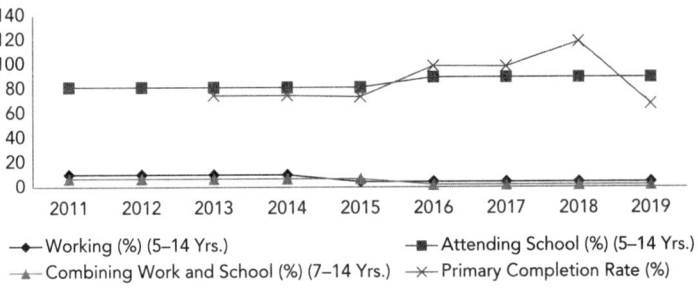

Children's school attendance (age group 5–14 years) remained at 81.2 per cent from 2011 to 2015, and it went up to 89.4 per cent and remained at that point from 2016 to 2019. The combination of work and school of children aged 7–14 years remained at 6.8 per cent from 2011 to 2015, and it decreased further and remained constant at 1.9 per cent from 2016 to 2019. The primary education rate was good with the exception of the year 2019 when it was 67.8 per cent. This was highest in 2018, that is, 118.6 per cent and in 2016 and 2017 it was 98.5 and 98.1 per cent, respectively. Data on completion rates were not available in 2011 and 2012, but in 2013 and 2014, the rate was 74.6 per cent.

A large number of children are usually involved in the garment industry in Bangladesh. As Leonie Barrie writes, the prevalence of female child labour in the garment sector in Bangladesh is always a matter of concern, and to be more precise, it is the female child labour that accounts for two-thirds of female labourers.[8] A study by Maria Quattri and Kevin Watkins[9] shows that about half of the children aged 14 years living in the slum areas of Dhaka were engaged in work, and most of them were engaged in export production of garments. The study critically examined and found that 15 per cent of children in Bangladesh in the age group of 6–14 years were out of school and engaged in work as child labourers. They had to work hard, and their average working hours too were long—longer than the stipulated working period of 42 hours set by the Bangladesh legislation. Many of the children worked—as the study found—64 hours per week on an average. The wage they received was low, much lower than the adults received. This trend is continuing even now. Interestingly, the government sector is the biggest sector in Bangladesh that offers employment to children, and many children are involved in export production.

Children in the garment industries of Bangladesh are mostly migrants from rural areas, and about half of them are illiterate, and a majority of them are girls. Children engaged in this sector are largely school dropouts, and it seems that the results of the parent's failure to send their children to school lead them to find employment in the industry works as sewing helpers and finishing helpers. D. Bhattacharya, in his 1996 essay,[10] notes how—because of legislations and interferences from trade unions, and the human and child rights' organizations—the Bangladesh Garment Manufacturers and Exporters Association (BGMEA) established schools for child workers in collaboration with the ILO, the UNICEF and the Ministry of Labour, Government of Bangladesh.

---

[8] Leonie Barrie, 'Child-labour Persists in Bangladesh Garment Sector' (9 December 2016), https://www.just-style.com/news/child-labour-persists-in-bangladesh-garment-sector_id129498.aspx

[9] Maria Quattri and Kevin Watkins, 'Child-labour and Education: A Survey of Slum-settlements in Dhaka,' The Overseas Development Institute, 2015, https://odi.org/en/publications/child-labour-and-education-a-survey-of-slum-settlements-in-dhaka/

[10] D. Bhattacharya, 'International Trade, Social Labelling and Developing Countries: The Case of Bangladesh's Governments Exports and Use of Child Labor,' *OpenEdition Journal* (1996), https://journals.openedition.org/sjep/1359

In the Bangladeshi garment industries, the children perform several tasks such as picking cotton, spinning yarn, cutting thread and sewing. These tasks can easily be done by little children with their small hands. But the wages the child labourers earn in these industries are pitiably low—much lower than what is called the 'living wage'. Parents withdraw their children, as one can notice, from school, and force them to work in garment industries and other jobs. Many international and government-owned factory brands such as H&M, C&A, Esprit, Marks and Spencer, GAP, VF, Corporation and Kmart Australia employ Bangladeshi child labourers, but give them low wages. Most of the readymade garment factories in Bangladesh are located at Ashulia, Gazipur and Narayanganj. The majority of women and girls employed as labourers work in factories located in these areas. Many case studies reveal that the Bangladeshi garment factories use child labourers—especially the girl children—more pervasively, along with paying less and engaging them in work for long hours. The ILO, the UNICEF, the UNESCO, the World Bank, the IMF and many non-governmental organizations have been long advocating the removal of child labourers from the readymade garment industry in Bangladesh. Despite this, many girl children are still employed in the garment sector—many of whom are in informal garment production units scattered in different parts of the country. Recently, the globally recognized brands depending on cheap labour have been trying to reduce girl children participation in the garment industry. Also, the US and European governments have promulgated legislation to the end that no garments would be imported from those countries which employ child labourers. As per a report in *The Himalayan Times*,[11] in 1992, about 10 per cent of workers working in the Bangladesh garment industry were girl children but the number has been reduced with each passing year.

Importantly, banning girls from the Bangladesh-based garment sector created another problem. The girls engaged in garment production units could earn money for their families. Withdrawing them from work forced them, in turn, to face an uncertain future. They had only option left after being sacked from employment and that was early marriage. The minimum marriage age laws are barely implemented in Bangladesh, and that is the principal reason behind premature weddings

---

[11] https://thehimalayantimes.com/opinion/bangladeshs-garment-industry-child-labour-options/

for teenaged girls. Banning factory employment for young girls in Bangladesh has really done more harm than good. It is required that a system of income augmenting mechanism should be evolved for the low-income families through which a decent standard of living can be maintained. This can only stop the burning problem of child labour in the less developed economies of the world.

In a 2015 study, UNICEF identified some of the grey areas in the readymade garment industry in Bangladesh which have affected children. In spite of its great impact on the economy, the Bangladeshi garment sector has exerted several negative effects on the well-being of workers—especially the women and children workers and their families. Some progress have been made on improving the working conditions, such as wages, working hours, health and safety. The said research highlights eight important impact areas which affect the rights of children. First, maternity protection provided to working women in the garment industry is inadequate. Special provisions such as 16 weeks paid maternity leave and elimination of maternity-related employment discrimination are absent which are important measures to protect the health of children and promote equal opportunities. Second, a lesser number of babies (below the age of six months) born to working women in garment industries are breastfed. The readymade garment sector knowingly overlooks the needs of breastfeeding mothers and their babies. In many industries, mothers do not have space or time to breastfeed. The UNICEF, in its study 'Analysis of the Situation of Children and Women in Bangladesh' (p. 89), completed in 2015, has estimated that only 56 per cent of babies aged less than six months are breastfed.[12] Third, child-care facilities are barely available in the government industry. Children's Act, 2013 (Act Number 24 of 2013) specifically mentions that factories having more than 40 workers should provide adequate childcare facilities for the children of women workers up to the age of six years. In some industries there, of course, are some facilities but the rooms provided for children are substandard and the amenities available are inadequate. Not only this, there is also the absence of trained and qualified caregivers in the readymade garment industries. There are some good-quality community-based child care centres run by civil society organizations, but these are available only for children above the age of two years. Therefore, these centres cannot

---

[12] See, for example, https://data.unicef.org/topic/nutrition/malnutrition/

completely fulfil the needs of parents engaged in the garment industry. Fourth, working women in the garment sector suffer from malnutrition and anaemia, and about 50 per cent of them belong to this category. The nutritional status of many women working there is very poor especially because low wages prevailing in this sector and along with hazardous workplaces and poor-quality drinking water, sanitation and hygiene standards in factories also pose threat to the health of working women and their children. Their probability of suffering from exposure to infections and communicable diseases and that of reproductive infections and diseases is also high.[13] Fifth, wages offered to women in the garment sector is not adequate enough to maintain a standard of living. Due to low wages, they are deprived of access to essential services such as education, healthcare, water, sanitation and hygiene. Parents cannot feed nutritious food to their children, and this also affects the decision of sending them to school. The children of garment workers have a high risk of dropping out of school and, thereafter, they are left with no other option than joining the garment industry as child labourers. The working hours for women in the garment industry are long, and in addition to this, they have to do overtime work for extra earnings. Children are deprived of the care of their parents, and they are more likely to face greater risks of accidents, exploitation and sexual abuse in the case of teenage girls. Sixth, many working women and children are engaged in the informal garment sector. They perform a variety of works related to the garment industry, such as embroidery, cutting/trimming, button stitching, etc. Poverty and low wage in this sector force workers to withdraw their children from school and engage them in work in order to contribute to family income. Seventh, poor income and longer working hours fail to provide garment sector workers a decent standard of living. Due to the unregulated growth of the ready-made garment sector, there has been a huge expansion of urban slums. Workers coming from rural areas prefer to stay nearer to the factories. This has given rise to urban slums with poor housing, insecure land tenure and lack of pure drinking water, toilet facilities and hygiene. All these make garment sector workers including women and children more vulnerable. Not much care has been given as such to improve the conditions of informal urban settlements majority of which are not

---

[13] BSR HER, *Female Factory Workers' Health Needs Assessment:* Bangladesh, 2010, https://www.herproject.org

recognized by the government. Proper care needs to be given by the government for housing for the labourers, and other facilities such as water, sanitation, hygiene to improve their living conditions. Finally, there is a shortage of qualified healthcare providers and facilities for government workers and their family members. There are provisions for basic healthcare facilities for factory workers and their family members in garment factories having more than 300 workers. However, this is absent in most of the factories. Similarly, there is a lack of education facilities for the children of factory workers. The parents' low income does not allow them to send their children to access education facilities.

The COVID-19 pandemic has had exerted a negative impact on the lives of the informal sector workers. Closure of schools and steady reduction of family income of vulnerable sections of society have exposed more and more children to child labour and sexual exploitation. The present days' UNICEF representative in Bangladesh, Mr Tomoo Hozumi, expressed his deep anguish on 12 June 2020, while discussing the present child-labour scenario in Bangladesh suffering from the Coronavirus infection. It has been suggested that a number of measures such as comprehensive social protection, access to credit for the poor, facilities in schools such as mid-day meals, exemption in school fees, etc., be adapted for tackling the crises of child labourers.

5.3. NEPAL

The survival of the majority of the population in Nepal largely depends on agriculture and allied activities—as Sunil Kumar Joshi writes in his 2013 work,[14] as more than 80 per cent of its people live on subsistence agriculture, and more importantly, 90 per cent of the total population lives in rural areas.[15] Of the different problems afflicting Nepal on a daily basis, that of child labour is among the graver ones. Nevertheless, various governmental agencies and non-governmental organizations of Nepal have been constantly working to address the diverse issues related to child labour. The Government of Nepal passed the Child Labour Act, 1992, and also ratified the ILO Convention Numbers 138 and

---

[14] Sunil K. Joshi, 'Child Labour Issues in Nepal,' *International Journal of Occupational Safety and Health* 3, no. 3 (2013).

[15] Also see Kamalesh Adhikari, *Farmers' Rights in Nepal* (Kathmandu: SAWTEE, 2008), 2.

182 in right earnest to reduce the problem of child labour. The *Nepal Labour Force Survey – 2008* estimated that 40.4 per cent of children in Nepal fall under the category of 'economically underprivileged', of which 51 per cent are child labourers. Poverty, illiteracy and lack of viable economic alternatives might be held responsible for pushing the Nepalese children into hazardous works. The under-18 Nepalese child labourers are forced to engage themselves in different sectors like agriculture, cottage industry, factory, plantation, domestic, catering, selling, manual labour, tourism and travel industries, rag-picking, prostitution, begging, and many more. Moreover, various forms of child labour can be found in Nepal even in the 21st century, and these include bonded child labour, forced child labour, girl trafficking, domestic child labour, industrial child labour, street child labour. As Yogender Gurung finds in his 1999 research paper, 'Child Migration to Kathmandu Valley City: Family and Other Factors in Context and Process', most of the Nepalese migrant child labourers come in large numbers from rural villages to urban areas and settle down in places where industries are located. The worst forms of child labour are performed in sectors such as brick kilns, construction work, sex tourism, carpet industry, etc. In the Nepalese urban areas—especially in Kathmandu—thousands of young girls below the age of 18 years are routinely engaged in 'entertainment-industry' such as cabin restaurants, dance bars, dohari restaurants and parlours. A study conducted in 2009 by the Department of Education/Education Management Information System, Nepal, gravely notes that these girls are often forced to engage in sexual activities, or are trafficked.

In order to protect its children's rights, Nepal signed an agreement at the United Nations Child Rights' Convention in 1990. It also ratified the ILO's Convention Number 138 on minimum age in 2003 and Convention Number 182 on the worst forms of child labour in 2004. Earlier, the Nepalese Government enforced the provisions of the Children's Act, 1992; the Child Labour Prohibition and Regulation Act, 2000; and the Kamaiya Labour (Prohibition) Act, 2002. All such initiatives created ample legal ground in Nepal for taking actions against the worst forms of child labour. The Government of Nepal also undertook administrative measures and promulgated acts to restrict child labour in different periods of time—some in the 1960s, one in 1970, another in 1995 and the other two in 2007. These are the Begging

Prohibition Act, 1962; the Prison Act, 1962; the Common Law Code, 1963; the Public Offence and Punishment Act, 1970; the Citizens' Rights Act, 1995; and the Foreign Employment Act, 2007.

The Government of Nepal had long identified the principal reason for child labour, and that is poverty. In order to eradicate poverty, a series of measures were introduced. Some of such important programmes/initiatives to eliminate child labour are the Nepalese Poverty Reduction Strategy, 2003; the 10th National Development Plan, 2002–2007; the National Master Plan on Child-labour, 2004–2014; the Three-Year-Interim-Plan, 2010–2013; the National Plan of Action on Education for All, 2001–2015; the School Sector Reform Program, 2009–2015; the National Plans of Action on Trafficking of Women and Children and Bonded Labour, 2001 and 2010; and the National Master Plan on Child Labour, 2011–2020. The National Master Plan, 2011–2020, aimed at eliminating child labour, while keeping in mind the endorsements' convention. The prime objective of the plan was to eliminate child labour completely from Nepal by 2020, and its worst forms by 2016. The Government of Nepal has been also committed to implementing the National Master Plan on the Elimination of Child Labour (2018–2028) in line with sustainable development goals. To implement the plans for the elimination of child labour successfully along with eradication of poverty, the Government of Nepal adopted measures concretely at a different level: that is, at the regional, district, and community levels. Labour Offices were established at Jhapa, Morang, Dhanusha, Parsa, Makawanpur, Kathmandu, Kaski, Rupandehi, Banke and Kailali. Different women and children's affairs offices were established in 75 districts of Nepal, and the District Child Welfare Boards started functioning in all the districts. In 30 Nepalese districts, Juvenile Benches were set up to protect the trafficked children. To help the trafficked and recovered women and children, the Police Women and Children Service Centres in 75 districts were established. To protect the children involved in child labour activities and adopt welfare measures for them, the Government of Nepal formed the Child Protection and Promotion Committees in 1,051 village development committees (VDCs).

The estimate of Nepalese child labour in different age groups in terms of residence, ecological zone and development regions has been shown in Table 5.8.

Table 5.8 Working Children Aged 5–11 Years (in Nepal) by Background Characteristics (%)

Background	Characteristics	Boys	Girls	Total
Age group	5–9	20.3	29.5	24.8
	10–14	51.5	65.9	58.3
Residence	Urban	17.2	29.4	23.0
	Rural	37.9	49.2	43.4
Ecological zone	Mountain	45.7	58.9	52.2
	Hill	41.5	49.6	45.4
	Terai	29.2	43.9	36.3
Development region	Eastern	40.5	51.7	45.9
	Central	33.1	45.2	38.8
	Western	29.5	37.3	33.2
	Mid-Western	44.2	56.6	50.4
	Far-Western	40.6	57.1	48.7
Nepal		36.1	47.6	41.7

Source: CDPS/ILO (1998); also see 'We Must Do Better: A Closer Look at the Contextual Factors That Drive Child Labour and Discipline in Nepal,' https://www.unicef.org/nepal/sites/unicef.org.nepal/files/2018-11/2.%20Child%20Labour%20%26%20Discipline%20NMICS%20further%20analysis-2018_05_31_final%20version.pdf

Data presented in Table 5.8 show that the number of aged children (boys and girls) is larger than children aged 5–9 years. Clubbing the data available on counting the boys and girls together, one can see that children aged 10–14 years represent more (58.3%) in workforce than children aged 5–9 years (24.8%). The overall girls' participation rate (47.6%) is higher than boys' labour force participation (36.1%). The Nepalese working children can be found as largely coming from the rural areas to join work located in urban areas. Working children's work participation is higher in the rural sector (49.2%) than urban areas (37.9%). Girl children's concentration is the highest (58.9%) in the mountain zone, followed by the far-western zone (57.1%) and mid-western zone (56.6%).

The distribution of working children in Nepal by major occupational group, sex, sector, region and age group has been reproduced in Table 5.9. Table 5.9 reflects that majority of children are engaged

Table 5.9 Distribution of Working Children, by Major Occupational Group, Sex, Sector, Region and Age Group

(a)	Currently Working Children	Service Workers	Agriculture and Fishery Workers	Crafts and Related Trades Workers	Plant and Machine Operators	Elementary Occupation	Others
	(b)	(c)	(d)	(e)	(f)	(g)	(h)
Nepal	100	2.9	81.0	3.1	0.3	12.5	0.2
Educational level							
No schooling	100	1.8	73.6	5.9	0.2	18.4	0.0
Primary	100	2.2	81.3	2.5	0.3	13.7	0.0
Secondary	100	4.6	82.8	3.1	0.4	8.8	0.4
Higher secondary	100	2.6	86.2	2.1	0.0	6.5	2.5
Sex							
Boys	100	3.9	80.9	3.6	0.6	10.7	0.3
Girls	100	2.1	81.0	2.6	0.1	14.0	0.1
Age group							
5–9 years	100	1.5	79.6	1.0	0.0	17.9	0.0
10–13 years	100	2.4	83.2	1.7	0.1	12.5	0.1
14–17 years	100	3.8	79.3	4.9	0.6	11.0	0.3

(Table 5.9 Continued)

(Table 5.9 Continued)

	Currently Working Children	Service Workers	Agriculture and Fishery Workers	Crafts and Related Trades Workers	Plant and Machine Operators	Elementary Occupation	Others
(a)	(b)	(c)	(d)	(e)	(f)	(g)	(h)
Sector							
Urban	100	14.3	53.8	9.3	0.4	20.8	1.5
Rural	100	2.2	82.8	2.7	0.3	12.0	0.1
Ecological belt							
Mountains	100	0.9	89.2	1.5	0.0	8.3	0.0
Hills	100	1.7	83.5	1.6	0.1	13.0	0.1
Terai	100	4.7	76.4	5.1	0.7	12.8	0.3

Source: Nepal Child Labour Report, Nepal Labour Force Survey, 2008; International Labour Organization (ILO), Central Bureau of Statistics of Nepal, 2011; also see https://www.ilo.org/wcmsp5/groups/public/---asia/---ro-bangkok/---ilo-kathmandu/documents/publication/wcms_182988.pdf

(a) Total Number of Children (Thousands)

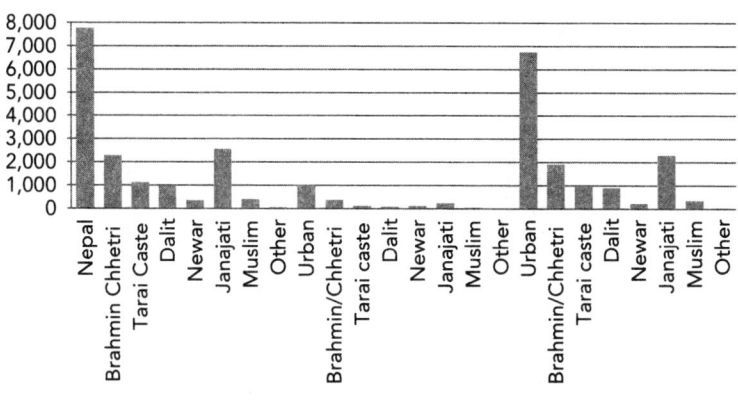

■ Total Number of Children (Thousands)

(b) Number of Working Children (Thousands)

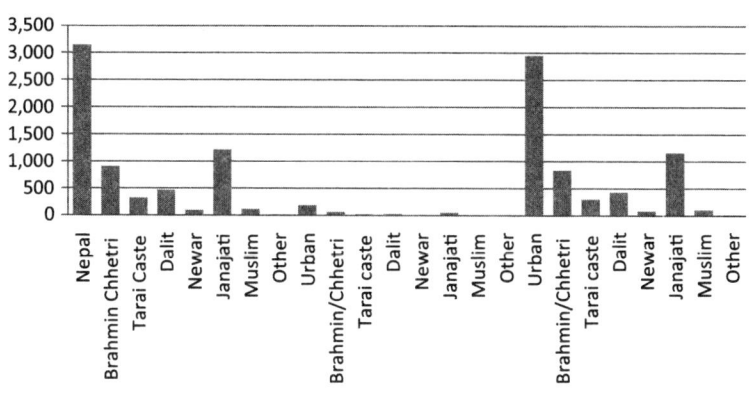

■ Number of Working Children (Thousands)

in agriculture and allied activities (81%). Only 3 per cent of them are employed in the service sector. The remaining children work in elementary occupations and craft and related works.

Table 5.10 represents the distribution of working children, child labour and children engaged in hazardous work, major ethnic groups and locality. In Nepal, the Janajati ethnic group of people represents the highest number of child labour. In this case, 47.7 per cent of

Table 5.10 Distribution of Working Children, Child Labour and Children Engaged in Hazardous Work, by Ethnic Group and Locality

Ethnic Group/ Locality	Total Number of Children (Thousands)	Number of Working Children (Thousands)	Percentage of Working Children	Number of Child Labour (Thousands)	Percentage of Child Labour	Number of Child Workers Engaged in Hazardous Work (Thousands)	Percentage of Child Workers Engaged in Hazardous Work
(a)	(b)	(c)	(d)	(e)	(f)	(g)	(h)
Nepal	7,770	3,143	40.4	1,599	50.9	621	19.7
Brahmin Chhetri	2,278	903	39.6	421	46.7	153	16.9
Tarai Caste	1,120	325	29.0	166	51.2	50	15.5
Dalit	990	463	46.8	280	60.4	128	27.6
Newar	356	97	27.1	39	40.3	16	17.0
Janajati	2,557	1,220	47.7	615	50.4	234	19.2
Muslim	401	117	29.1	68	58.4	35	30.0
Other	68	18	26.7	10	54.7	4	21.2
Urban	1,022	193	18.9	93	48.4	60	31.2
Brahmin/Chhetri	377	66	17.6	27	40.7	17	24.9
Tarai caste	123	24	19.2	14	57.8	8	33.0

Category						
Dalit	88	27	30.6	14	50.8	9	32.0
Newar	121	9	7.6	4	46.1	3	37.4
Janajati	249	56	22.6	28	49.7	19	34.7
Muslim	50	9	18.2	6	61.3	4	40.5
Other	14	2	12.9	1	74.1	1	44.1
Urban	6,748	2,949	43.7	1,506	51.1	560	19.0
Brahmin/Chhetri	1,901	836	44.0	394	47.1	136	16.3
Tarai caste	997	301	30.2	153	50.7	42	14.1
Dalit	902	436	48.4	266	61.0	119	27.4
Newar	235	87	37.1	35	39.6	13	14.9
Janajati	2,308	1,164	50.4	587	50.4	215	18.5
Muslim	350	107	30.7	62	58.2	31	29.1
Other	55	17	30.1	9	52.7	3	18.7

Source: Nepal Child Labour Report, Nepal Labour Force Survey, 2008; International Labour Organization (ILO), Central Bureau of Statistics of Nepal, 2011; also see https://www.ilo.org/wcmsp5/groups/public/---asia/---ro-bangkok/---ilo-kathmandu/documents/publication/wcms_182988.pdf

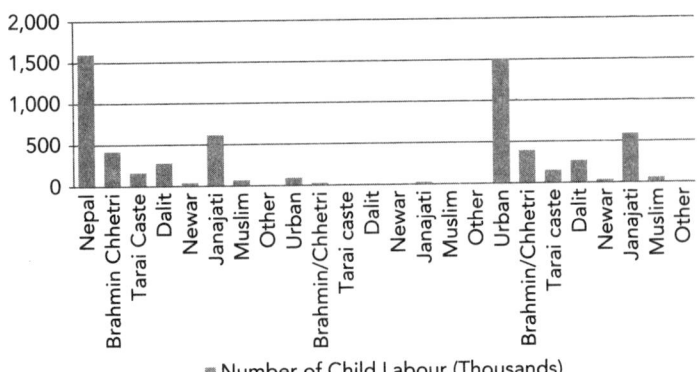

(a) Number of Child Labour (Thousands)

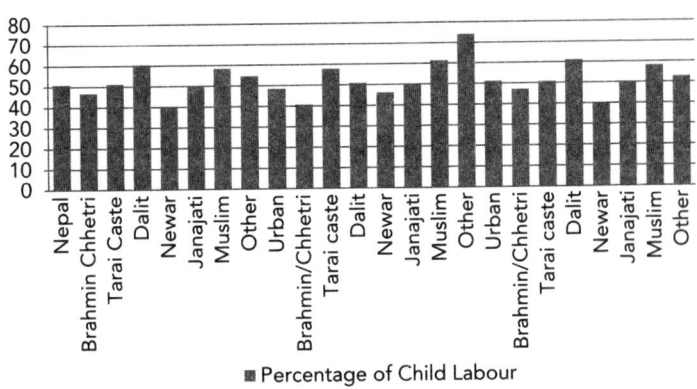

(b) Percentage of Child Labour

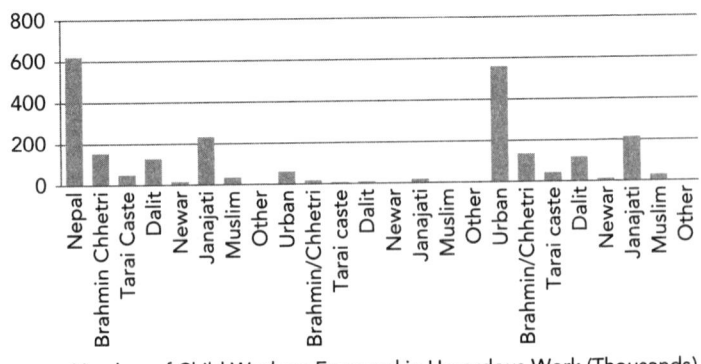

(c) Number of Child Workers Engaged in Hazardous Work (Thousands)

children could be found involved in different activities in Nepal. The second major group is the Dalit people who represent 46.8 per cent followed by the Brahmin group (39.6%). Terai and Muslims represent 29 per cent each. Hazardous works are mostly performed by the Muslim children, 30 per cent, followed by 27.6 per cent by the Dalit children.

The distribution of the Nepalese child labour and children in hazardous work only by the ethnic group has been reproduced in Table 5.11. Table 5.11 shows that the highest number of working children in hazardous work (in %) has been 37.7 per cent and their number is also highest as child labour which is 38.5 per cent among the Janajati ethnic group followed by Brahmin and Dalit communities (24.6% and 20.6%, respectively).

Working children, child labour and children engaged in hazardous jobs and their income and working hours have been shown in Table 5.12.

Data depicted in Table 5.12 shows that the Nepalese working children's median monthly income is low, and it is much lower for girls than boys. Moreover, rural children receive less compensation than urban children. Working hours per week increase with the increase in age. This is also true for the child labourers and children engaged in hazardous works. School attendance of child workers in general and children engaged in hazardous jobs, in particular, has been presented in Tables 5.13 and 5.14, respectively.

Table 5.14 shows the status of school attendance of working children in hazardous works in Nepal. The overall school attendance is 56.8 per cent. It is highest in the age group of 5–9 years, that is, 88.6 per cent, and lowest, that is, 38.3 per cent among the children aged 14–17 years age group.

In the Nepalese hill region, the percentage of school attendance is the highest (63.4%), and it is the lowest in the Terai region (48.2%).

The occupational statuses of child labourers have been portrayed in Tables 5.15 and 5.16.

Table 5.15 clearly reveals that many working children in Nepal face health hazards while at work, and about 20 per cent of such children experience such distress. Table 5.16 specifically shows that many of the children experience hardship while in work in sectors such as agriculture and fisheries, crafts and trade-related activities. Brick kilns

Table 5.11 Child Labour and Children Engaged in Hazardous Work, by Ethnic Group

Ethnic Group	Total number of Children (5–17 Years) (Thousands)	Number of Child Labour (Thousands)	Percentage of Child Labour	Number of Children Engaged in Hazardous Work (Thousands)	Percentage of Children in Hazardous Works
Nepal	7,770	1,599	100	621	100
Brahmin/Chhetri	2,278	421	26.3	153	24.6
Tarai Caste	11.20	166	10.4	50	8.1
Dalit	990	280	17.5	128	20.6
Newer	356	39	2.4	16	2.6
Janajati	2,557	615	38.5	234	37.7
Muslim	401	68	4.3	35	5.6
Others	68	10	0.6	4	0.6

Source: Nepal Child Labour Report, Nepal Labour Force Survey, 2008; International Labour Organization (ILO) Central Bureau of Statistics of Nepal, 2011; also see https://www.ilo.org/wcmsp5/groups/public/---asia/---ro-bangkok/---ilo-kathmandu/documents/publication/wcms_182988.pdf

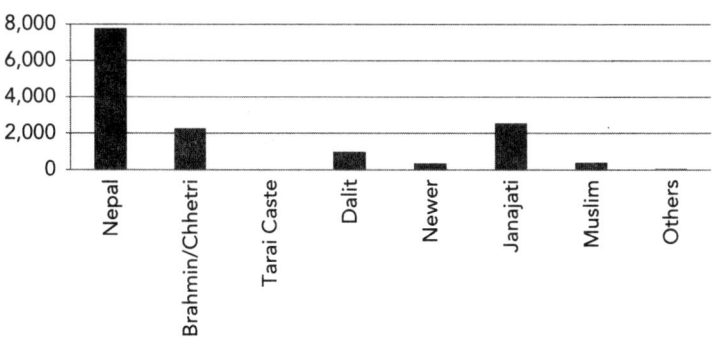

(a) Total number of Children (5–17 Years) (Thousands)

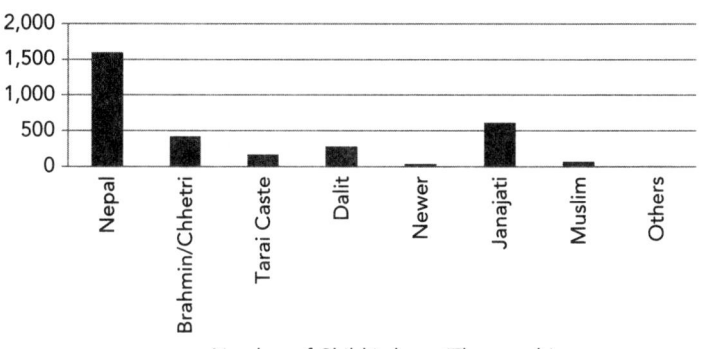

(b) Number of Child Labour (Thousands)

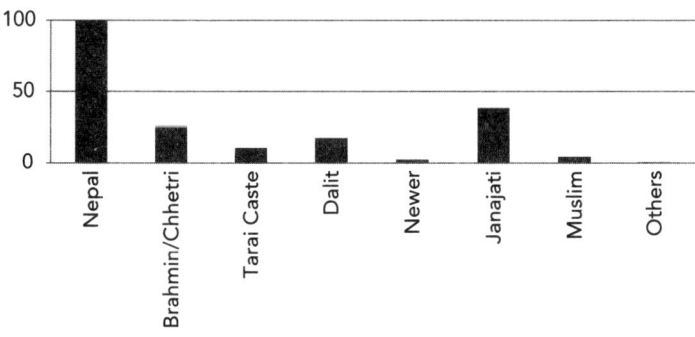

(c) Percentage of Child Labour

(d) Number of Children Engaged in Hazardous Work (Thousands)

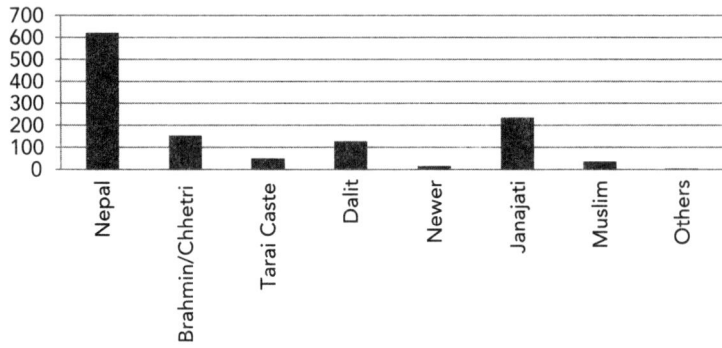

■ Number of Children Engaged in Hazardous Work (Thousands)

(e) Percentage of Children in Hazardous Works

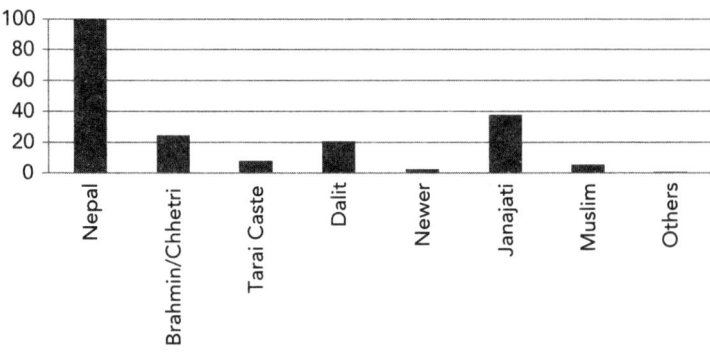

■ Percentage of Children in Hazardous Works

and carpet industries are some of the major industries where children are involved, and experience hazards.

The overall situation of child labour in Nepal is depicted in Table 5.17.

After the earthquake of 2015, the demand for bricks in Nepal has increased enormously and this sector has, in fact, been playing a much-needed role as a source of income for thousands of workers involved. Although the industry has been identified as an exploitative sector, it certainly has created an opportunity before the informal, migrant and working population in Nepal.

Table 5.12 Distribution of Average (Median) Monthly Income and Weekly Working Hours of Working Children, Child Labour and Children Engaged in Hazardous Child Labour, by Sex, Age Group and Urban/Rural Classification

	Working Children		Child Labour		Children Engaged in Hazardous Child Labour	
	Median Monthly Income (Rs.)	Average Working Hours per Week	Median Monthly Income (Rs.)	Average Working Hours per Week	Median Monthly Income (Rs.)	Average Working Hours per Week
Nepal	2,467	21.8	2,500	25.0	2,600	30.6
Urban	2,600	22.0	2,600	28.4	2,600	31.3
Rural	2,080	21.8	2,500	24.8	2,600	30.5
Sex						
Boys	2,500	21.5	2,882	25.2	3,000	32.6
Girls	1,733	22.1	2,123	24.9	2,427	29.2
Age Group						
5–9 years	1,733	13.1	1,733	13.1	1,083	6.9
10–13 years	1,300	17.9	1,300	22.5	1,700	13.1
14–17 years	2,427	27.8	2,817	42.6	2,817	42.6

Source: Nepal Child Labour Report, Nepal Labour Force Survey, 2008; International Labour Organization (ILO) Central Bureau of Statistics of Nepal, 2011; also see https://www.ilo.org/wcmsp5/groups/public/---asia/---ro-bangkok/---ilo-kathmandu/documents/publication/wcms_182988.pdf

Table 5.13 School Attendance of Child Workers, by Age Group, Sex, Locality and Region

	Thousands				Percentage		
	Child Population	No. of Child Workers	Attending School	Not Attending School	Total	Attending School	Not Attending School	Total
Nepal	7,770	3,143	1,177	422	1,599	73.6	26.4	100
Urban	1,022	193	62	31	93	66.6	33.4	100
Kathmandu Valley	267	20	7	7	14	47.3	52.7	100
Rural	6,748	2,949	1,115	391	1,506	74.0	26.0	100
Sex								
Boys	3,937	1,438	529	159	688	76.9	23.1	100
Girls	3,834	1,704	648	264	911	71.1	28.9	100
Age Group								
5–9 years	2,978	395	339	56	395	85.8	14.2	100

10–13 years	2,623	1,306	691	130	821	84.2	15.8	100
14–17 years	2,169	1,442	147	236	383	38.3	61.7	100
Ecological belt								
Mountains	542	283	122	35	157	77.8	22.2	100
Hills	3,300	1,511	640	153	792	80.7	19.3	100
Terai	3,929	1,348	415	235	650	63.9	36.1	100

Source: Nepal Child Labour Report, Nepal Labour Force Survey, 2008; International Labour Organization (ILO) Central Bureau of Statistics of Nepal, 2011; also see https://www.ilo.org/wcmsp5/groups/public/---asia/---ro-bangkok/---ilo-kathmandu/documents/publication/wcms_182988.pdf

Table 5.14 School Attendance of Children Engaged in Hazardous Child Labour, by Age Group, Sex, Locality and Region

	Thousands				Percentage		
	Child Population	Attending School	Not Attending School	Total	Attending School	Not Attending School	Total
(a)	(b)	(c)	(d)	(e)	(f)	(g)	(h)
Nepal	7,770	352	268	621	56.8	43.2	100
Urban	1,022	35	26	60	57.6	42.4	100
Kathmandu Valley	267	6	7	13	47.2	52.8	100
Rural	6,748	318	243	560	56.7	43.3	100
Sex							
Boys	3,937	140	108	248	56.6	43.4	100
Girls	3,834	212	161	373	56.9	43.1	100
Age Group							
5–9 years	2,978	63	8	71	88.6	11.4	100

10–13 years	2,623	143	24	167	85.6	14.4	100
14–17 years	2,169	147	236	383	38.3	61.7	100
Ecological belt							
Mountains	542	28	19	47	59.2	40.8	100
Hills	3,300	201	116	316	63.4	36.6	100
Terai	3,929	124	133	257	48.2	51.8	100

Source: Nepal Child Labour Report, Nepal Labour Force Survey, 2008; International Labour Organization (ILO) Central Bureau of Statistics of Nepal, 2011; also see https://www.ilo.org/wcmsp5/groups/public/---asia/---ro-bangkok/---ilo-kathmandu/documents/publication/wcms_182988.pdf

Table 5.15 Distribution of Child Labour, by Major Occupation (in Thousands)

Occupation	Urban			Rural			Total		
	Boys	Girls	Total	Boys	Girls	Total	Boys	Girls	Total
(a)	(b)	(c)	(d)	(e)	(f)	(g)	(h)	(i)	(j)
Nepal	48	46	93	640	866	1,506	688	911	1,599
Service workers and shop/market salesperson	19	21	40	470	625	1,095	489	646	1,135
Craft and related trades workers	9	5	14	36	34	70	45	39	84
Plant and machine operators, assemblers	1	0	1	6	1	7	7	1	8
Elementary occupation	19	20	39	128	206	333	147	225	372

Source: Nepal Child Labour Report, Nepal Labour Force Survey, 2008; International Labour Organization (ILO) Central Bureau of Statistics of Nepal, 2011; also see https://www.ilo.org/wcmsp5/groups/public/---asia/---ro-bangkok/---ilo-kathmandu/documents/publication/wcms_182988.pdf

Table 5.16 Distribution of Child Workers Engaged in Hazardous Works, by Major Occupation (in Thousands)

Occupation (a)	Urban			Rural			Total		
	Boys (b)	Girls (c)	Total (d)	Boys (e)	Girls (f)	Total (g)	Boys (h)	Girls (i)	Total (j)
Nepal	33	28	60	215	345	560	248	373	621
Service workers and shop/market salesperson	5	3	8	53	115	168	58	119	177
Craft and related trades workers	9	5	13	32	31	63	41	35	76
Plant and machine operators and assemblers	1	0	1	5	1	7	6	1	7
Elementary occupation	18	20	38	124	198	321	142	217	359

Source: Nepal Child Labour Report, Nepal Labour Force Survey, 2008 International Labour Organization (ILO) Central Bureau of Statistics of Nepal, 2011; also see https://www.ilo.org/wcmsp5/groups/public/---asia/---ro-bangkok/---ilo-kathmandu/documents/publication/wcms_182988.pdf

Table 5.17 *Statistics on Children's Work and Education*

Year	Working (% and Population) 5–14 Years	Attending School (%) 5–14 Years	Combining Work and School (%) 7–14 years	Primary Completion Rate %
2013	33.7 (2,097,163)	89.5	35.2	99.8
2014	33.7 (2,097,163	89.5	35.2	99.8
2015	33.7 (2,097,163)	89.5	35.2	105.7
2016	33.7 (6,755,852)	91.7	39.1	110.2
2017	37.2	91.7	39.1	112.8
2018	37.2	91.7	39.1	112.8
2019	37.2 (6,755,852)	91.7	39.1	120.4

Source: Child Labour and Forced Labour Report, Bureau of International Affairs, 2019; see https://www.dol.gov/agencies/ilab/reports/child-labor/list-of-goods for comparison.

As Deborah Andrews writes,[16] there are approximately 3000 brick-kilns in Nepal. They employ labourers in large numbers. However, the problem with these brick kilns is that many of them are unregistered, and exist in places where there is little government intervention and almost no intervention from non-governmental or civil society organizations. The consequent result is the exploitation of the workers, including the child labourers. More than 250,000 workers are engaged in these brick kilns, of whom as many as 60,000 are child labourers who are subjected to exploitative practices. Most of the workers are unskilled and most of them are migrants coming from rural Nepal and some of them from Northern India. Migrated kilns workers come and join work in the industry with their families. Consequently, women and children work together in the production of bricks. There is a practice in the Nepalese brick-laying industry: the provision of receiving cash in advance of the brick-laying season. The workers are required to stay in the brickfield and work for the entire season starting from April to October and repay the debt taken as advance. Some workers become successful in repaying debt, while others fail to do

---

[16] Deborah Andrews, 'A Better Brick: Addressing Child Labour in Nepal's Brick-Making Industry' (2016), https://stopchildlabor.org/?p=4325

so. Naturally, they return home after the season while being still in debt. They are obliged to return to the same brickfield in the following season to repay the debt. All the workers are paid by the number of bricks they produce—like the practice adopted for paying the beedi makers. Women and children who work under hazardous conditions are also paid accordingly. The number of bonded labourers created in this way cannot be estimated precisely because no such statistical data is maintained in any ways. Bricks produced by the brick kilns are used for internal usage, and hence international organizations cannot easily study the condition of the child labourers involved. The Global Fairness Initiative (GFI), since 2002, has been helping the Nepalese kiln workers—advocating fair wages, equal access to the market and generation of opportunities to end poverty. The project 'Better Brick Nepal', along with the Global Fairness Initiative, Brick Clean Group Nepal, Humanity United and Good Weave International, has been working since 2014 for good social prices on brick kilns and choices for consumer communities. These agencies regularly address the issues of child labour, bonded labour and decent working conditions for the labourers. It is strictly maintained that there should be no child labourer and bonded labourer in the Nepalese kilns, their working hours should be according to the standard norms, and the labourers should not be ill-treated. In fact, Nepal's legislation on child labour and the ILO Convention Number 138 restrict child labour under the age of 14 years. Other than trying to maintain this, the Government of Nepal has taken up measures to ensure compulsory education for every child. Unfortunately, the exploitative kiln-owners are reluctant to pay attention to the specific needs of children engaged in brick-kilns. They are far away from access to education. These owners also do not ensure child-care amenities for children up to the age of six years. They need to provide access to a nursery or child development centre for them, but this does not happen.

Another industry in Nepal that forces children to work under appalling conditions is the carpet weaving industry. These carpet weaving outlets put thousands of children into physical, mental, spiritual and moral hazards. Child labour in the Tibeto-Nepalese Carpet Industry faces extremely bad working conditions. Children are regularly found weaving carpets in dark, crowded, and filthy red-brick sheds. The wool-dust emanates while wool is knotted round metal-rods and it creates mentionable health hazards among the children—especially the girls. As Tom O'Neill writes,[17] the lives of these young female carpet weavers in Nepal are threatened by persistent illness, ill-health due to undernourishment, excessive physical stress, sexual abuse and psychological ailments arising out of their long absence from the family. They are always faced with a grim future.

5.4. PAKISTAN

Millions of children in Pakistan are forced into child labour because of poverty and unemployment. Rising prices of essential commodities and joblessness drive helpless children into the labour force instead of joining class.

A large number of children in Pakistan are involved in domestic chores, mining, fishing, construction, manufacturing and farming, and many of these children are exposed to health hazards. The Federal Bureau of Statistics and the ILO, while conducting a survey in 1996 on the state of child labour in Pakistan, found that the number of Pakistani child labourers aged 5–14 years is around 40 million: 73 per cent of them were boys, and 27 per cent were girls.

Like many other countries, Pakistan was initially reluctant to solve the problems of child labour. It had turned a blind eye even as millions of Pakistani children were engaged in factory works under poor working conditions. When the Government of Pakistan finally began to take adequate measures, the suppliers of exporting goods (especially soccer balls), for example, came under threat because this product was produced partially by child workers. The majority of the Pakistani soccer ball producing industries are located in Sialkot, and they regularly use child labourers in stitching soccer balls. Nevertheless, a credible threat for the Pakistani employers of child labourers came from the West-based consumers in the form of the Harkin Bill. This bill called for a ban on the inputs of goods produced by those industries that used child labour.

In face of hue and cry from within and without, Pakistan agreed to limit/remove child labour according to the UN mandate, and a policy initiative was adopted to ban hazardous labouring of children

---

[17] Tom O' Neill, 'Child Labour in the Tibeto-Nepalese Carpet Industry,' in *The World of Child Labour: A Historical Regional Survey*, ed. H. Hindman (New York: M.E. Sharpe, 2009).

under the age of 14 years. It also ensured the compulsory education of children up to the age of 16 years. In this context, most of the international conventions such as the ILO Convention Number 138 (minimum age), the ILO Convention Number 182 (worst forms of child labour), the UN-CRC Optimal Protocol on Armed Conflict, the UN-CRC Optimal Protocol on the Sale of Children, Child Prostitution and Child Pornography, and the Palermo Protocol on Trafficking in Persons were ratified. As Jonathan Silvers notes,[18] the Employment of Pakistani Children Act of 1991 strictly restricted the use of child labour in hazardous works. Another Act, known as The Bonded Labour Act of Pakistan, 1992, completely banned indentured servitude and the *peshgi* system. However, the Employment of Children Act is restricted to a few sectors and does not cover the sectors where there are larger number of children working in sectors like domestic activities, home-based cottage industries, agriculture, self-employed works and street vending. Interestingly, even enterprises employing a limited number of workers in Pakistan exploit workers regularly—including child labourers.

In the urban and semi-urban areas of Pakistan, a large number of underage children are engaged in small and unregistered establishments. Their employees usually do not obey the restrictive legislative provisions, and the work they perform, in fact, amount to work performed for large industries. Specialized Child-Labour Inspectors could have executed the Child Labour Acts, but, for many years, they were not appointed in Pakistan.

After the publication of the Child Labour Acts in Pakistan (in 1991 and 1992), the Federal Bureau of Statistics, Pakistan, conducted a child labour survey in 1996 and came to the conclusion that 3.3 million Pakistani children were economically active (out of total the then child-population of 40 million). The children were economically active principally to augment household income. However, these working children in Pakistan are regularly faced with very poor sanitation facilities. Polluted water available in factories affects the health of the working children. Long working hours, along with lack of supervision, bring in illnesses and injuries. These children are deprived of proper

---

[18] Jonathan Silvers, 'Child-labour in Pakistan,' *The Atlantic* (February 1996), https://www.theatlantic.com/magazine/archive/1996/02/child-labor-in-pakistan/304660/

medical care too. Many studies specifically mention the sexual harassment faced by minor Pakistani girls while working in sectors such as domestic works, brick kilns, carpet industry, soccer ball stitching, etc. They are—in fact—subjected regularly to physical, psychological and sexual violence, and exploitation. The writers seek to present the child labour survey data, arising out of the survey conducted by the National Federal Bureau of Statistics, Pakistan, in 1996, in Table 5.18. The child labour force participation rates in provinces are shown age-wise, sex-wise and area-wise in Table 5.19.

Child labour data presented in Table 5.19 shows the labour force participation rate among the children working in different sectors of the economy in Pakistan (all sectors together, and according to the rural-urban divide). One could notice that labour force participation is higher in rural areas than urban areas and it is more in the age group of 10–14 years. North-west Frontier Province exhibits 25.44 per cent workforce participation of which, boys represent 39.02 per cent while girls represent 11.58 per cent.

Children are regularly faced with the worst forms of child labour in different sectors of the economy of Pakistan. Statistics on Children's work and education are presented in Table 5.20. It reveals that children's overall representation in the workforce is 9.8 per cent, while 7.8 per cent are attending school in Pakistan. The interesting feature is that the primary completion rate is 71.1 per cent. The agriculture sector alone accommodates 69.4 per cent of working children. All these data have been represented in Table 5.20.

Based on a review of available information, Table 5.21 depicts children's work by sector and activity.

One of the worst forms of child labour prevalent in Pakistan is their employment in the brick kilns industry which is one of the most important forms of the building materials industry. It offers employment to more than 10 million people. But the problem associated with this industry is that it regularly employs more than 2 million underage children as workers who face physical torture and sexual abuse on a daily basis, along with long hours of work and a low wage rates. Working children face inhuman working conditions: for example, their hands are burnt while carrying baked bricks; they fall under the perpetual cycle of debt-trap over generations; and the women and girl children face sexual violence.

Table 5.18 *Child Labourers in Pakistan, 1996*

Provinces/Age-groups	Total	All Areas Boys	Girls	Total	Rural Boys	Girls	Total	Urban Boys	Girls
Pakistan	3,313,420	2,431,992	881,428	2,945,675	2,110,358	835,317	367,745	321,634	46,111
5–9	573,084	333,656	239,428	536,145	302,694	233,451	36,939	30,962	5,977
10–14	2,740,336	2,098,336	642,000	2,409,530	1,807,664	601,866	330,806	290,672	40,134
Punjab	1,943,305	1,414,787	528,518	1,704,577	1,212,330	492,247	238,728	202,457	36,271
5–9	217,817	147,836	69,981	192,973	127,710	65,263	24,844	20,126	4,718
10–14	1,725,488	1,266,951	458,537	1,511,604	1,084,620	426,984	213,884	182,331	31,553
Sindh	298,303	273,350	24,953	208,783	190,798	17,985	89,520	82,552	6,968
5–9	30,099	27,938	2,161	21,995	20,680	1,315	8,104	7,258	846
10–14	268,204	245,412	22,792	186,788	170,118	16,670	81,416	75,294	6,122
NWFP	1,058,089	730,471	327,618	1,121,147	696,207	324,940	36,942	34,264	2,678
5–9	323,201	155,915	167,286	319,375	152,502	166,873	3,826	3,413	413
10–14	734,888	574,556	160,332	701,772	543,705	158,067	33,116	30,851	2,265
Baluchistan	13,723	13,384	339	11,168	11,023	145	2,555	2,361	194
5–9	1,967	1,967	N/av	1,802	1,802	N/av	165	165	N/av
10–14	11,756	11,417	339	9,366	9,221	145	2,390	2,196	194

Source: National Federal Bureau of Statistics, 1996 Survey on Child Labour; also consult https://www.ilo.org/newdelhi/areasofwork/child-labour/publications/WCMS_436435/lang--en/index.htm

Table 5.19 Child Labour Force Participation Rates in Pakistan by Provinces, Age, Sex and Area

Age Group	All Areas			Rural			Urban		
	Both Sexes	Male	Female	Both Sexes	Male	Female	Both Sexes	Male	Female
				Pakistan					
5–9	2.65	2.98	2.30	3.39	3.64	3.11	0.64	1.08	0.20
10–14	14.86	22.17	7.15	18.71	27.47	9.56	5.95	10.9	1.50
5–14	8.72	11.78	4.54	10.26	14.16	6.05	3.24	5.60	0.82
				Punjab					
5–9	1.78	2.31	1.20	2.17	2.69	1.57	0.74	1.22	0.28
10–14	16.60	23.66	9.10	21.14	30.00	12.39	6.42	10.48	1.98
5–14	8.59	12.04	4.86	10.68	14.50	6.49	3.58	5.89	1.10
				Sindh					
5–9	0.66	1.20	0.10	0.81	1.48	0.10	0.43	0.78	0.09
10–14	6.64	11.71	1.18	8.08	14.28	1.49	4.71	8.34	0.74
5–14	3.46	6.18	0.59	4.16	7.37	0.75	2.49	4.50	0.40

	NWFP								
5–9	9.01	8.55	9.48	1.02	9.36	10.71	0.96	1.76	0.20
10–14	23.51	36.65	10.29	25.44	39.02	11.58	9.00	17.69	1.17
5–14	5.76	21.54	9.86	17.18	23.04	11.12	4.81	9.30	0.67
Baluchistan									
5–9	0.16	0.31	–	0.18	0.33	–	0.10	0.18	–
10–14	1.34	2.56	0.08	1.26	2.41	0.04	1.82	3.41	0.29
5–14	6.66	1.23	0.03	0.63	1.19	0.02	0.84	1.51	0.13

Source: Child Labour Survey, 1996.

Table 5.20 Statistics on Children's Work and Education

Children	Related Entity	Age	%
Working (% and Population)	All Pakistan	10–14	9.8 (2,261,704)
	Punjab Province	5–14	12.4
	Sindh Province	5–14	21.5
Working Children by Sector			
Agriculture	All Pakistan	10–14	69.4
Industry	All Pakistan	10–14	10.9
Services	All Pakistan	10–14	19.7
Attending School (%)	All Pakistan	10–14	78.0
	Punjab Province	5–14	77.1
	Sindh Province	5–14	60.6
Combining Work and School (%)	All Pakistan	10–14	0.8
	Punjab Province	7–14	8.2
	Sindh Province	7–14	11.6
Primary Completion Rate (%)	All Pakistan	71.1	
	Punjab Province		Unavailable
	Sindh Province		Unavailable

Source for primary completion rate: Data from 2018, published by the UNESCO Institute of Statistics, 2020 (5).
Source for all other data: International Labour Organization's analysis of statistics from Labour Force Study (LFS), 2017–2018; and Multiple Indicator Cluster Survey 5 (MICS 5), 2016 (6).

In Pakistan, like in several other nations, the bricklaying industry is an informal manufacturing sector, which provides seasonal employment to people coming from rural and semi-urban areas. Almost all the family members of the migrated workers including their wives and other female members, children including the girls are seasonally engaged. But, as Bisharat Ali writes on the 91st page of *Bricks and Bondage: Biler Report on Labour Rig in Pakistan* (July 2010), the working conditions prevailing in the Pakistani brick kilns are outrightly hazardous to human

Table 5.21 *Overview of Children's Work by Sector and Activity*

Sector/Industry Related Activity	Entity
Agriculture	Farming, including harvesting cotton, wheat and sugarcane
	Fishing, including deep sea fishing
Industry	Manufacturing glass bangles + surgical instruments + jewellery
	Weaving carpets + producing garments and tanning leather
	Producing bricks
	Mining coal + gemstones and crushing stone
Services	Domestic work (242,931)
	Working in hotels, restaurants, gas stations and automobile repair
	Scavenging + sorting garbage and recyclables, begging and street vending
Categorical worst forms of child labour#	Forced labour in agriculture, bricklaying, carpet weaving and coal mining
	Forced domestic work, sometimes as a result of human trafficking
	Commercial sexual exploitation, including use in the production of pornography, sometimes as a result of human trafficking
	Forced begging, sometimes as a result of human trafficking
	Forced recruitment of children by non-state armed groups for use in armed conflict
	Use in illicit activities, including trafficking and producing drugs

Source: https://www.ilo.org/newdelhi/areasofwork/child-labour/publications/WCMS_436435/lang--en/index.htm

Notes: + Determined by national law or regulation as hazardous and, as such, relevant to Article 3 (d) of ILO C.182.
Child labour understood as the worst forms of child labour *per se* under Article 3 (a)-(c) of ILO C.182.

health. Moreover, these bricklayers and their family members fall prey to debt traps regularly and over generations. The migrated Pakistani families working in brick kilns send their women and children into different stages of brick making in order to enhance their weekly wages, while simultaneously sacrificing their future enhanced income and education of children. Such workers become isolated from the political and social environment, and this does have a negative impact on their basic entitlements and human rights. Interestingly, in Pakistan, child labour is prohibited; debt bondage is banned; and bricklaying has been declared as hazardous work. In spite of all of these efforts, child labour is still used in this industry, carefully violating government norms. Social security benefits are regularly violated in most of the bricklaying industries. The NGO activities in Pakistan principally focus on eliminating child labour and debt bondage through education, and, to this end, the NGOs have been constantly organizing awareness campaigns to convince parents to send their children to school. They have also opened many special schools near the brick kilns and are in the task of highlighting the child labour issues in the international forum. Trade Unions in Pakistan have not been so much successful in the brick kilns, as many studies have revealed, especially in the case of child labour. But the NGOs are trying hard to do their bit.

5.5. AFGHANISTAN

Afghanistan is one of the poorest countries in the world, and its children regularly suffer from the worst forms of poverty, malnutrition and violence. The UNICEF, in a report on Afghanistan, had once identified it as 'worst place to be born in the world'.

Truly, the situation of Afghan children is outrightly critical. The child mortality rate is very high (the mortality rate for under five years of age children is 66%). More than one-third of newborns are underweight, and one woman out of eight dies during childbirth. Due to poverty (more than 45 per cent of the Afghans live in abject poverty), a very limited number of children are sent to school and are able to complete their primary education. More than 20 per cent of the impoverished Afghan children are involved in different forms of works such as street vending, water carrying, cardboard collecting, shoe polishing, taxi soliciting, domestic labouring, providing assistance to boutiques, and agriculture activities. Young Afghans often become victims of violence and sexual abuse. The incidents involving terrorist attacks on schools are common occurrences in Afghanistan. Other forms of Afghan child labour are found in sectors like handicrafts, automobile-repairing, wiring, blacksmithing, porting, selling woods, shopkeeping, working at restaurants, carpet weaving, litter collecting, street working or working at factories and workshops, shoe-making, begging, tailoring, participating in animal husbandry, car-washing, handworking and so on.

The major reason for the prevalence of child labour in Afghanistan is partly due to the continuous war between the government and the Taliban and partly due to poverty and corruption. The main reason—it is known—is the children's obligation to work for their families. They are forced to earn by working as metal workers, welders, miners, carpet makers, bricklayers, street vendors and as participants in commercial sex. Several research groups, government offices and NGOs in Afghanistan have identified several worst forms of child labour, such as the recruitment of children in armed conflict by non-state armed groups, forced recruitment of children by state armed groups for using them in armed conflict, usage of children in production and trafficking of drugs and pick-pocketing, their employment for domestic work, sexual exploitation as a result of human trafficking, and forcing children in begging and in the production of bricks and carpets. These issues remain unresolved even in this 21st century.

Afghanistan, like many other countries, ratified the key international conventions, such as the ILO Convention Number 138 (relating to minimum age), the ILO Convention Number 182 (regarding worst forms of child labour), the UN–CRC on optional protocol on Armed conflict, the UN–CRC on optional protocol on the sale of children, child prostitution and child pornography, and the Palermo Protocol on Trafficking in Persons. The Government of Afghanistan launched the first legislation on child labour known as the Child Rights' Protection Law (CRPL) or the Child Rights' Act in 2019. The child legislation defines the rights of children related to services, along with issues like the children's birth registration, health, education, vaccination and social protection. The law provides equal rights to boys and girls for availing compulsory education up to the secondary class free of cost.

The Government has taken strict action to protect children who suffered abuse, neglect, torture and sexual exploitation. Recruitment of children in armed conflict has been strictly banned and any violation of it has been declared to be a severely punishable offence.

In one of its 2019 studies, UNICEF found that 3.7 million school students were out of school in Afghanistan majority of whom—about 60 per cent—were girl children. The displacement of the population due to conflict, schools being used as military bases, militant attacks on schools, insufficient number of schools, high school fees, shortage of female teachers, sexual harassment and so on were internationally identified as the leading force for children's dropouts from school.

The Convention on the Rights of the Child (RC–1994) protects children against hazardous work, and the Government of Afghanistan has accommodated all the responsibilities, including the following: (a) the Government of Afghanistan recognize the right of every child to a standard of living for her/his all-round development; (b) the children's parents or their guardians are made responsible to provide the necessary conditions for their living; (c) the Government is determined to provide necessary materials to the parents or the guardians of children for basic minimum necessaries; (d) the Government makes arrangement for securing the recovery of maintenance for the children from their parents or persons responsible for their financial maintenance living within the country or from abroad; (e) the Government has recognized to protect the children from economic exploitation and hazardous work; and (f) the minimum working age and working hours have been specified. However, these have not been implemented everywhere in the Afghan industries. This needs constant watch and monitoring from the part of the Government.

Article 13(4) of the Labour Law of Afghanistan is understood to be required to be implemented in a better way in order to protect children working in hazardous jobs that injure their health, causing physical disability. Simultaneously, it needs to appoint more labour inspectors to cover the entire country—who would monitor hazardous industrial sectors giving full propriety. For the more effective usage of labour law it is necessary to amend them thoroughly—especially to empower the Ministry of Labour, Social Affairs, and other Departments for monitoring and enforcing child labour provisions. Alongside, it needs a constant dialogue and consultation with the civil society organizations through the incorporation of robust child protection measures. It is fervently

Table 5.22 *Statistics on Children's Work and Education*

Children	Age (Range in Years)	%
Working (% and population)	5–14	7.5 (673,949)
Attending school (%)	5–14	41.8
Combining work and school (%)	7–14	4.6
Primary completion rate (%)		85.6

Sources: 1. Primary completion rate—Data from 2018, as published by the UNESCO Institute for Statistics, 2020.
2. Other sata: ILO's Analysis of Statistics from Multiple Indicator Cluster Survey 4 (MICS-4), 2010–2011.
Note: Also consult the statistical data available on the https://www.ilo.org/wcmsp5/groups/public/@dgreports/@dcomm/documents/publication/wcms_575499.pdf

felt that the Child Protection Action Network should be expanded to all the provinces of Afghanistan to better monitor and implement provisions on working children at risk.

The writers would presently like to display the current statistics on children's work and education in Table 5.22.

The children's engagement in different sectors of the economy of Afghanistan has been represented in Table 5.23.

The brick kilns industry and carpet industry are the two major industries in Afghanistan that use child labourers on a large scale, and the works performed by children are hazardous and detrimental to their health. These children, in addition, are deprived of basic education,

Table 5.23 *Children's Work by Sector and Activity*

Sector/Industry	Activity
Agriculture	Farming including harvesting poppies
	Herding
Industry	Carpet weaving
	Construction, including gravelling, paving and painting
	Coal, gold and salt mining

(Table 5.23 Continued)

(Table 5.23 Continued)

Sector/Industry	Activity
	Bricklaying
	Working in metal workshops including in the production of doors, windows and water tanks
	Working as tinsmiths and welders
	Transporting water and goods, including across international borders
	Street work, including peddling, vending, shoe-shining, carrying goods and begging
	Collecting garbage
	Washing cars
	Selling goods in stores
	Collecting and selling firewood
	Repairing automobiles
	Tailoring in garment workshops
	Pushing loads on a wheelbarrow
	Working as waiters in restaurants
	Recruitment of children by non-state armed groups for use in armed conflict
	Forced recruitment of children by state armed groups for use in armed conflict
Categorical worst forms of child labour	Use in illicit activities, including in the production and trafficking of drugs and pickpocketing
	Domestic work as a result of human trafficking
	Commercial sex and exploitation, sometimes as a result of human trafficking
	Forced labour in begging and in the production of bricks and carpets, and for use as assistant truck drivers each sometimes as a result of human trafficking and commercial sexual exploitation, sometimes as a result of human trafficking

Source: https://www.hrw.org/sites/default/files/report_pdf/afghanistan0716_brochure_web.pdf

play and fun. The instance of child abuse in the metalwork industry is found when the children work as apprentices in making gates, doors, water tankers and windows. The abuses notwithstanding, they are involved in cutting sheets of metals, welding, lifting heavy items, etc. The tools children use in the Afghan metalwork industries are heavy and dangerous. Examples of such tools are hammers, anvils, chisels and blowtorches. We would now explain some of the important aspects of child labour engaged in these industries one by one.

In the Afghan bricklaying industry, hapless children work long hours with very little amount of pay. This effectively makes them 'bonded child labourers'. These 'bonded child labourers', along with their parents, work under conditions of servitude to pay off a debt. They have to continue working in the bricklaying industry until the debt is repaid. The Afghan children—at a very young age (some of them as young as five)—start working in this industry. The work they perform is laborious and exhausting, and the working hours are long: longer than 70 hours a week. Boys and teenage girls work 10 to 15 hours a day, and the shelter available to them is not liveable. They are particularly engaged in clearing the fields of rubble. They are also forced to arrange dried-out bricks in stacks. Water is fetched by them; and they bring sand used for making bricks.

The Afghan bonded labour families are employed in brick kilns. The season for making bricks starts in the month of March, and the work goes up to October. During this eight months' period, children cannot attend school. Not only this, the bonded labour families are forced to send their children to work in the bricklaying factories because they are not in a position to afford the transport cost and the other costs involved in sending their children to school. In a word, they cannot afford the opportunity costs of school attendance. The UNICEF and the Government of Afghanistan—under its Ministry of Education—have established several projects offering education to children who work in brick kilns industry. Several community-based schools were also established near the brick kilns. The first such project was started in 2010, and by December 2015, approximately 130,000 of the 380,000 odd impoverished Afghan students who got admitted to project-run schools, reached the fourth grade.

Later days' UNESCO data show that 10 per cent of children working in Kabul's Sukhroad brick kilns attended school in 2011. These were the brick kilns where the UNICEF's community based schooling (CBS) was in operation. Importantly, the school attendance of Afghan working children was only 5 per cent in the brick kilns where the CBS programme was not active. It has been alleged time and again by the families involved in the industry that proper attention was not given to establishing schools by the Afghan Government or by the CBS programme.

Another problem faced by the Afghan children in the brick kiln industries is the illness suffered by them due to hard physical labour, long working hours per day, and dangerous working conditions. Children face heatstroke, and they also experience other fatal illnesses such as malaria, asthma and silicosis while breathing in brick dust.

The writers would now like to present some of the data in Table 5.24 related to child labour as well as adult workers in the brick kiln industry in two provinces of Afghanistan (Kabul and Nangarhar)—based on the report commissioned by ILO–IPEC in 2011.

The report says that both adults and children work over 70 hours per week in a repetitive fashion, and these works expose them to sun, heat and blowing dust. Moreover, to make up their pitiable financial conditions, the families working at the Afghan brick kilns take advances from the kiln owners. The advances are made under

Table 5.24 Daily Wages of Brick Makers (Child and Adult)

District	Worker	Piece Rate per 1,000 Bricks	Bricks/Day	Wages per Day
Deh Sabz	Adult	370 AFA (7.76 USD)	1,100	407 AFA/8.54 USD
	Child		750	278 AFA/5.82 USD
	Family		2,320	854 AFA/18.01 USD
Surkhroad	Adult	270 AFA (5.67 USD)	1,100	297 AFA/6.23 USD
	Child		630	170 AFA/3.57 USD
	Family		2,240	605 AFA/12.69 USD

Source: ILO-IPEC Commissioned Report, 2011 based on the response of 186 households. One may consult 'They Bear All the Pain', published by the Hazardous Child Labour in Afghanistan, H.R.W., https://www.hrw.org/report/2016.07.15/

Table 5.25 Breakdown of Average Household Debt

District	Latest Loan Amount	Repaid Amount	Remaining Debt	Total Loans (5-Yr. average)
Deh Sabz	55,000 AFA 1,154 USD	21,400 AFA 449 USD	33,600 AFA 1,053 USD	133,900 AFA 2,810 USD
Sukhroad	64,800 AFA 1,360 USD	17,500 AFA 367 USD	473,000 AFA 1,266 USD	115,600 AFA 2,426 USD

Source: ILO-IPEC-commissioned Report, 2011 based on the response of 180 households. For details, see the ILO-IPEC-commissioned report, *Buried in Bricks: A Rapid Assessment of Bonded Labour in Afghan Brickkilns*, published in 2011 on the ILO website.

the condition that they would work (including their other family members and children) at the kilns at lower wages as is evident from the above table.

Due to the debt burden, the kiln worker families in Afghanistan cannot freely move from one industry to another. Their freedom of movement from one job to the other is very much limited due to the bindings of contracts. They have also limited access to the world outside the brick kilns, except when they go to pick up daily necessities or visit clinics or doctors. The breakdown of household debt in Afghanistan has been shown in Table 5.25.

The luxury axiom is followed in the brick kilns. That is, the term 'child non-work' is almost a 'luxury good' to the brick-kiln worker families. Due to poverty and heavy debt burden, they cannot send their children to school; but they send the children to the brick kilns for earning which is extremely necessary for family needs. It is clearly evident that only 15 per cent of children of workers' families attend school. That too is made possible because of the presence of a UNICEF-based pilot project providing school on kiln-sites which made schools accessible to the children.

The ILO–IPEC-commissioned report reveals that 56 per cent of workers in the Afghan brick kilns come from children below the age of 18 years—of whom 58 per cent are boys and 42 per cent girls. Children below the age of 15 years contribute to 47 per cent in the workforce participation, and the contribution of boys' here is 33 per cent, and that of girls is 14 per cent.

Table 5.26 Health and Development Risks of Brickmaking

Cause	Health and Developmental Risks
Manual labour in kilns and work conditions	1. Respiratory problems (e.g., asthma, chronic chest infections and silicosis) 2. Exposure to toxic fumes (when kilns use waste, such as tires and fuel) 3. Seasonal diseases including malaria 4. Physical injury: back and leg pain and injury 5. Heatstroke 6. Skin allergies and chapped skin from exposure to the elements
Living conditions and poverty	1. Illness related to poor hygiene and sanitation 2. Stunted growth 3. Malnutrition 4. Shortened lifespan

Source: ILO, 2011.

Writings like Michael Kamber article,[19] Madhura Swaminathan's 1998 essay[20] and the 2011 UNICEF report[21] have poignantly summed up the various problems faced by the Afghan brickmaking child labourers. Actually, any kind of brickmaking requires huge physical labour: continuous repetitive works under the sun, and blowing dust over longer hours. It thus exerts a mentionable negative effect on the health of both adult and child workers involved in brick kilns. The blowing dust creates respiratory problems—to reiterate—causing fatal diseases such as silicosis and asthma. The writers would now display a table (Table 5.26) that clearly focuses on the various health hazards that occur to labourers (including the child labourers) due to their working at the Afghan brick kilns.

The above-given report clearly explains the major reasons for the persistence of child labour in Afghanistan—especially what is prevalent in brick kilns. These reasons are the cycle of poverty, the cycle of

---

[19] Michael Kamber, 'In Afghanistan Kilns, a Cycle of Debt and Servitude,' *The New York Times*, 15 March 2011.

[20] Madhura Swaminathan, 'Economic Growth and the Persistence of Child Labour: Evidence from an Indian City,' *The World Development* 26, no. 8 (1998): 1513–1528.

[21] UNICEF, 'Sukhroad District Brick Kiln Project.'

dependence, the cycle of vulnerability and the cycle of debt burden. Intervention is considered to be essential from the government at the national and provisional levels and non-governmental national and international organizations to completely eradicate poverty from Afghanistan.

Carpet weaving is an important cottage industry in Afghanistan. This industry is basically a home-based small-scale enterprise, which employs labour from the family—especially the children and women. This industry employs more girls than boys for weaving carpets. Child labourers are used in huge numbers; more than 90 per cent of the Afghan child labourers are employed in this sector.

The Afghan carpet-weaving sector is indeed an important employment sector for children—engaging about 50 per cent of them in the total labour force. However, in recent years, Afghanistan is facing stiff competition from Pakistan, Iran and Turkey vis-à-vis the marketing of machine-spun carpets. Naturally, Afghanistan is inclining gradually towards making carpets at low cost in order to survive in the market competition. This has—interestingly—led to the employment of low-waged children in large numbers. Such children start working in carpet-weaving workshops from the age of six or seven years, and continue to work for long hours—approximately, 12 hours or more per day. This work is detrimental to their health as they suffer from respiratory diseases due to breathing the dust of wools.

Working children in the carpet industry also suffer from other ailments and physical injuries like carpal tunnel syndrome, neuralgia, swollen finger joints due to long-hour sittings and continuously performing monotonous and repetitive work using sharp equipment. Most of them suffer from eye problems due to working in poor lighting. However, the industry is thriving through illegal employment—as a 2018 report by the US Department of Labour Affairs has found out, four out of six carpet weavers in Afghanistan are children.

GoodWeave International has been constantly working in Afghanistan to reduce child labour engaged in hazardous works. Its objective is to withdraw children—especially the girl children—and send them to school. According to Australian Research and Management Consulting, the product of an independent evaluation of GoodWeave's programming in Afghanistan in 2013–2018, due to extreme poverty and societal perceptions, more than 675,000 children—aged 5–14 years—were forced to join the Afghan carpet weaving labour force in those 5 years, leaving behind chances of their schooling and for better living in future. However, as a result of government and non-governmental-interventions—the report says—there has been a spectacular reduction in child labour in the targeted group of people—especially in Kabul, Balkh and Jawzjian—and an increase in the enrolment of working children.

The Ministry of Labour, Social Affairs, Martyrs and Disabled (MOLSAMD), Government of Afghanistan, in collaboration with the ILO, published the National Child Labour Strategy and Action Plan 2018–2030 in 2018. Among other objectives, the main focus of the Action Plan is to adopt a straightforward strategy for the prevention and elimination of Afghan child labour. Four decades of continuous war in Afghanistan, along with poor socio-economic and security conditions, inward and outward migrations, and other factors have given rise to child labour in formal and informal hazardous works. The Action Plan also identifies that the issue of child labour is not only a moral problem; but is also related to issues such as child rights violations, and the lack of facilities for public health and basic education. The Action Plan Agency is determined and committed to eradicating the worst forms of child labour and improving their moral conditions through imparting education. It aims at completely eliminating child labour in Afghanistan by 2030, and ending its worst forms by 2025. While executing this policy, a set of strategies have been adopted. These are as follows: (a) Establishment of child labour knowledge base; (b) taking of a holistic approach, integrating government and non-government actors along with social partners to eliminate child labour; (c) improvement of the agencies of law, law enforcement and execution; (d) improvement social action and social protection mechanisms; (e) improvement of the conditions of households of working children; and (f) improvement of the institutional and technical capacities of actors.

It is being hoped that the Action Plan would be hugely successful in the long run.

5.6. INDIA

Child labour in every society and economy is a social evil which had its roots since ancient times. In India, most of the poor families use their children as workers who offer their labour to different sectors even as they work under exploitative conditions—leaving their schooling, games and fun. In India, child labourers could be found working as bonded labourers, child soldiers and products of trafficking. Children are also seen working in industries that are bad for health—such as brick kilns, carpet weaving factories, garment-making industries and domestic service (e.g., prostitution). These workings prevent children from going to school, and, instead, they are forced to acquire skills that they require to progress. As the compilers of various Indian child labour–related articles[22] opine, working children, who face violence, often grow up to develop a mental illness like depression, anxiety, hopelessness and loss of confidence. As Rajendra Srivastava writes,[23] nowadays, the term 'modern slavery' is being increasingly used to explain the exploitative conditions under which children are forced to do different jobs as forced labourers, bonded labourers, domestic servants and recruitees in war. This actually shows that the miseries of children have only increased.

In fact, child labour is a global phenomenon that is deep-rooted in the socio-cultural and economic conditions of every country. Its prevalence is the highest among the African nations and the lowest in the most advanced nations. One can always see a large number of working children in developing and less-developed countries.

To end the menace of child labour, the government-level initiatives in post-Independence India began in 1976 in a most sincere way when the UN's General Assembly announced 1979 as the 'International Year of the Child'. The objective of such an announcement was to create a worldwide consciousness regarding the promotion of the well-being of children less-privileged and at work. In fact, in every society children are considered to be the most important assets in terms of future growth and development. It is also true that the future of a country—whether it is so-called 'developed' or 'developing'—depends on how the children of that country are cared, reared and brought up with education and training. However, a significant number of parents, due to several reasons, fail to do so, and the children are forced to work as child labourers from a tender age. They work under pitiable conditions without their willingness and capacity and are exploited mercilessly. In India too, a large number of child labourers disguised or open—work in formal

---

[22] https://www.humanism.org
[23] Rajendra Srivastava, 'Children at Work, Child Labour and Modern Slavery in India: An Overview,' *Indian Paediatrics* 56, no. 15 (August 2019): 633–638.

and informal sectors of employment on a daily basis. Considering this grave situation of working children, the Government of India, in 1979, formed a Committee on Child Labour under the chairmanship of M. S. Gurupadaswamy. The Committee was entrusted to look into the reasons for the employment of child labour in detail, and into its consequent impact on society and economy. The Committee instructed the various state governments to form taskforces that would assist it in collecting data relating to child labour in the state. Three working groups were also formed separately to study the extent and dimensions of the problem, the adequacy of the existing legal framework, and to identify the various institutional arrangements for helping the working children as also to obviate employment of children in a longer perspective.

The Gurupadaswamy Committee defined 'child labour' as that part of 'child population who take part in paid or unpaid work', and it has—sadly—existed in India from the early times in history. Industrialization and urbanization have also forced a huge number of rural people in India to migrate to urban centres in search of jobs. Children too had to join work, and they had to face various kinds of health hazards. The employment of children into the labour force, as the Committee asserted, reduced the volume of employment for the adult workers, which, in fact, reduced the wages paid to the adults. The Gurupadaswamy Committee had identified some of the causes of child labour in India. These are listed as follows. First, there is a perception among the working classes that formal education has little relevance to their children. What they urgently require for their children is acquiring the necessary skills so that the children could help their families.

Second, chronic poverty is the root cause for the prevalence and continuation of child labour in India over generations. Parents desperately want their children to earn for the family. In some cases, children become the bread earners when their parents fail to earn adequate money for the family due to some reason.

Third, there are many works where children are more suitable than adults. In some cases, children are more active, agile and fast in completing the task than adult workers. Moreover, children are almost always paid less, and they have to work for long hours each day. In this way, child labour generates greater surplus value for the enterprises, and they become larger sources of profit.

Fourth, there are certain works which can be better performed by children, and children can better be managed by the employers. There are some crafts—*zari* and carpet, for example—that can be well-finished by the children, with the highest degree of sophistication and excellence. The tiny fingers of children can easily acquire the required skills in performing these tasks.

Fifth, Indian employers have always found it easier to train children than adults because it requires less cost to train them up. Moreover, children cannot become members of trade unions, which are often taken at task by the employers for 'misguiding workers' and for 'militantly fighting for their causes'. Sociologists and economists trying to understand these factors have also routinely noted that there are unmistakable links between child labour and schooling among poor families. In poor families, the guardians/parents regularly send their children to work instead of admitting/sending them to school and they do it as a kind of survival strategy. The Gurupadaswamy Committee especially cited the Third All Indian Education Survey results which stated that in 1965, the gross enrolment position for classes I to V was 14.36 per cent which rose to 79.16 per cent in 1973. This was 30.15 per cent in 1965 for classes VI to VIII which rose only to 34.72 per cent in 1973. This showed the high persistence of out-of-school children—about two-thirds—among the children in the age group of 11–13 years.

Sixth, the Committee identified that there was a distinct lack of schools, especially in the countryside. Many children—due to scarce and inaccessible schooling facilities—could not be admitted. Moreover, there was a very high dropout rate especially among the children of poor families, and more so among the female children of such families. The dropout rate was found to be very high in slum-areas, drought-prone areas and in poorer families—as also recorded in Perspective on Child in India, published by the Central Institute of Research and Training in Public Cooperation in 1975.

The Gurupadaswamy Committee, following its survey, suggested in detail the framing of a legislative framework in India for child labour (in Chapter III of its Report). One can remember that the writers too have attempted a discussion of child labour legislations in India in the First Chapter of the present book. Therefore, a further discussion regarding the issue need not be attempted. What, rather, is needed is a discussion in brief of the different supportive measures for child labour as proposed by the Gurupadaswamy Committee. The Committee notes with certainty that child labour is a social evil caused due to poverty and unemployment. The removal of poverty and unemployment may be the primary appropriate measures to solve the problem of child labour. Removal of child labour is not possible unless poverty is reduced to its lowest level. Wholehearted efforts and time are needed to tackle the situation. Only legislation cannot abolish it. Not only the employment of children in hazardous work should be banned there should also be minimum wages for parents of working children. This would influence the parents not to send their children to work—especially to do hazardous jobs. Stress was given towards finding out a meaningful and effective education policy. It was said that the education curriculum needed to be geared to bring the maximum of skills and competence in the child. To reduce dropouts among girls, they could be provided with some institutional arrangements in the schooling system itself— for example, providing crèche for young children. Due to insufficient arrangements for non-formal education for working children, night-shift schools were thought to be of great help. Provisions for providing educational facilities only to children working in the plantation were made according to the Plantation Labour Act. This needed to be extended. Educational facilities for child labour were required to be very extensive. To ensure the good health of working children, medical and health support were necessitated, and in the case of unrecognized sectors—like agriculture—the health facilities were recommended to be linked with the National Health Scheme. The Committee also suggested working out of schemes to provide supplementary nutrition to working children at subsidized rates extending up to rural areas. Proper housing facilities and time for joining recreation and cultural activities were necessitated too.

The sectors in which child labour is involved are not uniform throughout India. Some works have been identified as 'hazardous works', and legislations have been implemented to ban children to work in those sectors. Hazardous works in India are defined as follows: transport of passengers, goods or mails by railways, cinder picking, cleaning of an ash pit or building operation in the railway premises, work in a catering establishment at a railway station or with any other work where such work is done in close proximity to or between the railway lines, a port authority within the limits of any port, work relating to the selling of crackers and fireworks in shops, abattoirs, automobile workshops and garages, foundries, handling of toxic explosives, handloom and power loom industry, mines, plastic units and fibreglass workshops, domestic workers and servants, *dhabas*, diving, caring elephants and working in the circus, beedi making, carpet-weaving, cement industry, cloth industry, manufacture of matches, explosives and fireworks, mica-cutting and splitting, shellac manufacture, tanning, wool-cleaning, construction, manufacture of pencils, manufacturing process using toxic metals, etc. Cashew nut processing, *aggarbatti*-manufacturing, automobile repairs, brick kilns, detergent manufacturing, gem cutting and polishing, jute textiles, manufacturing process having exposure to lead such as primary and secondary smelting etc., manufacture of cement pipe, manufacture of glass, manufacture of dyes and dyestuff, manufacturing or handling of pesticides and insecticides, manufacturing or processing and handling of corrosive and toxic substances, manufacturing of burning coal, manufacturing of sport goods, moulding and processing of fibreglass and plastic, oil expelling and refinery, paper making, potteries and ceramic industry, polishing, moulding, cutting, welding and manufacturing of brass goods, processes in agriculture, sawmills, sericulture processing, skinning, dyeing, etc., stone breaking, tyre making and repairing, sari making, electroplating, graphite powdering, grinding, diamond cutting, extraction of slate from mines, rag-picking and scavenging, processes involving exposure to excessive heat and cold, mechanized fishing, food processing, beverage industry, timber handling and loading, mechanical lumbering, warehousing, etc. These have been outlined in the Child Labour (Prohibition and Regulation) Act (CLAPRA), 1986.

Child Labour (Prohibition and Regulation) Amendment Act, 2016 prohibits the employment of children in all occupations and adolescents in hazardous jobs and processes. A fine, the Act says, is imposed on those who employ adolescents to work. The list of hazardous jobs as mentioned in the 1986 Act, consisting of 83 jobs has been reduced and restricted, among others, to mining, explosives and occupations mentioned in the Factory Act. In the amendment act of 2016, it is specifically mentioned that a child cannot be employed for any work or process. But it cannot be applied to the child who helps his/her family or family-based enterprise. The work that the child does, should obviously be non-hazardous as listed in the Schedule. All such works, the amendment act mentions, can be done after school hours and during vacations. A child artist can work in the audio-visual entertainment industry such as advertisements, films, television serials or the like or sports activities and all such works can be performed by a child without hampering school education. Another commendable part of the Amendment Act of 2016 is the provision of punishment for any employer who employs any child or allows any child to work. Such employer is punishable with imprisonment for a period of not less than six months and a maximum for two years with fines ranging between ₹20,000 and up to ₹50,000 (The Child Labour [Prohibition and Regulations] Amendment Act, 2016, Ministry of Law and Justice of India, 30 July 2016). The Amendment Act allows, so to say, children to work in chemical mixing units, cotton farms, battery recycling units and brick kilns. Allowing children to work in family works and family-based enterprises may be a blow to the children belonging to depressed communities and children of poor families trapped in intergenerational debt bondage. Another flaw in the new Amendment is that the hours of work has not been clearly defined. Returning home from school, a child may be engaged in family work and how long he can be employed is not mentioned. This may ultimately hamper the child's education as well as his mental and physical growth. It is, in fact, the children from the underprivileged and other backward communities, who, more or less, represent 80 per cent of the total child labour force in India.[24]

Bihar, Uttar Pradesh, Rajasthan, Madhya Pradesh and Maharashtra are the five states of India that together use about half of the total child labour used in India. However, child labour has been drastically reduced in almost all the Indian states over the last two decades. The schemes introduced by the Government of India and the State governments such as the Right to Education, Mahatma Gandhi National Rural Empowerment Guarantee Act (MGNREGA), Mid-Day Meal, and setting up of schools and other programmes specific to the local conditions initiated by the government level or through private initiative have given rise to the scope of dramatic fall in child labour over decades. The highest concentration of child labour is in the states of Uttar Pradesh, Bihar, Rajasthan, Maharashtra and Madhya Pradesh—constituting about 55 per cent of the total working children in India. This is shown in Table 5.27.

According to the Indian Census 2011, of the total 259.6 million children in India, approximately 10.1 million were working children,

---

[24] Ruchira Gupta, 'A law that allows child labour', *The Hindu*, 10 August 2016. https://www.thehindu.com/opinion/columns/Ruchira-Gupta-Child-Labour-Prohibition-and-Regulation-Amendment-Act-2016-A-law-that-allows-child-labour/article56842404.ece

Table 5.27 Concentration of Child Labour

States	%	Number (Million)
Uttar Pradesh	21.5	2.18
Bihar	10.7	1.09
Rajasthan	8.4	0.85
Maharashtra	7.2	0.73
Madhya Pradesh	6.9	0.70

Source: Census of India, 2011; also see https://www.ilo.org/wcmsp5/groups/public/---asia/---ro-bangkok/---sro-new_delhi/documents/publication/wcms_557089.pdf

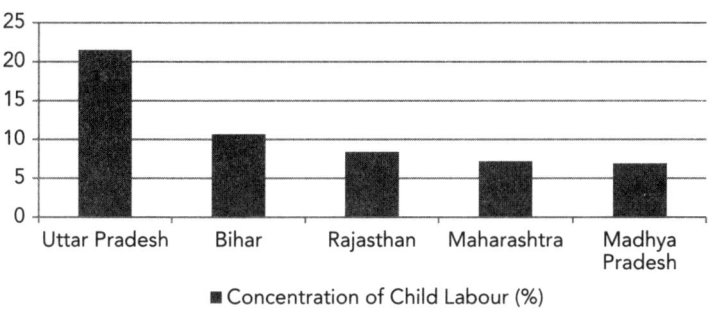

■ Concentration of Child Labour (%)

and in per cent it amounts to 3.9 per cent. Over 42.7 million children were out of school but the ray of hope is that there has been a sharp decline in it by 2.6 million between 2001 and 2011. The decline was more prominent in the rural areas. Working children and their distribution by type of work in 2011 is shown in Tables 5.28 and 5.29.

Table 5.28 Total Children and Their Number in Percentage Terms, 5–14 Years

Total number (millions)				%		
Rural	Urban	Total	Year	Rural	Urban	Total
11.4	1.3	12.7	2001	5.9	2.1	5.0
8.1	2.0	10.1	2011	4.3	2.9	3.9

Source: Census of India, 2001 and 2011; also see https://www.ilo.org/wcmsp5/groups/public/---asia/---ro-bangkok/---sro-new_delhi/documents/publication/wcms_557089.pdf

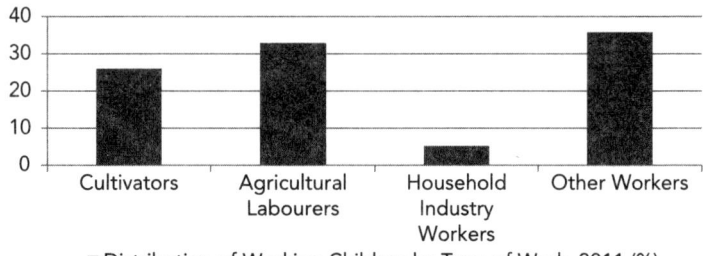

■ Distribution of Working Children by Type of Work, 2011 (%)

Table 5.29 *Distribution of Working Children by Type of Work, 2011*

Area of Work	%	Number (Million)
Cultivators	26.0	2.63
Agricultural labourers	32.9	3.33
Household industry workers	5.2	0.52
Other workers	35.8	3.62

Source: Census of India, 2001 and 2011; also see https://www.ilo.org/wcmsp5/groups/public/---asia/---ro-bangkok/---sro-new_delhi/documents/publication/wcms_557089.pdf

Comparing child labour census data for 1971, 1981, 1991, 2001 and 2011, one can clearly notice a declining trend across the country. The data shows that in 1971, the total number of working children amounted to 10,753,985 which rose to 13,640,870 in 1981. A declining trend was observed in 1991 when it declined to 1,12,85,349. Again it went up to 1,26,66,377 in 2001 and for the first time, it went down drastically to 43,53,247 in 2011. This is shown in Table 5.30. This is also portrayed in terms of a diagram. Over the decades there has been a decreasing trend in child labour all over the globe and in this context, India is no exception. Still, there are, according to Save the Child, 2016, over 8.3 million children in the age group of 5–14 years working in different sectors such as agriculture, manufacturing, mining and domestic service. The UNICEF, in 2017, had identified that there are some distinctive contributing factors leading to child labour in India, and these factors are migration, emergencies, lack of employment and poverty. These children are certainly being deprived of education and training. Child labour at a minor age face violence,

Table 5.30 State-wise Distribution of Working Children According to 1971, 1981, 1991, 2001 and 2011 Censuses in the Age Group of 5–14 Years

S. No.	Name of the State/UT	1971	1981	1991	2001****	2011
1	Andhra Pradesh	1,627,492	1,951,312	1,661,940	1,363,339	404,851
2	Assam*	239,349	**	327,598	351,416	99,512
3	Bihar	1,059,359	1,101,764	942,245	1,117,500	451,590
4	Gujarat	518,061	616,913	523,585	485,530	250,318
5	Haryana	137,826	194,189	109,691	253,491	53,492
6	Himachal Pradesh	71,384	99,624	56,438	107,774	15,001
7	Jammu & Kashmir	70,489	258,437	**	175,630	25,528
8	Karnataka	808,719	1,131,530	976,247	822,615	249,483
9	Kerala	111,801	92,854	34,800	26,156	21,757
10	Madhya Pradesh	1,112,319	1,698,597	1,352,563	1,065,259	286,310
11	Maharashtra	988,357	1,557,756	1,068,427	764,075	496,916
12	Chhattisgarh				364,572	63,884
13	Manipur	16,380	20,217	16,493	28,836	11,805
14	Meghalaya	30,440	44,916	34,633	53,940	18,839

(Table 5.30 Continued)

(Table 5.30 Continued)

S. No.	Name of the State/UT	1971	1981	1991	2001****	2011
15	Jharkhand				407,200	90,996
16	Uttaranchal/Uttarakhand				70,183	208,098
17	Nagaland	13,726	16,235	16,467	45,874	11,062
18	Orissa/Odisha	492,477	702,293	452,394	377,594	92,087
19	Punjab	232,774	216,939	142,868	177,268	90,353
20	Rajasthan	587,389	819,605	774,199	1,262,570	252,338
21	Sikkim	15,661	8561	5598	16457	2704
22	Tamil Nadu	713,305	975055	578889	418801	151437
23	Tripura	17,490	24,204	16,478	21,756	4,998
24	Uttar Pradesh	1,326,726	1,434,675	1,410,086	1,927,997	896,301
25	West Bengal	511,443	605,263	711,691	857,087	4,342,275
26	Andaman & Nicobar Island	572	1,309	1,265	1,960	999
27	Arunachal Pradesh	17,925	17,950	12,395	18,482	5,766
28	Chandigarh UT	1,086	1,986	1,870	3,779	3,135

29	Dadra & Nagar Haveli	3,102	3,615	4,416	4,274	1,054
30	Delhi UT	17,120	25,717	27,351	41,899	26,473
31	Daman and Diu UT	7,391	9,378	941	729	774
32	Goa			4,656	4,138	6,920
33	Lakshadweep UT	97	56	34	27	28
34	Mizoram ***		6,314	16,411	26,265	2,793
35	Pondicherry UT	3,725	3,606	2,680	1,904	1,421
	Total	**10,753,985**	**13,640,870**	**11,285,349**	**12,666,377**	**4,353,247**

Source: Census of India, 1971,1981,1991, 2001, 2011, Government of India.

Notes: * 1971 Census figures of Assam include the figures of Mizoram.

** Census could not be conducted.

*** Census figures of 1971 in respect of Mizoram included under Assam.

**** It includes marginal workers also.

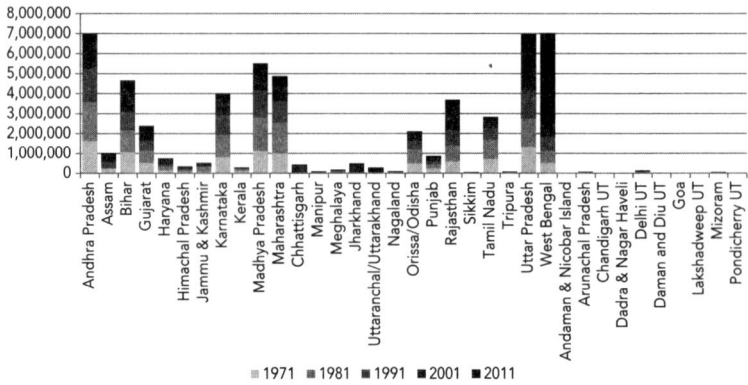

abuse and exploitation, and all these can lead to long-lasting mental illness and psychological traumas. As data reveal, the most concentration of child labour is found in the states of Bihar, Uttar Pradesh, Rajasthan, Madhya Pradesh and Maharashtra. It can be said that approximately a little over 50 per cent of child labour is found working in these five states alone, and it is Uttar Pradesh that accommodates over 20 per cent of India's child labour, according to survey reports presented by Save the Child, 2016.

Equal opportunity is regularly denied to Indian child labourers. Adequate care and education is neglected, and the various kinds of work these children do, lead to the loss of their childhood. As Srivastava writes, they fail to contribute to the growth of the nation because they do not understand their full potential for development. In 1997, India had ratified all the instrumental conventions on child labour—such as the ILO Convention Number 182 and Convention Number 138. The Child Labour Act, 1986 was also amended in 2016. The passage of the Juvenile Justice Act, 2015 and the Right to Education Act, 2009 gave emphasis on child care and protection of children and free education for all the children, respectively.

It was a herculean task before the Indian Government to rescue children forced to work in debt servitude and engage them in the mainstreams. To this end, the Government of India initiated the National Child Labour Project (NCLP) in 1988 under the care of the Indian Ministry of Labour and Employment. The objective of the programme was to withdraw the children engaged in hazardous works and put them in special schools. The special schools also had provisions for providing nutritious food, healthcare and vocational training to the children. There are some provisions for financial help in the form of grants-in-aids to the NGOs for initiating projects on child labour. The broad strategies of the NCLP are listed as follows:

1. To conduct a survey and identify working children
2. To indentify children involved in hazardous jobs
3. To withdraw children from hazardous jobs and under the care of *Sarva Siksha Abhiyan* (SSA)
4. To withdraw working children from work and admit them at the special schools run by the NCLP
5. To ensure that students admitted to special schools continued their studies for three years after which they would be mainstreamed
6. To provide vocational training to students
7. To provide nutritious food and healthcare facilities to students
8. To provide a fixed stipend to the students on a monthly basis

The functioning of NCLP, still now, is looked after by the 'project society' formed at the district level and the head of the district administration; District Magistrate and District Collector is the chairman of the society. Other members in the society are from different government departments, trade unions and NGOs. The Self-Help Groups, grass-roots organizations, Panchayats and municipalities, are also involved in the society for its smooth functioning. Each special school comprises three teachers/instructors of which two are general instructors and the other one is the vocational instructor. All the funds come from the Ministry of Labour and Employment directly to the district administration. Census data and National Sample Survey Organization (NSSO) data show that there has been a declining trend of child labour across the country because of these NCLP activities. This may also be due to initiatives undertaken by the Government of India, the state governments, various NGOs and international bodies such as the ILO, the IMF, the UNESCO and the World Bank.

The NCLP started its functioning in 1988, with 12 NCLP-projects in 12 child labour endemic districts of India. Its expansion over the past five-year plans has been shown in Table 5.31.

The NCLP has taken all-out efforts to set up special schools in different districts of India and the total number of schools under this scheme is 7,311, out of which 6,000 are very active in their activities.

Table 5.31 Expansion of NCLPs

Year	No. of NCLPs Sanctioned	No. of Districts Covered
1988	12	12
IX Plan	88	100
X Plan	150	250
XI Plan	21	271
Total	271	633

Source: Data released by the Ministry of Labour and Employment, Government of India, 2013.

On the basis of data received from India Education Diary Bureau Administration, 2020, it could be said that the total number of children mainstreamed through Special Training Centres set up under NCLP could be as high as 1.363 million.

The Child Labour (Prohibition and Regulation) Amendment Act, 2016, completely prohibits the employment of children below the age of 14 years in any occupation. It also prohibits adolescents in the age group of 14–18 years from employing them in hazardous jobs and processes. There are also provisions of punishment for employers for any violation of this act. For the first time in this amended Act, the following exceptions have been made. A child has been permitted to help his family enterprises—which are not hazardous—after his/her school hours, and during vacations. A child can also work as an artist in entertainment industry, including advertisement, films, serials or any other entertainments or sports activities except the circus, subject to certain conditions and safety measures and no such work affects the school education of the child.

Another important organization, Child Rights and You (CRY), was founded in 1979 by Mr Rippan Kapur and six of his friends. Mr Kapur was pained at seeing disparities between privileged and underprivileged children and children begging and working as servants. That is why he founded the CRY to help them.

Professor Jeroo Billimoria established the Childline in 1996, and, subsequently, the Government of India started Childline across India in 1998–1999. This is controlled and managed by the Ministry of Women and Child Development. Childline India Foundation is an NGO that operates a telephone helpline called 'Childline' for the children in distress, children who are homeless, and the children who are poor and due to poverty cannot go to school. The NGO collects money from different sources and spends the money for the benefit of child labour.

Save the Children India or Bal Raksha Bharat, another NGO established in 2008 has been constantly working to improve the lives of marginalized children in India. The NGO works in 19 states, and by 2018, it changed the lives of more than 10.1 million children (since 2008). The objective of the NGO is to spread education among underprivileged children, provide healthcare facilities and protect them from harm and abuse. In 2019 alone, Save the Children India reached 1.264 million children in distress.

The SOS: Children's Villages, India is an NGO aiming at the development of parentless children, women and children of vulnerable families. The NGO is based in Faridabad, and it also works with children and people in disaster-prone areas.

Another important movement in India to tackle child labouring was the Bachpan Bachao Andolan (Save Childhood Movement). The main architect of BBA, which was started in 1980, was the Nobel laureate Kailash Satyarthi. The objective of the movement is to wholesomely end the problem of child labour. Broadly speaking, it focuses on ending bonded labour, child labour and human trafficking, and providing education for all the children up to the age of 14 years. Through their able guidance and care, Satyarthi and his team converted it into a mass movement, identifying, liberating, rehabilitating and educating working children across the country. Due to his relentless efforts and his co-workers' dedication, it becomes possible for the concerned governmental authorities to rescue 92,028 child workers, as per a report[25] in 2021. However, the members of this movement have faced brutal physical attacks, and some of them have been even assassinated. Mr Kailash Satyarthi said that one of his colleagues was shot dead and another was beaten to death, and he has a broken shoulder and scars all over his body.

The rescue operations by BBA are usually done in the brothels or in the factories. But the owners of such families or brothels are often very powerful, have contacts with political leaders and police. Naturally, the participants of the BBA have to conduct raids without the help of the police. The BBA established the Mukti Ashram in 1991 and this is the first rescue home in India for bonded child labourers. The rescued

---

[25] https://www.bbba.org.in

children are provided food, clothing, medicine and psychological aid. In 1998, the Bal Ashram was set up in Rajasthan by the BBA. The objective of the Ashram is to provide long-term assistance to child labour including education. As a result of the concerted movement by the BBA, it has become possible to frame and implement legislation on child labour till the age of 14 years. The BBA was also successful in coordinating the historic Global March against Child Labour in 1998, covering 103 countries across the globe, as a result of which it had a great impact in advancing an international ban on child labour. The BBA is funded by various organizations—governmental and non-governmental.

Finally, one needs to mention the Pratham Education Foundation, which was established in 1995 as an Indian NGO aimed at providing education to children living in slum areas of Mumbai. The foundation aims at providing high-quality, low-cost education and interventions to address gaps in the education system.[26] The NGO's Teaching at the Right Level (TaRL) approach has exerted a great impact on the learning outcomes of children. *Pratham* was founded by Mr Madhav Chavan and Ms Farida Lambay. It also focuses on imparting quality pre-school education among underprivileged children in India. Its activities have been extended to 23 states and union territories, and it presently has chapters in the United States of America, the United Kingdom, Germany, Sweden and Australia. With the help of such NGOs, India is progressing a lot towards eradicating child labour.

As an NGO, Pratham tries to fill up the gaps in education systems in India. It provides innovative, low-cost and quality education both directly and through government systems reaching collectively to millions of children and thousands of school dropouts every year. The Pratham instructors work directly with children in the school or in the community. In the case of the 'partnership' model, Pratham, with governmental help, works closely at the state-level, district, city or even at the grassroot levels, and implements programmes with utmost sincerity, zeal and vigour. Pratham's efforts in imparting quality education and the methods of learning continue to serve as a model not only for India but its spectrum also spreads to other developing or less-advanced countries especially SSA, Asia and the Pacific and the Latin American countries.

Pratham's principal activities start with the children in the age group of 3–6 years. It gives special focus on their physical, language

---

[26] As per the information available on https://www.pratham.org

cognitive and socio-emotional development. To achieve this, local resources are used and caregivers are employed. Low-cost materials are used to improve children's basic abilities. In this context, five development domains are chosen for upliftment: physical development, socio-emotional development, cognitive development, language development and creative development. The NGO gives stress on children's 'motor-skills'—that is, children's brain, muscles and nervous system—must work together. Different tests are used to assess motor skills. Along with developing gross motor skills, children are being carefully trained for pre-writing abilities. To develop children's socio-emotional development, they are learned to adapt to a new setting and people. They are trained hard to work in groups, interact with people and develop interpersonal skills. To improve cognitive skills, children's pre-health abilities are improved through matching and counting along with improving knowledge of colours, shape, symbols and so on. In order to develop language skills, they are trained how to develop basic vocabulary and improve their ability to express ideas confidently before a person or a group of persons. Pratham also takes initiative in developing children's creative abilities, imagination and aesthetic appreciation.

Another of Pratham's important activities is conducting surveys and preparing a report on the schooling status and on the basic ability of students in the age group of 5–16 years to read and write in rural India. It started the activity in 2005, and in 2020, it completed 15th annual report known as 'Annual Status of Education Reports' (ASER). Since 2005, and up to 2014, the ASERs have provided estimates of the status of children and functional learning in the district, state and national levels for rural children in the age group of 3–6 years. Surveys were conducted to find out enrolment rates for rural children. Children in the age group of 5–16 years were examined on a one-on-one basis to assess their reading and writing abilities. Since 2016, ASER switched to an alternate cycle. The information collected up to 2014 were called 'Basic' which were conducted every other year including 2016, 2018, etc. In alternate years, ASER goes 'Beyond Basics' focusing on abilities, activities, awareness and aspirations of youth in the age group of 14–18 in 28 different districts of India. This was particularly followed in 2017. In 2019, an ASER survey was conducted on young children, aged 4–8 years, on their enrolment status and their abilities in 26 districts.

We hereby present in Table 5.32 the ASER, 2005 (state-wise) and comparative data between 2018 and 2020 surveyed by the ASER.

Table 5.32 Enrolment: All India—Age Group: 6–14 Years

States	% Children in Different Types of Schools				% Children Not in School		Total
	Government	Private	Madrasa	EGS	Never Enrolled	Dropout	
Andhra Pradesh: Data from 21 districts out of 22 districts	71.8	19.6	0.1	1.1	3.7	1.8	100
Arunachal Pradesh: Data from 3 out of 11 districts	81.4	13.4	0.0	0.2	3.1	3.1	100
Assam: Data from 8 out of 23 districts	77.5	13.8	0.7	0.6	4.4	3.2	100
Bihar Data from 34 out of 37 districts	72.1	9.1	3.7	1.6	10.3	3.5	100
Chhattisgarh Data from 15 out of 16 districts	90.9	4.4	0.0	0.1	1.2	0.2	100
Dadra & Nagar Haveli	97.2	2.1	0.0	0.1	0.4	0.2	100
Daman & Diu	81.4	16.9	0.0	0.0	0.1	0.7	100
Goa	72.2	27.7	0.0	0.0	0.1	0.2	100
Gujarat	87.8	7.5	0.6	0.6	1.3	2.3	100
Haryana: Data from 19 out of 20 districts	59.1	34.5	1.1	0.1	2.5	2.8	100
Himachal Pradesh: Data from 5 out of 12 districts	91.1	7.1	0.0	0.7	0.7	0.4	100

Jammu & Kashmir: Data from 7 out of 14 districts	78.0	17.2	0.3	1.8	1.4	1.3	100
Jharkhand: Data from 20 out 22 districts	71.9	10.9	1.4	6.1	6.4	3.4	100
Karnataka	88.5	9.5	0.1	0.0	0.3	1.6	100
Kerala	75.2	22.4	0.3	0.5	1.6	0.1	100
Madhya Pradesh: Data 40 out of 45 districts	83.5	8.5	0.2	3.8	1.2	2.8	100
Maharashtra	78.1	18.2	0.3	0.6	0.8	2.0	100
Manipur: Data from 3 out of 8 districts	33.6	52.4	0.0	0.3	10.5	3.3	100
Meghalaya: Data from 2 out 9 districts	48.4	41.9	0.0	1.5	5.2	3.0	100
Nagaland: Data from 2 out of 9 districts	70.9	10.2	0.1	0.0	7.3	11.5	100
Odisha	85.0	3.5	0.0	2.5	4.6	4.2	100
Punjab	69.9	25.5	0.0	0.2	2.0	2.4	100
Rajasthan	67.0	21.9	0.5	0.2	5.9	4.5	100
Tamil Nadu: Data from 28 out of 29 districts	78.2	18.4	0.7	0.0	0.3	2.3	100
Tripura: Data from 1 out of 6 districts	96.0	1.6	0.0	0.7	0.5	1.3	100
Uttar Pradesh:	63.0	28.0	0.6	0.2	4.4	2.9	100
Uttarakhand: 12 out of 13 districts	78.0	19.4	0.3	0.2	0.7	1.3	100
West Bengal: Data from 14 out of 17 districts	92.2	2.8	0.2	0.4	1.5	2.9	100

Source: ASER Reports, 2005.

Table 5.33 ASER: Children Enrolled in Different Types of Schools, 2018 and 2020 (Age Group 6–14 years)

Year	Types of Schools				Total
	Govt	Pvt	Others	Not in School	
2018	69.9	29.1	0.3	0.7	100
2020	72.6	26.6	0.5	0.3	100

Source: ASER Reports, 2018, 2020.

Table 5.33 shows the number of children enrolled in different types of schools, 2018 and 2020.

Bal Raksha Bharat or Save the Children, India, a non-profit organization established in 2008, is aimed at improving the conditions of lives of downtrodden children in India. Its headquarters are located at Gurugram, Delhi-NCR, India and the activities span over 19 states of India. The said NGO is a member of the International Save the Children Alliance. Since its establishment in 2008, it has surveyed and worked for more than 10.1 million children in rural and urban India. It provides quality education and healthcare facilities through the implementation of sustainable and community-driven projects. It has miraculously changed the lives of over 6.1 million people. In 2015, for example, the NGO reached 1.34 million children, and 0.13 million adults during crises like natural disasters and human-created crises (Save the Children India, 2018).

Save the Children India is determined to achieve sustainable development goals (SDGs) 2030 and for this, it has seven 'ideas' to materialize. They are thus termed:

1. Pneumonia: The Forgotten Killer
2. Under-nutrition: A Silent Emergency
3. Children are Ready for School
4. Ending Violence against Children
5. Rights for Children in Street Situations
6. Resilient and Climate-Smart Children
7. Triple Dividend of Investing and in Adolescents

Save the Children, India, amid the COVID-19 situation, has pleaded to protect a million children and their families. The NGO supplied a

5-litre oxygen concentrator to a special new-born Care Unit in Tonk, Rajasthan. The objective was to save the lives of babies. The NGO has disbursed 700 oxygen concentrators to public health centres (PHCs) across 11 states. Since the start of the pandemic, the NGO has exerted a positive influence on 0.56 million underprivileged and marginalized children. In 2021, the NGO implemented its initiatives in 57 districts covering 12 states of India and two union territories. Many children lost their parents and guardians during the coronavirus crisis during the second wave of the pandemic, and these children are being attended upon by the NGO.

During the pandemic, Save the Children, India had launched a mission to '#Protect A Million', the principal target of which is to reach an additional one million children and their families in 57 districts of 14 states and two union territories (as per a report by the *ANI/Business Wire India*, 21 May 2021). The NGO conducted a survey of urban and rural households of India regarding the impact of COVID-19. Data have been collected in two rounds, one on April 5–18, 2021, covering 7,455 households, and another on June 7–30, 2021, involving 7,022 households. Total 14 states—Assam, West Bengal, Bihar, Jharkhand, Uttar Pradesh, Himachal Pradesh, Madhya Pradesh, Maharashtra, Rajasthan, Tamil Nadu, Telangana, Andhra Pradesh, Karnataka, and Odisha and two union territories, Delhi and Jammu and Kashmir, have been covered. One adult in each family was interviewed over the telephone due to the pandemic.

The collected data was analysed, and it was revealed that 80 per cent of the respondents fail to afford basic necessities like food, water, electricity and gas. It has been found that vulnerability among the poor is increasing, thus the insecurity towards the social safety nets is also increasing. Being out of school, the children are being grossly exposed to domestic abuse and exploitation. The Childline India Helpline got 92,105 SOS calls seeking protection from abuse and violence in 11 days from March 20–31 2020. Also, the *Childline-1908* received approximately 0.31 million calls during this period. About 30 per cent of children sought protection against abuse and vigilance on children (as per a report in *The Hindu*, 8 April 2020). There is also an increasing trend of child trafficking during the crisis. The poor families living in the East Singhbhum district of northern Jharkhand state of India, for example, have been the target of child trafficking (as per the report of *The Telegraph*, 28 July 2020).

The findings that emerged from the survey during the pandemic can be enlisted as follows:

1. Eighty-four per cent urban households lacked livelihood opportunities;
2. Forty-three per cent rural households and sixty-one per cent urban households lacked sufficient food supply;
3. One-fourth of the surveyed households reported that they lost jobs and did not have any income;
4. Forty-five per cent households reported that they took loans for meeting day-to-day expenses;
5. Forty per cent respondents reported that their children did not receive support from school to continue their children's study;
6. Figty-three per cent respondents told that they did not know about Child Line.

Save the Children, India's efforts are to help the most vulnerable children during the pandemic—especially in 2020. Their achievements have been illustrated in Table 5.34 with the data taken from the website of the NGO.

The NGO has transformed the lives of more than 14 million children since 2008, through developmental activities in areas such as nutrition, healthcare, protection, education and response in times of unforeseen contingencies. Data presented in Table 5.34 shows that the NGO has extended healthcare and nutrition facilities alone in 2020 to vulnerable children numbering 162,656. The total number of children equipped to deal with the disaster is 634,448. Throughout 2020, 236,356 children were duly protected from different forms of harm, and access to quality education was provided by the NGO to 357,435 children.

Table 5.34 *Benefits the Vulnerable Children Received*

Benefits Children Received	Number of Children
Healthcare and nutrition	162,656
Equipped to deal with disasters	634,448
Protection from different forms of harm	236,356
Access to quality education and support	357,435

Source: Save the Children, 2020, www.savethechildren.in

Chapter 6

The Global Scenario

Child labour is a global problem—not unlike those related to poverty and threats to the environment. Since it is a global issue and affects almost all the countries around the world—some are more, some less—the solution to the problem needs to be formulated to address the issue globally.

The formulation of a solution to the problem of child labour is so complicated because it is really a tough task to define 'child labour'. It appears to be an impossible feat to come out to a real definition—especially because child labour depends on the socio-economic, cultural, religious and political conditions of the respective countries, regions and territories. In some settings, there are some works that are deemed very essential in respect of familial needs, and, simultaneously, such works make huge contributions to the growth and development of young children. Hence, in such a situation, it becomes problematic to identify 'child labour'. Rather, young generations involved in such works can adopt a sense of their responsibility; furthermore, this not only helps their own families but also benefits society as a whole.

It is indeed a herculean task to correctly define 'child labour'; it is even harder to calculate the number of 'child labourers' and it is also hard to assess its implications on the economy and society locally, regionally and globally. There is no problem with the works that the children perform gladly to support their families, while simultaneously acquiring knowledge for their future development through education and training—formally and/or informally. Only when children are forced to perform certain works against their wishes, it becomes a problem. They do such works under hazardous conditions, often at the cost of their health, education, and personal and social development.

Constraints and unpalatable circumstances force them to perform full-time works—sometimes beyond their capacity—from an early age. They even have to use dangerous machinery or handle toxic chemicals that are unhealthy for them, along with coping with long working hours and subjection to psychological and physical abuses.

As discussed in *Making Progress against Child Labour: Global Estimates and Trends 2000–2012*, published by the IPEC in 2019, the Millennium Development Goals adopted in 2000 gave much importance to tackling problems related to poverty and hunger. This had—as a result—left an impact on lowering the magnitude of global poverty. As one of its parts, the target of 8.7 of the Sustainable Development Goals is a reminder for everyone concerned that child labour in different forms needs to be abolished from the world by 2025.

Since 2000, there has been a remarkable decrease in the number of child labourers all around the world and the actual number has dropped by 94 million. An estimate tells that 152 million children are still being deprived of their rights to leisure and schooling (as recorded by the *Global Estimates of Child-Labour: Results and Trends, 2012–2016*, and the ILO, 2016–2017). This is an important fact that 39.3 per cent of total children in the entire world are child labourers, and of 152 million child labourers, 73 million are involved in hazardous works. The (usual) sectoral segregation of child labour is as under: agriculture: 70.9 per cent; industry: 11.9 per cent; and services: 17.2 per cent. A recent ILO estimate of child labour has been shown in Table 6.1.

Data depicted in Table 6.2 exhibit a declining trend in both the number of child labourers and that of children involved in hazardous jobs (in terms of percentage). The decline was more intense in 2008 and 2012 in total number, but slower between 2012 and 2016. Data shows that child labourers increased in number in Africa in spite of a number of steps undertaken by most of the African nations to reduce child labour. Another area of concern is the decline in the number of girls. A decrease in the number of male child labourers during 2012–2016 signifies an increase in the number of female child labourers.

As a result of wholehearted efforts of different countries—government, non-governmental and world organizations together—there has been a mentionable impact on the efforts to reduce child labour since 2000. The decline of child labour during 2000–2004 was −9.5 per cent. There was a −3.2 per cent decline during 2004–2008. The reduction was spectacular during 2008–2012 which was −22.0 per cent.

Table 6.1 Global Estimate of Child Labour, 2017

			Children in Employment		Of Which: Children in Child Labour		Of Which: Children in Hazardous Work	
			2012	2016	2012	2016	2012	2016
World (5–17 Years)		Number (000s)	264,427	218,019	167,956	151,622	85,344	72,525
		Prevalence (%)	16.7	13.8	10.6	9.6	5.4	4.6
Age range	15–14 years	Number (000s)	144,066	130,364	120,453	114,472	37,841	35,376
		Prevalence (%)	11.8	10.6	9.9	9.3	3.1	2.9
	15–17 years	Number (000s)	120,362	87,655	47,503	32,149	47,503	37,149
		Prevalence (%)	33.0	24.9	13.0	10.5	13.0	10.5
Sex (5–17 years)	Male	Number (000s)	148,327	123,190	99,766	87,521	55,048	44,774
		Prevalence (%)	18.1	15.0	12.2	10.7	6.7	5.5
	Female	Number (000s)	116,100	94,829	68,190	64,100	30,296	27,751
		Prevalence (%)	15.2	12.4	8.9	8.4	4.0	3.6
Region (5–17 years)	Africa	Number (000s)	–	99,117	–	72,113	–	31,538
		Prevalence (%)	–	27.1	–	19.6	–	8.6
	America	Number (000s)	–	17,725	–	10,735	–	6,553
		Prevalence (%)	–	8.8	–	5.3	–	3.2
	Asia and the Pacific	Number (000s)	129,358	90,236	–	62,077	–	28,469
		Prevalence (%)	15.5	10.7	–	7.4	–	3.4

(Table 6.1 Continued)

(Table 6.1 Continued)

World (5–17 Years)		Children in Employment		Of Which: Children in Child Labour		Of Which: Children in Hazardous Work	
		2012	2016	2012	2016	2012	2016
Europe and Central Asia	Number (000s)	–	8,773	–	5,534	–	5,349
	Prevalence (%)	–	6.5	–	4.1	–	4.0
Arab States	Number (000s)	–	1,868	–	1,162	–	616
	Prevalence (%)	–	4.6	–	**2.9	–	1.5

Source: Global Estimates of Child Labour, Results and Trends – 2012–2016 – ILO – 2017; see the report on https://www.ilo.org/global/publications/books/WCMS_575499/lang--en/index.htm

Table 6.2 Children's Involvement in Child Labour and Hazardous Work, 2000–2016

Year	Child Labour		Children in Hazardous Work	
	Number	%	Number	%
2000	245,500,000	16.0	170,500,000	11.1
2004	222,294,000	14.2	128,381,000	8.2
2008	215,209,000	13.6	115,314,000	7.3
2012	167,956,000	10.6	85,344,000	5.4
2016	151,622,000	9.6	72,525,000	4.6

Source: Global Estimates of Child Labour, Results and Trends – 2012–2016, ILO, 2017; see the report on https://www.ilo.org/global/publications/books/WCMS_575499/lang--en/index.htm

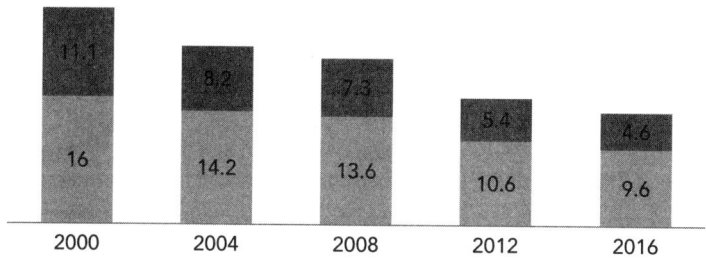

The declining trend continued during 2012–2016 which was −9.7 per cent; but the rate of decline is far below the rate that happened during 2008–2012, as is depicted in Table 6.3.

The intensity and severity of child labour across the globe are not uniform. In some regions, it is wide and severe, and in some other regions, it is less in terms of its absolute number and impact. Table 6.4 shows that Africa 'contributes' to the highest number of child labourers both in absolute terms and in percentage terms. Not only this, it represents the largest number of children involved in hazardous work. Asia-Pacific is the region which contains the second-largest number of child labourers and children engaged in hazardous jobs in absolute number and in percentage terms.

Table 6.3 Changes in Rates of Progress against Child Labour since 2000

Year	Decline (−) (%)
2000–2004	−9.5
2004–2008	−3.2
2008–2012	−22.0
2012–2016	−9.7

Source: Global Estimates of Child Labour, Results and Trends – 2012–2016, ILO, 2017; see the report on https://www.ilo.org/global/publications/books/WCMS_575499/lang--en/index.htm

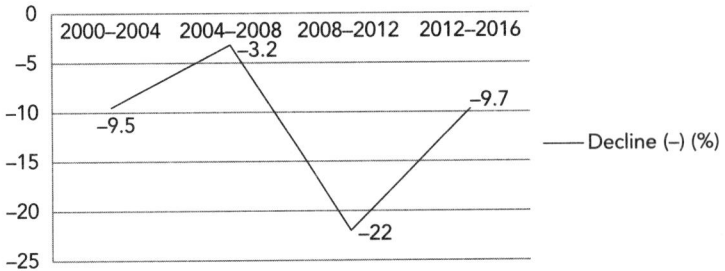

Table 6.4 Regional Profile of Child Labour and Hazardous Work

Region	Child Labour (Number 000s)	%	Children in Hazardous Work (Number 000s)	%
Africa	72,113	19.6	31,538	8.6
Arab States	1,162	2.9	616	1.5
Asia and the Pacific	62,077	7.4	28,469	3.4
Americas	10,735	5.3	6,553	3.2
Europe and Central Asia	5,534	4.1	5,349	4.0
World	151,622	9.6	72,525	4.6

Source: Global Estimates of Child Labour, Results and Trends – 2012–2016, ILO, 2017; see the report on https://www.ilo.org/global/publications/books/WCMS_575499/lang--en/index.htm

Table 6.5 *Child Labour and Hazardous Work by National Income*

National Income Grouping	Child Labour		Children in Hazardous Work	
	Number (000s)	%	Number (000s)	%
Low-income	65,203	19.4	29,664	8.8
Lower middle-income	58,184	8.5	33,465	4.9
Upper middle-income	26,209	6.6	7,751	2.0
High-income	2,025	1.2	1,645	1.0

Source: Global Estimates of Child Labour, Results and Trends – 2012–2016, ILO, 2017; see the report on https://www.ilo.org/global/publications/books/WCMS_575499/lang--en/index.htm

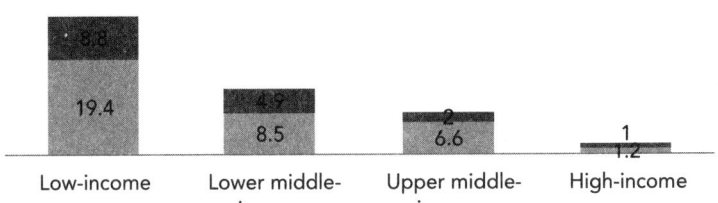

In Table 6.5, one can see that different countries have been grouped according to income—low-income, lower-middle-income, upper-middle-income countries—the child labour situation has been described accordingly. This shows that low-income countries have the highest number of child labourers (65,203,000 in number and 19.4%) and children in hazardous work (29,664,000 and 8.8%). Then come the lower-middle-income countries (absolute number 58,184,000 and 85%) and in hazardous work (33,465,000 and 4.9%). Upper-middle-income countries and high-income countries' contributions are 2.0 and 1 per cent, respectively.

Sector-wise distribution, as well as sex-wise distribution of child labourers, has been represented in Table 6.6. Africa, Europe and Central Asia represent the highest concentration of child labourers in agriculture, 85.1 and 76.7 per cent, respectively. Then comes the region

Table 6.6 Child Labour by Sector

		Agriculture	Industry	Services	Total
World		70.9	11.9	17.2	100
Region	Africa	85.1	3.7	11.2	100
	Arab States	60.3	12.4	27.4	100
	Americas	51.5	13.2	35.3	100
	Asia and the Pacific	57.5	21.4	21.1	100
	Europe and Central Asia	76.6	9.7	13.6	100
Sex	Male	71.5	12.4	16.1	100
	Female	70.3	11.1	18.6	100
Age range	5–14	78.0	7.4	14.5	100
	15–17	49.3	25.6	25.1	100

Source: Global Estimates of Child Labour, Results and Trends – 2012–2016, ILO, 2017; see the report on https://www.ilo.org/global/publications/books/WCMS_575499/lang--en/index.htm

of Asia-Pacific: 57.5 per cent in agriculture. In industry, it is 25.6 per cent, and in the services, it is 25.1 per cent.

The gender profile of child labourers (including those who are involved in hazardous works as shown in Table 6.7) reveals that boys in all age groups are more represented as child labourers and children in hazardous jobs. This, however, also needs to be remembered that domestic work performed by girls in their own houses are not counted as 'labour', and this may lead to more gender gap—especially because girls are more likely to engage in household work, and for this, no wage is paid. In fact, the work performed by girls is hardly given any importance—internationally so!

Finally, it might be said that child labour data presented in various reports fail to represent the actual picture throughout the globe. Numerous questions still remain regarding the availability of the quality of child labour data across countries and regions. A very limited amount of data is available—as *The ILO Report: Marking Progress against Child Labour, Global Estimate and Trends – 2000–2012*, says—especially in Eastern Europe and Central Asia, in the Pacific sub region, and in the

Table 6.7 *Gender Profile of Child Labourers, and Child Labourers in Hazardous Work, 2016*

Gender	Age (Years)	Child Labour		Children in Hazardous Work	
		Number (000s)	%	Number (000s)	%
Male	5–11	39,402	8.7	11,029	2.4
	12–14	24,582	13.3	10,208	5.5
	15–17	23,537	12.9	23,537	12.9
	5–17	87,521	10.7	44,774	5.5
Female	5–11	33,183	7.8	7,992	1.9
	12–14	17,035	10.0	6,147	3.6
	15–17	13,612	8.0	13,612	8.0
	5–17	64,100	8.4	27,751	3.6

Source: Global Estimates of Child Labour, Results and Trends, 2012–2016, ILO, 2017; see the report on https://www.ilo.org/global/publications/books/WCMS_575499/lang--en/index.htm

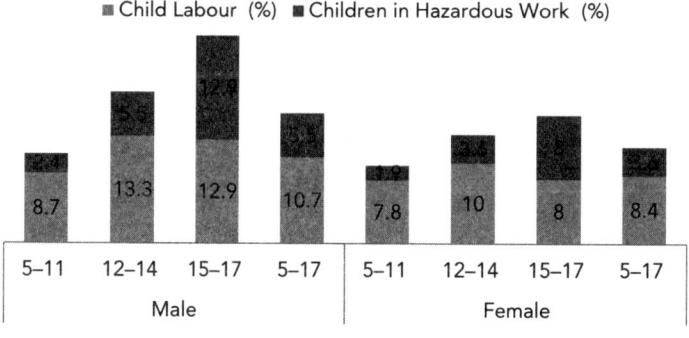

industrialized regions and select Asian countries. Child labour–related data is available in SSA, but there is a problem related to data on children engaged in hazardous work. It is also very difficult to compare data of a specific region collected over two different points of time, and also to compare data related to two markedly different regions. It is, therefore, necessary to establish fully-functional national statistical organizations. They could then be able to collect authentic data, which, in turn, could help in the international formulation of future policies towards the eradication of child labour.

Some of the reports forwarded by such organizations—when assessed together—could be found as suggesting a number of policies for the promotion of working children. These are as follows:

1. Children—boys and girls—should be provided free and good-quality basic education. It should be compulsory for all.
2. The report says that it is urgently required to protect the vulnerable sections of society by providing social safety. The *ILO Social Protection Floor Recommendation* (Number 202) of 2012 should be followed.
3. Employment opportunities should be expanded, and in this context, steps should be undertaken so that children indifferent impoverished families get ample educational opportunities to further their progress.
4. Legal framework for protecting working children against exploitation and protection in hazardous work should be strengthened to include the informal sector too.
5. Awareness should be created among the citizen regarding the benefits of education, the restrictions regarding the minimum working age of a child, and the necessities of health awareness and development costs for child labourers.
6. Target 8.7 of SDG calls for accelerated action against child labour and governments, workers' organizations, employers' organizations and other organizations must be committed to eradicating child labour completely. The main actors—the governments, the workers' organizations and the employers' organization together can formulate and develop public policy prescriptions to meet the needs of the affected people and their communities, as per *The Report of Global Estimates of Child-labour: Results and trends, 2012–2016*.
7. Free and compulsory quality education (up to a minimum age for admission) for the (prospective) working children can better serve as the main weapon to end child labour globally. Quality education can help children acquire training and can be suitable for candidates seeking employment in future.
8. Direct cash transfer to economically underprivileged families, supply of free books, free uniforms, free bags and other things necessary

for continuing education uninterruptedly can also help a lot in eradicating child labour. The impact of such assistance often has an intergenerational effect. The NCLP, taken up in India since 1988, has been playing a significant role in withdrawing children from work and sending them back to class while ensuring a direct cash transfer system for them. But the amount of cash transferred to families is not good; it is approximately ₹400 ($5.40) per month, along with provisions for mid-day meals. However, it is praiseworthy to note that about 50 per cent of students of the Indian NCLP-schools are girls who are coming from very poor and disintegrated families. The total number of NCLP schools is (presently) more than 7,000, out of which over 6,000 schools are fully functional. Approximately 10,000,00 odd students have been mainstreamed by 2016 under the NCLP all over India. However, the number of NCLP schools and that of the teachers/trainers need to be increased at least five times to tackle the child labour problem.

Chapter 7

Grassroots Experience from Rural India

7.1. INTRODUCTION: NCLP

One of the important developmental projects right across the globe, the NCLP scheme started working in India for fulfilling the following objectives: (a) ending child labour through identification and withdrawal of working children and preparing them for mainstream education and vocational training and ensuring employment for the cause of working children and their families; (b) withdrawal of adolescent workers from hazardous work and providing vocational training; (c) spreading awareness campaign amongst stakeholders and target communities; and (d) creating child labour monitoring, tracking and reporting systems.

7.2. SOME NCLP INITIATIVES

The NCLP began functioning in West Bengal (India) in 1995, initially in six districts: Burdwan, Dakshin Dinajpur, Uttar Dinajpur, North 24 Parganas, South 24 Parganas and Midnapore. Soon, the project opened 246 special schools for child labourers. Murshidabad and Kolkata came under the project during the Ninth Five-Year Plan. All other districts in Bengal were covered during Tenth Five-Year Plan. By 2008, the number of such special schools around West Bengal rose to 912, and the total number of admitted students increased to 0.0435 million. However, a matter of grave concern was that the total number of students admitted to such schools was only 5 per cent of the total number of child labourers identified, which amounted to 0.91 million.

Two NCLP evaluation surveys had been conducted so far in the state of West Bengal: one in 2001 and the other one in 2007. The first survey found that the project was hugely successful in admitting the students, especially those from below the poverty line (BPL) families. In fact, the maximum number of working children belongs to BPL families. During the surveys, it was noticed that they usually work in the fields of agriculture, domestic works and other informal sectors of employment. These special schools were partially successful in supplying mid-day meals to the working children who were admitted to schools monitored by NCLP. But the fact is, the infrastructure of these schools were usually pitiable—a very few schools were found to be suitable for children. Drinking water facilities were scarce, and so were lavatories. Kitchens for preparing mid-day meals were absent too. Nevertheless, due to the provisions of mid-day meals, the student attendance at such schools was usually good—about 75 per cent on an average. It was found that approximately 50 per cent of working children were withdrawn directly from work and admitted to these schools. The target (which was not completed) was to admit 100 per cent of the working children.

But there were/are impediments too. Lack of classrooms is one such. The two surveys revealed that three teachers, for example, were taking three different classes in a single room at different points in time. It seems to be outrightly pathetic and ridiculous. This happened because of meagre funds being allocated for the purpose. Essential furniture, such as chair, table, bench and blackboard, were hardly found in the classrooms. Due to lack of infrastructure, only 50 per cent of working children could be accommodated while numerous more could not be identified and/or withdrawn from work and admitted to the school. Most of the children engaged in the hazardous works—the surveys found—could not be accommodated to the NCLP schools. The students studying in the special schools could not be provided with the stipend because of a delay in the disbursement of funds from the Government of India.

Another important survey on the condition of child labourers in West Bengal was conducted by the Institute of Development Studies,

Kolkata (IDSK). Uttam Kumar Bhattacharya, in his paper[1] focuses in detail on this survey. The survey was conducted in five sample districts of West Bengal—Kolkata, South 24 Parganas, Murshidabad, Malda and Dakshin Dinajpur. The study found that almost all the schools had a single classroom, and teachers and students faced the same problem in the classroom because multiple classes would be held in a single room at a point of time.

Data regarding the operational procedures of special schools under the NCLP in the districts of West Bengal have been displayed in Table 7.1. The said data show that special schools were gradually started all over West Bengal between 1995 and 2006. During this period, 868 schools were set up in 17 districts, providing admission to a total of 32,337 students.

However, repeated surveys began to bring out the inadequacies of these schools in West Bengal. One usual feature would be the lack of electric connectivity. Seating arrangements in the classrooms would also be often inadequate. Building walls were made of mud or thatch, and roofs were tin-shaded. In many special schools, there would not be even any owned-building(s). Schools were held on the premises of government-aided schools. The IDSK survey also studied the course materials and the curriculum. The implementing agencies, along with teachers, framed the curriculum. Around 76 per cent of the special schools followed the formal curriculum, and almost all the special schools in the rural areas followed the formal curriculum. However, only 56 per cent of schools maintained admission registers. On one hand, the schools sincerely admitted students, maintained classes regularly, and the teachers' attendance was very remarkable. On the other hand, the healthcare facilities were inadequate, and only about 66 per cent of schools were found as providing school kits: including writing slates, uniforms and books. Even then, the delivery of such kits was irregular and untimely.

The second survey found that 20 per cent of students belonged to the scheduled caste communities, 2 per cent scheduled tribes and 5 per cent to the Other Backward Classes (OBC) category. Around 30 per cent of students could not explain their social category. However, in the matter of distributing study materials and caring for students,

---

[1] Uttam K. Bhattacharya, 'Education for Child Labour in West Bengal,' IDSK-Occasional Paper No. 15 (2008).

Table 7.1 Schools under the NCLP in the Districts of West Bengal, 2007–2008

Sl. No.	Name of the Districts	Year of Sanction	Year of Beginning of Operating	Number of Schools Sanctioned	Number of Schools Presently Operational	Number of Student Enrolled	
						Boys	Girls
1	Burdwan	1995	1995	47	46	1,124	1,140
2	Uttar (North) Dinajpur	1995	1995	40	40	902	1,048
3	Dakshin (South Dinajpur)	1995	1995	40	40	768	1,210
4	North 24 Parganas	1995	1995	40	38(40)$	958	942
5	South 24 Parganas	1995	1996	40	40	946	1,049
6	Murshidabad	1999	1999	140	140	2,779	4,221
7	Kolkata	1999	2001	40	40	934	1,066
8	Purba (East) Midnapore	2005	2005	23	23	NA	NA
9	Birbhum	2005	2005	55	55	NA	NA
10	Maldah	2005	2005	40	40	525	1,475
11	Purulia	2005	2005	90	48(90)*	1,298 (2,316)*	905 (2,184)*
12	Hooghly	2005	2005	32	32	818	782
13	Cooch Behar	2006	2006	19	19	NA	NA

(Table 7.1 Continued)

(Table 7.1 Continued)

Sl. No.	Name of the Districts	Year of Sanction	Year of Beginning of Operating	Number of Schools Sanctioned	Number of Schools Presently Operational	Number of Student Enrolled Boys	Number of Student Enrolled Girls
14	Bankura	2006	2006	62	47$	NA	NA
15	Nadia	2006	2007	100	13(14)*	385	265
					(100)$	(1,187)*	(813)*
16	Howrah	2006	2007	40	(16)$	NA	NA
17	Jalpaiguri	2006	2007	29(19$)	(19)$	NA	NA
			Total	868	649	32,337	
						(38,300)*	
				(872)*	(665)*	(23,434)**	
				(916)**	(630)**	(10,436 +12,998)***	
				(912)$	(869)$	(43,500)$	

Source: Government of West Bengal, Department of Labour (GoWBL) 2007; consult the data available on http://idsk.edu.in/wp-content/uploads/2015/07/OP-15.pdf

Notes: Break-up of male and female students was not available for each district from the Department of Labour, Government of West Bengal. Figures in brackets with single asterisk (*) are the revised data as on December, 2007. Figures with $ marks are from Labour Commissioner, Government of West Bengal as on 31 May 2008. Figures with double asterisks (**) are from the Ministry of Labour, Government of India. The District of Darjeeling could not start the NCLP scheme till August 2008.

no discrimination was noticed. The survey found that 70 per cent of sampled schools were successful in distributing stipends to students. The occasional delays in receipt of stipend were caused by delays in the disbursement of funds by the Government of India. Mid-day meals were provided by most of the special schools. The surveys' data revealed that a few schools could not cook meals, and those schools, instead of cooking food, provided bread, banana, eggs and soya beans. Health check-up facilities in rural area schools were not good, whereas in the urban areas they were relatively better. The surveys also found that the student's attendance was 75 per cent, and the dropout rates were less in the special schools—as compared to the condition in general government-aided schools. One problem however surfaced almost regularly. About 70 per cent of such schools could not maintain equipment for vocational classes. The situation was especially grim in the rural areas where the instances of maintenance of such equipment were a total of meagre 17 per cent. Also, most of the schools—it was frantically reported—did not receive educational kits on a regular basis. The data supplied by the Ministry of Labour, Government of West Bengal, 2012—shown in Table 7.2—display that there were 945 special schools in operation in West Bengal, and 46,403 students were enrolled in these schools.

Data available from grassroots-level survey conducted in 19 special schools working during 2013 has been presented in Table 7.3. The survey covered 30 per cent of parents from the sample school. The total number of households was 285. The survey covered enrolment, education of parents, literacy of children, the family size of children (caste-wise) and caste-wise and income-wise family division(s). Data presented in Table 7.2 show block-wise/subdivision-wise division of a number of special schools in the rural district of Cooch Behar of West Bengal State and student-intake (caste-wise).

Income-wise and caste-wise distribution of families of households is shown in Table 7.4.

Data presented in Table 7.4 show that maximum number of students admitted to special schools are from the scheduled-caste and Muslim families, 44.2 per cent and 40 per cent, respectively. Literacy and children size of surveyed families have been presented in Table 7.5.

Data presented in Table 7.5 show that per-family children size is 2.08. Maximum number of students is found in up to class IV, and only a few have continuous education from Class V to Class X.

Table 7.2 Child Labour and NCLP Schools in West Bengal

Sl. No.	District	Child Population (5–14 years age)	Child Labour (Percentage at Parentheses)	Number of Schools Operational under NCLP	Years of Operation	Child Labours Enrolled (%)
1	Darjeeling	371,091	10,341 (2.8)	21	NA	1,050 (2.3)
2	Jalpaiguri	863,702	31,901 (3.7)	19	2007	914 (1.96)
3	Cooch Behar	644,098	26,137 (4.1)	18	2007	900 (1.9)
4	U/Dinajpur	698,892	52,928 (7.6)	40	1995	2,000 (4.3)
5	U/Dinajpur	377,726	20,364 (5.4)	40	1995	2,000 (4.3)
6	Malda	928,902	88,556 (9.5)	40	2005	2,000 (4.3)
7	Murshidabad	1,637,356	87,968 (5.37)	140	1999	7,000 (15.1)
8	Birbhum	766,542	39,285 (5.1)	38	2005	1,900 (4.1)
9	Bardhaman	1,563,346	64,233 (4.1)	46	1995	2,300 (4.9)
10	Nadia	1,068,865	38,333 (3.6)	100	2007	5,000 (10.8)
11	24 Parganas (N)	1,905,879	55,619 (2.9)	40	1995	2,000 (4.3)
12	Hooghly	1,063,045	34,850 (3.3)	68	2006	3,400 (7.3)
13	Bankura	742,496	51,659 (6.9)	58	2007	2,463 (5.3)

14	Purulia	630,803	41,056 (6.5)	90	2006	4,500 (9.7)
15	Medinipur	2,333,062	95,739 (4.1)	31 (E) + 42 (W)	1999	1,582 (E) + 1,768 (W) = 3,350 (7.2)
16	Howrah	926,037	31,577 (3.4)	34	2007	1,667 (3.6)
17	Kolkata	742,868	30,810 (4.2)	40	2001	2,000 (4.3)
18	24 Parganas (S)	1,764,434	55,965 (3.2)	40	1995	1,959 (4.2)
	West Bengal	19,029,144	857,087 (4.5)	945	46,403	

Source: ILO (2007), Child Labour Facts & Figures: An Analysis of Census 2001, ILO-Geneva; GOWB (2012): Ministry of Labour (GOWBL), Labour in West Bengal, 2012, Kolkata; compare the data available on htps://core.ac.uk/download/pdf/211606082.pdf

Table 7.3 Schools reph the Number of Students (Gender-wise and Caste-wise) in the Northern West Bengal District of Cooch Behar

	Name of the School	Name of the Location and Address	Block/Subdivision	SC		ST		Others		Total	
				M	F	M	F	M	F	M	F
1	MUKTI Special School	Biswas Para 16 No. Jangal Bash, Post & Panchayat: Dewanganj, Block: Haldibari, Dist.- Cooch Behar	Haldibari	20	23	0	0	4	3	24	26
2	MUKTI Special School	Uttar Para, Word No. 9, Haldibari, Dist.- Cooch Behar	Haldibari	6	10	0	0	21	13	27	23
3	Sahebganj Mukti Special School	Vill.- Sahebganj, PO & GP: Sahebganj, Block: Dinhata-II, Dist-Cooch Behar	Dinhata-II	8	4	0	0	23	15	31	19
4	Barasimulguri Mukti Special School	Vill: Barosimulguri, PO& GP: Ghoksadanga, Block: Mathabhanga-II, Dist- Cooch Behar	Mathabhanga-A II	23	25	0	0	0	2	23	27
5	Patchhara Mukti Special School	Vill-D. Patchhara, Madal Para, PO& GP: Patchhara, Block: Cooch Behar-I, Dist.- Cooch Behar	Cooch Behar-I	23	9	0	0	8	10	21	19

	Name	Address	Location							
6	Tufanganj Mukti Special School	31, Natrional Highway, National Club More, Ward No. 7, Tufanganj Municipality, PO.Tufanganj, Dist.- Cooch Behar	Tufanganj	21	20	0	0	6	3	27	23
7	Barasimulgur Muti Special School	Vill& PO: Barasalbari, FP: Salbari-II, Block, Tufanganj-II, Dist: Cooch Behar	Tufanganj-II	9	8	1	6	12	14	22	28
8	Pan Bachatari Mukti Special School	Vill: Pan Bachatari, PO& GP: Bhotbari, Block Mekhliganj, Dist: Cooch Behar	Mekliganj	0	0	0	0	22	28	22	28
9	Takagachh-Rajarhat Mukti Special School	Vill: Damodarpur, PO: Takagachh, G.P.: Takagachh-Rajarhat, Block: Cooch Behar II, Dist: Cooch Behar	Cooch Behar-II	1	0	0	0	20	29	21	29
10	Sikarpur Mukti Special School	Vill: Shikarpur, PO: Colony Chamta, GP: Nakkatigachh, Block: Tufanjgnaj I, Dist: Cooch Behar	Tufanjganj-I	9	10	0	0	12	19	21	29

(Table 7.3 Continued)

(Table 7.3 Continued)

	Name of the School	Name of the Location and Address	Block/Subdivision	SC M	SC F	ST M	ST F	Others M	Others F	Total M	Total F
11	Taltala Mukti Special School	Vill. Taltala, PO: Depepare, Block: Tufanganj-I, Dist: 23 Cooch Behar	Tufanganj-I	21	16	0	0	5	8	26	24
12	Pachagar Mukti Special School	Vill: 28 Pachagar, PO& GP: Pachagar, Block: Mathabhanga-I, Dist.- Cooch Behar	Mathabhanga A-I	8	13	0	0	15	14	23	27
13	Paschim Galanwati Mukti Special School	Vill: Paschim Galanwari, GP: Galanwati, Block: Sitalkuchi, Dist: Cooch Behar	Sitalkuchi	5	2	0	0	23	20	28	22
14	Madhyavarali Mukti Special School	Vill: Madhyavarali, PO & GP: Sitai, Block: Sitai, Dist: Cooch Behar	Sitai	8	14	0	0	14	14	22	28
15	B.R.Charta Mukti Special School	Vill: B.R.Chatra, PO: & GP: B.R. Charta, Block: Sitai, Dist: Cooch Behar	Sitai	1	0	0	0	25	24	23	24
16	Cooch Behar Mukti Special School	Hazrapara, Bandherpar, Ward No. 16, Cooch Behar Municipality, PO: Cooch Behar	Cooch Behar	21	13	0	0	5	11	23	24

17	Mathabhanga Mukti Special School	Mainatali More, Ward No. 9, Mathabhanga Municipality, PO: Mathabhanga, Dist: Cooch Behar	Mathabhanga	3	6	0	0	26	15	29	21
18	Netaji Shishu Shramik Vidyalaya	Vill: Volka, Post: Matalhat, Block: Dinhata-I, Dist: Cooch Behar	Dinhata-I	10	14	0	0	13	13	23	27
19	Vivekananda Shishu Shramik Vidyalaya	Ward No. 9, Gopal Nagar Colony, Dinhata Municipality, PO: Dinhata, Dist: Cooch Behar	Dinhata	10	12	0	0	13	15	23	27
	Total			207	199	1	6	267	270	475	475

Source: Cooch Behar Zilla Shishu Shramik Kalyan Parishad (NCLP), Cooch Behar, 2013; compare the data available on https://core.ac.uk/download/pdf/211606082.pdf

Table 7.4 *Income-wise and Caste-wise Surveys of Households*

Income Group (Rs)	Number of Families (Caste-wise)			
	Scheduled Castes	Muslims	General Category (Other than Muslims)	Total
Up to 3,000	22	20	4	46
3,001–4,000	49	72	15	136
4001–5,000	31	19	19	69
Above 5,000	24	4	6	34
Total	126	115	44	285

Source: Field Survey, 2013 (Bhuimali, 2013); *Child Labour Survey Report: Cooch Behar District, 2013*, submitted by A. Bhuimali to Cooch Behar District Administration. It was a Government of West Bengal Project on Child Labour under the NCLP scheme.

The districts' select parents' educational status has been shown in Table 7.6.

Table 7.6 shows that 45 per cent of parents are illiterate, and 39.09 per cent of parents have education up to Class IV. They are only functionally literate, and, understandably, they are not capable of guiding and teaching their children properly. The data also show that illiteracy among the parents of the scheduled caste category and of Muslims is at a maximum level.

The survey—conducted by Bhuimali, with its results being published in his 2013 book—of special schools was based on certain parameters such as special schools' enrolment, attendance of students and teachers, employment of teaching-learning materials, mid-day meals, presence of school buildings and other facilities such as drinking water, toilet, playground, mainstreaming of students, coverage of target groups and convergence with different government departments, the roles of NGOs in monitoring schools, and the regularity of funds in giving salary to the special school teachers, contingency and stipends of students.

It was found that the NCLP schools were successful more or less in maintaining constant enrolment, and cooking and supplying mid-day meals. All the 19 special schools surveyed were found to be mud-built,

Table 7.5 Literacy and Children Size (Caste-wise) in the Household Survey

Category	1 illiterate		Up to Class IV		V–X		Above X		Total	
	Male	Female	Male	Female	Male	Female	Male	Female	Male	Female
Scheduled Caste	3	2	91	87	33	20	–	–	127	109
Muslim	7	14	105	91	18	38	1	–	131	143
General (Other than Muslim)	2	4	41	23	7	6	–	–	50	33
Total	12	20	237	201	58	64	1	–	308	285

Source: Field Survey, 2013 (Bhuimali, 2013); *Child Labour Survey Report: Cooch Behar District, 2013*, submitted by A. Bhuimali to Cooch Behar District Administration. It was a Government of West Bengal Project on Child Labour under the NCLP scheme.

Table 7.6 Educational Status of Parents

Caste	Illiterate			Up to Class IV			V–X			Above X			Total		
	Father	Mother	Total	Father	Mother	Total	Father	Mother	Total	Father	Mother	Total	Father	Mother	Total
Scheduled Caste	47	52	99	60	61	121	27	19	48	2	1	3	136	133	
Muslim	60	58	118	26	33	59	17	14	31	0	0	0	104	105	
General (Other than Muslims)	17	17	34	19	18	37	5	4	9	0	1	1	41	39	
Total	124	127	251	105	112	217	49	37	86	1	1	4	281	277	

Source: Field Survey – Bhuimali, 2013; *Child Labour Survey Report: Cooch Behar District, 2013*, submitted by A. Bhuimali to Cooch Behar District Administration. It was a Government of West Bengal Project on Child Labour under the NCLP scheme.

and there was not a single concrete-made building. In spite of this, the student attendance was noted to be very good: more than 76 per cent. It was understood that a regular supply of mid-day meals attracted the students. The plots where the schools were located did not belong to the school authorities. There was no playground and school boundary demarcation. School rooms were temporary in construction, room walls were made either of thatches or with tin or mud or jute drum, and the floors would be *kuccha*. The schools would be one-roomed and all the classes (from Class I–IV) would be held in one room. Naturally, there would not be a proper environment for the teaching-learning process. In such conditions, a huge investment was understood to be required if proper attention were to be given to the child labourers withdrawn from work and admitted to schools. The fund provided by the central government did not come regularly and directly to the respective NCLP headquarters. Direct cash transfer to the children's families also was irregular, and the amount was also meagre as ₹150 ($2.03) was given to each student as a stipend. As the cost of sending the children to special schools was very high, this could not be compensated with this meagre amount of stipend provided in the form of direct cash transfer. Presently, the amount has been increased to ₹400 ($5.40) per month, which, too, is meagre.

At any time, the maximum number of child labourers would be found in the rural districts, in the agriculture sector. To justify this, 200 farming families were surveyed in detail from four subdivisions of the northern West Bengal district of Cooch Behar—Mekhligunj, Dinhata, Tufanganj and Cooch Behar II. The results have been displayed in Table 7.7.

Data presented in Table 7.8 show that 35 children were directly involved in agricultural operation in Biswaspara village of Mekhligunj subdivision, 40 in Madhyavaratli of Dinhata, 20 in Tufanganj and 35 in Cooch Behar-II.

Table 7.8 shows that out of 130 children involved in agricultural work, 37 attended a special school, drew stipends and enjoyed mid-day meals; 47 of them completed their stipend-term education and joined high school. Forty-six of the children surveyed were completely out of school—they were doing nothing.

During the survey on child labour in the Cooch Behar district, many children were found involved in the tobacco industry: especially

Table 7.7 Agricultural Survey: Survey with 200 Farm Families

Subdivisions	Village	Number of Farm Families	No. of Children Involved in Agriculture
Mekhligunj	Biswaspara	50	35
Dinhata	Madhyavarali	50	40
Tufanganj	Barasalbari	50	20
Cooch Behar II	Damodarpur	50	35
Total		200	130

Source: Field Survey – Bhuimali, 2013; Child Labour Survey Report: Cooch Behar District, 2013, submitted by A. Bhuimali to Cooch Behar District Administration. It was a Government of West Bengal Project on Child Labour under the NCLP scheme.

Table 7.8 Agricultural Working Children in Activities: Attending Special School, Out of School and Joining High School

Nature of Work	No. of Students
Attending school	37
Joining high school	47
Out of school	46
Total	130

Source: Field Survey – Bhuimali, 2013; Child Labour Survey Report: Cooch Behar District, 2013, submitted by A. Bhuimali to Cooch Behar District Administration. It was a Government of West Bengal Project on Child Labour under the NCLP scheme.

in beedi making and production of tobacco. Tobacco and *tendu* leaves are usually required for making beedi. Beedi making started in West Bengal as a household industry. In course of time, it transformed itself into a huge industry with massive turnover and employment potentiality. Many states of India are involved in beedi rolling—the major states being Madhya Pradesh, Bihar, Odisha and West Bengal. Socially and economically weaker sections of the society—especially people belonging to the scheduled castes, scheduled tribes and minorities—are often engaged in beedi rolling. Children and women are also involved in this hazardous work.

One could have a clearer idea of the entire process of beedi making before s/he proceeds with this section further. Procurement of *tendu* leaves, procurement of tobacco, and beedi rolling and packaging are the different processes in beedi manufacturing. *Tendu* leaves are collected from the forest and processed. Tobacco is grown during the *Rabi* crops' season. Cooch Behar district is one of the few districts in West Bengal which is most suitable for tobacco cultivation. It is a labour-intensive technique—even more labour intensive than what is involved in rice or jute cultivation. Raw tobacco is directly procured from farmers. Sizing of *tendu* leaves, the filling of leaves with tobacco, and binding them constitute the third process of beedi making. This is done at either beedi factory or the houses of farmers/workers, mostly through contract systems. Packaging of the beedi sticks that have been rolled is the fourth process.

Tendu leaves, tobacco and other implements are supplied to the workers by agents or contractors. About 90 per cent of beedi making is done informally by women and children. The male workers, thereafter, check, roast, dry, label and pack the beedi sticks at factories. It is a hazardous work, and child labour is completely prohibited for all the activities related to beedi making. But the engagement of child labourers in tobacco cultivation and beedi-making process continues unabated.

Many reasons could be offered for engaging child labourers in this hazardous work. Some of them are listed thus. (a) It is highly labour intensive and requires less capital and less skill. Parents who work in the beedi industry can easily equip their children to the work without any formal training. (b) Child labourers can be easily dominated, subjugated and exploited by offering low wages and avoiding legal measures like leave and other benefits. (c) Lack of education and awareness among the parents, and large family size force children to join hazardous works to supplement the family income. (d) General literature and many studies show that dropout among girl children is highest in low-income families. Girls help their mothers with domestic chores. During leisure time, the girls are involved in beedi-rolling activity. Gender bias in this job increases the possibility of involving girl children in beedi-making work. (e) Subcontract system is followed in beedi rolling. The agents or subcontractors, on behalf of the owner or manufacturers, supply raw materials to beedi-making households. The families then start making beedi with the help of girl children and women in the family. It is very easy to exploit the beedi-making families under this subcontract system. (f) Tobacco merchants also exploit the tobacco leaf growers. Tobacco price is fixed unilaterally by the tobacco merchants; no role is played by the tobacco-leaf growers. Tobacco-leaf production is both labour-intensive and capital-intensive. This requires sufficient irrigation, chemical fertilizer and organic manure, pesticides and labour. However, the merchants cannot raise the price at their will because beedi smokers are usually from people of lower economic strata. As a result, both the tobacco-growers as well as the labourers are exploited. Children and women are forced to work in the beedi-making sector at a very low wage.

The process of beedi making is hazardous even for an aged person. Naturally, children are the worst sufferers. Beedi rollers do not wear protective clothing, gloves or masks, and are exposed to tobacco dust through their skin and by inhaling the harmful particles. Tobacco growers and beedi workers routinely suffer from bronchial asthma and tuberculosis. They also suffer pain and cramp in shoulders, neck, back, lower abdomen, and from anaemia and eye problems.

Data collected from two tobacco-growing villages (V-1 and V-2) of Mekhliganj subdivision have been presented in Tables 7.9 and 7.10.

Data presented in Table 7.9 show that 60 per cent of work was performed by the children from all categories of farmhouses (marginal, small and medium farmers). Children's participation is above 80 per cent

Table 7.9 *Tobacco-growing Village—Tikavita(V-1)*

Caste/Community	No. of Households Surveyed (Category-wise)			
	Marginal	Small	Medium	Total
Scheduled Castes (Rajbanshi)	60 (40)	40 (20)	20 (9)	120 (72)
Muslims	30 (26)	10 (6)	6 (3)	46 (37)
Total	90 (66)	50 (26)	26 (12)	166 (04)

Source: Field Survey, 2013; *Child Labour Survey Report: Cooch Behar District, 2013,* submitted by A. Bhuimali to Cooch Behar District Administration. It was a Government of West Bengal Project on Child Labour under the NCLP scheme.
Note: Figures in the parentheses indicate children's involvement in agriculture.

Table 7.10 *Tobacco-growing Village—Niztaraf (V-2)*

Caste/Community	No. of Households Surveyed (Category-wise)			
	Marginal	Small	Medium	Total
Scheduled Caste (Rajbanshi)	85 (112)	51 (26)	8 (3)	144 (41)
Muslims	11 (6)	5 (3)	2 (1)	18 (10)
General (other than Muslims)	2 (3)	1(1)	1(0)	4 (4)
Total	98 (121)	57 (30)	11 (4)	166 (155)

Source: Field Survey – Bhuimali, 2013; *Child Labour Survey Report: Cooch Behar District, 2013*, submitted by A. Bhuimali to Cooch Behar District Administration. It was a Government of West Bengal Project on Child Labour under the NCLP scheme.

Note: Figures in the parentheses indicate total number of children engaged in agricultural operation.

among Muslim families. The data also show that it is not possible to continue cultivation without the help of child labour. Tobacco is grown in the *Rabi season*. In the *Kharif season*, *aman*-paddy is grown, and during pre-*kharif season* jute and hybridized paddy is grown.

The second tobacco-growing village surveyed—Niztara——is 3 km north of the subdivisional headquarters of Mekhligunj. An even number of farmers, that is, 166 has been chosen for a detailed survey. The total number of farmers—marginal, small and medium—together was 166, of whom 155 were children who were engaged in agricultural activities. They worked through all the agricultural seasons—including that of the cultivation of raw tobacco, which is dangerous to health, especially of children. Total *Rajbanshi* (SC) farmers were 144 in number, of whom 141 were children who worked with their parents in agricultural activities. The irony was that the future of children—a total of 155 in number—was completely uncertain. Nobody could answer exactly what the children would do after completion of school education, or whether they would be able to complete their school education at all.

In earlier times, the situation of the towns was not good too. For example, a large number of children engaged in tea-stalls, hotels and restaurants, in Cooch Behar could be found toiling away at different locations like New Cooch Behar Station, Cooch Behar Bus Stand, Cooch Behar Kachari More, Chalkchaka and Rajen Choupathi, Pancharangi and Cooch Behar Hospital. Data regarding them, collected

Table 7.11 *Child Labourers Identified at Tea Stalls, Hotels, Restaurants in Cooch Behar Town, 2013*

Area Surveyed	No. of Shops, Tea Stalls, Hotels and Restaurants	No. of Workers Employed (Aged)	No. of Child Labour Found	Total Workers
New Cooch Behar Station	61	65	06	71
Cooch Behar Bus Stand	89	99	10	109
Cooch Behar Kachari More	14	18	07	25
Chalkchaka and Rajen Choupathi	28	32	03	35
Pancharangi	80	85	07	92
Cooch Behar Hospital More	80	89	13	102
Total	352	388	46	434

Source: Field Survey – Bhuimali, 2013; *Child Labour Survey Report: Cooch Behar District, 2013*, submitted by A. Bhuimali to Cooch Behar District Administration. It was a Government of West Bengal Project on Child Labour under the NCLP scheme.

from different locations of Cooch Behar town in 2013, has been presented in Table 7.11.

A child labour survey conducted in 352 shops, stalls, hotels and restaurants in Cooch Behar town showed that out of 434 workers engaged, 46 were found to be engaged as child labourers. Working children were also found to work throughout the day, and there was no fixed pay assigned to the child labourers.

The results of another child labour survey conducted with beedi-making households in four locations—Babupara (Tufangunj), Dudher Kuthi (Dewanbos), Ashrom Road (New Town, Cooch Behar) and Sunsuni Bazar (Cooch Behar)—have been presented in Table 7.12.

During interviews with members of the beedi-rolling households, it was found that the participation of child labourers was very

Table 7.12 Beedi Rolling in the District of Cooch Behar

Area	No. of Persons Involved	Child Labourers Involved
Babupara (Tufangunj)	24	NIL
Dudher Kuthi (Dewanbos)	28	4
Ashram Road (New Town)	25	NIL
Sunsuni Bazar (Cooch Behar)	24	2
Total	101	6

Source: Field Survey – Bhuimali, 2013; *Child Labour Survey Report: Cooch Behar District, 2013*, submitted by A. Bhuimali to Cooch Behar District Administration. It was a Government of West Bengal Project on Child Labour under the NCLP scheme.

low—only six girl children were involved in beedi rolling. It might be a fact that parents did not disclose the exact number of children engaged in this work.

7.3. THE BANAMALI ECONOMY

Parentless children and the children of the poverty-stricken families have no option but to join work as a survival strategy for their own and for their families. The writers can cite a few cases in which one could particularly notice all the family members—parents and children—working together. In doing so, they are just able to manage the bare minimum necessities. They cannot care for their own health and education. One of the respondents of a survey, Ms Taranga—a destitute coming from Nilphamari, Rangpur area of Dinajpur district, Bangladesh—migrated with his family members to Siliguri (India) around 1971. They were five members in the family—Taranga, her husband, a son and two daughters. All worked together and just managed to live from hand to mouth. After a few years, she was suddenly abandoned by her husband. It was a bolt from the blue for Ms Taranga—she became restless and no one was there to help her. She worked, for some time, as a domestic help. Her daughters and son joined hands with their mother. It was thus, an addition of three children to the workforce but they had to leave their school. In this way, child labour increases. In addition, their dream of overcoming poverty and economic distress remains unfulfilled.

Another respondent (to a survey interview), Mr Sunil, lived with his family members in a remote rural area of the district of Dakshin Dinajpur in West Bengal. Similar story has been covered by Jeffrey Sachs in his 2004 publication. Mr Sunil's forefathers were the landless farmers who cultivated only the land owned by the *zamindars*. They gradually lost their cultivating rights, and ultimately became daily-wage workers in the farmland of others. His father, Mr Babua, was a daily-wage farm worker and his mother was a domestic help. After finishing her domestic chores, Mr Sunil's mother would go to work on foot to Udai, an adjacent village, 2 kilometres away from her own hamlet. She worked there for the whole day, and would come back in the evening. Coming back to home, she would join in the household work. Her three daughters and three sons remained at home uncared. The elder daughter, Ms Aruna, looked after her younger brothers and sisters and completed the tasks that remained unfinished. Three children of the family—Mr Sunil, Mr Sushil and Mr Anil—became child labourers, working with others as the village cow tenders. They could not come out of poverty. Due to the existence of a very weak social protection system, they still remain below the poverty line as being among the poorest of the poor.

Another person living in the village—Mr Dukhiram—was a beggar. He was quite intelligent and was well-known in the locality. There were a total of six members in his family: his wife and his four children. He was a good storyteller. He would tell people mesmerizing stories through his attractive voice, good narrative style and mesmerizing personality. He spoke very quietly and intelligently and narrated incidents from the life of ordinary villagers. He was a wily man and was famous for being a 'skilful apothecary' with 'unconventional ways of treatment' (Bhuimali, 2020). He and his residence were always at the helm of main attraction to numerous children and inquisitive people all around. After his death, the family members, the children (three daughters and the son) and the mother became guardianless and destitute. Three children became domestic workers. The family began to live in a poverty trap in the Dakshin Dinajpur's village of Uday. There was almost no health facility for them; there was no nearby secondary school and roads, and earlier the road connectivity was also very poor. All these contributed negatively to the growth of the family. This was the story of almost everyone in rural West Bengal during the 1950s—1980s.

Another story of a family (supplying child labourers) living in the village was that of the Banamalis'. Their forefathers were the tenants under the Zamindari system. They too lost their tenancy after the abolition of Zamindari system. They became landless and were converted into daily agricultural workers, while the children were forced to engage in domestic sectors and farms as 'child labourers'. The family would have to survive on a single meal every day for about 30 years, from 1960 to 1990. The female members would, in the morning, collect a few leafy vegetables, lentils and wood for fuel for preparing and cooking the lone meal in the evening—in accompaniment of laughter and mirth, and of fish trapped from nearby water sources. The whole family is still living in the village without any mentionable economic and educational upliftment. Globalization could not influence the family in any way. Social protection failed to improve the economy of the family. However, presently the said family members are successful in managing two square meals a day, (probably) financially aided by Mr Janjalu—a member of the family—who pulls a hand cart or sometimes drives an auto rickshaw.

The above stories focus on the miseries of different families living in the remote, rural areas of Bengal. They belong to the so-called 'Banamali economy', a situation where people give up their all hopes and aspirations to get out of poverty traps.

We can present below the so-called 'Banamali-economy'—of people trapped in extreme poverty—in a diagram. The below diagram represents the 'Banamali economy' applicable for families that remain poor for generations (three generations here) and have to survive on one meal a day.

In the diagram, B represents the Banamali economy.

G-1 = Generation 1, G-2 = Generation 2, G-3 = Generation 3, and G-4 = Generation 4.

BF = Banamali's Father, BS = Banamali's son, BGS = Banamali's Grand Son.

The diagram shows the families living under extremely extreme poverty for generations, and there is no ray of hope of getting out of poverty. Here Banamali's father was a tenant farmer. He belongs to the poor category. He had tenancy right which he lost with the disappearance of the Zamindari system. In his later life, he experienced extreme poverty. His son began his working life as a child labourer at the age of 7 years. He and his family lived under extremely extreme

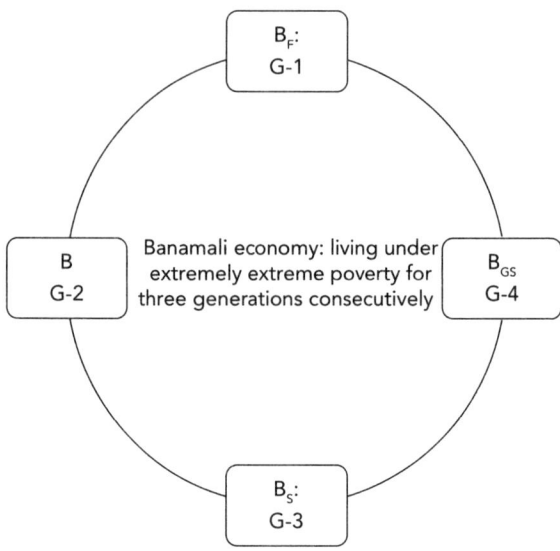

poverty and could manage a square meal a day. That poverty which Mr Banamali acquired/inherited from his father continued. It easily went to his son Mr Janjalu and his family. He too was able to manage a single meal for his family. Thus, for the three generations, extreme poverty continued. Now the turn is on the fourth generation. He has two children—one boy and a girl, who, respectively, are studying in Class IX and Class XI respectively. They are taking two meals a day. Slight improvement has been noticed. There may perhaps be a slight improvement in the social protection cover. Health facilities have been dramatically improved, and there is a good sign of improvement in education with direct cash transfer by the government. This is a very recent phenomenon.

Here the writers have indentified three categories of poor people who can be given special attention in order to get out them of poverty.

They are:

1. Poor—capable of managing two square meals, and involving women and children with low income, low education, low saving.
2. Extreme poor—managing two square meals, involving women, with low income, low education, very meagre saving.
3. Extremely extreme poor—managing one square meal, with low income, no education and no savings.

People from all the above three categories lack resources: natural and those based on human capital. They have very limited access to food, education, health and other necessities. They are involved in working in informal sectors and have an extremely meagre income per day. They obviously have low education and cannot take care of their health. They need special care—a special boost—coming from outside. It could be government-level assistance, assistance from an individual endeavour, or assistance from government-level organizations. Foreign government-level donors also sometimes come forward to solve the problem. Only then could the issue of the production of child labourers from these impoverished families be addressed and solved.

Chapter 8

Impact of COVID-19 Pandemic

8.1. INTRODUCTION

The entire globe has seen a significant improvement in the struggle to eradicate child labour, especially since 2000. In 2020, however, the COVID-19 pandemic has entirely changed the situation, and the formal and informal sectors, which employed child labourers, have come under direct threat. The pandemic has had exerted a direct negative impact upon the whole global economy, affecting employment in agriculture, industry and the service sector. This has increased the volume of poverty, unemployment and vulnerability among commoners—be it in the developed, developing or least-developed countries. The condition of people from poor families is extremely serious. Urgent action is required to address and rectify the harms and tolls done or taken by the COVID-19 virus.

Although it is very difficult to quantify the actual losses the whole globe has incurred, one could easily detect how the situation has intensified instances of economic crises while disrupting the supply chain and stalling manufacturing. Household income has fallen down abruptly—especially in families engaged in the informal sector of the economy. The pandemic has exerted a direct impact upon women and children. As a survival strategy, children are being increasingly forced to work under exploitative and hazardous conditions. Those who are already in work are facing harder working conditions such as longer-than-usual hours of work, with less wage and provisions for working under more stringent conditions. Along with this, gender inequality has increased, increasing the miseries of girl children. Closure of schools for a long period of time has contributed to severe numbers of school dropouts, especially among low-income families. This, in turn, is increasing the number of child labour.

8.2. POLICY PRESCRIPTION

The ILO has identified four policy prescriptions to tackle the COVID-19 crisis: (a) stimulating the economy and employment, (b) supporting enterprises, employment and income, (c) protecting workers and (d) relying on social dialogue for solutions. To make the prescribed policies effective, the ILO has advised governments, employers' and workers' organizations to work together for overcoming health, social and economic crises. Like the ILO, the UNICEF has also been advocating the following: keeping children healthy and well-fed; supplying vulnerable children with water, sanitation and hygiene; keeping children under learning; supporting families in need; protecting children from exploitation and abuse; and protecting refugee and migrant children and children affected by conflict.

It has been estimated by numerous e-surveys that the COVID-19 virus has affected four billion people living in slums, informal settlements and poor housing, and those working in the informal economy. Their livelihoods have been crippled. The World Bank, in a 22 April 2020 report, estimates that due to the ongoing pandemic situation, the number of poorest of the poor people around the world would increase from 40 million to 60 million by the end of 2020. This, undoubtedly, has had exerted a negative impact on the race to curb child labour.

Due to the ongoing pandemic, there has been a drastic fall in the standard of living—especially among the socially unprotected people. This is due to the decreasing chances of employment. During this period, wages have fallen, and working hours have increased drastically. This has increased economic crises in families. This also has given rise to uncertainties regarding the family income. In many cases, families are becoming increasingly dependent on children, who are being forced to work as child labourers.

8.3. IMPACT ASSESSMENT

The crisis has been increasing economic informality. Evidence shows that formal sectors of employment had been reduced in number, and this increased the dependence on the informal sector. Child labour is presently being found in the informal sectors. If dependency on the informal sector increases, so will be the possibility of increasing child labour. Children are becoming more and more vulnerable in such situations, and are facing increased exposure to hazards and exploitation in different sectors of the economy—particularly in agriculture and domestic work—and they are sometimes facing sexual violence. Due to natural hazards or other causes, children are being left behind or left alone. Thus, they are becoming less protected and more vulnerable to the worst forms of work. As an example, as M. Brulisauer[1] writes in 2015, when Nepal experienced a devastating earthquake. All sorts of social protection failed, and this led to increased human trafficking.

Usually, millions of people from Asia, Africa, Latin American countries work in the European countries and the United States of America. A huge amount of remittances thus earned go to the poor countries. Business closure due to lockdown measures, understandably, has reduced the volumes of remittances to be sent to the households of the workers. This has increased the suffering among the family members of the migrant workers living abroad. Less remittance means less income. Due to the COVID-19 pandemic, there has been a decline in remittances as well as the migrants due to the closure of industries. Forced returns of migrant workers have negatively impacted the migrants' families and their children.

Contraction of business activities and that of production activities have resulted in the downturn of the supply of money and the availability of credit in the economy. This is a global phenomenon. Due to the coronavirus pandemic, there has been a 3 per cent reduction in global trade ('COVID-19 and Child Labour: A Time of Crisis, a Time to Act', ILO, 2020). Credit contraction and reduction in trade and FDI have made developing countries credit short. This has, in turn, become responsible for turning people from low-income households into bonded labourers. Travel and tourism have also been contracted due to the coronavirus effect. This has further contracted employment in this sector in a large number.

---

[1] M. Brulisauer, 'Human Trafficking in the Post-Earthquake in Nepal: Impacts of the Disaster on Methods for Victim recruitment,' *MAS ETH (Development and Cooperation)*, December 2015.

For more than one year, the educational institutions of all types—schools, colleges, research institutes and other institutes of higher learning—have remained closed due to pandemic and this has in fact affected about 1.6 billion school students all over the globe, as a UNESCO-study of 2020 reveals ('Education from Disruption to Recovery: Global Monitoring of Schools Closures caused by COVID-19'). Some good schools across the world have shifted to online teaching. But many students—more than 50 per cent of those enrolled worldwide—fail to avail this opportunity due to financial hardship and lack of Internet facilities. Most of such students live in remote rural areas and semi-urban areas and have no access to the Internet. They are, in fact, being left behind—perhaps too far behind—and may not be able to reach to those who have advanced further due to access of Internet. Schools provide students with not only education but also social protection through free mixing and interaction. These have been affected, and had, in turn, been influential in shoving pupils towards becoming labourers. Moreover, due to the closure of schools, students from economically and socially backward communities are leaving school en masse, and many of them are abandoning their studies forever.

Dropping out from schools in this way may force these children to join work as child labourers. They cannot be good workers in future because it is not possible to acquire skills with such meagre education. They may be forced to join work in the informal sector and domestic service. This has already happened in many of the SSA countries and those in Asia and the Pacific region. Post-COVID-19 effects may permanently force many students to informal sector's hazardous and exploitative work—as had long before opined, for a different situation, by Frankenberg et al.[2]

The present crisis has shocked the whole world infinitesimally. Economies have downsized, social life has been disrupted, education system has collapsed, and, on 8 September 2021, total deaths due to the COVID-19 pandemic rose to 4.56 million, globally and that of coronavirus-affected people went up to 219 million on the same day. This in fact, understandably, has forced millions of more children to work as child labour. Table 8.1 illustrates this trend.

---

[2] E. Frankenberg, E. B. Sikoki, C. Sumantri, W. Suriastini, and D. Thomas, 'Education, Vulnerability, and Resilience after a Natural Disaster,' *Ecology and Society* 18, no. 2 (2013): 16.

Table 8.1 Child Labour and Hazardous Work: Trends

		Children Aged 5–17 Years in Child Labour				Children Aged 5–17 Years in Hazardous Work			
		2016		2020		2016		2020	
		%	No.	%	No.	%	No.	%	No.
World Total		9.6	151,600	9.6	160,000	4.6	72,500	4.7	79,000
Sex	Girls	8.4	64,100	7.8	62,900	3.6	27,800	3.6	28,800
	Boys	10.7	87,500	11.2	97,000	5.5	44,800	5.8	50,200
Age	5–11 years	8.3	72,600	9.7	89,300	2.2	19,000	2.8	25,900
	12–14 years	11.7	41,900	9.3	35,600	4.6	16,400	4.8	18,100
	15–17 years	10.5	37,100	9.5	35,000	10.5	37,100	9.5	35,000
ILO regions	Africa	19.6	72,100	21.6	92,200	8.6	31,500	9.7	41,400
	Sub-Saharan Africa	22.4	70,000	23.9	86,600	9.8	30,500	10.7	38,600
	Arab States	2.9	1,200	5.8	2,400	1.5	600	4.5	1,900
	Asia and the Pacific	7.4	62,100	5.6	48,700	3.4	28,500	2.6	22,200
	Americas	5.3	10,700	4.3	8,300	3.2	6,600	2.9	5,700
	Latin America and the Caribbean	7.3	10,500	6.0	8,200	4.4	6,300	4.0	5,500
	Europe and Central Asia	4.1	5,500	5.7	8,300	4.0	5,300	5.5	7,900

National Income Grouping								
Low income	19.4	65,200	26.2	65,000	8.8	29,700	11.6	28,700
Lower middle income	8.5	58,200	9.0	69,700	4.9	33,500	4.3	33,600
Upper middle income	6.6	26,200	4.9	23,700	2.0	7,800	3.2	15,300
High income	1.2	2,000	0.9	1,600	1.0	1,600	0.8	1,500

Source: International Labour Organization and United Nations Children's Fund 2021.
Notes: 1. Numbers are expressed in thousands and have been rounded.
2. Tread data are not available for SDG and UNICEF regions.

The data presented in Table 8.1 clearly show global trends of child labour and hazardous works. The data make a comparison between the numbers of working children in 2016 and 2020 (aged 5–17 years) and those engaged in hazardous work. These show sex-wise, age-wise data as well as data from the ILO-serviced regions like Africa, SSA, Arab States, Asia and the Pacific, Americas, Latin America and the Caribbean and Europe and Central Asia. National income grouping has also been made and the segregation of income of countries is made into four subheadings, that is, low-income, lower-middle income, upper-middle-income and high-income countries. What the data lack is the unavailability of data for SDG and UNICEF-served regions. Analysing data of the child labourers, it reveals that there is no change, in percentage terms of child labourers' numbers, between 2016 and 2020, which remains constant at 9.6 per cent, but in terms of their numbers, there is an increase from 151,600,000 in 2016 to 160,000,000 in 2020 worldwide. Sex-wise distribution of working children shows that girl child's contribution goes on increasing if the data between 2016 and 2020 are compared. In percentage terms, it shows that girls' participation decreased from 8.4 per cent in 2016 to 7.8 per cent in 2020. In the case of working boys' engagement, data purport an enhancement of their employment from 10.7 per cent in 2016 to 11.2 per cent in 2020. The involvement of child labour in hazardous jobs indicates that girls' proportion of working involvement remained the same at 3.8 per cent between 2016 and 2020, while in the case of involvement of boys', it increased from 5.5 per cent in 2016 to 5.8 per cent in 2020. Their engagement in hazardous work has also increased for both boys and girls. In the case of working girls, it increased from 27,800,000 in 2016 to 28,800,000 in number in 2020 and for working boys, this increased from 44,800,000 in 2016 to 50,200,000 in 2020.

Analysing data of child labour from the ILO-serviced regions, the table shows that there has been a marked enlargement of child labour in the African region from 19.6 per cent in 2016 to 21.6 per cent in 2020 and in terms of number it increased from 72,100,000 in 2016 to 92,200,000 in 2020. Similar trends have been noticed in the case of engagement of working children in percentage terms and in number. In percentage terms, the data show that it increases from 8.6 per cent in 2016 to 9.7 per cent in 2020 and it increases from

31,500,000 in 2016 to 41, 400,000 in 2020. This is very alarming, and this goes against the SDGs. Child labour data and that of their engagement in hazardous jobs pertaining to the SSA continent alone show the presence of 22.4 per cent child labour in 2016, which again went up to 23.9 per cent in 2020 and their participation in hazardous jobs increased from 9.8 per cent in 2016 to 10.7 per cent in 2020 and in terms of their number is increased from 30,500,000 to 38,600,000 respectively. The second highest contributors to child labour in the ILO-serviced regions are Asia and the Pacific and then follow the Latin America and the Caribbean regions. The prevalence of child labour and their engagement in hazardous work goes on declining in arrayed countries in terms of their income. In this case, we observe a marked declining trend of child labour, that is, it is the highest in the low-income countries. Then follow the lower-income countries and then the upper-middle-income countries. This is the lowest in both percentage terms and in number in the high-income countries, as the ILO–UNICEF data present.

The ILO and UNICEF used data collected from 106 countries of the world to generate the estimates and the standard deviations of the 2020 global and regional estimates due to sampling variability. The variation is the indicator of children in employment, as suggested, and was calculated by running the econometric model 150 times. The data collected and tabulated by the ILO-UNICEF have been portrayed in Table 8.2.

Table 8.2 exhibits child labour aged 5–17 years in employment. The data show that the worldwide data for child labour are 222,088,000 (13.3%) in number in 2020. The highest number is found in SSA, that is, 32.0 per cent and the total number of child labour is 110,766,000. Then come Latin America and the Caribbean (9.1%) followed by Europe and Central Asia (8.2%), Arab States (8.1%) and Asia and the Pacific (7.8%).

The pandemic has created mounting problems regarding health-related issues in countries where health is under-resourced and social protection is not strong: not capable enough of accommodating the affected people and saving the families from health and economic hazards. The deaths due to the COVID-19 pandemic may increase child labour. Death of earning member who is bread-winner may force children to compulsorily join work—sometimes in abusive work.

Table 8.2 *Children Aged 5–17 Years in Employment*

	Children in Employment (Thousands)	Children in Employment (Percentage)	Standard Deviation (Percentage Points)
World	222,088	13.3	1.0
Africa	124,122	29.1	0.8
Sub-Saharan Africa	115,766	32.0	0.8
Americas	14,672	7.5	0.6
Latin America and the Caribbean	12,422	9.1	0.7
Arab States	3,447	8.1	–
Asia and the Pacific	67,960	7.8	1.8
Europe and Central Asia	11,886	8.2	0.7

Source: International Labour Organization and United Nations Children's Fund 2021.
Note: The table shows regional groupings used for ILO reporting.

In this case, child labour becomes the survival strategy (as suggested by Alam in his 2008 work; and also by S. Bazen and C. Salmon in the 2008 publication).

Initially, countries throughout the world faced many problems in accommodating patients. They took a number of months to cope with the situation. The damage was to the United States of America, Italy, Germany and many developing countries, including India and Brazil. To combat the COVID-19 pandemic, the countries require wide-ranging social protection coverage like providing direct cash transfer, health facilities, jobs and food security. Around 190 countries of the world have adopted 937 social protection measures to combat COVID-19, as U. Gentilini writes in his article.[3]

Health crises and economic and labour market shocks due to the pandemic have created vulnerability among 152 million children workers all over the world. The ILO, as the *Secretariat of Alliance 8.7*, has

---

[3] U. Gentilini, 'SP Links 22—Global Social Protection Covid-Response v.10!' *The Weekly Social Protection Links*, 22 May 2020.

adopted the key role in coordinating the network of 250 organizations to address the threats of coronavirus-affected communities.

A brief by Guy Ryder, the ILO Director-General, has stated that COVID-19 may result in a rise in poor which, in turn, may increase in child labour. This is what the affected families could only do as a means of living. In the same way, UNICEF Executive Director Henrietta Fore has pointed out that due to the rise in poverty, school closure and a decrease in social services, many children are being pushed into the workforce. Most of the works, children are doing presently are exploitative in nature, and there might be gender discrimination. More girls may be found joining work in agriculture and domestic services. As remedies, the brief suggested increasing social protection, easier access to credit, providing decent work to the adults, adopting measures to withdraw children from work and getting them back to schools.

Reports jointly produced by the Human Rights Watch, Initiative for Social and Economic Rights (ISER) in Uganda and Friends of the Nation (FoN) in Ghana, under the title 'I must work to Eat: COVID-19, Poverty and Child Labour in Ghana, Nepal and Uganda' (26 May 2021), mentions that due to the closure of schools and joblessness in the informal sector and the consequent decline of income of millions of families, children are being increasingly forced to enter the workforce. This is the survival strategy of the hapless families. Distressed children have no options but to participate in the workforce for longer hours and to work under hazardous and exploitative conditions. The pandemic has exerted adverse effects upon the children's rights such as their rights to lead a decent standard of living, their rights to education and protection from child labour. The report examines the rise in child labour and poverty in three countries—Ghana, Nepal and Uganda—during the pandemic. The countries, as mentioned, have shown remarkable stride in ending child labour during pre-COVID-19. However, during the pandemic, the number of child labour and their plight has risen sharply. Interviews of children in Nepal, Ghana and Uganda clearly indicate that COVID-19 has exerted a negative impact upon the family income. The income-earners have lost their jobs due to business closure during lockdown, transportation restrictions and decreasing consumer demand. Children have reported that they have been spending days with little food, and sometimes without food. They cannot buy food, sugar, salt and water. The report says that due to a sharp fall in income and school closure, there has been an increasing number of child labour in Nepal, Ghana and Uganda. Children in Uganda and Ghana are forced to work at gold mines. They are forced to carry heavy bags of ore and crash ore or their pieces with their soft small hands. They face breathing problems due to the presence of dust and fumes coming from the processing machines. Some children are paid a daily wage rate and the rest receive their wage in terms of processed ore. The wages they receive are being used for buying food and other necessaries.

Cash allowances that exist in Nepal, Ghana and Uganda for eradicating poverty have been enhanced during the pandemic. The Uganda government has placed 'COVID-19 Budget' in June 2020 which is more than 12.36 per cent of the previous year's budget. The objective is to spend the additional allocation, among others, for social protection. But the fact is that this effort has failed to reach the targeted households with children.

Nepal's COVID-19 relief initiatives consist of providing food assistance packages to labourers in the informal sector and those who are in dire need. This has been funded by the local and the provincial government, the report says.

Ghana's Livelihood Empowerment against Poverty (LEAP) programme of 2008 enlarged its activities during the coronavirus crisis. In 2020, LEAP alone provided direct cash allowances to millions of people amounting to approximately 5 per cent of Ghana's total population. LEAP's hotline witnessed a spike in calls from families who were in urgent need of additional assistance. The weekly survey on a sample of LEAP beneficiaries between April and August 2020 found that the pandemic has exerted a negative impact on a large number of families. Therefore, the LEAP disbursed an additional fund to the pandemic-affected families in May 2020.

In order to achieve universal social protection in areas such as children, maternity, disability and old age the ILO had made an estimate of spending, averaging 3.3 per cent of GDP, for the low- and middle-income countries. The average spending gap, the ILO says, between the current expenditure and achieving universal coverage is 1.9 per cent of GDP in 2019 and due to COVID-19, this in 2020, has gone up to 2.2 per cent of the GDP. The universal coverage in SSA is estimated at 5.2 per cent and for children, it is 0.8 per cent. For the South Asia region, the universal coverage is 2.8 per cent of the GDP and for the children, it is 0.6 per cent. In arranging additional funds, it is suggested, for the purpose of tackling the pandemic, to re-allocate public expenditures increase tax revenues and reduce consumption. Another way is through tax evasion and international assistance and cooperation.

The economic vitality of every country essentially depends on its children's well-being. Children living in the SSA region are already struggling desperately against a lot of challenges due to adverse climate like cyclones, droughts, floods, landslides, conflicts, and so on. As a new set of challenges, the SSA families are facing falling income and assets, high cost of living, reduced access to social goods and services (as per a 2020 UNICEF study titled 'COVID-19: A Catastrophe for Children in SSA—Cash Transfers and a Marshall Plan can help'). The advent of coronavirus disease has, in fact, pushed the entire SSA into deep economic recession, and put millions of people into abject poverty—affecting mostly children and women. The region is already a challenging place for SSA children. The pandemic has added too many problems to the children of the poverty-stricken families of this region, putting them under stress and severe crises. More than 50 per cent of the children of the region are now facing food insecurity. More than 50 million students have lost access to mid-day meals due to the closure of schools (as per the same 2020 UNESCO report). More than 250 million students are out of school due to the ravages of the pandemic along with other 100 million students who were already out of school even before the onset of the pandemic.

To face the challenge of the COVID-19 pandemic, Mohamed Fall of UNESCO has suggested expanding the cash transfer programmes to the really needy families. He has been referred to in the 20 November 2020 report, 'COVID-19: A Catastrophe for Children in SSA—Cash Transfers and a Marshall Planren Help'). Professor Abhijit V. Banerjee has also prescribed direct cash transfer and expansion of 100 days works in India to cope with the pandemic. This can really and effectively boost the economic growth process already stalled and enlarge social protection cover. But the fact is that the state governments have been suffering from fund constraints. It should be mentioned that the external assistance provided to the SSA countries by the G-20 countries is inadequate in relation to present demand.

To meet up the problem of fund shortage, it has been suggested to properly execute out-of-the-box financing approaches such as selling

IMF gold reserves, issuing long-term bonds and materializing the proposal for starting cross-border fractional taxes. This can only effectively help to reopen the schools after the pandemic and put millions of out-of-school children back to studying.

While discussing any crisis, the world always witnesses that the impacts had been gender-neutral. COVID-19 crisis is no exception. Women from poor and marginalized families are facing greater shock such as loss of livelihood and increased exploitation and violence. In the whole world, women are more than 70 per cent of the active population, but they are not at par with their male counterparts in terms of working hours and pay. The gender gap in payments in the health sector is 28 per cent, which is far larger than that overall gender gap in payment, that is, 16 per cent. This means that more and more women are pushed into extreme poverty than men. The UN Women, 2020 says that coronavirus would push 96 million people throughout the world into extreme poverty by the end of 2021. Of this, 47 million would be women and girls, and this would increase the total number of women and girls under abject poverty to 435 million. The per-head and per-day income of a woman or a girl would dwindle to $1.90 or less. The gender-poverty gap especially among women aged 25–34 years is widening in 2021, and there will soon be 1.18 women under extreme poverty for every 100 men. By the end of 2030, this will be 121.

Women paid labour and women-run businesses have been severely reduced because of the ongoing pandemic. There are some sectors when women are represented more than men. Food service, for example, is run largely by women. Also, retail and entertainment are managed by women and girls. About 40 per cent of women are presently working in the hard-hit sectors compared to 36.6 per cent of employed men. Globally, more than 58 per cent of women are presently engaged in the informal sector and it is the informal sector that is mostly affected by the coronavirus. Another sector where women are largely concentrated is the domestic sector. In the domestic sector, 80 per cent of workers are women. Due to the pandemic, the conditions of these workers have worsened. Seventy-two per cent of domestic workers have so far lost their jobs, the *UN Women Report, 2020,* says. The joblessness among the women and girls would exert a snowball effect on their lives for years to come. The negative economic challenges which women and girls face can best be tackled if the initiatives such as direct income support, support for women-led businesses, and support to women workers especially in the informal sector are provided by the governments and businesses.

8.4. INDIAN PERSPECTIVE

Vulnerabilities in the Indian economy have been exposed due to COVID-19 pandemic, and these have been more due to the second wave in some of the states of India. How has the Indian economy been affected due to Coronavirus can be seen if we go into deeper in the analysis of tourism, aviation and retail sector, GDP growth, migrant workers, women, agriculture and micro and small enterprises (MSMEs), education, etc.

Nationwide lockdown was imposed on 24 March 2020 and it continued for more or less one year. Due to this, the Indian economy faced devastative impacts and people's sources of livelihood, such as shops, eateries, factories, transport, services and businesses, were shattered. Different organizations dealing with the Indian statistics estimate that due to COVID-19 the economy contracted by 8 per cent in 2021. The Economic Survey 2020–2021 sees the growth would be 11 per cent in 2022. But the IMF has revised its estimate which says it would increase from 11.5 per cent estimated in January 2021, to 12.5 per cent for 2022. As per Dun and Bradstreet Global Report, India experienced negative growth of 4.5 per cent during the 2020 fiscal year. The report also forecasts that it would not be possible for the Asian nations to come back to their pre-pandemic situation very quickly. It calls for a special focus on some specific sectors of the economy to cope with the situation. This obviously requires resources and time to reach the target.

Due to coronavirus, the Indian economy witnessed an unprecedented unemployment rate of over six per cent. The closure of manufacturing and service sectors contracted the employment of workers. In India, more than 90 per cent of employment comes from the informal sector. The travel and tourism industry has been making an important contribution to the economy contributing to GDP growth with the creation of huge employment—more than 26.7 million jobs. Due to lockdown, daily-wage workers—the urban poor and migrant workers/labourers alike—have been left without work. This has further put workers under stress and strain, accentuated by no movement of buses and trains. Thousands of labourers, as we could notice, ended up walking back to their own shelters with their families. There was no food and drink with them. They were walking and walking and failed to maintain social distancing. Hundreds of migrant workers died of hunger and diseases. Central and State governments and many social organizations had to come forward to help the distressed migrant workers who lost their jobs and were on the street without any hope of how to survive. Thus, coronavirus has further deteriorated India's hunger and malnutrition woes. The millions of informal-sector workers have been the worst victims of it.

The lockdown made it clear that migrant workers are extremely poor and vulnerable to hunger, and they have been the worst sufferers (along with their women and children) during the COVID-19 pandemic. The death toll in India due to this pandemic is 0.44 million, and that of Coronavirus infection cases is 33.2 million (as of 9 September 2021).

The coronavirus crisis has turned millions of Indian underprivileged families more vulnerable and destitute. An online survey was conducted by Jean Dreze and Reetika Khare on 1400 school children of underprivileged households in 15 states and union territories in August 2021. The report says that almost all the parents of children from poor families in rural India want reopening of the schools closed down due to COVID-19. Students living in rural areas as shown in Table 8.5 lack amenities of online classes such as mobile phones and the Internet. Most of such households belong to scheduled castes (SC) and scheduled tribes (ST) communities. Students' abilities to read and write have been declined and the dropout rates among them have been reduced abnormally. Attendance of SC and ST students had been very low, about 4 per cent and that of 15 per cent among other category students, the study says. About 98 per cent of parents wanted immediate reopening of schools at the earliest. Only 8 per cent of students, as reported, attended online classes regularly and 37 per cent did not attend at all. In the urban areas, students had better access to online classes wherein 23 parent guardians agreed that their children had adequate online class facilities and in rural areas, only 8 per cent of parents agreed upon it. The data collected by Dreze and Khare during the lockdown period of 2021 as shown in Table 8.3 represent that urban children were the gainers from online classes if compared with the children in rural areas in terms of the supply of study materials, online access, ability to read and write, etc.

Table 8.3 Experience of Online Study among Online Children

% of Sample Children	Urban (%)	Rural (%)
Satisfied with online study material	29.0	20.00
Has adequate online access	44.0	25.00
Ability to read and write declined	65.0	70.00
Online classes/videos difficult to follow	46.0	43.00
Connectivity problems (often or sometimes)	57.0	65.00
Own smartphone	11.0	12.00
Live classes not just videos	27.0	12.00

Source: School survey conducted by Dreze and Khare, 2021.

Table 8.4 Children's Attendance in Urban and Rural Areas

Students' Attendance	Urban Areas (%)	Rural Areas (%)
Studying online regularly	24.0	8.0
Not studying at all nowadays	19.0	3.0
Not met their teachers in last 30 days	51.0	58.0
Not have a test or exam in 3 months	52.0	71.0
Not met their teachers in last 30 days	51.0	58.0

Source: School survey conducted by Dreze and Khare, 2021.

School survey conducted by Dreze and Khare in 2021 as shown in Table 8.4 in relation to children's attendance in urban and rural areas remarkably portrays a distinction of school attendance among the children in urban and the rural areas. The lockdown decision was taken hastily, resulting in the loss of millions of jobs and an exodus of migration of informal sector workers from urban to rural areas. Certainly, this led to the soaring of unemployment from 8.35 per cent to 23.52 per cent during April–August 2020.[4]

A large number of MSMEs were not in operation and that was the biggest concern to the millions of workers involved in the MSMEs. This also had a direct impact on the GDP growth rate; since more than

---

[4] CMIE, September 2020; Kavaljit Singh, 'Covid-19 India Economic Recovery,' *The Wire*.

Table 8.5 Students Locked (Community-wise)

Students	SC/ST (%)	Others (%)
Without smartphone	55.0	38.0
Not studying at all	43.0	25.0
Studying regularly	22.0	4.0
Studying online	4.0	15.0
Children watched online, not just videos	5.0	29.0
Parents of online children satisfied with online study material	13.0	26.0
Unable to read more than few letters	45.0	24.0
Literacy rate	61.0	77.0
Parents' feeling about the children's ability to read and write declined	83.0	66.0

Source: School survey conducted by Dreze and Khare, 2021.

30 per cent of our GDP comes from this sector. All India Manufacturers Organization Survey, June 2020, shows that due to the closure of 35 per cent of MSMEs and 43 per cent of self-employed enterprises, 120 million workers lost their jobs. Consumer goods sector, readymade garments and logistic companies suffered most during this period. Another affected sector was the e-commerce industry. Due to the lack of a database of migrant workers—available neither with the Central government nor with the state government—it was rendered very difficult to estimate exactly the total number of suffering migrant workers. A rough estimate reveals that about 10 million migrant workers returned to their native places while enduring hardships. Social protection programmes including the direct cash transfer, subsidized food and daily necessities of the Central Government and the State Governments assisted these workers a great deal even as they reeled under the unprecedented economic shock.

The two waves of the COVID-19 pandemic necessitated a concrete policy initiative on the part of Central and State governments, especially with respect to inclusive societal and health system response along with the specific thrust on a vulnerable population. The UN Policy Brief-Impact of COVID-19 on Women's Health (2020) and ILO-data (2020) tell that women throughout the globe earn less, save less and possess less secure jobs than men, and more than 70 per cent of women of developing countries are involved in informal employment. In India, women have suffered more than men due to the loss of jobs. The ILO, in the *Rapid Assessment of the Impact of the COVID-19 Crisis on Employment*, has warned that those who have lost their work and income are casual workers and the self-employed. In India, three-fourths of employment is non-regular either engaged in casual work or self-employed. Using 2020 population figures, the *ILO Report* finds that 118 million workers are casually employed and represent 25 per cent of the total workforce and slightly more than half of 246 million are self-employed.

The Indian agriculture sector provides 43 per cent employment and its contribution to GDP is 16.5 per cent. COVID-19 crisis has been creating problems for this sector in many ways. Non-availability of migrant workers has been disrupting agricultural activities and supply chains. Northwest India has faced severe problems in many agricultural activities. In this part of India, among others, wheat and pulses are enormously grown over thousands of hectares of land. However, because of transportation problems, supply chains have been disrupted. Due to such problems and many other related issues, prices of wheat, vegetables and other crops have fallen drastically. Closure of shops, hotels and restaurants has reduced the demand for agricultural goods and services along with the sale of milk and milk products. Also, the demand for chicken has fallen due to misinformation on social media that chickens are the carriers of COVID-19. A large number of farmers—marginal, small, medium and large—and workers, daily-wage and permanent, are facing enormous numbers of problems. The farmers who are the producers of perishable items fail to sell their products due to the stress in the supply chain. Agricultural workers have also faced a problem because of restrictions in the free mobility from one place to other due to coronavirus.

Children of daily-wage earners and casual workers are the worst sufferers in these pandemic times. These families have become vulnerable and it has a great impact upon their children. The families do not have work and their livelihood and earnings are under threat. They do not have savings to buy food and other necessities. The children in these low-income families are being forced to join the workforce and this has repeatedly been reported by the media. The majority of these children join work in agriculture on cotton, chilli, paddy, vegetables and other farm products. Both boys and girls are being forced to join the workforce, and the children—especially the girl children—are being trafficked by the unscrupulous middlemen. It is a grave fact that COVID-19 has increased the miseries of child labour in India like that of other affected countries of the world. We can, in brief, discuss the following child labour sufferings and related issues caused due to coronavirus crisis:

1. Children are forced to work because their guardians/parents engaged in informal sector employment have lost their jobs due to the COVID-19 pandemic. This they do in order to supplement family income as a survival strategy. Not only this, children, during the COVID-19 period, joined farm works and family-based firms in large numbers.
2. Children perform work like that of adults but the wage they receive is less than the adults for the same work. The entrepreneurs are encouraged to employ the children because this helps overcome financial losses. COVID-19 helps reverse migration, that is, migration from the urban areas to the rural areas. This creates a shortage in the labour supply in urban areas.
3. Children, especially girl children, face pressure. They have to perform domestic work along with looking after their siblings. Naturally, there is every possibility of more school dropouts among the girl children.
4. With the rise in coronavirus crisis, there increases the livelihood crisis among the people engaged in informal sector employment. There has been a closure of many of the non-government (informal sector) enterprises. This gives rise to the possibility of human trafficking and many of the working children are already being trafficked. The spread of the second wave has opened up the possibility of more child labour trafficking, especially the girl children. Reverse migration forced migrated workers along with their family members to move back to their native places. Workers and their family members coming back to villages face huge livelihood crises. The children in such working groups become more vulnerable particularly trafficking.
5. Due to the second wave of COVID-19, educational institutions have again been closed. Many of the students living in rural areas do not have access to Internet facilities. Naturally, they cannot avail the online class facility. This negatively impacts the children living in

areas with no Internet connectivity. This makes students detached from school, which again can lead to dropouts among the students of poor income households and force them to join the workforce.
6. The Factories Act, 1948, has been modified, through an ordinance, by some of the industrially developed states of India—Gujarat, Punjab, Himachal Pradesh, Uttar Pradesh, Maharashtra, Rajasthan, Madhya Pradesh, Odisha and Assam. This modification, experts opine, might weaken the enforcement of child labour legislation. The amendment has extended the working hours per day from 8 hours to 12 hours. This might have a negative impact on working children and adolescent workers.
7. Apart from governmental-level initiatives, there must be more action-oriented programmes to be undertaken by civil society organizations. In this respect, one might mention the initiatives undertaken by Mr Kailash Satyarthi, a Nobel Laureate, who for the last 40 years has been constantly engaged for the cause of ending poverty. He started his 100 million campaign in 2016 along with his Kailash Satyarthi Children's Foundation, wherein he engages 100 million young people around the globe to speak out for more than 100 million child workers. The ILO, in 2017, identifies that there are 10 million children in the workforce who are the victims of extreme poverty. Mr Satyarthi has a dream of ending child labour from the globe in his lifetime. He strongly believes that there are enough resources available on this planet capable of ending child labour. What is required, he considers, is the feeling of comparison for others. Civil society organizations can strengthen government efforts to identify vulnerable children who are not regularly coming to school and have every possibility of being trafficked. The NGOs can well conduct rescue operations in assistance with the Ministry of Labour and Employment's protocols. They can initiate awareness campaigns about the implications of legal provisions of child labour, their rights and their voices. They can also make people aware of the social protection measures provided to vulnerable families.
8. Child labourers are tortured and harassed in many ways. But the actual number of cases remains far larger than the complaints made and FIRs lodged. NGOs can better take up the issue and find out the actual positions of cases reported and complaints made. Kailash Satyarthi Children's Foundation has observed the situation and presented data in Table 8.6.

Table 8.6 *Total Number of Child Labour in India under CLPRA during 2014–2016*

Status	Total No. of Child Labour as per Census 2011	No. of FIRs Filed Under CLPRA During 2014–2016	Child Labourers Rescued Under CLPRA 2014–2016
Assam	284,812	6	6
Bihar	1,088,509	4	4
Chhattisgarh	257,773	3	3
Delhi	36,317	145	511
Kerala	45,436	5	6
Madhya Pradesh	700,239	6	6
Rajasthan	848,386	31	48
Uttarakhand	82,431	3	3
Haryana	123,202	4	4
Jharkhand	400,276	2	2
Maharashtra	727,932	234	340
Karnataka	421,345	63	143
Andhra Pradesh	343,973	2	2
Telangana	329,030	15	21
Total	10,128,663	602	1,318

Source: Kailash Satyarthi Children's Foundation, 2019.

Data presented above shows that only 1,318 child workers have been rescued out of 10,128,663 working children. The number of FIRs filed under CLPRA during 2014–2016 has been only 602. Only Delhi and Maharashtra reported a higher number of FIRs filed and children rescued. In other states, these are very low.

The budget allocation under NCLP during 2016–2017, 2017–2018 and 2018–2019 has been shown in Table 8.7.

In conclusion, one could say that we desperately need to adopt special means in order to cope with the second wave of coronavirus infections which have crossed 250,000 per day for the last few days. The government should respond with fiscal measures as per the need.

Table 8.7 Budget Allocation under NCLP During 2016–2019

Schemes	Percent Distribution of ...as per 2018–2019 Budget Estimates	Financial Year-wise Budget (in Curve)			Total Budgetary Allocation in Last Three Years (in Curve)
		2016–2017	2017–2018	2018–2019	
NCLP including grants-in-aid to voluntary agencies	92%	128	147	110	385
Reimbursement of assistance to bonded labour Central Sector Scheme for Rehabilitation of bonded labours-2016	8%	12	13	10	35
Total	100%	140	160	120	420

Source: 34th Standing Committee report on Demand for Grants (2018–2019), Ministry of Labour and Employment, Government of India.

The second wave has been spreading infections, and more deaths are occurring. To control this, many states are putting restrictions on the movement of people. The Union Government has announced Atmanirbhar Bharat package to perk up the economy and to prepare for greater uncertainty that the country is going to face shortly. But it has become very difficult to arrange treatment of patients due to the sudden start of the second wave on a very large scale. In this huge wave, inadequate hospital beds and insufficient availability of oxygen cylinders in relation to the number of patients is observed. Vaccination is also going on but it seems shortage of supply. Both central and state governments should work together to bring the situation under control. The second wave has spread infections not only in urban areas but also in the hinterland. It is being reported by different Indian newspapers that the wave has entered into rural areas of Uttar Pradesh and Tamil Nadu. Even Tier-2 cities of Tamil Nadu have been severely affected. In the first wave, the Coronavirus infections impacted much more in the urban areas of India. During this phase, consumer goods sector failed to motivate the urban sector. This means that consumer demand from urban India has been restricted. During the second wave, the consumer goods sector would not be able to equally influence the rural sector as it had done during the first phase. There is every possibility of shrinking the consumer goods demand. This might, in turn, lead to an increase in the number of child labourers.

Chapter 9

Conclusion and Policy Recommendations

The COVID-19 pandemic has reversed the progress against child labour witnessed globally, especially since 2000. On the World Day against Child Labour, 12 June 2021, the ILO and the UNICEF published *Child Labour, 2020: Trends and the Road Forward*. The main focus of this book—as also of the two international organizations—is to examine how the pandemic has severely affected the progress towards the eradication of child labour, and how the crisis is to be overcome globally. The book and other surveys have revealed that in the pandemic situation, numerous children, instead of being nurtured and cared, are pushed to work within the home and outside. During childhood, they need to be provided quality education, healthcare, social protection and time for play and fun. Why do these children have to work instead of going to school? A lot of issues are associated with this question. Due to hard labour at the place of work, their body and mind do not permit them to learn and prosper. Humanitarian efforts against child labouring seem to fall flat.

Before the outbreak of the COVID-19 pandemic, the total number of child labour was 160 million. Of them, 97 million child labourers were male and 63 million were females. The Global Estimate, 2020 mentions that for the last four years—from 2016 onwards—the world has miserably failed to make progress in reducing child labour. This suggests that the international target of ending child labour completely by 2025 would not be possible until and unless some concerted efforts are being made. The coronavirus-ravaged situation has made the situation more awful. In the last four years, the overall number of child labourers has risen by 8 million, while the number of children engaged in hazardous work has gone up by 6.5 million. One good news to be shared here is that there has been continuous progress against child labouring in Asia, the Pacific and Latin America and the Caribbean regions. In Asia and the Pacific, the trend since 2008 is as follows: 2008: −13.3 per cent, 2012: −9.3 per cent, 2016: −7.4 per cent, and 2020: −5.6 per cent. In Latin America and the Caribbean, it is: 2008: −10.0 per cent, 2012: −8.8 per cent, 2016: −7.3 per cent, and in 2020: −6.0 per cent. The estimate also finds that SSA has been mentionably successful in lowering poverty. Still more than 40 per cent of people in this region live under abject poverty. The problem is that there exists persistent inequality in many parts of the region and GDP per capita declines and remains low. All these exert adverse impacts upon child labour. Child labour is three times larger in the rural setting than the urban areas and it is more intense in the agriculture sector. The engagement of child labour in agriculture throughout the globe is 70 per cent. It is highest in SSA (81.5%) and lowest in Europe and North America (44.1%). The estimate says that children are not safe even in the family in terms of distribution in hazardous work.

The estimate focuses on the fact that since 2008, there is a declining trend of child labour till 2020 among children aged 12–14 years; but an alarming increase is noticeable during 2016–2020 among the younger children aged 5–11 years. Comparing among the boys and the girls, girl child labourers represent a faster declining trend than boys. This alarming condition is the result of the coronavirus ravages. The informal sector employees, as we mentioned earlier, have suffered the most. The people employed in these sectors have lost their jobs and are now very desperate to find out alternatives. In such a situation, children are being pushed into work, and, in most cases, in hazardous work. The prolonged closure of schools has also aggravated the number of child labourers. Their working hours have also increased due to coronavirus, and so is the closure of schools. The estimate cites testimonies collected by the Human Rights Watch which says that 81 new children have been pushed to work in order to support their families during the pandemic in Ghana, Nepal and Uganda. To tackle the situation, the estimate has suggested a number of measures to be adopted by the countries. These include:

1. Extending social protection: this can reduce poverty and economic uncertainty;
2. Providing good-quality schooling and skill-enhancing training;
3. Registering every birth;
4. Expanding decent work: this can deliver a fair income for the family;
5. Protecting rural population: it urgently requires a well-conceived and well-designed social protection coverage combining social insurance and tax-based social assistance;
6. Learning skills and training of rural youth: this can help in achieving a substantial increase in farm productivity and hence the family income of the rural people; and
7. Direct cash transfer to low-income families in an uninterrupted manner, which can reduce child labour and send the prospective labourers to school.

Child labour has an intergenerational effect that directly harms children mentally, physically, socially and morally. It restricts children to attend school and separate them from their families and relations. Working children are exposed to exploitation and hazards. Child labour is actually the effect of extreme poverty throughout the world. This is added to by malnutrition, chronic illness, violence, abuse and exploitation as by-products. COVID-19 crisis, as expected, may give rise to the global extreme poverty to 150 million by 2021 (as per estimation by the World Bank, 7 October 2020). This may lead to an increase in the number of child labourers.

Due to industrialization and agricultural revolution, and due to the overall growth of different sectors of the global economy, the share of people living in extreme poverty has started to decline sharply. This has been noticed over the last two centuries. The improvement in global health, education, communication and connectivity has been phenomenal and astounding. Every country in the entire globe is improving with its limited capacity and with the help of foreign aid, through its proper utilization of natural and human resources. SDG Number 1 sets the target: there will be the complete eradication of extreme poverty by 2030. The achieving of a movement above the international poverty line—$1.90 per day (set in 2017 by the World Bank)—would depend a lot on the true representative for all the countries, and on the availability of local resources, people's desire and the government's /leader's initiatives. In every sphere, there is a need for a strong social protection mechanism spreading to all the poor irrespective of political, religious, social and cultural affiliation. The only consideration that we need to make is attending to the economic condition. Poor families, especially those who live in extreme poverty, are usually trapped in poverty for generations, and some are forever a number of new entrants. They have no or limited access to critical resources—education, health, finance, land and other opportunities. They need to be attended upon if child labouring is to be ended.

The issue of child labour and that of ending poverty is not an issue specific to a country or region. Rather, it is a global issue like that of global warming and climate change, civil wars or pandemic situations, COVID-19, etc., which have regional, and, sometimes, global implications. Thus, to resolve the issue of poverty and that of child labour, one needs a composite action plan to be initiated by the global leaders and global policymakers who think good for future generations covering the entire globe. In this context, one could reiterate that the SDG Target 8.7 is set to end child labour by 2025.

The ILO, the UNICEF, and the World Bank's UCW published report—*Joining Forces against Child-Labour, 2010*—and this report aimed at making an international platform for combating child labour. Nevertheless, these organizations have been jointly working with employers' and workers' organizations, civil society organizations and national governments to eliminate child labour from the globe forever. Without ending child labour, it is not possible to achieve other goals such as millennium development goals, universal primary enrolment, education for all, poverty reduction and decent work.

It is a fact that child labour exists because (a) people directly or indirectly accept it, (b) children's rights are not protected, (c) education is not compulsory and free, (d) international agreements are not observed, (e) poor and vulnerable children are excluded, (f) child labour is cheap, (g) decency is absent and (h) enough funds are not available for the benefit of child labour.

9.1. WHAT TO BE DONE—THEN?

Child labour is a global problem, and naturally, we need a global solution. Our preceding discussions show that the highest number of child labour is noticed in low-income countries. In terms of number, working children are higher in middle-income countries. In terms of regions, Africa ranks the top position, Asia and the Pacific rank second.

We plead for the establishment of a free school in such countries where children are regularly rescued from hazardous work. They could be admitted to schools, and food and accommodation should be provided. This, of course, requires a huge investment. There should be a global fund for the cause of improvement of child labour. All countries—developed and less developed—together can make the fund to be accumulated. From this fund, expenses could be borne for imparting quality education to the destitute children engaged in hazardous work. Free hostel facilities—food, clothing, books, tuitions and other expenses—should be provided free of cost.

Poverty is the main cause of child labour in most of the African nations and Asia and the Pacific. There are many other causes behind the increase in the number of child labourers. Social protection measures should be made more strong and sufficient so that no child should work and every child should go to school.

In most of the developing countries, there are a huge number of children working in agriculture. More than two-thirds of these children work in agriculture and family operations. They work together with their family members during the agricultural seasons. National legislations on child labour do not cover children engaged in agriculture. Labour enforcement also does not cover children working in forests or herding livestock. They should be included more and more under such legislations. Children involved in farming activities do not find time to attend school. They thus attain a low level of education that limits their access to better opportunities in future. These children are being deprived of decent work. They have been left with one option and that is to migrate to urban areas. This puts the children at risk of trafficking. These issues need to be addressed immediately.

An important question is how should one stop child labour in agriculture? The simple answer to this question is reducing poverty in rural areas. The FAO and the ILO together are working in this sector, and are in search of finding a solution. They suggest that improved technology and better agricultural practices are to be adopted more intensely so that no children are engaged in agricultural operations.

Verisk Maplecroft has compiled a Child Labour Index (CLI) to assess the intensity and severity of child labour. The main elements in calculating the index are both quantitative and qualitative data, the major considerations being the severity and frequency of violations, a country's adoption of laws and international treaties, the ability and will of a country to enforce those laws through active intervention of government agencies. The index is constructed with the help of inputs, available at the ILO, the UNOs, the U.S. Department of Labour, the U.S. State Department, the World Bank, the UNESCO and others. The 2019 CLI accesses 198 countries and manufacturing hubs. According to this index, no remarkable improvement against child labour has been noticed in the countries like China, India, Bangladesh, Vietnam and Cambodia—particularly in the ranking. India's performance is very poor in this respect. India's CLI is only 3.05 out of 10, the worst score being 0.00.

The 10 worst performers, according to the 2019 index, are shown in Table 9.1.

Table 9.1 *Ten Worst Performing Countries, 2019*

Countries	Worst Performing Ranks
North Korea	1
Somalia	2
South Sudan	3
Eritrea	4
Central African Republic	5
Sudan	6
Venezuela	7
Papua New Guinea	8
Chad	9
Mozambique	10

Source: Verisk Maplecroft, 2019.

The index identifies that East Africa is the highest risk zone and 82 countries are high-risk countries which include India (ranked 47th), China (ranked 98th), Ethiopia (30th), Bangladesh (ranked 44th), Turkey (63rd) and Vietnam (81st).

This study defines 'worst countries' as those countries where children are compelled to work under the worst conditions and in dangerous sectors such as sex trading, war, etc. They are even engaged to work in logging, mining, fishing, begging and household working.

The CLI clearly shows that worst performing countries are either the so-called 'less-developed' or 'developing' in nature and the worst performing countries belong to the poor economic strata. Paul Collier, in his rigorous study on the poor,[1] finds four specific barriers which hinder the economic progression of the poor nations. They are: (a) the scarcity of natural resources; (b) the existence of landlocked locations surrounded by so-called 'unproductive' neighbours; (c) poor governance; and (d) the existence of a state of ongoing conflict. Nobody is a single bread-earner in the families of these poor nations. Only collective earnings by parents and children help these families to survive. Because of poor social protection measures, these children cannot have access to education, health facilities and nutrition. Devoid of resources and opportunities, such families remain poor for generations. This is the picture found everywhere in the world, albeit with little amounts of variations. It is extremely severe and intense in the poorest nations, and less in the relatively 'developed' or 'advanced' countries. It is evident that due to the ravages of COVID-19, the world would not be able to eliminate child labour completely by 2025. To achieve this mammoth task—the Global Estimate, 2020 says—the global progress should be 18 times faster than the progress achieved during the last decades. A pre-COVID-19 projection of child labourers in 2025 was around 140 million. However, the conditions have aggravated. Many more children—than what was previously estimated—would be shoved towards becoming child labourers by 2025.

So, one could, in conclusion, say that the end of child labour needs numerous efforts and careful planning. However, it should also be said that this is not an impossible task. The sustainable development goal

---

[1] Paul Collier, *The Bottom Billion Why the Poorest Countries Are Failing and What Can Be Done about It* (New York: Oxford University Press, 2007).

(SDG) of ending child labour by 2025 would not be achieved until it is tagged with complete eradication of poverty by 2030. Nevertheless, global collective action, along with social safety net, can make millions of working children turn towards school with smiling faces and full potentiality where their dreams would start to materialize. Only then we would see that there would be no child labourer in the entire world for generations to come. To make a real impact on the efforts to end child labour from the globe for good, social workers, reformers and intellectuals need to undertake a holistic approach and collaborate with all the stakeholders. This includes providing as many opportunities as possible to every child to develop his/her physical and mental growth in full potential. This entirely depends on the full achievement of entitlements by all the children living in various societies, as has been propounded by Amartya Sen (in his 1981 and 1995 publications) and by Nussbaum (in his 2003 and 2011 works).[2]

---

[2] M. Nussbaum, 'Capabilities as Fundamental Entitlements: Sen and Social Justice,' *Feminist Economics* 9, no. 2–3 (2003): 33–59; M. Nussbaum, 'Capabilities, Entitlements, Rights: Supplementation and Critique,' *Journal of Human Development and Capabilities* 12, no. 1 (2011): 23–37.

Bibliography

AD Haut-Rhin. In Childhood in Nineteenth-century France, edited by Heywood Colin, 129. Cambridge: Cambridge University Press,1988.
Annual Status of Education Report (Rural). Pratham Resource Center: Mumbai, 2005.
ASER 2020 wave 1 findings. Pratham Resource Center: Mumbai, 2020.
ASER Reports (Rural), 2018. Provisional. Pratham Resource Center: Mumbai, 2005.
Bhuimali, Anil. *Rural Cooperative and Economic Development*. New Delhi: Sarup and Sons, 2003.
———. *Child Labour Survey Report: Cooch Behar District, 2013*. Kolkata: Press of the Government of West Bengal, 2013.
Bhuimali, Anil. *Words yet Unspoken: An Autobiography*. New Delhi: Authors Press, 2000.
Banerjee, Abhijit V., and Duflo Esther. *Poor Economics: A Radical Rethinking of the Way to Fight Global Poverty*. New York: Public Affairs, 2011.
———. *Good Economics for Hard Times*. New York: Public Affairs, 2019.
Carlton, Frank Tracy. *The History and Problems of Organised Labour*. Boston: D.C. Heath and Company, 1920.
Child Labour Survey, 'Federal Bureau of Statistics,' Pakistan (1996).
Clark, Ross. Panic over rising covid-19 case numbers is as irrational as it is dangerous. *The Telegraph*, July 28, 2020. https://www.telegraph.co.uk/news/2020/07/28/panic-rising-covid-19-case-numbers-irrational-dangerous/
CMEI. Unemployment rate falls to 6.67% in September from 8.35% in August. *Business Today*, October 5, 2020.
Coronavirus lockdown: Govt. helpline receives 92,000 calls on child abuse and violence in 11 days. *The Hindu*, April 8, 2020. https://www.thehindu.com/news/national/coronavirus-lockdown-govt-helpline-receives-92000-calls-on-child-abuse-and-violence-in-11-days/article31287468.ece
De Neve, Mieke.' Child Labour in Ghent from 1830-1914. Magazine for Industrial Culture 10.37 (1992): 5-45.
De Weerdt, Denise. The Working Conditions from 1876 to 1914. In *History of the Socialist Workers'Movement in Belgium*, edited by Jan Dhont, Antwerp: Ontwikkeling,1960.
Dreze, Jean, and Amartya Sen. *India: Development and Participation*. Oxford: Oxford University Press, 1996.

International Labour Organization. *Implementation Report 2011: IPEC action against child labour: Highlights 2010.* 2011. https://www.ilo.org/ipec/Informationresources/WCMS_IPEC_PUB_15735/lang--en/index.htm

Lieten, G. K. 'Introduction: The Worst Forms of Child Labour in Latin America.' In *Hazardous Child Labour in Latin America*. New York: Springer, 2011.

Mitchell, B. R. *European Historical Statistics* 1750-1975 (2nd rev ed.) London: Macmillan,1981.

Sachs, Jeffrey D. *The End of Poverty: How We Can Make It Happen in Our Lifetime.* London: Penguin Books, 2005.

Satyarthi, Kailash. *Every Child Matters.* New Delhi: Prabhat Prakashan, 2018.

Save the Children. India touches lives in the grassroot level with protect a million mission. *ANI/ Business Wire India,* May 21, 2021. https://www.aninews.in/news/business/save-the-children-india-touches-lives-in-the-grassroot-level-with-protect-a-million-mission20210521095219/

Scholliers, Peter. 'Grown-ups, boys and girls in the Ghent cotton industry: The Voortman mills, 1835–1914.' In *Social History* 20, no. 2 (1995): 201–218.

Sen, Amartya. *Poverty and Famines: An Essay on Entitlement and Deprivation.* Oxford: Clarendon Press, 1981.

Sen, Amartya. 'Ford, Economics and Entitlements.' In *The Political Economy of Hunger,* edited by J. Dreze, A. Sen, and A. Hussain, 50–68. Oxford: Clarendon Press, 1995.

———. *Development as Freedom.* New York: Alfred A. Knopf, 1999.

Singh, Kavaljit. COVID-19 Has Pushed the Indian Economy into a Tailspin: But There's a Way Out. *The Wire,* September 21, 2020. https://thewire.in/economy/covid-19-india-economic-recovery

UNESCO. *Text of the convention for the safeguarding of the intangible cultural heritage.* Paris, 2003. https://ich.unesco.org/en/convention

UNICEF Nepal Working Paper Series (2017). *We must do better: A closer look at the contextual factors that drive child labour and discipline.* Nepal, 1998. https://www.unicef.org/nepal/sites/unicef.org.nepal/files/2018-11/2.%20Child%20Labour%20%26%20Discipline%20NMICS%20further%20analysis-2018_05_31_final%20version.pdf

Verisk Maplecroft-2019 Survey Reports". Refer to, for example, Deb Sibnath et al.(eds), Disadvantaged Children in India, Singapore: Springer, 2019 p. 91.

Vorst, Bessie Van. *The Cry of the Children: A Study of Child Labour.* New York: Moffat, Yardaw Company, 1908.

About the Authors

Anil Bhuimali is a Professor of Economics, University of North Bengal (West Bengal, India), and the former Vice-Chancellor of Raiganj University (West Bengal). He is a senior economist, academician and administrator, with specialization in child labour. He has written and edited over 50 books and published a large number of essays in different anthologies. Professor Bhuimali was conferred the award of Banga Ratna by the Government of West Bengal and has earned many other international awards and accolades. He has presented a number of seminar papers at international conferences and seminars, and lectured on various economic issues in India and abroad.

Partha Chatterjee is the Minister-in-Charge of the Department of Industry, Commerce and Enterprises, Government of West Bengal. Other than performing his administrative works, he is also interested in academia and has published a mentionable number of books and articles. He has many international visitations to his credit, and has presented papers and lectured on various economic issues in India and abroad.

Index

Afghanistan, 256
  Action Plan Agency, 266
  breakdown of average household debt, 263
  brick kilns industry and carpet industry, 259
  carpet-weaving sector, 265
  child mortality rate, 256
  child non-work, 263
  children's work by sector and activity, 259
  Convention on the Rights of the Child (RC–1994), 258
  daily wages of brick makers, 262
  forms of child labour, 257
  health and development risks of brickmaking, 264
  ILO–IPEC-commissioned report, 263
  statistics, children's work and education, 259
Africa
  child labour, 161
  children's education, 172
  children working, 163
  self-sufficiency, 161
American Federation of Labour (AFL), 70
Asia
  child labourers, 203
Australia
  child adolescent participation, 150
  child labour, 142–151
  occupation, significant child employment, 151
  Queensland population and workforce participation rates, 149

Bal Raksha Bharat, 286
Bangladesh, 206
  agriculture and non-agriculture sectors, child labour, 210
  banning girls from garment sector, 222
  child population and labour force participation, 208
  children, 211
  children in hazardous works by industry, 217
  children in the garment industries, 221
  children's activity status and household income level, 213
  children's work and education, 220
  COVID-19 pandemic, 225
  distribution of child labour, 215
  garment industries, 222
  National Child Labour Elimination Policy–2010, 214
  RMG sector, 223
  UNICEF and child labour, 214
Belgian
  child labour
    crafts and industries, 86
    children, 82
    government report, engagement of children at factories, 84
  Belgian anti-child labour law in 1889, 90

Belgium
  abject poverty, 19th-century, 82
  abusive conditions, child labour, 91
  child labour in factories, 1843, 85
  child labour in Ghent factories, 83
  children statistics, 90
  Industrial Revolution, 81
  literacy by gender, 1866-1910, 97
  school education expansion after independence, 96
  wages paid to children, 95
  Bombay Factory Commission, 1884, 10

child employment, 1851–1881, 73
Childhood and Child-labour in the British Industrial Revolution, 76
child labour
  abusive conditions in Belgium, 91
  Africa, 161, 172
  Asa Matsuoka's view, 45–48
  Australia, 142–151
  beedi making, 318
  Bessie Van Vorst's views, 23–29
  British Census of 1841, 71
  changes in rates of progress agains, 294
  children's involvement in labour and hazardous, 293
  China, 152–159
  Colin Heywood's perspective, 19–23
  COVID-19 pandemi, 326
  crafts and industries Belgian, 86
  defined by ILO, 61
  definitions, 61
  equal opportunity, 278
  European Nations, 67
  France, 99
  Ghana, 201
  Ghent factories, 83
  G. K. Lieten's views, 40–41
  global estimate, 291
  global phenomenon, 267
  Gurupadaswamy Committe, 268
  income sector, 296
  Indian perspective, 4–10
  intergenerational effect, 351
  Katrina Honeyman's perspective, 14–19
  Malawian tobacco farming, 181
  Mughal regime, 6
  national incom, 295
  NCLP schools in West Benga, 306
  post-Industrial Revolution concern, 62
  poverty, 204, 353
  reasons, 6
  reasons of existence, 352
  regional profile, 294
  Sally Atkinson-Sheppard, view, 41–44
  Samuel Slater, 114
  Sub-Saharan Africa, 162
  tea stalls/hotels, 320
  Textbook for University students, 29
  The Functions of Women in Industry, 110
  United Nations Convention on the Rights of the Child, 64
  USA, 114–128
Child Labour Act, 249
Child Labour Act 1916, 70
Child Labour Act, 1986, 278
Child Labour Index (CLI), 354
  10 worst performers, 2019, 354
child labour Kailash Satyarthi's work, 49–60
child labour Kaushik Basu's views, 33–39
Child Labour (Prohibition and Regulation) Amendment Act, 2016, 271
Children's Bureau Act of 1912, 70
Child Rights and You (CRY), 280

Chimney Sweepers Act, 1788, 70
China
  child labour, 152–159
  percentage of child labour, 157
Cocoa Research Institute of Ghana (CRIG), 201
COID-19 pandemic
  child labour, 326
COVID-19 pandemic
  budget allocation during 2016–2019, 347
  impact assessment, 327–339
  Indian perspective, 339–348
  policy prescription, 327
  students locked (community-wise), 342

England
  Industrial Revolution, 75
  working children, 74

Factories Act, 1881, 9
Factories Act, 1948, 345
Factory Act 1833, 70
France
  child labour, 99
  child labouring in 18th century, 103
  child labour reforms, 105
  China of Europe, 99
  composition of males and females in mills, 1822, 107
  employers, 111
  participation rates of youth, 1851, 106
  Pregnancy and Suckling Allowances Policy, 100
  women and minor children's engagement in mining, 108

gender profile
  child labourer, 297
Ghana, 200

child labour, 172, 201
children involved in household chores, 171
children's work, 202
children's work and education, 202
cocoa-trees, 200
distribution of working children, 171
economy, 200
fishing, 201
Ghana Cocoa Board (COCOBOD), 200
Ghent
  daily wages of children, 96
  height and weight of children working in cotton industry, 94
  textile workers in Voortman Cotton Mill, 88
  working hours, 1840–1914, 93
GoodWeave International, 265
Gurupadaswamy Committee, 268

Harkin Bill, 248
Health and Morals of the Apprentices Act, 1802, 76
Human Rights Watch, 350

India
  benefits, vulnerable children, 288
  bonded labour, 5
  child labour, 266
  Child Labour Act, 198, 278
  Committee on Child Labour, 268
  concentration of child labour, 273
  CR, 280
  distribution of working children, 201, 274
  Gurupadaswamy Committee, 268
  NCL, 278
  povert, 268
  public health centres (PHCs), 287
  schools with number of students, 308

state-wise distribution of working
  children, 275
Indian Factories Act, 1881, 9
Industrial Revolution
  Japan, 129
  USA, 116
Initiative for Social and Economic
  Rights (ISER), 335
Institute of Development Studies,
  Kolkata (IDSK), 302
International Labour Organization
  (ILO), 352
International Programme on the
  Elimination of Child Labour
  (IPEC), 64
International Save the Children
  Alliance, 286
Ivory Coast
  children's work, 198
  children's work and education,
    197
  cocoa farms, 196
  National-level Child Labour Unit,
    200
  WACAP programme, 198

Japan
  characteristics of workforce, 137
  child labour, 128–142
  child labour by factory-size and
    gender, 135
  child labourers in select industries,
    136
  children in industrial employment,
    134
  employment structure, 140
  entry age of interviewed women,
    143
  feudal system, 131
  Industrial Revolution, 129
  school attendance—children, 141
  sizable number of child workers,
    130
  underage children, 133
  working conditions of child
    workers, 138
Japanese Industrial Revolution, 132

Labour Law of Afghanistan
  Article 13(4), 258
laissez-faire capitalism, 68
Law against Child-labour
  first, 6
Library of Congress
  Africana Collections, 160
Livelihood Empowerment against
  Poverty (LEAP) programme, 336

Malawi
  activity status of children, 185
  adolescent, activity status, 186
  child labour in tobacco farming,
    181
  children aged 14–17 years in child
    labour, 183
  national legislation, child labour,
    182
Malawi National Child Labour Survey
  (MNCLS), 183
Ministry of Labour, Social
  Affairs, Martyrs and Disabled
  (MOLSAMD), 266
Mulock Commission, 9

National Agency for Rural
  Development (ANADER), 199
National Child Labour Committee
  (NCLC), 127
National Child Labour Project
  (NCLP), 278, 300
  agricultural survey, 316
  agricultural working children in
    activities, 316
  beedi rolling, 321
  child labour and school in West
    Bengal, 306

educational status of parent, 314
expansion, 280
functioning, 279
income and caste-wise household, 312
initiative, 301
initiatives evaluation survey, 301
literacy and children size (caste-wise), 313
objective, 300
schools under, 303
schools with number of students, 308
strategies, 279
tobacco-growing village, 318–319
National Child Labour Survey (NCLS), 169
national income
   child labour, 295
Nepal, 225
   agreement, United Nations Child Rights' Convention, 226
   carpet-weaving industry, 247
   child labour hazardous work, 236
   Child Labour Prohibition and Regulation Act, 2000, 226
   Children's Act, 1992, 226
   children's work and education, 246
   distribution of working children, 229, 232
   hazardous works and child worker, 245
   Kamaiya Labour (Prohibition) Act, 2002, 226
   monthly income and weekly working hours of children, 239
   National Master Plan on the Elimination of Child Labour (2018-2028), 227
   Nepal Labour Force Survey – 2008, 226
   occupation, child labour, 244
   school attendance of children, 242
   school attendance of child worker, 240
   working children, 228
Nihon no kasoshakai, 129

Ōto mine disaster, 1903
   age structure of deceased, 142

Pakistan
   child labour, 248
   child labourers, 199, 251
   children, 248
   children's work by sector and activity, 255
   employment in the brick kilns industry, 250
   statistics on children's work and education, 254
parish apprenticeship system, 15
Pratham Education Foundation, 282
Pregnancy and Suckling Allowances Policy, 100
prepubescent, 1
public health centres (PHCs), 287

reports
   British Parliamentary Report, 1819, 71
   Council of Europe—Commissioner of Human Rights, 66

Save the Children India, 286
SOS – Children's Villages, India, 281
Sub-Saharan Africa
   child labour, 162
   children condition, 165
   educational status of children, 167
   HIV/AIDS-pandemic, 166
   HIV/AIDS-prevalence and children orphaned, 165
Sustainable Development Goal (SDG) Number, 351

Tanzania, 187
   adolescents' activity status, 194
   child labour estimates, 189
   children in child labour, 191
   children's activity status, 193
   children's work and education, 188
   involvement in child labour, 190
   out-of-school children, 195
   working children, 188
Teaching at the Right Level (TaRL), 282
The Child Labour (Prohibition and Regulation) Amendment Act, 2016, 280
trans-Atlantic slave trade, 116

Unbeaten Tracks in Japan, 130
United Kingdom
   child labour, 69
   English Industrial Revolution, 68
   first jobs, 77
   laissez-faire capitalism, 68
   occupation status of children aged 5-14, 80
   Victorian era, 74
United Nations Children's Fund (UNICEF), 352
United States of America (USA)
   child labour, 114–128
   child labour legislations, 125
   distribution of child labourers, 120
   first federal child labour-law, 127
   Industrial Revolution, 116
   non-agricultural occupations of children, 122
   occupation of children, 121
   passage of anti-child-labour laws, 125
   proportion of children, 123
   State Child Labour Law, 70
   trans-Atlantic slave trade, 116

Wales
   working children, 74
Walsh-Healey Act, 1936, 70
West Bengal
   child labour and NCLP-school, 306
World Day against Child Labour, 349
World Report on Child Labour, 63

Zambia
   school attendance, effect of orphanhood, 168
Zimbabwe
   children's work and education, 174
   children's work overview, 175
   international conventions on child labour, 176
   laws and regulations on child labour, 177